ICATION

ok is dedicated to my wife, Donna, who has put up with years of carboys in every room, suspicious smells menting new ingredients, the fruit press on the kitchen counter when she is trying to prepare meals, rom supplies and equipment, and a chest freezer usually full of Ziploc bags of grapes or fruit destined for ation that covered up meats and vegetables frozen for consumption. She has also suffered from hundreds of neglect while I tended to my website and blog—hours I can never repay, neglect I can never undo.

dedicated to my stepson Scott, who has tended to me, the house, and the property during very long days ts when I was glued to the keyboard while writing this book. His contribution was never unnoticed.

: is dedicated to my late parents, Jack and Rosalie Keller, who left this world too soon to see the fruits of this bor but did enjoy years of exotic wines from some of the recipes contained herein. I miss them both terribly.

Jack B. Keller, Jr.
Pleasanton, Texas

OWLEDGMENTS

acknowledge the folks at Adventure Publications and AdventureKEEN for inviting this book and for all the have provided. I especially wish to acknowledge Travis Bryant and Jonathan Norberg for the overall design, psomer for marketing and media relations, and last but certainly not least, Brett Ortler for guiding and e work and stepping in when health issues sidelined me. Without their efforts, this book would not have hed.

hank Daniel Pambianchi for agreeing to be technical editor and reviewer for this book. As the saying ou can swing it, go first class." Daniel is first class. He not only is a prolific author, his *Techniques in Home* g is a go-to classic and belongs in every winemaker's library.

cknowledge the many years of fellowship with past and present members of the San Antonio Regional d. I thank them for all they have taught me and for their forgiveness for the meetings I missed while y deadline and facing medical challenges.

to acknowledge my wife Donna for her long patience in seeing this work come together and my stepson tending to my needs as I spent 14–18 hours a day glued to the keyboard for three months straight. eir support, I doubt the timeline agreed to would have been met.

Jack B. Keller, Jr.
Pleasanton, Texas

n by Travis Bryant

by Travis Bryant and Jonathan Norberg

rett Ortler

bianchi, Technical Editor

lustration credits on page 363

5 4 3 2

aking: The Simple Way to Make Delicious Wine
021
021 by Jack B. Keller, Jr. (died 2020)
Adventure Publications
AdventureKEEN
treet South
innesota 55008
6
republications.net
ved
a
193-947-4 (pbk.); ISBN 978-1-59193-948-1 (ebook)

Home
WINEMAKING

JACK B. KELLER, JR.

with DANIEL PAMBIANCHI,
Technical Editor

Adventure Publications
Cambridge, Minnesota

DEI

This b
from fe
clutter
fermen
of hour

It is als
and nig

Finally,
writing

AKN

I wish to
help the
Liliane C
editing t
been fini

I wish to
goes, "If
Winemak

I wish to
Wine Gu
racing to

I also wis
Scott for
Without t

Cover des
Book desig
Edited by
Daniel Pan
Photo and

10 9 8 7 6

Home Wine
First Edition
Copyright ©
Published by
An imprint o
310 Garfield
Cambridge,
(800) 678-70
www.advent
All rights res
Printed in Ch
ISBN 978-1-5

TABLE OF CONTENTS

INTRODUCTION

Winemaking isn't difficult. The ancient ancestors of the Sumerians made wine 7,000 or possibly 8,000 years ago, so you probably can too. Your wine will be much better than theirs; it likely often was undrinkable stuff that turned into vinegar or smelled horrible, and they tolerated it by adding pine resin or seawater.

Grape wine actually makes itself. The ancient inhabitants of Georgia (circa 8,000 years ago) made large earthenware vessels called *qvevri*, shaped similar to amphora without handles, which they buried in the cool ground for storing grains, nuts, roots, and other edibles. Eventually, someone used one to store grapes, and the weight of the grapes crushed those on the bottom, and the wild yeasts on their skins did what yeasts do: ferment.

When the ancients smelled the odors associated with fermentation, I'm sure they thought storing grapes like this was a bad idea. But, as time passed, the fermentation odors disappeared, replaced by an almost fragrant odor never encountered before. When the vessel was opened, a heady, pleasant-smelling liquid was discovered, and someone tasted it. As more and more was tasted, the participants became intoxicated. Not only did it taste good, but it also made them feel good too.

To these people, the wine was a religious experience—so say their descendants. They've been making the stuff this way ever since—just grapes, no added anything, in *qvevri* buried in the ground. Good batches are reported to be more than just good—some exquisite. We don't hear anything about the bad batches.

This book, on the other hand, will teach you how to make good wine every time, and some of it will be exceptional, some even exquisite.

A Personal Journey

When I was in the second grade, we happened to live about three blocks from my maternal grandparents. One Saturday morning while my father was at work, my mother walked my sister and me to their house. I went out to the garage and found my grandfather making wine from the pears from the tree next to the garage.

He cut up pears then crushed them in a rather large earthenware crock with a length of 4x4 lumber, one end of which was whittled down to resemble the end of a baseball bat. I announced I wanted to help, so he sent me on chores that I realized much later were intended to get me out of his hair while he crushed the chopped up pears. Satisfied, at last, he poured a lot of sugar over them, had me turn on the hose while he filled the crock to a certain level he magically understood and then stirred it with the hand-whittled paddle for what seemed like forever.

I even got to stir it while my grandfather went into the house for a bit. My arms were about to fall off when he returned. He thanked me for my assistance by saying, "This will be our wine—yours and mine."

I was thrilled, but never tasted or even saw "our wine" in the coming years. It didn't matter. It existed, and I helped make it.

This was my introduction to winemaking. I didn't understand how the crushed pears, sugar, and water would become wine or how I'd helped, but it was exciting and even a little romantic. As my grandfather worked, he paused now and then to take a sip from a glass of last year's pear wine. He told me, "Never drink your wine until you are making more." Though the math escaped me at the time, he meant that each batch of wine should be at least a year old.

When my grandfather went into the house to clean up, I sneaked a sip from his glass. It was mildly sweet, had a strange effect on my tongue, and didn't taste anything like the pears I knew. I quickly took a second sip. I liked it.

I carried the memories of that experience with me for over 20 years before I returned from my third tour in Vietnam to receive my inheritance from my grandfather, who had passed away during my tour. My inheritance included a cigar box full of wine recipes cut from newspapers, magazines and books, others written out in pencil on pages from various sized note pads, the backs of envelopes, and pieces of cardstock. It is a treasure I still have, although none of the recipes stand up to modern standards without severe modification.

This Book Is for You

Perhaps some of you share similar memories of a grandfather or grandmother, mother, father, uncle, or other family member magically transforming pears, apples, blackberries, figs, elderberries, or rhubarb into wine. If you're like me, you only saw one aspect of the whole process and lacked a vision of the entirety. That's not enough knowledge to make wine. That's why I've written this book for you.

Many of you may have helped friends make wine. The first wine I helped a friend make was a dandelion wine I made with an Army buddy, Bob Keller (no relation). He had the recipe and orchestrated the process. I always seemed to get the job of crushing Campden tablets into powder using a mortar and pestle. We were supposed to age it 15–18 months before sampling, but we were impatient and popped the first cork at about seven months. It was a mistake. We wasted the second bottle at a year—well, we drank it anyway. At almost exactly 18 months, we tasted an excellently transformed wine and became believers of the recommendations tucked away in recipes. This book was actually born in

that moment, although I wouldn't think of a book for another four decades. Over time, I learned more about every aspect of winemaking I've encountered, and that knowledge has taken me here.

Perhaps some of you have made or helped make a wine which was disappointing when you sampled it too early or too late. Or perhaps you lacked one of the recipe ingredients and skipped it, thinking the recipe would come out OK anyway, but it didn't. What went wrong? How could one ingredient you'd never heard of spoil your crab apple wine? Well, this book is for you.

Some of you, I know, have made kit wines—wine made from a kit that contains everything you need to make a good wine except water. You know most of the steps to make wine except creating it from scratch—gathering and measuring the additives in the various envelopes that accompanied the kit. You want to expand your knowledge and make blueberry wine all by yourself. This book is for you.

Some of you have been making good wine, even exceptional wine, from scratch, perhaps for years, and are very experienced. You don't really need a beginner's book. But any book written by someone who has made dozens of grand champion or best of show wines might—just might—contain a few insights worth the price of the book. So hopefully this book is for you, too.

You can make wine out of all sorts of things; in fact, when it comes to potential winemaking ingredients, there are no restrictions except this: it must be made from a nontoxic ingredient, and that base ingredient must be fermentable. To illustrate this, I present you with three tales of some perhaps surprising wines.

Bermuda Grass Clippings Wine

At a meeting of a not-so-local wine club I belonged to many years ago, which was comprised mainly of snobs who believed all wines must be from *Vitis vinifera* grapes, preferably red, and that non-grape wines were a travesty, it was my turn to give the "program," meaning I had to talk about something. Had I remembered it was my turn at this meeting, I would have brought in some non-grape wines—perhaps a tomato wine, zucchini wine or an oak leaf wine—to taste, which would have irked the attendees to no end. But I had forgotten, so I just got up and talked.

My theme was, "You can make wine out of anything both nontoxic and fermentable." As examples, I mentioned acorns, dried mushrooms, grapevine prunings, eggplant, parsnips, and anything else I knew would disrupt their sensibilities. My talk was relatively short, with about half of it on how to leach the tannins out of acorns and bamboo roots. After the "presentation," there were no questions.

At the following meeting a month later, one of the members slapped a large paper grocery bag into my chest and said, "Here, ferment this." The top of the bag was folded over and sealed with a dozen or so staples. I set it beside a sofa and ignored it until I left. In my car, I carefully opened the bag and peeked inside. It was filled with about three pounds of Bermuda grass clippings.

Once at home, I wasted no time in bringing three quarts of water to boil in a stockpot while slowly feeding it the grass clippings. I stirred them until they wilted into near-nothingness, reduced the heat, placed a lid on the pot, and went into the living room to watch some TV. An hour later I strained the water into another pot through a colander and a tea towel, set the colander of cooked grass in the sink to cool before discarding and repeated this process with the remainder of the clippings.

When all was said and done I had just under a half gallon of grass clipping-infused water, which I later brought up to a gallon. While the water was still hot, I stirred in my sugar, acid blend, and yeast nutrient. When the water cooled, I tasted it to judge whether to add tannin, which I did—just a pinch. About then I added yeast, stretched a clean towel over the pot, and left it. It took two days to get a nice fermentation, but once started, it took off, finishing just shy of semi-sweet.

I patiently waited for my turn to bring the "mystery wine." The bottle was wrapped in a brown paper bag suitable for wine and sealed just under the rim with masking tape. There would be no peeking. When the tasting time arrived, I poured each member a nice splash and left them to debate it. After discussing the possibilities a while, each member wrote his guess on a slip of paper which I collected and

sorted. I announced that the wine with the most votes was Chenin Blanc, with Chablis taking second place—unusual because the wine tasted like neither.

I then tore off the masking tape and pulled out the bottle with a prominent label reading "Bermuda Grass Clippings Wine." Watching their faces pleased me to no end. I later entered a bottle of this wine in a local competition and took third place in the "Novelty" category.

Dwarf Nettle Wine

A far-back portion of our property is cursed with dwarf nettles. While not as much of a nuisance as stinging nettles they are nonetheless irritable. One day I had just begun weed-eating them when I noticed that the new growth at the tops lacked the irritable hairs of the older leaves and stems below. I retired the weed-eater and fetched a bucket, gloves, and pruning shears. Within a short time, I had a bucket full of dwarf nettle tops.

In the kitchen, I took my largest stockpot, placed in it a gallon of water, and set that to boil. I slowly fed my nettle tops into the boiling water. Although the bucket was larger than the stockpot and filled with nettle tops, they all managed to wilt. I set the pot to a low boil, placed the top on it, and left it to itself for a little over an hour. The water was drained into another pot, and the colander of cooked nettles was divided—some were chopped and eaten as one would eat cooked spinach and the rest were added to the compost pile. The ones I ate weren't bad at all, just overcooked.

While the nettle water cooled, I added sugar, acid in the form of one squeezed lemon and two squeezed oranges, grape tannin, and yeast nutrient and stirred until completely dissolved. I also added three very thin slices of ginger, as pure nettle wines tend to lack character. When nearly cooled to room temperature, I sprinkled yeast over the water, placed the lid on the pot and set it aside. The next evening the kitchen began harboring the odors of fermentation.

Eight months later, I entered my last bottle of Dwarf Nettle Wine in the local county fair's winemaking competition as a novelty wine. It won a Reserve Grand Champion rosette and every drop of it was consumed at the post-competition tasting.

Texas Sandbur Wine

For 11 years, we were blessed to own an English Springer Spaniel named Colita (Coli for short). When we moved to Pleasanton, Texas, we were cursed to have a section of yard overgrown with *Cenchrus echinatus*, the Texas Sandbur. The half-dozen to a dozen sharp spikelets on each seed stem grabbed whatever passed by them. For reasons I never understood, Coli never learned to avoid them.

One day I got home from work to find my wife sitting on the tiled floor next to Coli, using a fork to pull the dozens of spiked seeds from Coli's long hair. I was immediately sent outside to mow down the sandburs. As I approached the infested area with my mower, I noticed a gentle breeze sending the seed stalks loaded with spikes waving gently to and fro. It was actually beautiful, for in those thousands of burs I saw wine.

Wearing rawhide gloves, I picked the seed stems while the seeds were still green and tossed them into a bucket. When my back ached sufficiently, I went inside and used a fork's tines to strip the spikelets off the stems. When done, I made two more trips outside to "harvest" more burrs. When at last I had a quart of only burrs, I placed them in a 2-quart pot and added two quarts of water. I stirred them occasionally while bringing them to a medium boil, then put on the lid and left them. Twenty to thirty minutes later, I strained them and saved the dark-green water.

I assumed some tannin was present, but no sugar or acids. I developed a recipe from those assumptions. I proceeded as with the previous two wines, only omitting the tannin, and lastly adding more water to make a gallon. The finished wine was neither dry nor sweet, but in between—this is how I preferred my white wines at that time. The color was light straw, with only the very faintest hint that it had once been green. It was nicely flavored but without any noticeable aroma. Despite this deficiency, it won a silver medal in an East Texas wine competition.

A Shared Pattern

From the above tales, it should be obvious that a winemaking pattern is evident. The pattern is there because these wines were made from grass, weeds, and under-ripe seeds. These require boiling the main ingredient—called the **base**—to extract whatever sugars, acids, flavors, and other essences that are present. Boiling the base is not a common practice in winemaking, but in the above examples, boiling was the most practical way to proceed.

So how does one know when to boil and when to press, as with grapes? There are several ways to prepare a base for fermentation. Sometimes it is obvious which one to use, and sometimes it isn't. Often there is more than one way, usually dictated by available equipment. I'm sure my grandfather would have preferred to have a crusher to prepare his pears, but he certainly couldn't afford to buy one. His method of crushing the pears worked for him and is the method I used for many years when I started making wine.

In the next chapters, we'll discuss this and many other choices you'll be confronted with when making wine, but at the same time, you have a great deal of latitude to determine how to follow the directions. For example, when a recipe calls for crushing or pressing, I've known folks who sawed off the end of a baseball bat and used the bat as the plunger—much like my grandfather did with his customized piece of 4 x 4 lumber.

Equipment and Supplies

To use this book, you'll need certain equipment that most beginners avoid, but the modest expense is worth it. If you purchase the following items, you will have everything you need to start out, and even to become an intermediate or advanced winemaker.

For one thing, you'll absolutely need a gram scale. When a recipe calls for one (and only one) gram of a certain additive, there just isn't any reliable way to measure it without one. You can buy a digital gram scale for about $10. Get one that can measure at least to one tenth of a gram (0.1 gram).

You'll also need a sulfur dioxide (SO_2) test kit because you'll need to make adjustments to your sulfite additions at the end of each recipe. I cannot predict how much SO_2 will bind with the suspended solids in your wine, so you'll have to measure it. This test kit costs about $20.

The biggest expense will be a pH meter, which should cost around $50, possibly as much as $60. You can use certain litmus test strips to get you in the ballpark of where your pH should be, but they will not be accurate enough for reliability.

If you just can't wait to start a wine while collecting the above instruments, you can take a chance at making a wine with the following:

Basic Gear Checklist
- Hydrometer
- Primary fermenter
- Secondary fermenter (you'll actually need two)
- Airlock
- Siphon hose
- Five wine bottles (screw caps)
- 2 oz. potassium metabisulfite
- 1 oz. tartaric acid
- 2 oz. pectic enzyme
- 1 oz. grape tannin (powder)
- 2 oz. potassium sorbate
- 2 oz. yeast nutrient

Some of the additives will probably only be sold in larger quantities.

Measuring the potassium metabisulfite will be impossible without a gram scale, so you might as well add it to your list. You won't be able to measure acidity, so let your taste buds put you in the ballpark.

Start with Clean, Sanitized Gear

Before you start a batch of wine, make sure you clean, and then sanitize, your gear. These are two distinct steps. As you might expect, cleaning your gear simply involves scrubbing your gear until you can no longer see/feel any soiled materials. There are a variety of cleaning products, such as Easy Clean and One Step, that you can use in this process, and specialized scrub brushes for secondaries can be quite helpful.

After cleaning your gear, you also need to sanitize it before making each batch. This is important. Bacteria, wild yeast, and other contaminants are too small to see and could still be lurking, waiting to ruin your next batch of wine. For that, use Potassium Metabisulfite. It takes two ounces to sanitize a gallon of water. After using the solution, the equipment should not be rinsed; let it drip-dry instead. You'll also need to sanitize any other gear/equipment (primaries, tubing, weights, yarn, etc.) that will come into contact with your wine, for it too can harbor contaminants.

Once your gear is clean, sanitized, and dry, you're ready to make wine.

This Book . . .

In this book, I will try to guide you from fruit to wine as simply as possible, while at the same time letting you know that it requires a certain exactitude.

With that goal in mind, I welcome you to home winemaking.

CHAPTER ONE
ESSENTIAL CONCEPTS

This book was written to help you move from start to finish as simply as possible, while respecting you enough to demystify winemaking and make it understandable. Let me explain.

Ages ago, during my bachelor years, a lady I was dating cooked me a wonderful meal. After dessert, I asked her an innocent question about a spice she used in her glazed carrots. I think it was tarragon (which I have added to my glazed carrots ever since). She became very fidgety and suddenly, with quivering lips suggesting she was about to cry (which she did), she said, "I don't know. I just followed the recipe."

I didn't think any less of her, but she may have thought less of herself and was obviously embarrassed. She had followed a recipe and made the dish, yet she could not remember what was in it or why. Fast forward to winemaking.

Understanding the Recipes

You will be making wines according to recipes, but after you read the first few chapters of this book, you will know what you are adding and why. Unless you're making wine from traditional wine grapes, you'll be adding sugar to ensure a certain amount of alcohol by volume, as well as acid and probably tannin to give the wine structure, character and style, pectic enzyme to release the juice and help the breakdown of its pectin, nutrients for the yeast, and sulfites for a host of reasons.

In short, you will not only be following recipes but will know what you are doing along the way. The only thing you may not understand is why the wine is set aside for periods and then racked.

These periods of rest mimic what the author did when making a successful recipe. If a recipe calls for racking a wine to allow it to show clarity, and yours shows clarity sooner than the prescribed time period, you can shorten one of the rest periods without adverse consequence. The recipes are guidelines, not hard-and-fast rules. They are flexible, to a point.

The bulk of the skills you need to become a proficient winemaker are in these first few chapters. And you'll build upon that knowledge in successive chapters. Some of that knowledge is contextual, and some is hands-on, but both are needed.

An Honest Approach

Many books for the beginner are a bit too simple. They list the ingredients, sketch out a method, and hope you can deal with whatever happens along the way. This book differs in that I want you to understand why and when my recipes call for the ingredients/steps that give birth to wine. This, in turn, will help you take pride in your clean, flavorful wines.

Each recipe is written to stand on its own, with all the steps you need, so once you've acclimated yourself to the introductory material, go ahead and jump from a berry wine to a flower wine and then to fruit wine or tropical fruit wine or even a root wine.

You probably will refer back to this chapter until the concepts and language become your own, but these look-backs are expected. Eventually, it will all become routine. When asked to measure some aspect of the wine, we expect the first half-dozen times you'll read instructions for making such a measurement, but in time, with repetition, it will become routine. And when it does, you'll no longer feel like a beginner.

Advanced Concepts

Like anything else, winemaking can involve optional more advanced concepts and techniques which, if executed properly, can improve the final product or completely change the wine type or style. The advanced concepts largely involve organic chemistry, of which I am as much of a fan as I have to be. Generally, they are more scientific, but some are matters of technique. They are not essential to making good or even great wine at home.

To give you a solid introduction, I'll cover basic concepts, as well as advanced ones below; truth to be told, the distinction between the two is often a sometimes blurry line. Fining, for example, is a basic technique, but when addressing certain winemaking problems can be an advanced procedure. Regardless, the essential concepts are addressed below as a lexicon for winemaking. Because of the fine and sometimes blurry lines, certain advanced concepts are also briefly addressed or simply mentioned in passing.

Don't Skip the Text Below, Really

Lexicons are usually arranged alphabetically and can read like a glossary, as you will find below. In navigating it, you will undoubtedly see terms you think you already understand. The temptation to skip them will be natural, but I implore you not to do so. They are listed because they have a direct bearing on how this book is to be interpreted, understood, and followed. The descriptions are as complete as need be for introductory purposes. Some concepts are addressed in later chapters as necessary.

Chapter 1 covers the essential concepts that will build your knowledge base, whether you recognize the terms at first. Reading the lexicon will make the tools, processes and tasks discussed in Chapter 2 much easier to understand. If you want to double-check the meaning of a term, look first in the index or check in Chapter 2.

The Very Basics of Winemaking

If you are new to winemaking it will help you understand the lexicon better if you understand the basics of winemaking itself.

It begins with the selection of the base ingredient the wine will be made from. Whether they be fruit, berries or flowers, they must be fresh, fully developed, and the best of that ingredient you can find. They will be turned into a fermentable form called a must, and it is from this that you will make the wine.

The must is then prepped for fermentation by adjusting its chemistry. Yeast is added and fermentation begins. The wine is transferred from the primary fermenter to a secondary. When fermentation is complete the wine is racked off its lees into another secondary. The wine might be racked at intervals three or even four times, each time becoming clearer.

When the wine is clear, it is allowed to rest and maturate (mature) until it is what the winemaker wants. It is then stabilized and bottled. It will then age in the bottles for a specified period before tasting.

Stripped to its essentials, these are the basics of winemaking.

The Basic Chemistry of Winemaking

When we prep the must for fermentation by adjusting its chemistry, do so gently and purposefully. If the must is not at the volume we desire, that is corrected with juice, concentrate, or sweetened water. The wine is brought to a certain specific gravity which determines the alcohol content of the finished wine.

The acidity of the wine is measured and adjusted if required. Acid has two faces. One face is titratable (or total) acidity, commonly called TA, which is the total concentration of acid in the must. The other face is pH, which is a measure of the

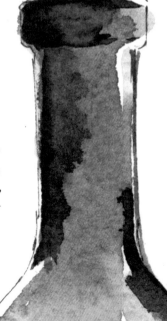

strength of the acids present. pH is the inverse of TA, meaning the lower the pH (strength of the acids) the higher the TA (concentration of the acids). Of the two, pH is the more important throughout the winemaking process to the end product, wine. If acid reduction is required, calcium carbonate is added sparingly.

Tannins are polyphenolic compounds that add texture to wines, especially red wines. They contribute to mouthfeel and body. Their bitterness is a balance against the sourness of excessive acidity. White wines naturally have reduced tannins.

Pectin is a water-soluble polysaccharide found in most fruit. It binds the cell walls of the fruit together. It is undesirable as it forms a haze in wines. It is broken down both in the preparation of the must for fermentation and the clarification of the wine with an enzyme called pectinase.

Potassium metabisulfite is a salt of metabisulfite with a pungent odor that is added to both must and wine to achieve an aseptic level of microbiological stability. It plays many roles in winemaking and is an essential compound to understand. Its active ingredient, once it is added to wine, is sulfur dioxide.

With these basics behind us, let's explore the lexicon for winemaking for details.

A Lexicon for Winemaking

Acetic Acid: An organic acid that imparts the sour taste to vinegar; it's formed by the action of bacteria belonging to the genus *Acetobacter*. Some acetic acid, however, is produced by yeast during fermentation.

Acetobacter: The principal bacteria genus, consisting of many species, responsible for converting alcohol into acetic acid—vinegar—in the presence of oxygen.

Acidity: Acid helps balance the wine and gives it structure. It is responsible for freshness, tartness, and crisp taste. If wine has too much acid the wine tastes too tart; if there's too little, it tastes flat or insipid. Acid isn't just necessary for good taste; it also repels harmful microorganisms. Yeast also require some acid in the winemaking process.

Acid performs other vital services; its tartness helps offset a wine's fruity sweetness, and it dampens the burning taste of pure alcohol by making it seem sweeter than it is. Later in the process, acid facilitates chemical changes that help develop the aroma of the base as well as bottle bouquet (see page 21). Acid also helps mature and age the wine. The greater the acidity, the lower the pH, which, in general, helps slow down the rate of oxidation, and stronger acids (lower pH) require less sulfite to stabilize the wine.

Acids in wine usually originate from the acids present in the base and acid added by the winemaker. In grapes, the more important acids include tartaric, malic and some citric acid, although citric is unstable and easily metabolized into other compounds. Malic or citric usually are the dominant acids in fruit, berry and other non-grape base ingredients and are almost always supplemented with acid additions. Finally, some acids, such as lactic, succinic, and acetic are actually created in small amounts by the yeast during fermentation. Some of these may gain importance after the primary fermentation is complete: lactic acid may be welcome while acetic acid (think vinegar) is not.

There are two measures of acidity, TA and pH. TA measures the titratable (or total) acid in the wine, or the concentration of acids, while pH measures the relative strength of those acids; pH is the inverse of TA. The lower the pH, the stronger the acid, and, generally, the higher the TA will be (indicating more acid). It is pH, not TA, that indicates how well a must or wine can combat oxidation and microbial invasion. It also influences how much SO_2 (see page 69) is needed to keep a wine aseptic (free of harmful microorganisms).

Table 1. Probable TA Ranges for Table Wines

WINE TYPE	TA RANGE (g/L)
Sherry	5.0–6.0
Red, Non-Grape	5.0–6.0
White, Non-Grape	5.0–6.5
Red Grape, Dry, Demi-Sec	6.0–7.0
Red Grape, Sweet	6.5–8.0
White Grape, Dry, Demi-Sec	6.5–7.5
White Grape, Sweet	7.0–8.5
Dessert, Sweet	7.5–10.5

Data for Table 1 from Jack Keller's *Winemaking Home Page*, Internet, September 2010

Note: These are "probable" ranges because the actual TA should depend on the acid required to balance the dryness or sweetness of the wine. A TA of 10.0 or higher in non-dessert wines is tolerable if that is what is required to balance the wine.

The pH of wines can vary greatly, but there are some magic numbers to take note of. At the start of fermentation, white wines and rosés should have a pH of 3.1–3.3. A pH below 3.1 will be highly acidic, and the yeast may not respond well to it. Red wines should have a pH of 3.3–3.4. A pH above 3.55 will be at risk of contamination by bacteria and invites faster oxidation. Consider pH 3.41–3.54 a buffer zone, with 3.55 being the barrier you do not wish to cross.

So, how much acid are we talking about? Different wines tolerate different levels of acidity. The numbers are somewhat variable because acid is a key ingredient in a wine's balance, along with sugar, tannin, and alcohol, and many different combinations/proportions of each can result in a balanced wine. But generally, the acid levels shown on Table 1 correspond to those specific types of wine.

Airlock: A device that fits into a **bung** and is designed so that air can escape the **secondary** but also has a liquid trap that prevents air from entering the secondary fermenter. The liquid is usually water, water mixed with a little glycerol, or water containing 3-10 percent **sulfur dioxide**, or a spirit such as vodka. When recipes say to "affix an airlock" or words similar in meaning, it means to insert a bung containing an airlock into the mouth of the secondary.

Anthocyanins: In grapes, these are the pigments that contribute the red and purple colors to wines. In most other fruits, they provide bright reds, purples, blues, and indigos.

Antioxidant: Additives such as ascorbic acid and sulfur dioxide which, when added in the right quantities, protect against oxidation, especially when the wine is exposed to the air during processes such as racking, filtering, and bottling.

Base: The base is the primary flavor ingredient, and there may be more than one in a given wine. In home winemaking, the rules behind naming wines follow a certain logic that may not be apparent at first. Apart from water, the first-named ingredient is usually the one with the greatest volume in the recipe. So if you're making a wine with more strawberries than raspberries, it's strawberry-raspberry wine, but there are exceptions and sometimes the ingredient providing the most flavor "names" the wine.

Bases and Naming Wines: When it comes to naming conventions, there are a few others that have been informally adopted to keep in mind.

- **Flower bases** are always named first, even when a second ingredient has the dominant flavor, such as hibiscus-kiwi wine or rose petal-strawberry wine.
- **Herbal and spice** ingredients are always named first, regardless of their volume, such as cinnamon-pineapple wine. Multiple herbal ingredients are usually named by their flavor appearance when the wine is consumed, such as parsley-basil-sage wine.
- **Body-building** ingredients, such as grape concentrate, raisins or sultanas, are usually not named, but since they do influence the flavor somewhat may

be named at the discretion of the winemaker. An example might be cactus blossom-sultana wine.

- **Multiple flavors**, such as Concord-blackberry-blueberry wine, typically are blends of two or more finished wines with the forward flavor (the one you taste first) declared first in the name, but multiple flavors could also be two bases, such as blackberries and blueberries, fermented together. When co-fermented, even in 50-50 proportions, one flavor usually dominates the whole and it's the first-named ingredient in the wine's name.
- **Chocolate** is a forward-flavor ingredient that nonetheless traditionally takes a back seat in the wine's name, as in strawberry-chocolate wine.
- **Rhubarb** is a popular base where it grows because it tends to adopt the flavor of whatever other base it ferments with and therefore it also takes a back seat in the name regardless of its volume, as in raspberry-rhubarb wine.

Names can be as specific as the winemaker wants them to be. I once made wine from a wild grape that I couldn't identify with certainty and added to it a noble grape variety I could, but in fairness I named it "Grape-Grape Wine." The judges got a chuckle out of it, but only a second-place chuckle.

Note: The rules aren't "official"; it's just how things are usually done, but feel free to do it another way if it pleases you.

Bottle Sickness: A period following bottling during which the wine seems dull, uninspiring, and possibly unpalatable. This is a temporary condition that usually lasts no longer than a month, and rarely two. Because all wines experience bottle sickness to some degree, never consume a wine immediately after bottling, even if the recipe says you may drink it right away.

Bottle sickness can occur after any period of agitation. Traveling a long distance is a prime example. Another is a short distance where the bottle is laid on its side and free to roll with the turns of a vehicle.

Bottle Aging: Once the wine is stored anaerobically (bottled, without access to oxygen), the wine undergoes reductive aging. In this process, chemical changes occur (including polymerization, esterification, and micro-oxygenation), and these changes are what propel the wine to its apex, and eventually its inevitable decline. During this journey, the wine constantly undergoes chemical changes that may result in a perceived delicate but defined bouquet, subtle but complex flavors, a smoother texture and mouthfeel, and, rarely, a silkiness in taste and finish. Even if the wine doesn't reach such heights, it will still improve in most ways, resulting in a good wine.

Entire chapters have been written on the chemistry of bottle aging, so I'm not going to summarize that here. Let us just say it is real, very dynamic—the same wine cannot be consumed on two consecutive days due to subtle chemical changes—and the process can go very well or very wrong (see **Wine Storage**).

Bouquet: The complex, vaporous scent(s) released when a cask or bottle is opened, derived from volatile acids, esters, and other aromatic compounds formed during aging. Bouquet may rapidly dissipate or be slowly released if the wine is warmed in your hand and swirled in the glass, but when gone, the wine is left with the fragrance of the fruit or another base from which the wine was made. This fragrance is the aroma of the base ingredient(s).

Bulk Aging (Maturation): See **Maturation (Bulk Aging).**

Bung: This is the rubber stopper with a hole in it to accommodate the airlock. Bungs come in various sizes and fit the various sizes of jug mouths. It is best to bring your secondary to a local home brew shop and get the jug fitted with the correct size. A proper fit is one with half the bung in the jug and half out.

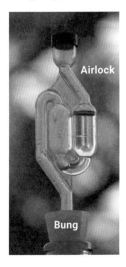

Airlock

Bung

Caramelized: The taste and/or odor of caramel is achieved by heating a sweet wine. In non-grape wines, this characteristic is often produced by cooking the fruit to extract the juice, set the color, or extract polyphenolic compounds from the skins. The browning of sugar most often produces this character, which is why recipes say to bring water to boiling, remove from heat, and *then* add sugar. A juice that is steam-extracted will not be caramelized, but steaming may set the pectin, making it very difficult to remove. The perception of some caramel is desired in some wines (e.g. sweet Sherries) but considered a fault in most others.

Chaptalize: To add sugar to a must or juice to increase its alcohol potential. The word is a method named after Frenchman Jean-Antoine Chaptal, who in 1801 accurately calculated the amount of sugar to add to a juice to increase potential alcohol.

Citric Acid: The principal organic acid in citrus and many other fruits. It is a minor acid in grapes. When added to wines, it is always added after fermentation has finished. It should be avoided, if possible, in red wines, as it is converted into undesirable substances during red winemaking. It is used in whites only to push the acidity up a small amount.

Clarify: The process of how a wine becomes clear. This occurs when all of the yeast and microscopic bits of pulp from the base ingredients settle to the bottom of the secondary fermenter, leaving a clear wine without haze. A wine that has clarified entirely and is crystal clear is called brilliant.

Complexity: A wine with multiple layers of bouquet, aromas, flavors, and nuances, all of which are perfectly balanced, harmonious, and delightful.

Decant: To pour clear wine gently from a bottle into a serving container (decanter or carafe) so as not to disturb the bottle sediments and thereby leave them behind. Decant also can mean allowing a wine to "breathe" before one serves it.

Degas: The process of removing dissolved carbon dioxide from a wine to bring it to stillness. Vigorous stirring, either manual or mechanical, or applying a vacuum are the two most common ways of achieving this. When using a vacuum, be very careful. The author once used too much vacuum and, an instant after the wine degassed, the 5-gallon carboy imploded, releasing glass and wine over a wide area. It required two hours to clean up.

Demi-Sec: A French term that means "semi-dry" and indicates a wine that is neither dry nor sweet, but closer to dry than sweet. Although usually reserved for sparkling wines, it is gaining frequent use when describing still wines. Wine is usually perceived as demi-sec when its specific gravity is in the range of 1.000 to 1.003. It is usually Americanized as Semi-Dry.

Diammonium Phosphate (DAP): One of the major ingredients in many yeast nutrients and energizers, serving as their basic source of nitrogen. Also known as DAP. There is much that could be written about DAP and, in commercial winemaking, how its dosage is calculated, but when it comes to home winemaking, we are only going to be adding predetermined, but sufficient, doses.

Earthy: Non-grape wines with an unpleasant odor/taste of damp soil are often described as earthy. Most wines made from roots (beet, carrot, parsnip, rutabagas, turnip) possess an earthy quality that diminishes to neutral over time—usually two years, but possibly more—and should not be served until neutralized by age. In homemade wines, whenever earthiness is perceived, it is a fault, though it may be desirable in some red wines.

Enzyme: Any of the numerous protein molecules produced by living organisms (including yeast) and functioning as catalysts in biochemical reactions. Even though they are derived from living materials, enzymes are not alive. Enzymes emerge intact from the catalytic reactions they produce and are denatured (rendered inactive) by pH extremes and high temperatures. Usually, an enzyme acts only on a specific molecule (substrate), so an enzyme that acts upon pectin will not act upon starch. In winemaking, most of the essential enzymes are produced by yeast, but some are not and must be introduced by the winemaker. Some of the more important enzymes in winemaking are:

- **Amylase:** An enzyme that catalyzes the hydrolysis of starch, producing maltose and dextrin.
- **Cellulase:** Any of several enzymes that catalyze the breakdown of cellulose.
- **Invertase:** An enzyme that catalyzes the hydrolysis of sucrose into an equal mixture of glucose and fructose.
- **Lactase:** An enzyme that catalyzes the breakdown of lactose, resulting in glucose and galactose.
- **Lipase:** Any of a group of enzymes that catalyze the hydrolysis of triglycerides into glycerol and fatty acids.
- **Maltase:** An enzyme that catalyzes the breakdown of maltose to glucose.
- **Pectinase:** An enzyme that catalyzes the breakdown of pectin to pectic acid and methanol.
- **Zymase:** The name given to the group of enzymes that yeast use to transform sugar into alcohol.

Esters: Volatile, aromatic, organic compounds formed during alcoholic fermentation and by the chemical interaction of the wine's alcohol, acids, and other components during maturation.

Ethanol: An alcohol, C_2H_5OH, produced as the principal alcohol in an alcohol fermentation by yeast. Also, known as *ethyl alcohol*.

Ethyl Acetate: An ester produced by fermentation. When ethyl acetate exists in sufficient quantity, it produces a slightly sweet, fruity, vinegary smell. Too much is considered a flaw, detectable as a nail polish remover smell and can occur in wines affected by advanced oxidation.

Fermentation Vessels: There are usually two classes of containers in which we conduct fermentation.

Primary fermenters: These are large-mouthed for easy access. They make it easy to add base and other ingredients and manipulate and extract solids from the must when desired. These containers were traditionally glazed earthenware crocks or large stockpots made of enameled metal. They gave way to glass jars, food-grade plastic buckets, and stainless steel pots.

Primaries must be larger—it's recommended they are twice as large—than the amount of must placed in them. This is because any solids in the must will be lifted to the surface by carbon dioxide created by the yeast during fermentation. The lifted material or foam will form a "cap" on the surface that rises above the liquid. Even base material contained in cotton or nylon straining bags will rise and float above the surface. These bags and any cap that forms will need to be "punched down" several times per day until time for removal. These actions prevent the material from drying out and becoming a breeding ground for unwanted microorganisms capable of ruining your wine.

There are many specialized containers made of plastic or stainless steel specifically produced for primary fermentation. Unless you simply like spending money, these are not necessary. Food-grade plastic buckets come in a variety of sizes that will satisfy most home winemakers' needs. In the many years I have been making wine I have never needed more primary space than my assortment of primaries allows. Also, I have never found enough money lying around to spend on what I really don't need.

Secondary fermenters: These are relatively small-mouthed jugs, demijohns or carboys into which the fermenting liquid in the primary is transferred at the appropriate time and in which fermentation will finish under an airlock. The primary is sealed with a rubber or similar elastic material called a bung. A bung is a stopper-like closure with a hole in it to accommodate an airlock. The airlock allows CO_2 produced by the yeast to escape the container while preventing atmospheric gases (especially oxygen) from entering. This moves the yeast from an aerobic environment (the primary) into an anaerobic environment (the secondary).

Plastic secondary containers are much lighter than glass carboys. While I have neither owned nor used any of these products, I see no reason to avoid them except as vessels for maturation beyond 90 days. In the long term, nothing beats glass or stainless steel.

As with primaries, there are many specially designed plastic or stainless steel secondary vessels designed to make the winemaker's job easier. Some claim to combine the jobs of both primary and secondary. They may, but not without considerable work that is not guaranteed to produce safer results than transfer from primary to secondary and then *racking* (see page 60) from one secondary to another when needed.

Finish: The final flavor, texture, and impression that remains on the palate after a wine is swallowed. A finish may be brief or long, the longer being preferred as long as it is pleasant. Many off-flavors can spoil a finish. These can range in severity (in competition judging) from a blemish to a deficiency to a fault, while a favorable finish only strengthens the positive score.

Flat: A taste denoting a wine with insufficient total acidity. The taste is truly flat, lifeless, and wholly wrong. Technically, it is the absence of the sour taste. This taste appears in wines with a pH greater than 3.75 and a titratable acidity less than 0.5%. Wine with an opposite fault—too much total acidity—is known as *acidulous*.

Fructose: This is one of two simple (reducing) fermentable sugars in grapes and other fruit, the other being glucose. Isolated, fructose is approximately twice as sweet as glucose. In wine, a higher fructose concentration will result in a heightened sweetness threshold (i.e. it will be sweeter).

Gassy: A wine with carbonation, usually produced by a secondary fermentation in the bottle, but sometimes also unexpectedly and unintentionally produced by malolactic (bacterial) or alcohol (yeast) fermentation.

Geranium: A fault caused by sorbic acid degradation, usually the addition of potassium sorbate to a wine that has undergone malolactic fermentation. This scent is characterized by the odor of geraniums, which is produced by 2-ethoxy-hexa-3,5-diene.

Glucose: One of two simple fermentable sugars in grapes and other fruit, the other being fructose. Glucose is approximately half as sweet as fructose.

Glycerol: A colorless, odorless, slightly sweet, syrupy substance produced naturally during fermentation that gives the palate an impression of smoothness in a wine. Also known as *glycerin*.

Gross Lees: Theses are loose sediments containing a large quantity of fine pulp from the fruit or other base materials from which the wine is made as well as dead yeast cells. The gross lees precipitate, but do not compact well on their own and therefore are loosely layered in the wine. Gross lees can be compacted somewhat by adding gelatin to the wine, or they can be coarsely filtered or, in commercial winemaking, centrifuged to recover much of the wine trapped within them.

Herbaceous: An odor suggestive of herbs or broken green stems of plants. It is a positive characteristic if just suggestive of the base and not too pronounced, but a fault if it's excessive or stems from spoilage.

Hot Wine: A wine with excessive alcohol that creates a burning, prickly sensation in the mouth.

Hydrogen Sulfide: H_2S for short, hydrogen sulfide is produced in all wines when yeast metabolizes various forms of sulfur. In excess, it creates an undesirable, rotten-egg-like smell in wine. If not corrected, the wine will be ruined, as the gas will transform into mercaptan with skunky odors, and eventually disulfides, with sewage-like smells.

Hydrolysis: The cleavage of a chemical compound via reaction with water, such as the dissociation of a dissolved salt or the catalytic conversion of starch to glucose. Also, the breaking down of a chemical compound into two or more simpler compounds via a reaction with water. Some proteins and complex carbohydrates in wine are broken down by hydrolysis that is catalyzed by enzymes that were added to the must or created by the yeast.

Hydrolyze: To undergo hydrolysis, or to break up by reacting with water (see *hydrolysis*).

Hydrometer: Although a simple instrument for measuring the amount of sugars dissolved in a must or wine through the measurement of *specific gravity (SG)*, it is *the* essential instrument in winemaking. See pages 31 and 55.

Inoculate: To add an active, selected culture of yeast or malolactic bacteria to a must, juice or an unfinished wine.

Lees: Just about (not quite, but just about) anything that precipitates from the wine before it is consumed can be called lees.

Technically, lees are suspended solids from the winemaking process and include particles of ingredients, dead yeast cells, precipitated proteins and tannins, and MLF culture.

- **Gross Lees:** Larger particles form the bulk of what is called the gross lees. These lees are thicker and looser than fine lees and contain more wine interspersed that could be lost when racking if the lees are discarded. Many winemakers rack down to the gross lees, then rack the gross lees into a container to be compacted so the contained wine can be recovered. That is one way to recover otherwise lost wine. Another is to fine the wine with gelatin before racking to compact the gross lees *in situ*. This, too, recovers the wine from the lees.
- **Fine Lees:** When the yeasts begin their die-off, they fall to the bottom and form a thin layer of very fine lees. These lees are well compacted and contain very little wine to be lost.

There is another use for the fine lees if you are going to be around for at least three months after your scheduled racking. Inspect the lees. If fine lees are depositing on top of the gross lees, rack immediately and allow a clean deposit of fine lees. Then leave the wine on the fine lees (a process called *sur lie*—pronounced sur lee—French, meaning leave on lees) and stir them thoroughly every week or so for at least three months. This process is called *bâtonnage*—pronounced *bah-toe-nawge*—French, meaning stir into the wine. *Bâtonnage* is usually conducted for a year, but some effect can be noted after three months, but a year is far better.

The effects of *sur lie* and *bâtonnage* are pronounced after a year. These include:

enhanced flavors and complex aromas; reduced astringency; increased roundness, volume and length to the palate; and a host of other benefits.

These positive effects occur because of the complex chemistry involved in yeast cell autolysis (decay). When yeasts die and decay their cell walls start to break down and release a whole host of beneficial substances into the wine. As the yeast is dead, there's no life left in the cell walls to fend off these attacks. Think of it as a slow, chemical dismantling.

Malic Acid: The dominant organic acid in young grapes, which slowly diminishes as the grapes ripen; malic acid is considered the sharpest-tasting of the acids in grapes. It also is the dominant acid in many fruit and berries such as apples and blackberries. 0.9 g/L (3.4 g/gal.) will raise the acidity of a must or wine by 1%.

Maturation (Bulk Aging): The period in between when fermentation, both primary and secondary, ends and the wine is finished and ready for bottling is called maturation. In reality, this phase should be thought of as oxidative maturation, for it occurs within the conditions in which exposure to O_2 exists. During this time the wine might be fined, could be undergoing *sur lie* and *bâtonnage*, might be oaked, or could simply be sitting unpampered by itself. Along the way, it loses its yeasty and spritzy characters and begins an odyssey of change.

To appreciate maturation, think of it as a journey of chemical evolution. When fermentation ends, the wine is raw. It has all the building blocks required for its type and style, but those blocks, as well as the components that make up each of them, do not blend well yet. And so their chemical components begin to react to and with each other, interacting, combining, and changing until an approximate equilibrium of mostly new compounds is attained. It is at this point, or as close to it as the winemaker can estimate, that oxidative maturation ends.

Several esters are produced during fermentation and these produce the fresh, fruity character of young wines, especially white wines and some reds. The chemical compounds produced that are responsible for these esters continue to evolve during maturation. Some become more obvious, some less, and some are preparing for an appearance later in the future. The aromas donated by the base, and the developing, but still embryonic, bouquet are not static.

Concurrently, maturation (and aging) can affect the wine's acidity, presenting small but perceptible losses. Esterification of acids removes components (carboxyl groups) intricately related to the sour sensation. The instability of tartrates in wine results in deacidification. The polymerization of tannins and their subunits with themselves, proteins, pigments (anthocyanins), peptides, and sugars (polysaccharides), especially in red wines, is responsible for the most perceptible changes during maturation—assuming the wine wasn't

A hydrometer

allowed early oxidation. Within weeks, an increase in astringency may be perceived in the wine; this results from a greater astringency in medium-size tannins, predominately from oak, as opposed to fewer large-size tannins. However, the relentless binding of tannins with other components results in further reductions in bitterness and astringency. This process (called glycosylation) does two things. It further lessens the astringency of the tannins while eventually slightly increasing the perceived sweetness of the wine. Along the way, the wine loses some of its fresh fruitiness. After bottling, it will lose much of the rest.

What happens in the bottle will probably remain a mystery, but the wine will deliver hints when consumed. Depending on the type and rate of oxygenation, the underlying taste and aroma components of the base will undergo changes consistent with their chemistry, revealing glimpses of the recent past. When consumed, the wine will release a bouquet while eventually slightly increasing the perceived sweetness of the wine. Along the way, the wine loses some of its fresh fruitiness. After bottling, it will lose much of the rest.

When consumed, the wine will release a bouquet of previously non-existent esters and new aromas constructed on its journey. Aromas are dictated by the base.

Bouquet is dictated by the entirety of the process. See **Bulk Aging (Maturation).**

Must: Must is the base prepared for and during initial primary fermentation. Except for recipes where a base is prepared by boiling and straining, bases are usually chopped, crushed, mashed, or otherwise rendered to juice that will make the wine. In this condition, it is added to a **primary** container with water and other additives, and then it is called a must. For country wines (i.e., wines not made from traditional wine grapes), the must typically contains the prepared base, water, perhaps a body-enhancer, added sugar, acid, sulfites, pectic enzyme, yeast nutrient, and yeast.

The undissolved solids in the must eventually have to be removed so the remaining liquid can be further fermented and then clarified for bottling. For the home winemaker, straining or containing the pulp are the most common and practical practices. Filtering a wine is a step reserved for polishing a clear or nearly clear wine, not for straining visibly suspended solids. Attempting this will burn out your filter's pump.

Straining catches larger pulp for further processing or disposal. Certain fruit or berries tend to disintegrate during fermentation, so straining such materials is not an option, but containing them is easy. Traditional methods of containment include cotton bags, cotton mesh bags like those used by painters, or nylon mesh straining bags designed for this purpose. Nylon stockings also have a place in winemaking. The bags are tied closed and contain the solids for easy eventual removal from the liquid.

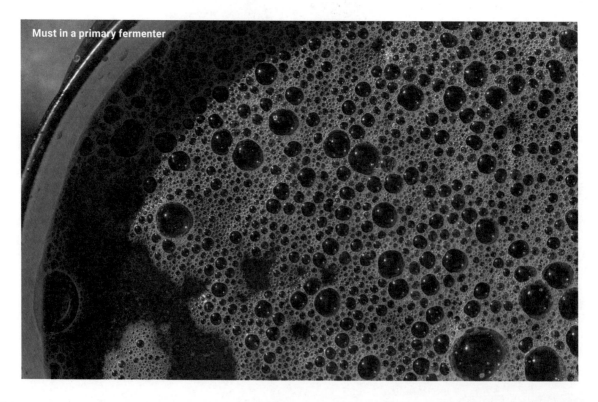

Must in a primary fermenter

Nose: The smell of a wine, combining both its aroma and bouquet, thereby revealing the character of the base from which it was made and the character of its maturation.

Off: An unexpected, indistinct, slightly offensive odor or taste in wine, which is considered a minor fault.

Oxidation: The process of reaction between many molecular components of wine with oxygen, resulting eventually in a darkening (browning) of the wine and the development of undesirable odors and flavors.

Pectin: A water-soluble carbohydrate (polysaccharide) that binds cell walls together, especially in ripe fruit; it can ruin a wine by causing an unsightly haze or, in severe cases, a gelatinous mass to form. Luckily, the enzyme pectinase can break down pectin molecules and prevent them from causing any haze.

pH: A chemical shorthand for [p]otential of [H]ydrogen, used to express relative acidity or alkalinity in solution, in terms of strength rather than amount, on a logarithmic scale. A pH of 7 is neutral; above 7 increases in alkalinity and below 7 increases in acidity. Because the scale is logarithmic, a pH of 3 is ten times more acidic than a pH of 4, but a pH of 2 is 100 times more acidic than a pH of 4. (See **Acidity.**)

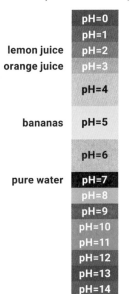

white/rosé wine: 3.1–3.3

red wine: 3.3–3.4

pH 3.41–3.54: buffer zone for wines; you do not want your wine to exceed 3.54

pH of 3.55 and higher: DANGER ZONE; contamination by bacteria and rapid oxidation possible.

Pomace: The residue of pressed pulp, skins, and pips of apples, grapes, or any fruit after pressing. When pressed under great pressure, a pomace cake or brick results. Pomace from appropriate fruit can be ameliorated with sugar, water, and yeast nutrients (possibly acid and tannin will also be required) and a second wine can be made. The pomace provides enough flavor for a reduced volume of wine and should contain enough viable yeast (assuming the pulp was pressed after an initial period of fermentation) to continue fermentation.

Potassium Bitartrate: A salt of potassium and tartaric acid which can precipitate out of wine as crystals under chilled conditions. Cold processing white, rosé, and overly acidic red wines is aimed at precipitating this salt, after which the wine is racked cold off the crystals to prevent them from dissolving into the wine as it warms and then precipitating in the bottle.

Potential Alcohol: The potential amount of alcohol that can be expected from a given must based on its measured specific gravity. (See **Specific Gravity.**)

Residual Sugar: The amount of sugar, both fermentable and unfermentable, left in a wine after fermentation is complete or permanently halted by stabilization.

Fermentation is complete when either all the fermentable sugar has been converted by the yeast into alcohol and carbon dioxide as byproducts or when the concentration of alcohol produced reaches a level that is toxic to the yeast, and they die. Fermentation is permanently halted by stabilization through several means involving intervention by the winemaker.

Sachet: A paper, foil, mylar, or plastic packet of dehydrated, freeze-dried, dried, or active dried yeast. A sachet typically holds 5 grams of product, although 8-gram sachets are becoming common.

Sauerkraut: An odor in wines, attributed to lactic acid, that have undergone excessive malolactic fermentation. This fault is most often found in wines made from malic-dominate bases (such as blackberry) which undergo unchecked malolactic fermentation.

Sec: French for dry. A wine becomes dry when all or most of the sugar within it has been converted through fermentation into alcohol and carbon dioxide. Wine is usually perceived as dry when residual sugar is at or below a specific gravity of 0.995.

Second Wine: A wine made from the pomace or strained pulp obtained from making the first wine is a second wine. A second wine will require that the pomace or pulp be ameliorated with water, sugar, yeast nutrients, and possibly acid and tannin, but usually not a pectic enzyme. Sulfites, however, should be introduced at once to achieve a free SO_2 of 45–55 ppm. A second wine cannot usually be made in the same volume as the original wine from which the pomace or pulp was obtained, but a volume of ⅓ to ⅔ the original is usually attainable.

Semi-dry: (See *Demi-sec*.) The term denoting a wine as neither dry nor sweet, but closer to dry than sweet. Although usually reserved for sparkling wines, it is gaining frequent use describing still wines. Wine is usually perceived as semi-dry when its specific gravity is in the range of 1.000 to 1.003. The French call such wine **demi-sec**, which has been bastardized into the half-English, half-French term semi-sec.

Semi-Sec: See *Demi-Sec* and *Semi-dry*.

Semi-Sweet: The term denoting a wine as neither dry nor sweet, but closer to sweet than dry. Although usually reserved for sparkling wines, it is gaining frequent use describing still wines. Wine is usually perceived as semi-sweet when its specific gravity is in the range of 1.004 to 1.007. The French term for this type of wine is *demi-doux*.

Silky: An incredibly smooth, lush, and finely textured wine. The French term is *soyeux*.

Skunky: A severe off-odor caused by mercaptan formation. See *Hydrogen Sulfide*.

Sourness: A tart taste in wines, associated with acids, is perceived as sour. The degree of sourness in acid is a function of the pH of the wine and its titratable acidity. In technical terms, it is the hydrogen ion (actually, the hydronium ion) that stimulates the sour taste on the taste buds. The order of decreasing sourness of the primary organic acids in wine is tartaric, malic, citric, lactic, and succinic. Wines with a pH less than 3.1

or a titratable acidity more than 0.9% will taste sour unless balanced with an appropriate amount of residual sugar.

Specific Gravity: In winemaking, specific gravity (SG) is the ratio of any liquid's density to the density of pure water at a given temperature, with pure water having an SG of 1.000 at a tested temperature. Specific gravity is very important in winemaking because we start with a must whose liquid is heavier than water (i.e., whose SG is higher than 1.000) and ferment it until its SG is near or below 1.000. This reduction in SG is caused by the fermentation of sugars (which are heavier than water) into ethanol (with a SG of 0.789, considerably lighter than water).

A completely dry wine, with no residual (unfermented) sugar, very rarely will have a density below 0.990.

A finished wine with an SG higher than 1.000 (for example, 1.008) will contain some residual sugar and be perceptibly sweet, while finished wines with an SG lower than 1.000 (for example 0.996) are perceived as slightly to very dry. It is essential to measure

Measuring specific gravity with a hydrometer

a must's SG with a hydrometer before yeast is introduced to know the must's potential alcohol (PA) and again when fermentation is finished to know the wine's true alcohol as a percentage of volume, which is also known as percent alcohol by volume (ABV).

Today's hydrometers also display the results in degrees Brix, another unit of measure of a liquid's sugar content and preferred by many. One degree Brix equals one percent of sugar by weight. A *refractometer* is another instrument that measures Brix. I have both instruments and use the refractometer to measure the Brix of a grape or fruit or berry in the field but use the hydrometer in the winemaking processes (from preparing the must and into the bottling process). My references in this book will be SG, not Brix.

Stuck Fermentation: A fermentation that has started but then stops before converting all fermentable sugar into alcohol and carbon dioxide or before reaching the toxicity level of the particular yeast strain(s) involved. A stuck fermentation is usually due to an imbalance in the ingredients or to temperature extremes unacceptable to the yeast.

Sucrose: A natural, crystalline disaccharide found in grapes, most fruit, and many plants. This is the type of refined sugar obtained from sugar cane, sugar beets and other sources which, when added to a must or juice to make up for deficiencies in natural sugar, must be hydrolyzed (inverted) into *fructose* and *sucrose* by acids and enzymes in the yeast before it can be used as fuel for fermentation. The winemaker can invert the sugar before adding to the must to save the yeast some work.

Sulfur Dioxide: Appropriate amounts of sulfur dioxide (SO_2) are used in winemaking for their antioxidant, antimicrobial, and preservative properties, but SO_2 also possesses additional benefits. It inhibits the activity of wild yeast strains so desired strains have time to dominate the fermentation, it slows browning initially and during aging and, if a *malolactic fermentation (MLF)* is desired later (or not at all), SO_2 will delay or stop it from occurring, depending on the SO_2 level maintained.

It is helpful to think of SO_2 as an antimicrobial, an antioxidant, and as a preservative during different phases of winemaking, while never forgetting the other benefits that overlap. Very early, SO_2 is introduced primarily for its antimicrobial benefits, to kill unwanted microbes and stun unwanted wild yeast affixed to the base. During this phase, we want oxygen (O_2) in our must because the wine yeast strain we introduce needs O_2 to propagate. But once the yeast saturates the must we deny it O_2, forcing it to make alcohol instead of more yeast. Here, the antioxidant benefits of SO_2 are appreciated. Finally, during maturation and bottling, we rely upon the preservative properties of SO_2 to make our wine last more than a year. But the other roles are always there.

Adding and maintaining an aseptic level of SO_2 is rather complicated. It involves adding a sulfite salt which dissociates into molecular SO_2 (for protection against microbial spoilage) and bisulfite (for protection against chemical oxidation), each in amounts dependent upon the must's or wine's pH, temperature, and to a lesser degree its alcoholic content. Here, however, we will try to simplify the concepts so you will understand how to add and maintain an aseptic level of SO_2.

SO_2 is usually introduced through the addition of **Campden tablets** or sulfite salts of potassium (e.g., **potassium metabisulfite**) or sodium (e.g., sodium bisulfite), although we will not discuss sodium bisulfite here. The appropriate amount to use under controlled conditions is determined by several factors, including the amount of free SO_2 already in the must or wine, the amount desired after the addition, and the wine's pH.

There are some numbers that operate behind the scene during calculations. Except for the first one, you probably won't be aware of them directly, but you need to know they are there.

- Only 57.6% of the sulfite will dissociate and become free to bind with constituents of the must or wine now and in the future. This is a fact. You can't change it.
- 93 to 99% of the amount of sulfite dissociated is ionized bisulfite (HSO_3^-).
- 0.7 to 7% of the amount of sulfite dissociated is molecular SO_2.
- The sum of bisulfite and molecular SO_2 concentrations is referred to as free SO_2.

Both HSO_3^- and SO_2 play important roles in ensuring the health of a must or wine, but it is the molecular SO_2 that is of key importance for our wine. Each is delivered in dose amounts primarily dictated by how much free SO_2 is already present in the wine, the wine's pH, and how much free SO_2 is needed. That last one is tricky. Because only 57.6% of the sulfite will dissociate, and because some of what dissociates will become bound fairly rapidly, one needs to add more than what is merely needed. The 57.6% is built into the calculations in this book (Chapter 2), but the rest is up to you. Every winemaker adopts a strategy that makes him or her comfortable. Personally, I like to build up sulfite level 25% above what is needed as a fudge factor. But with successive additions of sulfite, the fudge factor can be reduced. The things that bind with SO_2 will largely have already been bound by the time we stabilize, until we back sweeten.

Adding SO_2 to your wine will be covered in Chapter 2 but it is worth noting that in the recipes in this book the compound SO_2 refers to all three forms combined.

Sultana: A small, pale golden-green grape originating in Smyrna, Turkey. It is the most widely planted variety in California, where it goes by the name of Thompson Seedless. It is the common "white" or "golden" raisin sold in America.

Sweetness: We all recognize this taste sensation most commonly associated with wines with residual sugars (glucose and fructose), glycerol, ethanol, and 2,3-butanediol (the latter in trace amounts). While the threshold for detecting sweetness (as sugars) is about 1% by volume, the threshold for classifying a wine as sweet is commonly 2% by volume (specific gravity of 1.008) for a wine with 12% alcohol by volume. Sweetness does appear to soften some flavor components and blend with others to enhance their recognition. A wine with poor fruit flavor as a dry wine may possess more recognizable fruitiness when sweetened.

Tannin: Tannins are found in the leaves, stems, skins, and seeds of most fruit and berries. Tannins are polyphenolic compounds with an affinity for binding to and precipitating proteins. If there were just one tannin compound, it would be considerably less difficult to characterize it, but there are several, if not many. And this is just counting the tannins in the plant parts being made into wine. If  one adds oak (chips or extract) to the wine, then there are many more.

Once tannins are incorporated into the must and subjected to fermentation, the chemistry gets very complicated. While you don't need to delve into all those details, there are few things to understand.

Tannin compounds not only bind to proteins but also to each other and many other constituents of wine. Tannin compounds can both break apart into subunits, which also bind to things and can link together and to other constituents to form "long chains" which are heavier and more susceptible to precipitation than a tannin molecule bound to a single protein.

Tannins contribute to mouthfeel through astringency and bitterness. It is thought that tannins bind with proteins in saliva and precipitate them out, leaving a feeling of astringency. Astringency is characterized by a feeling of dryness and friction within the mouth. In its extreme, it is often described as the cheeks being drawn inward and the tongue being lifted. These are physical feelings rather than elements of taste, but the fact is that astringency contributes to mouthfeel in notable ways. A Cabernet Sauvignon with heavy tannins is described as both heavy in the mouth and chewable.

Tartaric Acid: The strongest organic acid in grapes. It is considered the best acid for raising the acidity in an acid-deficient must or wine. 1 g/L (3.8 g/gal.) will raise acidity 1%.

Texture: The impression on the palate delivered by dense, intense, and full-bodied wines.

Thin: A wine lacking body. A wine with a viscosity approximately the same as water.

Titratable Acidity: Also called TA and sometimes total acidity, titratable acidity is the sum of the fixed and volatile acids present in a wine. This is determined by a chemical process called titration. The titratable acidity is usually expressed in terms of tartaric acid, even though the other acids are also measured. Titratable acidity is expressed either as a percentage or as grams per liter. For example, 0.7% TA is the same as 7 grams per liter (or 7 g/L) TA.

Ullage: See *Bottling*.

Unctuous: The thick, often unpleasant, almost syrupy texture of too-sweet wine.

Vinegar: "Sour wine," caused by vinegar-producing bacteria, most notably *Aceto-bacter*. These bacteria are usually airborne but also carried by the so-called vinegar fly (also known as the fruit fly).

Volatile Acidity: Also known as VA, volatile acidity is the acidity produced by volatile acids as opposed to fixed acids. Fixed (non-volatile) acids are those occurring naturally in the grape or fruit base, those added by the vintner, and those non-volatile acids created during fermentation which are stable-fixed. Volatile acids are those created during fermentation or reduction processes (aging) and they are unstable, or those created during spoilage by *Acetobacter*. They can be altered through further reduction or they can evaporate from the wine altogether. Acetic acid and butyric acid are the two most notable volatile acids in wine. In small amounts, VA contributes to a wine's *bouquet*, which is transitory, but if VA is too intense, it will spoil the wine.

Wild Yeast: Any mixture of the thousands of yeast strains that may be airborne or found naturally on fruit; wild yeast does not refer to the cultured wine yeast deliberately added to a must. Grapes, fruit and the air often contain spoilage bacteria, molds or yeast which can destroy a wine's quality, but if no spoilage yeast or

Wild yeast on Oregon grape berries

bacteria are present in the must during the fermentation process, wild yeast can produce an acceptable wine. Due to the risk from spoilage organisms, prudent winemakers treat their must with an aseptic dose of sulfite to kill non-yeast organisms, stun wild yeasts into temporary inactivity, and thereby allow their own choice of cultured yeast to dominate the fermentation. Also, see **Yeast.**

Wine Cellaring (storage): Wine aged at 80 degrees F. will age quickly and decline before the damage is noticed. Cork closures cellared in dry climates will dry out, permitting oxygen to enter the bottle; the wine will oxidize quickly and probably leak all over the place.

Wine racks displayed in open rooms will suffer premature browning from exposure to sunlight and possibly fluorescent lighting.

The miracle that happens inside the bottle is of no consequence if the wine is abused during aging. Home winemakers may not be able to achieve ideal cellar temperatures or humidity; however, there are still many ways to protect the wine.

If wine racks cannot be located in dark, semi-humid areas with stable temperatures, wine can still be stored fairly safely. Empty cardboard wine cases can usually be obtained from wine and liquor stores. Wine can safely be stored in these with corked bottles inserted upside down. If the box has no closure, any cover that will protect the wine from light will do: cardboard, folded newspaper, old towels, etc.

The cases can then be stored in any area with a fairly stable temperature. This kind of "cellar" may not live up to the image portrayed in movies of the 2,000-bottle wine cellar with floor-to-ceiling wine racks, but it is practical if a suitable basement, cellar, walk-in closet, under-stairs storage, or other areas simply do not exist. Avoid using a laundry room if possible due to excessive vibrations from the washing machine, and it should go without saying that the garage is probably the worst location of all.

More than one winemaker has laid his bottles horizontally under the bed, and that is a fairly safe location.

Wine Stabilizer: *Potassium sorbate*, sold by the brand name "Sorbistat K," which produces sorbic acid when added to the wine. When active fermentation has ceased, and the wine is racked the final time after clearing, ½ teaspoon added to 1 gallon of wine will prevent future fermentation. ***Sodium benzoate***, sold as "Stabilizing Tablets," is another type of fermentation inhibitor. These are primarily used with sweet wines and sparkling wines, but may be added to table wines which exhibit difficulty in maintaining clarity after fining or are sweetened to some degree. For sweet wines, the final sugar syrup and stabilizer may be added at the same time. Also, see ***Potassium Sorbate*** and ***Sodium Benzoate.***

Wine Yeast: Yeast cultured especially for winemaking, with such desirable attributes as high alcohol tolerance, firmer sediment formation, and less flavor fluctuation. Wine yeasts are usually obtained from a winemaking/brewing specialty shop or by mail order. See entries for ***Yeast*** on starting a culture before adding to a must.

Winemaking Environment: The wine-maker must provide a near-constant environment favorable to *fermentation* and *maturation*. Here we are talking about maintaining the temperature, humidity, and light requirements most favorable to the healthy biological and chemical progression required to make wine. Ideally, temperature should not exceed 70 degrees F., humidity should be maintained between 55 and 70 percent, and exposure to filtered sunlight and fluorescent lighting should be zero. For most home winemakers, these are impractical, if not impossible, goals. But we do the best we can.

Wine-laden carboys should be stored in basements, closets, specialty built cabinets, or dedicated rooms where lighting can be mitigated. In the absence of these options, we cover them with cloth, opaque plastic (black trash bags are ideal light blockers), mylar, cardboard, or you can just stick them in dark corners and hope for the best. Be sure to store wine in an insulated, temperature controlled-room, as this will limit the changes from day to night. For most of us, we don't have much control over humidity, but it can be moderated by a home cooling system. Air conditioning removes humidity, but it also removes heat.

If you cannot meet all of these requirements, don't be discouraged. The author cannot meet them either and has made award-winning wines for decades. Indeed, the overwhelming majority of all people who make wine at home, including those in the tropics, deserts and far north, cannot meet them, and they do just fine. The environmental goals are just ideals for which we aim.

Wood Aging: This is the process of maturing wine in barrels or casks before bottling. This process allows young wines to soften and absorb some of the wood's flavors and tannins and allows the wine's flavors to become concentrated through slight evaporation through the wood. White oak is the overwhelming wood of choice for wood aging, although mesquite, hickory, pecan, apple, orange, and cherry wood can also contribute unique qualities to wines aged with their chips or shavings. The taste a wood tends to impart in wine reflects the wood's smell. Also, see *Oaking*.

Woody: A wine fault denoting too much (too long) contact with wood, usually oak.

Yeast: Single-cell microorganisms (they are fungi, actually) characterized by asexual reproduction by budding, and in the process synthesize carbohydrates (saccharides) into energy, carbon dioxide, and alcohol. Yeast have been used for thousands of years to make bread and alcoholic beverages. While over 1,500 species of yeast have been identified, almost all wine is made using the species *Saccharomyces cerevisiae*.

- **Wild Yeast:** *Saccharomyces cerevisiae* is a yeast species found naturally on grapes and other fruit, but so are many other genera and species that exhibit less than desirable traits. Many strains of *S. cerevisiae* have been isolated that exhibit traits favorable to making wine. Since we are unable to separate the desirable yeasts from the undesirable, treat all wild yeasts the same: expose them to a dose of SO_2 calculated to render them dormant for a while, during which we introduce a selected culture of yeast proven to be tolerant of SO_2. By the time that the dormant wild yeast decide the environment is favorable to them, the inoculated culture has already dominated the must to the point where the wild yeast cannot survive, they are literally crowded out and starved of O_2.

- **Wine Yeast:** There are dozens of cultured wine yeasts, each isolated and selected for specific traits favorable to the process of winemaking or to the wine itself. Some are more tolerant to SO_2 than most, others are more alcohol tolerant, while others produce more precursors for fruity or floral esters. Some are recommended for red wines, others for white.

Selecting an appropriate yeast strain is but one of the chores some winemakers agonize over, while others select an all-purpose strain and stick with it batch after batch after batch. Over time, most amateur winemakers keep 2–4 specific strains in their refrigerator, proven tools for almost any challenge. At one time, I had 29 strains I evaluated for efficacy across many varieties of base ingredients. Today I keep seven or eight strains that I know will produce most styles of wine I choose to make from just about anything I chose to turn into wine.

One responsibility of the winemaker is to know just what a particular yeast needs in terms of nitrogen, other nutrients, and temperature needs. I have troubleshooted many batches of wine that have just given up before completing fermentation. Too many times, the fault was selecting a yeast strain that could not handle the amount of sugar in the must or using a yeast strain with high nitrogen needs and then not providing enough nitrogen.

Yeast Energizer: There are many proprietary blends of DAP, magnesium sulfate, yeast hulls, and vitamin B complex that are used to energize yeast activity from start to finish, and also to supplement mead, berry, herb, spice, and vegetable wines.

For other wines, if you use both types of nutrients, you should not encounter a stuck or sluggish fermentation. A stuck fermentation is one where yeast activity never adequately starts or stops before fermentation is complete. A sluggish fermentation is one where yeast activity slows and might become stuck. While there are several other reasons a fermentation could become stuck or sluggish, inadequate nutrition is the number one cause. If you do encounter either one, a yeast energizer should solve the problem.

Yeast energizer contains multiple sources of nitrogen as well as yeast hulls and vitamin B complex. It should not be confused with complete yeast nutrient. However, there are products, Super-Ferment is an example, that combine yeast nutrient with yeast energizer. Generally, such products are best used with mead, herb, spice and vegetable wines, but are useful with other bases as well.

Yeast Nutrient: In most musts, the chosen yeast requires more nutrients than is found naturally in the original materials used to make the wine. The exceptions are specific wine grapes that are grown in the right vineyard, with the right climate, in the right year and married to a specific wine yeast suited for just one wine style. Assume a lug of these exceptional grapes fell into your lap. You would need a wine laboratory to determine the exceptional quality of the grapes and recommend the correct yeast to produce the wine style you desire. Assume, as a beginner, that all musts require yeast nutrients.

Yeast nutrients come in two forms, generic yeast nutrient, and complete yeast nutrient. You may need both.

Yeast Starter: The winemaker has the awesome responsibility of getting the yeast started. There are several ways of doing this. You can sprinkle it on the top and wait a couple of days to see if it is just a slow starter or it simply isn't starting at all. You can sprinkle it on the top and stir it in and suffer the same agony. Or you can make a yeast starter solution and know within three or four hours whether it's going to start or not.

You might well be wondering why not assume it's going to start: why all this worry? There are two reasons it might not start. First, it might be too old. Yeast packets and jars bear a "best used by" date of two years from the packaging date. I've been in stores that have some winemaking supplies tucked away in a corner and found yeast packets eight years and more past their best used by dates.

But the yeast may have been dead when they arrived at the store. Dried yeast cultures preferably should be stored and transported under refrigeration. They rarely are. Sealed inside of cargo trailers and box trucks, they can bake in the summer heat. The quickest way to prove

Wine yeast, up-close

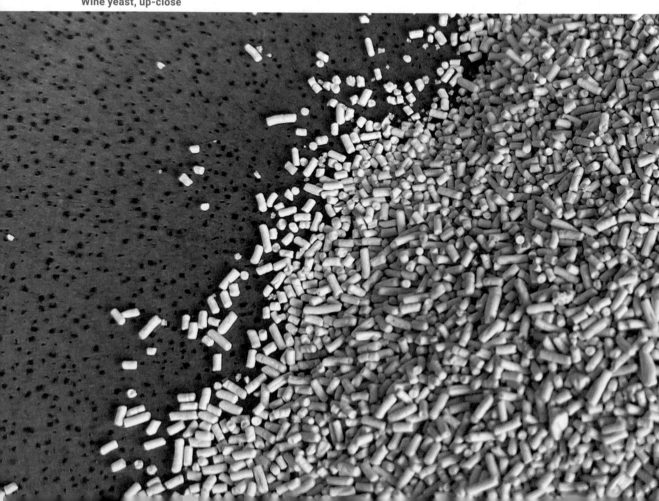

or disprove the viability of a yeast culture is to make a yeast starter solution.

First, let's explore the idea behind it all. Healthy rehydrated yeasts in a favorable environment will double their population every 2–3 hours. A 5–8-gram packet of wine yeast contains around 20 billion dehydrated yeast cells. When hydrated in a friendly environment, they will show viability within 15–30 minutes and will begin propagating within 2–4 hours, doubling in numbers as each cell grows a second cell through a process known as budding. Once propagation begins, it can continue every 2–3 hours until their numbers reach a density where resources required for propagation—sugar, nutrients, O_2—become too scarce. At this point, the yeast will stop propagating and settle down to just making CO_2 and ethanol.

Zest: While "zest" is a quality a good, fresh wine might possess, when mentioned as an ingredient in the recipes in this book, zest refers to the grated rind of lemon, orange, grapefruit, or lime. Only the colored portion of the rind is used, as the white pith is bitter and will spoil the batch. When a recipe calls for two lemons, both the zest and the extracted juice are intended unless otherwise noted.

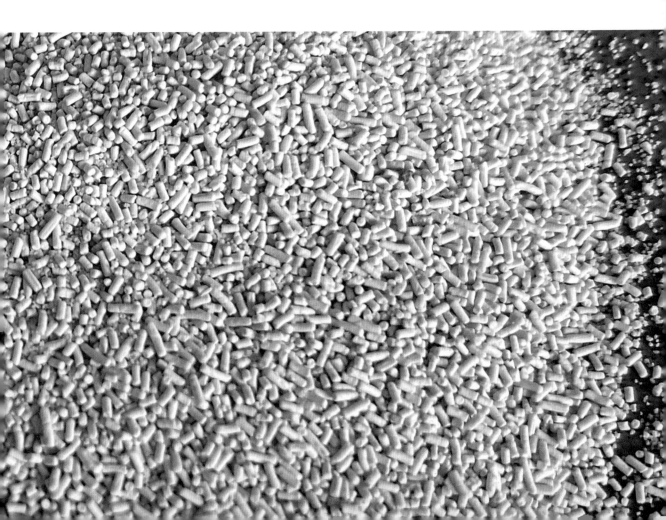

CHAPTER TWO
A WINEMAKER'S TOOLS

If Chapter 1 left you feeling a little dizzy, relax. It's called information overload, and it happens to everyone who makes wine. Maybe not at the outset, but eventually. In a while, you'll understand why that learning curve is necessary and never really ever over.

A winemaker's tools help you apply essential concepts that aren't self-evident. This chapter will provide the missing links between many essential concepts and their real-world applications. It will also introduce and flesh out a few more.

Acid

We previously learned that there are two measures of acidity, TA and pH. TA measures the titratable (or total) acid in the wine, or the concentration of acids, while pH measures the relative strength of those acids; pH is the inverse of TA, meaning the lower the pH (the stronger the acids), the higher the TA (the more acids) generally. These do not measure the same things. TA can be expressed as g/L or as a percentage (*e.g.*, 6.5 g/L = .65% TA), but pH can only be expressed as a logarithmic value (*e.g.*, 3.4 pH).

TA: Titratable acidity is the ability of an alkaline base to neutralize acids in wine and is easily measurable using an acid test kit. Total acidity is the total amount of acid in wine and would be the better measure of TA if there were a simple way to measure it in one's home, but there isn't. But the two are so close to each other that the terms practically mean the same thing. So just think of TA as a rough equivalent for total acidity; it will make no difference to the wine. To determine total acidity of your wine, you need to determine the TA of your wine in a process called titration. You can also taste the TA levels, but that is something no one can teach you.

Acid Blend: Non-grape musts are almost always deficient in acid, and acid needs to be added. Home brew and winemaking shops sell a generic product called acid blend, which usually contains equal amounts of tartaric, malic, and citric acids. I do not recommend using this product in this ratio as microorganisms can easily convert citric acid into other compounds, including acetic acid, rendering one-third of your addition unstable and unreliable.

It is far safer to make your own acid blend by purchasing and mixing equal parts of tartaric and malic acid. Both are sold in a crystalline form. You need not make more than a 2- or 4-ounce batch at a time unless you are making large batches of wine. Store the acids and the blend in airtight containers in a dark, cool place (like a cabinet or closet). If you want to add some citric acid to your blend, minimize it to no more than 20%. In this book, we generally add specific acids as required rather that a blend, but the blends will work as substitutes for the specifics.

Testing for TA: Testing the TA of a must or wine is simple if you have the correct equipment and reagents. If you don't, there are numerous inexpensive acid test kits. Country Wines has a Wine Acid Titration Kit for a little

A pH meter and common wine-making chemicals

over $10. Vintner's has an Acid Test Kit for just under that price. And there are others as well. Look for a kit that contains a graduated test tube, a syringe, sodium hydroxide (NaOH) with a concentration of 0.2N, and phenolphthalein (pronounced "fee nol fa lein").

Testing is simple and straightforward. The only thing you need to supply (besides the must or wine to be tested) is distilled water. Just follow the instructions and you'll obtain the TA of your must or wine. The distilled water is a necessity. The usual method of testing is to place 15 mL of must/wine into a graduated test tube, add distilled water to bring the volume to approximately 100 mL, followed by three drops of phenolphthalein. Shake the sample to mix thoroughly. Draw 10 mL of 0.2N sodium hydroxide into a syringe and slowly add 0.5 mL to the test tube, shaking it to mix. I recommend wearing rubber gloves because sodium hydroxide is caustic. The color will change: white wines will turn pink, and red wines will turn dark gray. Wait at least a minute to see if the color changes back to its original hue. If it does, add another 0.5 mL of sodium hydroxide to the tube and repeat the color change steps. Repeat this procedure until the color does not change back to its original hue. Then calculate the amount of sodium hydroxide added to the sample. Every 1 mL equates to 1 g/L of TA. If you added 5.5 mL of 0.2N sodium hydroxide, the TA would be 5.5 g/L. Perform this test in good, strong light because with red wines it can be very difficult to recognize the final color change. An easy alternative method of determining your TA is using a pH meter and titrating to an endpoint of 8.2.

pH: The abbreviation pH is short for potential of Hydrogen, and refers to a logarithmic scale measuring the concentration of hydrogen ions in a substance; the lower half of the scale consists of acidic materials, with alkaloids on the upper half. This simply means that the lower the number is on the scale, the higher the acidity. Note: Because the scale is logarithmic, it means that a substance with a pH of 3 is 10 times more acidic than one with a pH of 4. A substance with a pH of 2 is 100 times more acidic than one with a pH of 4.

Most wines have a pH between pH 3.0–3.5. A pH of 3.55 is considered a safe threshold for sound wine, as certain harmful bacteria can more easily tolerate higher pH. Additionally, oxidation occurs much more rapidly at pH 3.55 and above, and this is something SO_2 will struggle to resist. In the other direction, some wines with pH as low as 3.0 are very drinkable if the acid is offset by residual sugar, glycerol (also called glycerine, produced during fermentation), and alcohol to create a **balance** between sweetness and tartness.

Some winemakers swear by pH and never look at TA. In this book, we will generally go by pH but be aware of TA when needed to bring the taste of acid into a tolerable window. The numbers matter, but so do your taste buds.

TA is easy to measure with a TA testing kit or with a pH meter, although each test uses consumables, which eventually have to be replaced. Supplies are plentiful: check eBay.

pH meter: While we are not going to rely entirely on pH, when we need to measure it, we wish to do so accurately. To do this, we will need a *pH meter*. This will require you to invest in an inexpensive pH meter with ATC (automatic temperature compensation). By inexpensive, I mean

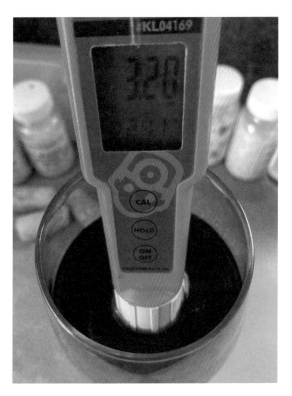

between \$50 and \$70, not the cheap \$5 to \$10 mini-meters for testing water. Stay away from those that measure plus/minus 0.1 pH accuracy with single-point calibration. You will appreciate one with plus/minus 0.01 pH accuracy, usually with 2- or 3-point calibration. Remember that in a logarithmic scale—hundredths matter. Every pH meter comes with its own operating instructions, so consult them before using yours.

Litmus Strips: If you need to save up for a pH meter, you can at least get an idea of where your wine's pH might be by using winemaker's litmus strips. Their accuracy can be off by as much as a factor of 10, but they usually will tell you if you're within or close to the window where wine resides: pH 3.0–3.5. It is helpful if you can find a litmus test graduated to increments of 0.5. Hydrion makes such a pH strip, with a pH range of 0.0–6.0.

Testing for TA with a pH meter: This is so simple it should be illegal. You only need your pH meter, a 10-mL plastic syringe, your pH meter calibration solutions (for pH 4 and pH 7), fresh 0.2N sodium hydroxide (NaOH), distilled water which has been boiled and then cooled, and a completely degassed sample of your must or wine. You will also need a beaker (glass) of about 250 mL (1 cup) capacity (a glass measuring cup would work fine). Remember, only measure TA before adding yeast and when you are sure fermentation has ended.

To start off, follow the manufacturer's instructions to calibrate your pH meter, first to pH 7, and then to pH 4.

Clean the syringe with the distilled water and measure 15 mL of your wine in the beaker—enough to contact your pH meter's electrode. Place the pH meter in the beaker, ensuring the electrode has good contact with the wine. Measure the wine's pH and leave the meter on and in the beaker.

Clean the syringe very well with the distilled water and draw exactly 10 mL of NaOH. For safety's sake, you should be wearing rubber gloves, as NaOH is very caustic. Also, remember that 10 mL is the same as 10 cc.

With one hand, hold the beaker and pH meter and with the other begin adding the NaOH, 1 mL at a time, Swirl the beaker after each addition and monitor the pH.

Continue adding NaOH and monitoring the pH. When the pH passes 7.0, slow down the amount of NaOH added. It is very easy to overshoot the endpoint, so add 1 drop at a time at pH 7.0 and higher and swirl after each drop. Pay close attention to the pH monitor reading.

When the endpoint of pH 8.2 is reached, look carefully at the syringe and write down the amount of NaOH used to reach the endpoint. The number of mL used is the TA of the wine. For example, if you used 7.3 mL, the TA is 7.3 g/L, or 0.73%.

Dispose of the wine in the beaker, return unused NaOH to the bottle it came from, and clean the syringe thoroughly with the distilled water. Rinse the pH meter electrode with the distilled water. Blow on the electrode to speed up its drying, and then rinse it again with the distilled water, help it dry, and then either use it to measure the TA of another must or wine or return it to its storage bin. Be careful not to touch the electrode with your hands.

Adjusting TA and pH: Most of the recipes in book this will require the addition of acid either because the base contains too little acid (*e.g.*, plums, pears, figs) or practically none at all (*e.g.*, dandelions, parsnips, nettle tips), or because the addition of water dilutes the natural acidity level too much.

Raising Acidity: This is far simpler than reducing it. To raise (increase) TA, you simply add acid. Acid corrections must occur before fermentation if possible, or if not, as soon as possible. The addition of 1 g/L (3.8 g/gal.) of tartaric acid will raise the TA by 1 g/L (0.1%). Only minor adjustments should be made after fermentation, as they will taste harsher as the wine ages.

When adjusting acid, proceed in baby steps, even if you know you have a way to go. Very large adjustments can skewer the actual results for a few hours. A good process is to make an adjustment, stir the must well to integrate the adjustment, wait 30 minutes, and then continue adjusting further.

Reducing TA: The reducing agent of choice is water. Most non-grape bases will require dilution with water to get you to a gallon, and water will dilute the TA. Never make your acid reductions before your must is fully diluted. Also, consider that fermentation can reduce TA by 0.5 to 1.0 g/L. If malic acid is the major acid present, Lalvin 71B wine yeast can metabolize 20–35 percent more malic acid than most other yeasts, so if you use it, assume the TA will be reduced by 1 g/L. Dilute the must first, measure TA, and then decide if you need to reduce the acidity more and by how much, factoring in a loss of 0.5 to 1 g/L to fermentation. However much is left to reduce must be reduced with a buffer.

The buffers of choice for reducing TA are calcium carbonate and potassium bicarbonate. Either buffer will work, but potassium bicarbonate is the least desirable option if your major acid is not tartaric. It's the go-to choice for grapes but few other bases. So, for non-grape wines, the buffer of choice will be calcium carbonate. Note: When using calcium carbonate, the must cannot be cooler than 60 degrees F.

Calcium carbonate: The must should be treated after *amelioration* (diluting with water) but before fermentation. The must should not be cooler than 60 degrees F. Adding calcium carbonate will cause a dramatic reaction in the must. There's no better way to describe it, except there will be an eruption of foam that will rise almost as high or higher as the height of the must. That means if your primary is only 2 gallons and you're making 1 gallon of wine, the foam could almost reach the rim of the primary. Indeed, it might surpass it, making a giant mess to clean up. My primary for 1-gallon batches is a 3-gallon glass canister with a lid obtained at Walmart. What is really nice about it is that you can see the wine, the lees, and the tip of the racking cane.

The desired dose is 0.66 g/L (2.5 g/gal.) to lower TA by 1 g/L (0.1%). Lowering the acidity by more than 1 g/L should be done in 1 g/L stages. Add 1 g/L, stir well despite the rising foam. It will take 2–3 hours for the must to settle down, perhaps even longer. When it is settled and calm, stir in another adjustment. A total dosage of 3 g/L is the maximum that can be added without the possible detection of a chalky taste in the wine. Notice the word used was "possible." Taste the wine. Ask someone else to taste it. Then decide if you can add more.

The calcium carbonate will turn excess acid into calcium tartrate crystals, which will precipitate over time. Post-fermentation, the wine should be matured for at least three months to ensure the crystals settle in secondaries rather than in bottles.

Potassium Bicarbonate: When making wine from grapes, potassium bicarbonate is the buffer of choice. A 0.66 g/L addition will reduce TA by 1 g/L. The addition of potassium bicarbonate releases a great deal of CO_2. When adding to any must or wine, the containment vessel (primary) should have at least 50% free headspace to contain the large amount of foam produced. The operative phrase was "at least." In addition, it should not be added to very cold musts or wines as most of the released CO_2 will then remain dissolved in the wine, creating a carbonation problem requiring considerable attention.

Reducing pH: One of the downsides to making a white wine from, say, dandelions, is that dandelions have such a low natural acidity that I have never been able to measure it. The natural TA is 0–0.5 g/L, and the pH is around 7. It is, therefore, necessary to raise TA while at the same time lowering pH. In both cases, the jump to the desired numbers is quite a leap. Adding tartaric acid will send you well on your way to your desired numbers. You will not reach both numbers at the same time because TA and pH are not proportional. The final additions are "fine-tuning" and can be done with malic and even citric acid if necessary.

As pointed out in Chapter 1, rosé and white wines should be adjusted to as close to pH 3.3 as possible. Red wines should be adjusted to pH 3.4. If recipes specify using acid blend, this is just for the initial addition. Remember, you'll be using your own blend of tartaric and malic acids. For all further adjustments, use tartaric acid. The age-old rule-of-thumb for tartaric acid additions is that 1 g/L of tartaric acid will reduce the pH by 0.1, except that every 4 g/L of tartaric only decreases the pH by up to 3 g/L due to what is called the buffering effect in acid chemistry.

There is a tendency to measure the pH and calculate the tartaric acid addition based on this rule-of-thumb. For small adjustments of 1–3 g/L, this is fine, but if your adjustment is more than 4 g/L of tartaric acid, it is prudent to conduct a bench trial to better guide you to the amount of tartaric acid to add.

Bench Trials: To conduct a bench trial, dissolve 10 grams of tartaric acid in 15–20 mL of distilled water. Use only distilled water. Add more distilled water to bring the total to 100 mL, making a 10% solution. Now set out 5 glasses or beakers, and to each add exactly 100 mL of your juice or strained must. The first is your control, so set it aside. To the next 4 add 1, 2, 3, and 4 mL of the 10% solution, respectively. Each mL of the 10% solution in 100 mL of distilled water is equivalent to 1 g/L of tartaric acid or 1 g/L in a 100-mL sample of juice or must. Using your pH meter, measure the pH in each glass. When one of the glasses meets your target, you know how much tartaric acid to add to your must/juice/wine to achieve your desired pH. If none of the glasses meet your needs, add more 10% solution to total 5, 6, 7, and 8 mL of solution. Sooner or later you'll meet your mark.

Meeting your mark is just part of conducting a bench trial where taste will be affected. So taste the juice or wine in the glass that hit your target. If it is too tart, you'll want to find the sweet spot between it and the dose before it. If it's too flat, you have a way to go.

A word about Acidex™: As you delve into the literature of winemaking, at some point you will probably run across a product called Acidex and its step-child Acidex Super-K. These are both avenues into what is known as double-salt precipitation that reduces high acidity levels by reducing both tartaric and malic acids. Don't go there. The products are only specified for grape musts and wines and even then carry a certain amount of risk. Reviews and anecdotal testimony offer mixed results. At best, double-salt precipitation is an advanced technique for grape wines, and such products shouldn't be used in non-grape wines.

Acid Blend: See **Acid**, subsection **TA**.

Airlock: Also referred to as a fermentation trap, this marvelous invention has an S-shaped airway that allows you to close it off with a little water, metabisulfite solution, or vodka. The CO_2 produced by the yeast rises through the airlock, forces its way through the liquid as bubbles, and escapes to contribute to climate change. These come in a variety of sizes and shapes, none holding an advantage over the others.

Amelioration: This is a fancy word often thought to mean "to add water." It is sometimes used interchangeably with dilution, although that is usually technically incorrect. Dilution refers to making something thinner. Amelioration refers to improving something that's unsatisfactory. We ameliorate to improve a juice that has, for example, high acidity, or astringency or herbaceousness.

We usually ameliorate to correct high acidity. But we can also ameliorate to correct astringency, as with persimmons.

Acidity is inversely proportional to the volume of the must/wine. If we double the volume with water, the TA will be halved, but the pH will only be affected slightly because the strength of the acid has not changed all that much. We cannot calculate the pH change without knowing more than we want about the acid present. So we'll pretend there is no change in our pH.

Autolysis: The decomposition of dead yeast cells that can be favorable or unfavorable, depending on the wine, the yeast, and the process involved. The favorable process can occur in wines that are aged *sur lie* ("on the lees"). Certain wines such as Chardonnay and Sauvignon Blanc benefit from autolysis because they gain complexity during the process that enhances their structure and mouthfeel. They gain extra body and aromatic complexity. Aging *sur lie* is usually conducted with an accompanying regime of periodic lee stirring that can result in a creamy, viscous mouthfeel.

Amylase: An enzyme that catalyzes hydrolysis of starch into dextrin and maltose. It can effectively be used to neutralize starch haze, which emerges from the active fermentation of starchy ingredients, such as root vegetables, or residual starch haze post-fermentation. It is used only when starch is the obvious culprit.

Balance: The pleasurable, proportional correctness of a wine's many aromatic and taste components in harmony, but especially alcohol, acidity, sugar, and tannin, describes balance. The taste or aroma of the base ingredient (fruit, flower, or another botanical component), or its absence, may also be said to contribute to balance, although this is a minor consideration and should more correctly be associated with the wine's character. A wine is balanced when its acidity, tannins, alcohol, and sweetness all sit around the table as equals. No one of them has ascendancy over the other three. Each plays a unique part. Body also contributes to balance.

Acidity softens with time. A wine bottled with just a bit too much acidity may have perfect acidity in a year or two. So which acidity expresses a correct balance? Here we enter a world of nuance. If we know where the wine is in its evolution, we should have an idea of where it is going. We can then say the wine "is balanced today" or the wine "is balanced next year," not "will be balanced" but "is" because we know it to be true. It takes experience to know that, or think we know it. The beginning winemaker should stay rooted in the here and now.

Tannins, and the phenolic family they belong to, are such a nuisance at times, but when they aren't, they are usually in deficiency or balance. If they cannot be noted at all when they should be (as in a big red) their absence is a deficiency, but their absence in a white is no big deal. The recipes in this book slip a little tannin in every white wine simply because it adds to the notion of "wine." We don't want astringency in our lemon wine, but we don't simply want an alcoholic lemonade either. Tannins put a little snap in there without cracking the whip.

Alcohol can be sweet, or it can be hot, or it can even be a no-show. How is this? Well, if there's too much alcohol, it's on the hot side. If you want heat, drink spirits. Wine is more refined. But if there isn't enough alcohol, it's the same as a no-show. You know it when you taste it because it's not there. And then there can be a slight sweetness in alcohol. It is about age. A slightly aggressive alcohol profile gets smoothed and rounded out with time, and this mitigation hits the palate as a slight shift toward the sweet side.

Sweetness, not sugar, is what is at the table. Sure, sweetness includes the sugars, but it also includes the sweet perception of aged alcohol, glycerol, and the "sweetness" of oak tannin as opposed to the "bitterness" of grape tannin.

To muck things up a bit, an awful lot of people think that "body" belongs in a

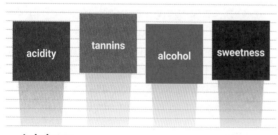

In balance

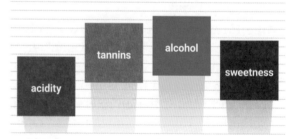

Out of balance

conversation of balance. They argue that a wine without body is out of balance with its potential, but now we're entering the world of metaphysics. Every wine judging score sheet I have ever seen has an item on it called "body." A wine either has it, or it doesn't. Whether it belongs at the balance table is the debate, with no fixed resolution in sight. You may opt either way without argument from this author.

Blending: The process of combining different wines to create a composite that's better than any of the individual wines. The wines blended might be from different varieties, vintages, or regions, have aged in different circumstances (in wood vs. without), or even be wines made from different fruit. Blending is often used to balance high TA wines with low TA ones. For our purposes, we will almost always be referring to blending wines of different fruit or other bases.

Blending Trials: When blending wines, conduct bench trials with measured quantities that are smaller than the whole to get it right. Some winemakers like to use 75.7 mL because it is 2% of 1 U.S. gallon, and results can be multiplied by 50 to arrive at the total addition of the blender (wine to add) to the blended (wine receiving the blender).

Trials are conducted by usually setting up 5 glasses containing the same amount of wine to be blended. One glass is the control sample (untouched) and is set aside. To the remaining 4 glasses, we add differing measured amounts of the blender, such as 5 mL, 10 mL, 15 mL, and 20 mL. Now we taste each glass, starting with the least amount of blender. It may be that 5 mL and 10 mL are not enough,

but 15 mL is a bit much. The correct amount is between 10 mL and 15 mL.

We can move the 10 mL glass to number 2 (remember, number 1 is our control) and the 15 mL glass to number 5. To glass 3 we might add 12 mL, and to 4 we might add 13 mL. Now we taste again. Chances are we'll find our perfect blend. Suppose 10 mL is still not enough, but 12 mL is too much. By deduction, the solution is 11 mL.

Bottling: Transferring the wine to bottles should be done as gently as possible so as not to agitate it and introduce unwanted O_2. This can be done as simply as running a hose from a secondary to a lower bottle, initiating suction that pulls the wine down the hose, and allowing the wine to enter a tilted bottle or an upright one when the exit end of the hose has a ***bottling tip*** attached. The latter is a device with a valve inside that closes when the hose is lifted from the bottom and opens when pressed. There are variations of this device.

The bottle is filled to within a half- to three-quarters of an inch of where the bottom of the closure (cork or screw cap) will be. This minimizes the ***ullage***, or airspace, in the bottle.

Bottles are then labeled and stood upright for three days to allow the headspace, or ullage, to equilibrate with the wine. Screw-capped bottles need not be so pampered. They can immediately be stood up, laid on their sides or stored upside down, the latter so you can read the labels while lying on the floor on your back, sober or otherwise.

Closures: There has long been a debate as to whether natural cork, synthetic cork, or screw caps offered the best closure for the wine bottle. In terms of permitting premature oxidation, the screw cap has surely proven in 10-year side-by-side trials to allow almost no passage of post-bottling O_2 into the container.

In terms of wine development due to micro-oxygenation, the natural cork is without peer. By natural cork, I mean one that is 100% a homogeneous piece of cork, not bits of pieces of cork bound together to form an amalgamated "cork" closure.

Corker: For the home winemaker, there are hand corkers and floor corkers.

- **Hand corker:** These come in a variety of designs, each of which utilizes a different mechanical principle to get the cork in the bottle. The simplest one is a plunger-type and utilizes your brute strength to force the cork into the bottle, requiring more force than you might imagine. An improvement on the plunger-type is the lever-type, which harnesses lever action to push the cork and requires less brute force. There are several designs of lever-type hand corkers, including double-lever types, some of which require an extra set of hands to operate easily. The compression-type hand corker uses the same principles as are used in certain floor models.

- **Floor corker:** These are celebrated for their ease of use and adaptability. When the corker is open, a bottle is stood upright on a spring-loaded pedestal while a cork is inserted into a chamber walled-in by four movable brass irises. When the handle is in a backward or open position, the chamber is open so it can receive a cork. When the lever is brought forward, the irises close ever tighter around the cork and compress it, while at the same time a steel plunger is driven down to push the cork down out of the chamber and into the wine bottle. The plunger is adjustable and can drive the cork to specific depths. When the operation is complete, the lever is again laid back, opening the chamber and releasing the bottle. One can cork bottles as fast as one can remove a corked bottle, position an uncorked one, load a cork into the chamber, swing the lever forward to cork the bottle and back again to release the newly corked bottle. A floor corker is essential to making corking an effortless and enjoyable task.

Ullage: The airspace between the wine and the bottom of whatever contains it—the bottom of an airlock or the bottom of a cork. This airspace is critically important in the healthy development of wine. Any such space is filled with air, of which roughly 20% is O_2. In the case of an airlock, it will be removed several times (testing, racking, tasting) and each time that airspace (ullage) will be replenished with fresh air containing 20% O_2, which will be dissolved into the wine while you are adding sulfites to keep the stuff out. In the bottle, the 20% oxygen in the space above the wine will interact with the wine over time and contribute to its eventual oxidation. While this is a given, there is no reason to provide more oxygen than necessary, so if you are thinking, if a half-inch is good then a quarter-inch should be better. No. Changes in temperature and atmospheric pressure will cause the wine to expand and contract periodically. The expanding ullage will push against the cork and over time cause it to lose its grip on the walls of the bottle. You don't want that—one-half-inch to three-quarter-inch.

Capsule: A foil, plastic, or mylar sleeve that fits over the cork of a corked bottle, giving it a finished appearance. The capsule is heat sensitive and easily shrunk around the bottle with a directed heat source such as a blow-dryer.

Calcium Carbonate: See *Acid*, subsection *Reducing TA*.

Fining: A fermenting wine is cloudy because of the incredible number of yeast and other particulates in suspension. As the sugar in the must gets consumed by the yeast or the yeast produce too much alcohol to survive in, wholesale death occurs, and any suspended yeast cells begin falling to the bottom of the secondary. In theory, when the last yeast cell is dead and all particulates have precipitated, the wine should be perfectly clear. If it isn't, we look for reasons. Usually, pectin creates a slight haze and a dose of pectic enzyme does the trick. If not, the problem most likely is something in suspension, and so we turn to a fining agent to clear the wine.

Most of what is suspended in the wine will carry a positive or negative charge. Fining agents also carry a positive or negative charge. Opposite charges attract, so if we use the correct fining agent in the correct dosage, most of what is in suspension will have a fining agent particle attached to it and, having gained mass and weight, will fall to the bottom, with other particulates falling by gravity, leaving the wine clear.

Two-part fining agents include a positively-charged agent and one that is negatively-charged. They are added at different, spaced times (follow the instructions on the packet) so that they don't merely attract each other. Between the two, they should get everything in suspension. Any haze that remains should be removed by an appropriate enzyme or other fining agent.

Fining Agents: There are many individual fining agents on the market, each preferred by advanced or commercial winemakers who learned their trade years ago, in college or under the apprenticeship of a seasoned master winemaker. Many fining agents are less expensive than what will be recommended here, but those recommended here are simpler to use and will get the job done. Generally speaking other fining agents are complex, more advanced tools than are suited for the beginner.

We'll only be using four fining agents: polyvinylpolypyrrolidone (sold as PVPP or Polyclar), bentonite, and gelatin, as the need arises, and then we'll follow the directions supplied by the manufacturer as there are various formulations. So, where is the fourth?

Aside from these three, our approach is to ensure that when you need to use a fining agent and do not know if you are dealing with positive or negative charged particles, or if they are charged, you need to get the job done anyway with as little fuss as possible. For that peace of mind, we'll be using the 2-part fining system utilizing products such as Super-Kleer KC or Kitosol 40.

Polyvinylpolypyrrolidone (PVPP or Polyclar): An inert, synthetic polymer used in both red and white wine to reduce the level of phenolic compounds associated with browning and astringency through hydrogen bonding, PVPP is effective against a wide variety of low molecular weight polyphenols. It can remove oxidized flavors and aromas to an extent without itself impacting flavor or aroma, and it can reduce or remove bitterness.

PVPP should be used early on to freshen a wine. Since there are several manufacturers, always follow the accompanying instructions and rack soon after use as instructed.

Bentonite: This is a very fine clay used as a fining or clarifying agent in wine to remove proteins, to achieve Heat Stabilization, or to remove another fining agent. Bentonite has a negative, attracting charge which attracts positively charged particles suspended in wine and carries them to the lees at it settles. It is especially effective at fining yeast, and other persistent protein-based particles. It helps polish the wine to brilliance, purify the color, and reduce certain off-flavors.

Bentonite is mixed with water to form a slurry, which has to sit a while to set (allow the clay to absorb as much water as it is capable of absorbing). It is then stirred into the wine, post-fermentation, gently but thoroughly. The wine is then gently stirred every hour for the remainder of the day (at least four times) to

maintain its suspension and attract more suspended particles. The colder the wine, the stronger bentonite's charge will be and the better its effectiveness. The wine is later racked off the bentonite lees.

Because bentonite deposits vary in the strength of the charge of its particles, bentonites from different mines have slightly different instructions. Follow the manufacturer's instructions for its use.

Gelatin: A natural extractant from animal parts, gelatin is well-suited to reduce larger molecular suspended phenols and tannins. It reduces or removes bitterness and astringency and improves mouthfeel.

Gelatin is primarily for use in red wines because it would strip a white of what few tannins it possesses, although it is possible to "seed" white wine with tannin before gelatin fining in order to leave the wine's natural tannins in place, but that process is beyond the scope of this book.

Follow the manufacturer's instructions on mixing the gelatin and carefully calculate the dose. Excess gelatin can create protein instability and actually cause cloudiness in white wine.

Within three days of its use, the wine should be fined with a negatively charged fining agent such as Kieselsol or racked. This points to the problem with most fining agents—they do half the job and rely on another to finish the job. At one time, I had seven different fining agents in my refrigerator with notes on what to use prior or next and the preferred order of use. After using Super-Kleer™ just once, I began reducing my inventory of fining agents.

Gelatin will deteriorate over time, so always purchase fresh gelatin before use.

Super-Kleer KC™: This product consists of premeasured and packaged portions of kieselsol and chitosan. Its strength is that the two components provide positive and negative charges, ensuring that the widest range of suspended solids will be fined. The kieselsol is added first and a minimum time later (1–3 days, but I

recommend 2–3 days) the chitosan is dissolved in warm water and gently stirred in. Wine will clear in 24–48 hours, but this will not remove pectin haze or reactants to hard water.

Super-Kleer KC costs about $3–4 per dose. An alternate product using the same ingredients is Kitosol 40, which is considerably more expensive and no more effective.

Gram Scale: We will be working with additives measured in grams, and for this, a gram scale is a necessity. Although there are rough conversions (e.g., ½ teaspoon equals X grams), they are indeed rough. Harbor Freight sells gram scales for under $10, both in the store and online.

Hydrometer: A hydrometer is a weighted glass bulb with printed scales for comparing the density of a liquid with that of distilled water. There are many variants of the hydrometer. Some have only one scale, some two, but most have three, specific gravity (for measuring dissolved sugar), degrees Brix (another scale for measuring dissolved sugar), and potential alcohol (PA).

The bulb is larger in diameter on the weighted end than along the portion containing the scale, which, by comparison, is rather skinny. The hydrometer is used in conjunction with a test cylinder that holds a sample of the liquid to be queried, usually about a cup. It is useful to think of both items, together, as the hydrometer, however inaccurate that may be. Next to the airlock, the hydrometer is the most useful tool a winemaker can possess. The hydrometer is to the winemaker what the compass is to the mariner.

The specific gravity (SG) scale will usually read from 0.990 to 1.120. The SG of distilled water is 1.000. If you fill a test cylinder with water and float your hydrometer in it, the water surface should rest at the 1.000 calibration mark. As you dissolve sugar (or anything else) in the water, the hydrometer will float higher because the density, or weight, of the dissolved sugar and other suspended solids) is holding it up against a known scale. One pound of sugar dissolved in one U.S. gallon of water will float the hydrometer to the 1.046 level. A reading of 46 is the gravity of the dissolved sugar, but 1.046 is the specific gravity; it's specific to distilled water. You can say, "a gravity of 46" or "a specific gravity of 1.046." To be accurate and well-understood in conveying the measurement, use SG.

Table 2 (see page 57) shows some hydrometer Specific Gravity (SG) readings and the Potential Alcohol of that SG. The third column shows the amount of sugar in a US gallon to achieve that SG reading, while the fourth column shows the amount of sugar required to be added to a US gallon (containing no sugar until now) to achieve the same SG. The final column shows how the volume of a US gallon increases as the sugar is added to reach the SG shown.

I have demonstrated, through careful tests, that sugars containing residual molasses (brown sugar, Demerara, Turbinado, Muscovado, Sugar-in-the-Raw, etc.) raise the specific gravity a little higher than processed white sugar, but the difference is negligible in 1-gallon batches. With 5- or 6-gallon batches, it registers a noticeable difference. But the shift in flavor profile offsets that difference.

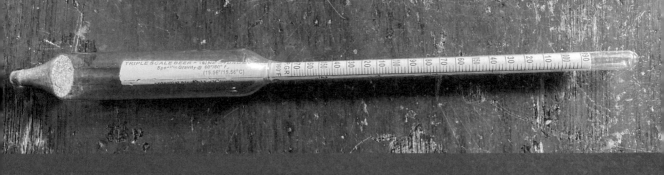

How to Use a Hydrometer

An amount of liquid, either wine or juice strained from the must, is placed in the test cylinder and the glass bulb is lowered into it. How much liquid? Usually ½ to 1 cup, just enough so that the glass bulb floats freely from the bottom. Because bubbles of air and carbon dioxide (CO_2) gas can attach themselves to the glass instrument, it is necessary to spin it in the cylinder to dislodge them. Also, wine contains CO_2 so samples should be degassed as much as possible to get more accurate hydrometer readings.

When the instrument stops spinning and bobbing and comes to rest, get down at eye level with where the scale is at the top of the test liquid. It is natural for liquids to rise slightly around objects they embrace. You will see this rise at the test cylinder wall and the floating instrument. The rise above the actual level of the liquid is called the meniscus. You read the scale where it intersects the bottom of the meniscus, the true level of the liquid.

Whatever the number is, write it down! It is a good (and very useful) habit to create a log page for the wine you are making. Here you should make a note of everything— all ingredients (and how much of each), all measurements, all calculations, all lengths of time between steps you take, etc. I cannot tell you from memory how I made a Best in Class Black Cherry Wine in 1996, but I can turn to my wine log for the wine and it is all there, including where I bought the black cherries. Yes, I posted the basic recipe for this wine on my website, but it is generic for that attempt. In my wine log, I note exactly how much acid I added, when I tested for sulfites, how much I added to raise the free SO_2, and much more. Get in the habit of writing it down!

When all is said and done, and the fermentation appears to be finished, measure the SG again. This number should be somewhere between 0.990 and 1.000. (this is known as fermenting to dryness). Suppose your must had a starting SG of 1.096. Fermented to 1.000, the wine would have an ABV of 13% (read the PA scale for 1.096 and it is 13%). That brings us to 1.000. Now suppose your wine finished with an actual SG of 0.992. That extra 0.008 below 1.000 means something. Use the table on page 57 to obtain the approximate value in ABV—I say approximate because the values below 1.000 are all fractions with many digits right of the decimal point, which have been rounded up or down as appropriate.

Thus, if we add 1.1% ABV to 13% ABV, we arrive at a finished ABV of approximately 14.1%.

Also, please note that fermentation produces heat from the activity of the yeast. Most hydrometers are calibrated to give correct readings at 60 or 68 degrees F. Higher temperatures thin the wine somewhat and result in lower readings than you'd get at the calibrated temperature. For details on how to adjust for your temperature, see the table on page 57.

Fermentation temperatures above 95 degrees F. put your yeast at risk. Don't allow it to go that high. You can cool a fermentation down in several ways. Here are two.

Place the primary or secondary in a pan of cold water and then later add a few ice cubes to the water. Add more at half-hour intervals—not too many at any time or you risk putting the yeast in shock, which

is every bit as bad. The goal is a gradual lowering of the temperature. Use a thermometer to monitor your process.

A second method is to wrap a damp towel around the vessel and allow evaporation to drop the temperature (a reduction of 8–10 degrees is not uncommon). You can aim a fan at the vessel to speed up evaporation and increase cooling slightly, but remember to keep the towel damp and not let it dry out.

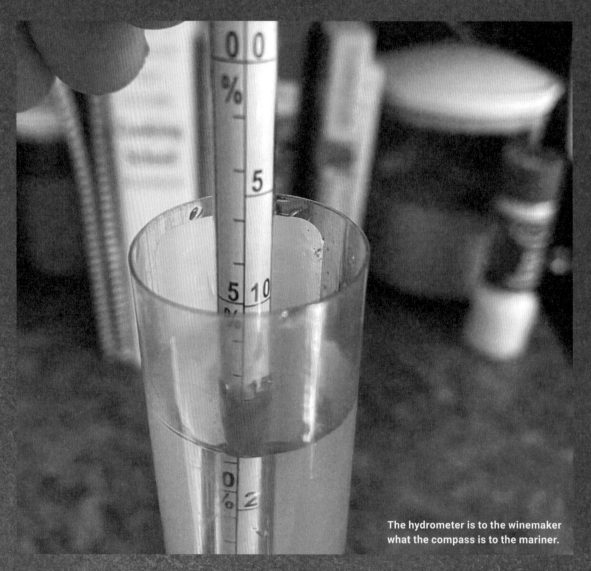

The hydrometer is to the winemaker what the compass is to the mariner.

Table 2. Specific Gravity, Potential Alcohol & Sugar

SPECIFIC GRAVITY	POTENTIAL ALCOHOL (% ABV)	AMOUNT OF SUGAR IN US GALLON	AMOUNT OF SUGAR ADDED TO US GAL.	VOLUME WITH SUGAR ADDED TO US GAL.
1.010	0.9	1.7 oz.	2.1 oz.	1 gal. 0.8 oz.
1.015	1.6	3.4 oz.	4.2 oz.	1 gal. 2.4 oz.
1.020	2.3	5.8 oz.	6.7 oz.	1 gal. 4.0 oz.
1.025	3.0	7.5 oz.	8.3 oz.	1 gal. 5.6 oz.
1.030	3.7	10 oz.	10.8 oz.	1 gal. 6.4 oz.
1.035	4.4	12.5 oz.	13.3 oz.	1 gal. 8.0 oz.
1.040	5.1	14.0 oz.	15.0 oz.	1 gal. 8.8 oz.
1.045	5.8	15.8 oz.	1 lb 0.7 oz.	1 gal. 10.4 oz.
1.050	6.5	1 lb 1.5 oz.	1 lb 3.3 oz.	1 gal. 11.2 oz.
1.055	7.2	1 lb 3.0 oz.	1 lb 4.8 oz.	1 gal. 12.8 oz.
1.060	7.8	1 lb 5.0 oz.	1 lb 6.5 oz.	1 gal. 13.6 oz.
1.065	8.6	1 lb 6.5 oz.	1 lb 9.0 oz.	1 gal. 15.2 oz.
1.070	9.2	1 lb 8.0 oz.	1 lb 11.5 oz.	1 gal. 16.0 oz.
1.075	9.9	1 lb 9.8 oz.	1 lb 14.0 oz.	1 gal. 17.6 oz.
1.080	10.6	1 lb 11.5 oz.	1 lb 15.6 oz.	1 gal. 18.4 oz.
1.085	11.3	1 lb 14.0 oz.	2 lb 2.2 oz.	1 gal. 20.0 oz.
1.090	12.0	1 lb 15.6 oz.	2 lb 4.6 oz.	1 gal. 21.6 oz.
1.095	12.7	2 lb 1.3 oz.	2 lb 7.2 oz.	1 gal. 22.4 oz.
1.100	13.4	2 lb 3.0 oz.	2 lb 9.6 oz.	1 gal. 24.0 oz.

Data for Table 2 derived from Jack Keller's *Winemaking Home Page*, Internet, October 2016

Table 3. Potential Alcohol Below 1.000

FINAL SPECIFIC GRAVITY	ADD TO STARTING POTENTIAL ALCOHOL
1.000	0.0
0.998	0.3
0.996	0.6
0.994	0.8
0.992	1.1
0.990	1.4

Table 4. Adjusting Hydrometer Reading for Temperature

DEGREES F.	ADD SG TO READING
70	0.001
77	0.002
84	0.003
95	0.005
Above 95	Don't Go There

Invert Sugar: The product of the hydrolysis of sucrose, which is glucose and fructose. Yeast ferment invert sugar more rapidly than sucrose, such as simple cane sugar, because they do not have to break the sucrose down into glucose and fructose themselves. Invert sugar can be made by dissolving two parts sugar into one part water, adding two teaspoons lemon juice per pound of sugar, bringing this almost to a boil, and holding it there for 30 minutes (without allowing it to boil). If not to be used immediately upon cooling, this can be poured into a sealable jar, sealed, and cooled in the refrigerator. Invert sugar can be used to sweeten finished wine as long as potassium sorbate is used to prevent re-fermentation.

Jelly-Bag: A bag used to isolate or strain the solid fermentation media from the wine.

They are similar to nylon straining bags, but shorter and usually fitted with a drawstring so they can be closed and hung while the liquid drips from the pulp. They can also be made of cotton or linen for containing ground spices.

Litmus Strips: See *Acid* subsection *pH*.

Malolactic Fermentation (MLF): When malic acid is predominant and too high, MLF may be the best way to reduce some of that acid. MLF is enabled by malolactic bacteria (MLB) that may hitchhike in on the fruit being fermented or be introduced by the winemaker in a commercial culture of selected bacteria. The latter is preferred over the wild bacteria, much like selected cultures of wine yeast are preferred over wild yeast. MLF is an advanced tool not covered in this book.

Methylated Spirits: Denatured alcohol is used to check if a hazy wine is caused by pectin. Add 3–4 fluid ounces of methylated spirit to a fluid ounce of wine. If jelly-like clots or strings form, then the problem is most likely pectin and the wine should be treated with a pectic enzyme.

Mincer: A powered or manual device for chopping fruit, grain, vegetables, or meats into very small pieces. The size of the pieces can usually be regulated by changing chopping blades. This device is very useful for chopping large quantities of fruit, especially dried fruit and raisins. Fruit with hard seeds should be de-seeded before mincing.

Nutrient: Food for yeast or malolactic bacteria, containing nitrogenous matter, yeast-tolerant acid, vitamins, and certain minerals. While sugar is the main food for yeast, nutrients are the "growth hormones," so to speak, and essential to a healthy, complete fermentation.

Oaking: The process of immersing oak chips, shavings, particles, cubes, "beans," or sticks into wine to simulate having aged the wine in an oak barrel or keg. The oak may be natural or toasted (light, medium, or heavy toast). Oaking allows young wines to soften and absorb some of the wood's flavors and tannins. However, most light, delicate wines should not be oaked.

Pectic Enzyme: The enzyme pectinase is available in powdered or liquid form. When it encounters pectin, it catalyzes the breakdown of pectin molecules. We will be using the powdered form as it is most easily prescribed in quantity—

1 teaspoon, ½ teaspoon, etc.—and has a much longer shelf life.

We use it initially to counter any pectin released by ingredients and prevent it from cursing our wine with pectin haze. That early addition also helps break down molecular barriers that prevent the juices in the base from freely flowing. It will never make them flow freely, but it sure helps release them.

Without going into the biochemistry of the process, pectinase engages pectin, and when finished with that engagement is available to engage more, if encountered. It is not "used up," but some are always engaged and not available (think of it as temporarily bound and not free for immediate use elsewhere). In the end, there may not be enough to completely rid a wine of all pectin, resulting in a slight haze we'd rather not see there.

When asked in a recipe to check clarity and correct if necessary, we add a bit more and evaluate the results. "A bit more" can be as much as half of what was initially used. If the amount added fails to eliminate the haze, we add a bit more (maybe ¼ of our initial addition) and continue doing so until the haze is gone or, if nothing has changed, switch to another enzyme, such as amylase if we have a starch base.

Residual pectinase isn't harmful and imparts no taste or other sensory characteristics. Still, we always want to use it minimally and not just dump teaspoon after teaspoon into our wine. It is a soluble solid and will add density to your wine, skewing SG readings. When our hydrometer reads 1.000, we want to know it is measuring sugar, not sugar and pectin.

In commercial winemaking pectic enzyme generally refers to a cocktail of enzymes that each attack different parts of the pectin molecules most common in grapes. We are not primarily making wine with grapes, and when we do turn to grapes, we may be using native (wild) grapes or hybrids of native and European grapes such as Concord, Niagara, Diamond, etc. For these grapes, our pectinase-based enzyme will work just fine.

pH: See *Acid* subsection *pH*.

pH meter: See *Acid* subsection *pH*.

Potassium Bicarbonate: See *Acid* subsection *Reducing TA*.

Potassium Metabisulfite: One of two salts of sulfite which may be used to sanitize winemaking equipment and utensils (the other being *Sodium Metabisulfite*). Campden tablets are the tablet form of potassium metabisulfite. (Campden tablets of sodium metabisulfite are also available.) Its action, in water or wine, inhibits harmful bacteria through the release of sulfur dioxide, a powerful antiseptic. (Also see *Sulfur dioxide*.)

It can be used for sanitizing equipment and washing fruit from which wine will be made. For equipment, a 1% solution (10 grams dissolved in 1 liter of water) is sufficient for washing and rinsing. After using the solution, the equipment should not be rinsed again.

For protecting the must, a 10% solution is made (10 grams dissolved in 100 mL of water). Three milliliters of this 10% solution added to a U.S. gallon of must will add approximately 45 ppm of sulfur dioxide (SO_2) to the must. One should wait at least 12 hours after adding this to the must before adding the yeast.

Both bottles of solution (1% and 10%) should clearly be labeled with the respective strength, active compound, and date formulated to prevent disastrous mistakes; both may be stored in a cool, dark place for several months without affecting potency. Potassium metabisulfite has a shelf life of about a year. In other words, you will need to replace it every year. When you buy it, write the date a year from then on the label, so you'll know when you have to replace it.

Potassium Sorbate: Sold under the brand name "Sorbistat K" (among others) and affectionately as "wine stabilizer," potassium sorbate produces sorbic acid when added to the wine. It serves two purposes. When active fermentation has ceased, and the wine is racked the final time after clearing, ½ teaspoon added to 1 gallon of wine will render any surviving yeast incapable of multiplying. Yeast living at that moment can continue fermenting any residual sugar into alcohol and CO_2, but when they are inhibited, no new yeast will be able to cause future fermentation. It should always be used in conjunction with potassium metabisulfite as the wine will not be truly stabilized without them both. It is primarily used with sweet wines and sparkling wines but should be added to table wines which are sweetened before bottling.

Press: To use pressure to force the juice out of fruit pulp, or a device used to achieve this result. Home winemakers have found ingenious ways to press their fruit without spending big bucks. Early on, I used two pieces of plywood, about 2 x 2 feet and ½ inch thick. My straining bag with fruit was placed between them, and I then loaded the upper piece with a layer of bricks, then additional bricks stacked in layers until the addition of more bricks yielded no new juice. The bottom piece of plywood had a channel routered around it, near the edges, that exited to the outside where I placed a bucket to collect the juice—sanitizing the plywood before and after use was a chore that eventually motivated me into purchasing a basket press.

Primary Fermenter: It is useful to have a variety of primary sizes. I've found that 2- and 3-gallon primaries are perfect for 1-gallon batches. You can usually cheaply acquire food-grade plastic buckets, with lids, from your local donut bakery. There are two donut chains I hit ages ago and scored 2-, 3-, 5-, and 8-gallon buckets for $8 total. Each of these originally contained gelled fillings or prepared toppings.

Punching Down the Cap: The process of pushing the layer (cap) of skins, seeds, and pulp, which are lifted to the surface by CO_2 released by yeast, down into the juice during fermentation. This facilitates the extraction of color, flavor, acids, and tannins and, equally important, ensures that the cap doesn't dry out and develop unwanted mold.

Racking: As fermentation concludes, rising CO_2 diminishes and is unable to keep large, small, and micro solids in suspension. They then begin falling and create sediment called lees. It is necessary to siphon the wine off the lees to improve clarity and prevent off-flavors and odors as the lees decompose. This process of siphoning the wine from a lees laden fermenter to a clean, sanitized fermenter is called racking. Racking the wine off the lees allows clarification and aids in stabilization. A **Racking Hose** or tubing is used and can be attached to a **Racking Cane** to make this task easier.

Because racking agitates the wine, it drives SO_2 out while allowing O_2 in. Repeated racking lowers free SO_2 levels and places the wine at risk. Thus, racking should be done only when necessary.

Racking Cane: A stiff, plastic tube, usually "L"-shaped, that is attached to the racking hose to make racking easier. A protective cap is placed over the lower end of the cane that allows liquid to be drawn into the cane from above rather than below while keeping most large solids out. The cap allows the tip of the cane to be lowered close to the lees without unduly disturbing them. The lower tip of the racking cane should initially be held about midway between the surface and the lees and gradually lowered as the volume decreases due to the siphoning.

Racking Hose: A flexible, clear plastic hose, usually ⅜ inch in inner diameter, used to siphon wine from one vessel to another. It is used in both racking and bottling operations.

Secondary Fermenter: For the beginner, it is suggested you begin making wine from scratch with 1-gallon batches. All recipes in this book are 1-gallon batches. These allow you to learn and master the basics with the least resources invested.

A secondary fermenter

Remember, any batch requires two secondaries: one for fermentation and the other to rack into, at which point the used one can be cleaned and sanitized, and their roles reversed.

In a less plasticized age, it was easy to collect 1-gallon secondaries. You walked into any supermarket and bought a gallon of apple juice or cider. It's not so easy anymore, although gallon glass jugs of cider are still around if you look hard.

The next best glass secondary for small batches is the 4-liter jug. Buy your favorite wine in bulk and re-use the jug. But when you re-use it, you are making four liters of wine, not a gallon. No worry, you'll still put away five bottles and then have a couple of glasses left over for the winemaker.

Sodium Benzoate: Often sold as "Stabilizing Tablets," sodium benzoate is used, one crushed tablet per gallon of wine, to stop future fermentation. It is used when active fermentation has ceased, and the wine has been racked a final time after clearing. It is generally used with sweet wines and sparkling wines but may be added to table wines which exhibit difficulty in maintaining clarity after fining. For sweet wines, the final sugar syrup and crushed tablet may be added at the same time. When using it to stabilize a wine, it must be used in conjunction with an aseptic dose of *potassium metabisulfite*. When used, it is used instead of *potassium sorbate*. In this book, we only use *potassium sorbate*. See *Potassium Sorbate*.

Sodium Metabisulfite: One of two compounds commonly used to sanitize winemaking equipment and utensils, the other being *potassium metabisulfite*. Sodium metabisulfite is also sold in the sodium bisulfite form. Either form, in must or wine, inhibits harmful microorganisms through the release of sulfur dioxide (SO_2), a powerful antiseptic. It can be used for sanitizing equipment, but the U.S. government prohibits its inclusion in commercial wine and thus should not be used to protect the must from which wine is to be made.

Some winemakers prefer to use the sodium salt for sanitizing equipment and the potassium for protecting the wine. This book does not endorse such a procedure, as the residual sodium cannot help but make its way into the wine. Also, having two solutions on hand is an accident waiting to happen. See *Potassium Metabisulfite*.

Sorbate: See *Potassium Sorbate.*

Stabilization: Fermented wine has run its course in terms of fermentation, and the yeasts have begun their great die-off. If they do so before all the available sugar is consumed, the wine is inherently unstable. Almost all finished wines contain a few live yeast cells and various microorganisms that could spell disaster for the wine if bottled. Other conditions may exist that produce undesirable effects.

Stabilization is a multi-layered process as there are several types of stabilization. No wine will need each type of stabilization, but all will need the first, and many will need two. Ignore at your own risk.

Microbiological Stabilization: Yeast, malolactic bacteria and many other microorganisms can go dormant if their environment changes too much. If they determine they cannot survive the change they either die off or wait to see if the environment becomes more favorable. If, during dormancy, they decide that they can survive, they begin doing what nature programmed them to do. Yeast will consume sugar and continue the primary fermentation. Malolactic bacteria will metabolize any residual malic acid and continue the secondary fermentation. Other bacteria can turn the wine rancid. If the wine has been bottled, any one of these scenarios can ruin your wine. That's why microbiological stabilization is important.

Microbiological stabilization is achieved by raising the SO_2 to an aseptic level of 30 mg/L or more and adding ½ teaspoon of potassium sorbate per gallon. The SO_2 takes care of everything but the yeast, and the potassium sorbate dissociates as sorbic acid and prevents the growth and activity of yeast, thereby rendering them incapable of further reproduction. They still have to die, but neither the SO$_2$ nor the sorbate will kill them. They die naturally, and since they are the last of the culture that made the wine, we hope they rest in peace.

Cold Stabilization: Dissolved molecules of tartaric acid can bind and react with excess potassium to form what is called potassium bitartrate, which is unstable. Potassium bitartrate can precipitate out of solution as crystals over time and with minor changes in ambient temperature. In white wines, the crystals look like broken glass and are unsightly. In red wines, the crystals are largely unnoticed until the bottle is almost empty. Potassium bitartrate is cream of tartar and harmless if consumed, but the crystals can be removed from the wine before it is bottled.

The wine has to be chilled to near freezing for potassium bitartrate to precipitate completely. The kitchen refrigerator can accommodate gallon jugs, but a 5-gallon carboy will occupy most of its space. When upgrading to a newer model, many winemakers keep an old refrigerator just to cold stabilize their wines. Others age their wines until winter comes, but don't set your carboys outside and forget them. If the contents freeze, the carboys will burst. You've been warned. Check the carboys every few hours and bring them inside if ice begins forming on their inner walls. When the ice melts, they can be brought back outside until ice reforms. Just be vigilant. It is best to bring them outside on cold nights that do not reach freezing.

Heat Stabilization: A wine possessing an excess of proteins can react unfavorably to warm temperatures. The proteins can break down and precipitate out of solution in two phases. First, the clear wine becomes hazy or even cloudy. Second, the protein molecules begin binding to each other and form a loose deposit of fluff in the bottle. While this fluff has little if any effect on the taste of the wine, the swirling fluff is unsightly and reflects unfavorably on the winemaker. This is almost exclusively a white wine and rosé problem and a white grape wine problem at that. I say almost exclusively because a very few non-grape white wines can experience this problem.

Fining with bentonite will produce a bond between the bentonite and proteins which, upon settling to the bottom, allows us to rack the wine off the deposit. There are four things to say here. First, bentonite will strip some of the flavor and aroma from the wine if used excessively. Second, there are different bentonites, and some produce compact lees while others produce loose, fluffy lees. The latter, which is sodium-based bentonite (not calcium-based), is more desirable because it is more reactive and thus, less of it is required, and it alters the character of the wine the least. Third, the only way to determine how much bentonite is required is through bench trials, trying 0.25 g/L, 0.50 g/L etc. to a maximum of 1.0 g/L until the least amount that gets the job done is determined. Fourth, because the lees will be loose and fluffy, it would be prudent to fine the wine a second time, after the bentonite has settled, with a small amount of gelatin, which helps clear the wine and compacts the bentonite.

Starter Solution: A solution of water, juice, sugar, and nutrients into which a culture of yeast is introduced and encouraged to multiply as quickly as possible before adding to a must. The purpose of the starter solution is to achieve a greater density of yeast than contained in the original culture sample; this way, the cultured yeast will quickly dominate the fermentation process, literally smothering out any wild yeast that might be present. It is also used to restart a **Stuck Fermentation**. See **Yeast Starter** for a method of creating a starter solution.

Straining Bags: Containing the pulp of fruit and berries makes the whole process easy when the pulp needs to be separated from the liquid. This is especially true of strawberries, kiwi fruit, raspberries, blackberries, and other fruit or berries that completely fall apart during fermentation. Containment is the solution.

Cotton bags have long been used for this purpose and I used them for years; I still have a couple. Yeast have no problem getting through the cotton weave. The bags can be washed for reuse but have one important drawback. As the cotton soaks up sugars, either added or naturally in the contained pulp, yeast attack the cotton to get at the sugars, and after a dozen or so uses the bags are weakened and can burst when removed from the primary or pressed.

Cotton mesh painter bags suffer the same drawback to a lesser extent but also are not as efficient as nylon straining bags designed for larger capacities and easy tie-offs. Nylon straining bags come in different mesh sizes useful in making beer and wine, but in winemaking, smaller mesh sizes usually are more desired. These bags can be cleaned, sanitized, and reused many times.

Women's nylons and pantyhose are really useful for the above-mentioned fruit and berries. They stretch quite a bit and hold far more material than you might imagine. Cut the feet off around calf-high, but get your partner's permission before you raid her stash of pantyhose. If they are your own pantyhose, please carry on. Use sanitized yarn to tie them closed.

Raw sugar

Sugar: Without sugars (and yeast) there could be no wine. Yeast convert sugars, through enzymatic actions, into alcohol and CO_2. In the process, there is a little bit that the yeast convert into energy for their own metabolic needs. Thus, sugars provide both the fuel for the yeast and the raw materials for the alcohol in our wines.

When chaptalizing a must (adding sugar), there are many choices, each bringing something different to the wine. Some of these are:

Bar Sugar: This sugar's crystal size is the finest of all the types of granulated sugar. It is ideal for sweetening finished wine because it dissolves easily. It is also called "superfine" or "ultrafine" sugar. In England, a sugar very similar to bar sugar is known as caster or castor, named after the type of shaker in which it is often packaged. Commercially, it can be purchased as "Baker's Sugar."

Barbados Sugar: A British specialty brown sugar, very dark brown, with a particularly strong molasses flavor. The crystals are slightly coarser and stickier in texture than "regular" brown sugar. Also, known as ***Muscovado Sugar***. It delivers a heavier-tasting, molasses-like sweetness that is often an acquired taste.

Brown Sugar: Sugar crystals coated in a molasses syrup with natural flavor and color. Many sugar refiners produce brown sugar by boiling a special molasses syrup until brown sugar crystals form. A centrifuge spins the crystals dry. Some of the syrup remains, giving the sugar its brown color and molasses flavor. Other manufacturers produce brown sugar by blending a special molasses syrup with white sugar crystals. Dark brown sugar has more color and a stronger molasses flavor than light brown sugar. Lighter brown sugars are more commonly used in winemaking than darker ones, as the richer molasses flavors in the darker sugar tend to mask the flavor profile of the wine's base, but both have their place.

Demerara Sugar: A light brown sugar with large golden crystals that are slightly sticky. While this sugar is often expensive, it has a unique, unmatched flavor that in turn gives the wine a unique flavor profile and character.

Dextrose: An isomer form (the invert) of glucose, actually called dextroglucose (D-glucose) with a right-axis polarization (a.k.a. "right-handed glucose"); it is found naturally in sweet fruits and honey.

Fructose: One of two simple (reducing) fermentable sugars in grapes and other fruit, the other being glucose. Isolated, fructose is approximately twice as sweet as glucose. In wine, a higher fructose concentration will result in a heightened sweetness threshold.

Galactose: Sometimes called lactose, although it is not lactose proper—lactose is a disaccharide of galactose and glucose. It is not desired as a residual sugar in wine, as it oxidizes to form mucic acid.

Glucose: One of two simple fermentable sugars in grapes and other fruit, the other being fructose. Glucose is approximately half as sweet as fructose. An isomer form of glucose, dextrose, is considered to be glucose.

Honey: Honey varieties vary widely; they generally are a complex mixture of right-axis glucose (about 30% dextrose), left-axis fructose (about 38 to 40% levulose), maltose (about 7%), and a surprising number of other sugars (3 to 5%; see ***Sugars and Honey,*** pg. 68) in water with proteins, minerals, pollens, bee parts, and other solids interspersed. Honey purity and quality also vary widely, as do the "varieties" of honey. "Variety" is attributed to the predominant flower

Barbados sugar · Brown sugar · Demerara sugar · Honey

Invert sugar · Jaggery · Molasses · Piloncillo

the bees visited while making the honey (such as clover, orange, wildflower, raspberry, sage, heather, etc.). Only purified honey should be used in winemaking—the purer the better.

Invert Sugar: The product of the hydrolysis of sucrose, which is glucose and fructose. Yeast ferment invert sugar more rapidly than sucrose, such as simple cane sugar, because they do not have to break the sucrose down into glucose and fructose themselves. Invert sugar can be made by dissolving two parts sugar into one part water, adding two teaspoons lemon juice per pound of sugar, bringing this almost to a boil, and holding it there for 30 minutes (without allowing it to boil). If not to be used immediately upon cooling, this can be poured into a sealable

jar, sealed, and cooled in the refrigerator. Invert sugar can be used to sweeten finished wine as long as potassium sorbate is used to prevent re-fermentation.

Jaggery: Raw or semi-refined palm sugar, made in the East Indies by evaporating the fresh juice of several kinds of palm trees, but specifically that of the palmyra.

Lactose: A sugar comprising one glucose molecule linked to a galactose molecule and found only in milk products. It has a slightly sweet taste and is much less soluble in water than most other sugars. The human body breaks it down into galactose and glucose. Because it is not ordinarily fermentable until separated into its component sugars, it can be used to boost residual sweetness.

Levulose: An isomer form (the invert) of fructose, with a left-axis polarization (a.k.a. "left-handed fructose") found naturally in sweet fruits and honey.

Maltose: A crystalline sugar formed from starch (specifically malt) and the amylolytic ferment of saliva and pancreatic juice. It consists of two linked glucose molecules and is completely fermentable.

Molasses: The filtered residue of sugar refinement after the crystallized portion has been removed. "Light molasses" is roughly 90% sugar, while "blackstrap molasses" is only 50% sugar and 50% refinement residue. It may have sulfur compounds added to sterilize and stabilize it. This makes it generally undesirable as sugar for wine, as it could encourage the formation of hydrogen sulfide. It is similar to treacle. Molasses can be used to add complexity to a finished wine prior to bottling if it is for personal consumption. Otherwise, honey is a better choice.

Muscovado Sugar. See ***Barbados Sugar.***

Piloncillo: A Latin American brown sugar, which is semi-refined and granulated. It is sometimes sold in solid cone-shaped cakes, where the sugar is scraped off the cake as needed. The taste is quite different than American brown sugar, which is actually refined sugar to which molasses has been added. It can be used to sweeten a wine prior to bottling and create a unique flavor profile.

Raffinose: A complex sugar (trisaccharide) found primarily in grains, legumes, and some vegetables. It has little value in winemaking and is only slightly sweet.

Raw Sugar: Crystalline sugar obtained from the evaporation of cane, beet, maple, or some other syrup. Raw cane sugar is sold as "Sucanat." Raw beet sugar is said to be unsavory. Raw sugar should not be equated with the product "Sugar in the Raw."

Rock Candy: Large sucrose crystals, usually clear but may be tinted with flavorings. Some people drop a piece of rock candy in the wine bottle before filling it, where it slowly dissolves and sweetens the wine.

Stachyose: A complex sugar (tetrasaccharide) found in a few grains, most legumes, and some vegetables. It has little value in winemaking and is less sweet than raffinose.

Sucrose: A natural, crystalline disaccharide found in grapes, most fruit, and many plants. This is the type of refined sugar obtained from sugar cane, sugar beets and other sources which, when added to a must or juice to make up for deficiencies in natural sugar, must be hydrolyzed (inverted) into fructose and glucose by acids and enzymes in the yeast before it can be used as fuel for fermentation. It can also be inverted by the winemaker before adding to the must or wine.

Sugar in the Raw: See ***Turbinado Sugar.***

Treacle: The inverted sugar made from the residue of refinement and very similar in taste to molasses, although treacle is generally darker. There is even a "black treacle" with roughly the same taste as "blackstrap molasses." If you like the taste, it is more useful in winemaking than molasses.

Turbinado Sugar: A raw sugar that has been partially processed, removing some of the surface molasses. It is a blond color with a mild brown sugar flavor that enhances some wine bases like no other sugar can. It is marketed as Turbinado Sugar and as Sugar in the Raw.

Sugars and Honey: We tend to think of honey as liquid sugar, a super-thick syrup flavored with various flower nectars. Many winemakers add a little honey to wine to give it a mellow but sweet finish, as honey contains a number of sugars, and not all of them are fermentable. But the overwhelming majority of them, given enough time, will ferment. The very complexity of some requires a long time for the yeast to break them down into a fermentable form.

Over 75% of the sugars in honey are dextrose, levulose, and maltose. Sucrose—common table sugar—usually comprises only about 1–½% of the total. A small quantity might be brachyose (isomaltose), erlose, kojibiose, maltulose, panose, theanderose, turanose, and other exotic disaccharides and oligosaccharides. Yeast can eventually reduce all that can be reduced into fermentable sugars, but it sometimes takes quite a few steps and therefore quite a while. People wonder why meads take so long to ferment out. You just read the answer.

Conventional wisdom says that 1.25 pounds of honey can be substituted for 1 pound of sugar in any wine recipe to produce an equivalent amount of alcohol; substitute honey for all of the sugar and you make some form of honey wine or mead. The 1.25 pounds of honey for 1 pound of sugar is based on the fact that most honey averages around 80% solids, give or take 2%. The math is reliable on average, so don't worry about the give or take.

Sulfur Dioxide

Appropriate amounts of sulfur dioxide (SO_2) are used in winemaking for their antioxidant, antimicrobial, and preservative properties, but SO_2 also possesses additional benefits. The nine benefits of sulfur dioxide on wine that I like to cite are:

- Antioxidant properties (limits undesirable reactions of wine substances with oxygen)
- Can inhibit most wild yeast
- Inhibits acetic acid bacteria (think vinegar)
- Inhibits lactic acid bacteria*
- Helps prevent browning
- Helps stabilize color in red wines
- Keeps wine fresher
- Allows longer storage of wine
- Sanitizing agent for winemaking equipment

*If an MLF is desired later or not at all, SO_2 will delay or stop it from occurring, depending on the SO_2 level maintained. Usually, 40 mg/L or higher will prevent MLF from occurring, but the SO_2 does not kill the ML bacteria. It only creates an environment inhospitable for the bacteria to flourish. When the SO_2 level drops below that mark, which it will over time, MLF may occur.

It is useful to expound upon some information from Chapter 1 and above.

- Only 57.6% of the sulfite will dissociate as SO_2 and become available to protect wine. While this is theoretically true, in reality, many variables are at work to decrease that number. The age of the metabisulfite is the easiest variable to understand. You'll probably never achieve 57.6%, but our calculations pretend you can. Don't worry. They work.
- 93 to 99 percent of the amount of sulfite dissociated is ionized bisulfite or free SO_2 (HSO_3-). This is the form that provides antimicrobial protection.
- 0.7 to 7 percent of the amount of sulfite added is molecular SO_2. This is the form that provides antimicrobial protection.

Both HSO_3- and molecular SO_2 play important roles in ensuring the health of a must or wine, but it is the molecular SO_2 that is the more important of the two in our wine. Each is delivered in dose amounts primarily dictated by how much free SO_2 is already present in the wine, the wine's pH, and how much is needed.

It is easy to say too much about SO_2, but one should remember that between any consecutive two points listed above are four additional values. For example, between pH 3.50 and 3.55 are 3.51, 3.52, 3.53, and 3.54, which is why a pH meter capable of +/- 0.01 accuracy is so important. One must extrapolate values between the points on the tables, above. For example, a reading of pH 3.53 for a red wine (Table 6), which falls midway between 3.50 (25 mg/L) and 3.55 (29 mg/L) of free SO_2, is extrapolated as 27.5 mg/L, the midway point between the two.

Table 5. Free SO$_2$/pH points for white wine stabilized at 0.80 mg/L molecular SO$_2$ in mg/L

pH	2.90	2.95	3.00	3.05	3.10	3.15	3.20	3.25	3.30	3.35
SO$_2$	11	12	13	15	16	19	21	23	26	29

pH	3.40	3.45	3.50	3.55	3.60	3.65	3.70	3.75	3.80	3.85
SO$_2$	32	37	40	46	50	57	63	72	79	91

Table 6. Free SO$_2$/pH points for red wine stabilized at 0.50 mg/L molecular SO$_2$ in mg/L

pH	2.90	2.95	3.00	3.05	3.10	3.15	3.20	3.25	3.30	3.35
SO$_2$	7	7	8	9	10	12	13	15	16	18

pH	3.40	3.45	3.50	3.55	3.60	3.65	3.70	3.75	3.80	3.85
SO$_2$	20	23	25	29	31	36	39	45	49	57

Data for Tables 5 and 6 derived from *2018–2019 Gusmer Enterprises, Inc. Wine Products Catalog*, the chart on page 64. Napa, CA: Gusmer Enterprises, Inc., 2018

Using Campden tablets: I will place a heavy bet that every other winemaking book out there aimed at the beginner suggests using Campden tablets to deliver SO$_2$ to your must or wine. The main arguments are that they are so convenient, and they deliver a known dose.

This book will suggest just the opposite. Do not use Campden tablets.

To deliver the appropriate amount of SO$_2$, one needs to know the amount of SO$_2$ in different doses of Campden, a whole tablet, a half tablet, a quarter tablet, and so on. You also need to know if the tablets contain potassium metabisulfite or sodium bisulfite and whether they were manufactured for the British market or the American market. I'll bet dollars to donuts you cannot learn these things. Why are they important?

Potassium metabisulfite and sodium bisulfite aren't the same things and not the same strength; they do not contain the same amount of sulfite. Therefore the dosages differ, slightly, but they differ. If they were manufactured for the British market, they contain a set dose for one Imperial gallon: 4.5 liters. If they were manufactured for the American market, they contain a set dose for a US gallon: 3.785 liters. So again, the dosages differ, slightly, but they differ. Finally, potassium is better than sodium, as we want to limit our intake of the latter for health reasons. The different doses outweigh the convenience of crushing a tablet. It is better to measure the crystalline potassium metabisulfite salt on a gram scale.

Finally, if you ever were to crush a Campden tablet for use in winemaking, you would need a mortar and pestle. It is not all that easy or quick to pulverize that hard tablet into a fine, dissolvable powder. After reducing it to a powder, it still has to be dissolved before adding to your primary or secondary. Suppose you draw off 2 cups of juice and add the powder. It will take you 3–4 minutes (or longer) of constant stirring to get that powder to dissolve. I did this often for almost a year before concluding there's nothing convenient about Campden tablets.

Using potassium metabisulfite: There are two ways to add potassium metabisulfite to your must or wine. You can weigh the calculated dose of the crystalline salt each time an addition is required, or you can make a known-strength solution and calculate your additions using that.

The first way works with the solid (crystalline) form of the salt. You can weigh and add it to your must or wine directly, or you can dissolve the salt in a little water or juice and then stir that into the whole batch. The first method is fairly straightforward and the one used in this book.

If you need to add 0.5 gram, you weigh out that much, stir it into some water, juice, or wine until dissolved, and stir that into the primary. When racking, add the sulfite to the wine the day before it is racked or add it to the new secondary.

Making up a solution (below) and adding it works just as well. Many people think it works better.

Adding the solid: Adding the potassium metabisulfite to the must or wine requires very little math. The following calculations were already done for you to simplify the recipes, but it is important you know how to do them.

You need to know the amount of SO_2 you have to add, by weight. Suppose you want to add 28 mg/L to your 1-gallon batch of wine. We need to remember four things:
- 1 gal. = 3.785 L
- We will convert mg/L to grams needed
- SO_2 = 57.6% of potassium metabisulfite by weight, or 0.576
- 1000 converts mg/L (parts per million, or ppm) to g/L and mL to liters

The formula for adding the solid form of potassium metabisulfite is:

$$\frac{\text{desired free } SO_2 \text{ mg/L x 3.785 L/gal. x gal. of wine}}{1000 \times 0.576} = \text{grams potassium metabisulfite}$$

The following math solves the amount of potassium metabisulfite needed to provide 28 mg/L (ppm) of SO_2 in one gallon of juice or wine:

$$\frac{28 \text{ mg/L x 3.785 L/gal. x 1 gal.}}{1000 \times 0.576} = 0.18 \text{ g}$$

If we needed 28 mg/L for a 5-gallon batch, we would simply replace the 1 gallon with 5 gallons:

$$\frac{28 \text{ mg/L x 3.785 L/gal. x 5 gal.}}{1000 \text{ x } 0.576} = 0.92 \text{ g}$$

It should be stressed that the examples above were all based on the need to produce a certain amount of molecular SO_2 and raise the wine to an aseptic level. Both tasks are pH-dependent, and it makes no difference if you are adding this to red or white wine, each with its own molecular SO_2 needs; the formula will comply with Tables 5 and 6 and get the right answer. There isn't one formula for reds and another for whites.

Adding the solution: The easiest method to make up a stock 10% metabisulfite solution is to weigh out 10 grams of potassium metabisulfite and dissolve it in 75 mL of cool water. Once completely dissolved, carefully add cool water until the total liquid is 100 mL. You now have 10 g/100 mL or 100 g/L (100 mg/mL), a 10% potassium metabisulfite solution.

The previous formula need only be adjusted to account for the %SO_2 solution as mg/mL:

$$\frac{\text{desired free } SO_2 \text{ mg/L x 3.785 L/gal. x gal. of wine}}{100 \text{ mg/mL x } 0.576} = \text{ volume potassium metabisulfite}$$

Using the same problem as in ***adding the solid***, we add the 10% SO_2 solution to the equation as 100 mg/mL:

$$\frac{28 \text{ mg/L x 3.785 L/gal. x 5 gal.}}{100 \text{ mg/mL x } 0.576} = 9.2 \text{ mL}$$

Storing your sulfite solution: Metabisulfite solutions degrade rather quickly in storage. Always date the jar/bottle with an expiration date three months from when the solution was made. The culprit is O_2, always up to no good after helping our yeast culture get a running start. The sulfites simply oxidize during storage. Use glass, not plastic, containers with tight-fitting closures. Measure what you need and close the jar up again. Be mindful of the airspace above the solution. As that space grows, the O_2 available for oxidation increases. It is helpful to have several empty containers in various sizes so you can transfer the solution to a smaller one as the solution is used up.

While we are on the subject of the shelf life of the 10% solution, you need to know that you will need to replace your potassium metabisulfite every year. When you buy it, write the date a year from then on the label so you'll know when you have to replace it.

Final thoughts on SO$_2$: We must never lose sight of the fact that some of the SO$_2$ we add will become bound, some lost to racking and bottling, and some lost to oxidation during maturation and bottle aging. We will never really have what we added except for the first few minutes after adding it. When asked to add a certain amount, which will remain fairly constant throughout the recipes that follow, we must do it. And the amount added must be as accurate as our digital gram scales can weigh it.

Sur Lie Aging: French for "on the lees," this is the process of leaving the lees in the wine for a few months to a year, accompanied by a regime of periodic stirring. Certain wines such as Chardonnay and Sauvignon Blanc benefit from autolysis because they gain complexity during the process that enhances their structure and mouthfeel. It gives them extra body and increases their aromatic complexity. Aging *sur lie* with lees stirring can result in a creamy, viscous mouthfeel. See **Autolysis.**

Sweet Reserve: A sample of the original juice from which a wine is made is used to sweeten the finished wine after fermenting to dryness and stabilizing. The sweet reserve is either refrigerated or frozen until needed. When making a sweet reserve from whole fruit, such as strawberries, peaches, or plums, the fruit must be crushed and pressed, and the juice stood in a tall, clear, glass bottle in a refrigerator until the juice separates (*i.e.*, pulp sediment settles to the bottom of the bottle). The clear juice is very carefully racked off the sediment and stored for the reserve. The sediment can be lightly pressed through a double layer of sanitized muslin cloth, and the liquid obtained allowed to separate again, with the clear juice again removed and stored with the sweet reserve. The advantage of using a sweet reserve to sweeten a stabilized dry wine is that it adds sweetness, fresh flavor, and natural aroma to the wine. It may also improve the color of the finished wine somewhat.

Tannins: We noted earlier that acid gives structure to your wine, assuming it is in balance with other components: tannin, sugar, alcohol, and aromatics. What acids contribute to structure tannins contribute to complexity.

Tannins arrive from two, possibly three, sources. They originate in the base and are transferred to the must during maceration (fermentation on the pulp). They also originate in oak, whether barrel, chips, or extract, and again are extracted by the wine. In the absence of a tannic base, they may also be added by the winemaker in the form of powdered grape or oak tannin or liquid extracts. In this book, we use powdered grape tannin.

Balanced tannins present a sensory equilibrium between tannins originating in the base (or added by the winemaker) and those extracted from oak. Balanced tannins age more gracefully than those out of balance and are often described as soft, smooth, or silky. Over time, tannins polymerize with themselves and other polyphenols, changing in stages and forming longer molecular chains that are perceived as less harsh, more rounded, and softer.

Tartaric Acid: An acid found in grapes and several other fruits, tartaric is the strongest organic acid in our musts/wines.

Thermometer: For both primaries and secondaries, there are digital thermometers for winemaking that stick to the outside of the vessel or float inside. The outside models are convenient because they are non-intrusive and can be left on for the duration of the fermentation, offering a reading at a glance.

Yeast Nutrient: In most musts, our chosen yeast requires nutrients over what is naturally found therein. The exceptions are specific wine grapes grown in a perfect climate and with a perfect yeast for a given style. Assume a lug of these exceptional grapes fell into your lap. You would need a wine laboratory to figure what to do next, so assume, as a beginner, that all musts require yeast nutrients.

If you walk into any home brew shop or visit their online store, you'll find a generic product called yeast nutrient. With rare exceptions, this is diammonium phosphate (DAP), a nutrient rich in nitrogen, and one of the best bargains in the shop.

Generic yeast nutrient is often not enough for many fermentations. Yeasts also need micronutrients, key vitamins, minerals, free amino acids, sterols, and unsaturated fatty acids, that may not be available in the must and certainly are not available in DAP alone. Complete yeast nutrients are available in products such as Fermaid K and Superfood. These alone are often all that is needed, but if your yeast requires high nitrogen, then supplementation with DAP will be needed at the beginning of fermentation and halfway through it to ensure the wine will finish dry.

Most home winemaking recipes (even those on my website) almost always specify one teaspoon of yeast nutrient per gallon of wine. Although this is 4–5 times what is needed for the rare must requiring little if any added nutrients, it does provide a yeast with high nitrogen demands a more than adequate supply. However, yeast with high nutritional demands will probably still require a micronutrient supplement, in which case you should use 1 g/gal. of DAP and 1 g/gal. of supplement and be prepared to add more DAP if the wine does not appear it will finish dry.

Yeast Starter Solution: The "use by" dates on the yeast packets are mere suggestions. I have used yeast nine years past that date with success using a yeast starter. The starter compounds the number of viable yeast cells over time. Yeasts can propagate every 2–3 hours, so in theory, the yeast population of a culture can double every 2–3 hours. That means that in 8 hours, the population potentially can increase 16-fold, 12 hours 64-fold, and so on. Use the entire packet, even for 1-gallon batches, to build a super yeast starter that will kick-start a fermentation almost at once.

What to Do

To 1 cup lukewarm water (about 100–102 degrees F.) dissolve ¼ tsp sugar and a pinch of yeast nutrient. Add yeast culture, stir, cover the container, and set in a warm place.

After 2 hours, add ¼ cup water.

After another 2 hours, add ¼ cup water, ¼ tsp sugar, and a pinch of yeast nutrient. Stir.

After another 2 hours, add ¼ cup water.

After another 2 hours, add a pinch of yeast nutrient and ¼ cup of juice from your must.

Repeat the last step every 2 hours until you pitch the yeast starter. Stir well.

I like to husband a starter solution for at least 12 hours. If it is an old packet and starts slowly, that's usually enough time to develop a healthy culture, but if not, we can always increase the time.

Yeast Strain Selection: Selecting the correct wine yeast strain is one of the most important decisions the winemaker will make. With literally dozens and dozens of strains to select from, the task seems daunting. But the fact is that most strains are developed for specific *Vitis vinifera* varieties, specific styles, harvests, or other situations that most home winemakers will not encounter.

There are a handful of strains that are most useful for our needs. Over the years I have used over 60 cultures—the exact number is unknown because I did not take notes for several years. I even imported over 20 yeasts from the United Kingdom and Germany, with postage usually costing more than the yeasts. I had very good records of 60–62 yeast cultures until a water leak ruined a box of notes on many subjects.

Lemon zest

But a half dozen strains had become so routine that they became my go-to strains, my yeast toolbox as it were. A couple of other strains are always on standby for specific needs, and I keep a database of strains so I can search it when a need arises.

I keep about 30 sachets of yeast in a plastic box in my refrigerator to always have my favorite strains on hand, including 2–4 of each of my favorite go-to strains. You might only want a third that many if you make a lot of wine unless you buy your yeast when you make the wine.

Zest: There is a difference of opinion in the use of citrus zest in winemaking. One camp believes the oils in the zest hamper and can even stall fermentation. The other camp, where this author sleeps, says bull roar. Having used zest in my winemaking almost from the beginning, I have never experienced any negative effects on fermentations.

The Best Yeast Strains for Country Wines

- **Lalvin 71B**: Can metabolize 20–35% more malic acid than other yeasts, noted for producing fruity reds and rounder, smoother, more aromatic wines that tend to mature quickly. This is a great, go-to yeast for off-dry fruit wines. Temperature range is 60–85 degrees F., 14% ABV.
- **Lalvin BA11**: Promotes clean, aromatic, varietal characteristics, excellent esters, intensified mouthfeel, and lingering flavors in white fruit wines. Temperature range is 68–86 degrees F., 16% ABV.
- **Lalvin EC1118**: One of the most popular wine yeasts in the world. Low foam, productive at low temperatures, good for heavy suspended pulps, produces very compact lees, fast fermenter. A preferred choice in making sparkling wines, restarting stuck fermentations, low pH musts, excellent sensory properties. Temperature range 39–95 degrees F., 18% ABV.
- **Lalvin K1**: Tends to express freshness in fruit, produce flowery esters with good retention, ferments well under stressed conditions, and dominates almost any fermentation. Can restart stuck fermentation and ferment to 20% ABV if nutrients and nitrogen are sufficient. Temperature range is 59–86 degrees F.
- **Lalvin R2**: Use this yeast whenever a Sauternes strain is desired. It has an excellent temperature range, contributes esters, rarely sticks, and fermentation is fast. Temperature range is 42–86 degrees F., 16% ABV.
- **Lalvin RC-212**: A traditional Burgundy strain famous for big reds, it is suitable for black and red fruit. Tolerant of concurrent MLF, high temperatures, has excellent color stability. Requires high nitrogen and nutrients. Temperature range is 68–86 degrees F., 14–16 percent ABV.
- **Lalvin DV10**: The original Champagne isolate with relatively low oxygen and nitrogen demands. Known for clean fermentations that respect varietal character. Both reds and whites, and excellent for country wines. Fast fermenter under stressful conditions of low pH. High total SO_2 tolerance. Low foaming with low volatile acid production. Temperature range is 50–96 degrees F., 18% ABV.
- **Red Star Côte des Blancs**: Excellent for white wines as well as grapes,

fruit, cider, mead. Moderate-to-slow but steady fermentation. It brings out floral and fruity qualities, especially in the bouquet. Temperature range is 50–80 degrees F., 12–14 percent ABV.

Keep yeast refrigerated. Don't use partial packets for 1-gallon batches. Use the whole 5- or 8- gram packet. Once the packet is opened, the yeasts are exposed to air and will begin a slow deterioration, no matter how well you reseal the packet. Don't pinch pennies on yeast. Yeast is cheap.

CHAPTER THREE
PUTTING IT ALL TOGETHER

You may well be wondering how all this fits together. We'll be using the language introduced in Chapters 1 and 2, so if you have to refer back to them that's all right. My first winemaking book, a thin paperback, did not explain things well upfront, and I was constantly highlighting key procedures as they were introduced so I could find them more easily when thumbing back through previous pages looking for meanings. I've tried my best to spare you that time-wasting chore.

Demystifying Winemaking: A Crash Course in Wine-Making

There are endless books on making wine from grapes, the perfect fruit for making balanced wines. They contain just about the right proportions of sugars, acids, tannins, pigments, and everything else you need to make good wine. Other fruits are not so blessed.

Making wines from other fruits and materials is a bit complicated, not because they lack sufficient sugar, which is easily added, but because they possess acid levels all over the place. Our biggest challenge is to measure and adjust their acid content. This is almost always done before fermentation is initiated, but there are exceptions.

Making non-grape wines can be divided into several steps, none of which are trivial. Some require considerable time. While some country winemaking books rush you to have drinkable wine in 3–4 months, we will allow the wine to mature and age according to its nature. For some wines, this may take as long as it takes many grape wines to complete the same journey.

The Basic Steps for Making Country Wine

1. First, inspect your ingredients for quality and ripeness, culling out any with damage, bruises, moldy or rotten parts, or those that aren't quite ripe.

2. Base ingredients are chopped, crushed, mashed, or otherwise prepared for fermentation. Appropriate amounts of sugar, acid, tannin, enzymes, nutrients, SO_2 and water are carefully combined.

3. An appropriate dry wine yeast is rehydrated and added to the must.

4. Fermentation carried out aerobically is closely managed. Skins, pulp, and seeds undergo a modest fermentation but then are removed, drained or pressed, and discarded. Additional nutrients may be added. The juice is transferred to a secondary and aerobic fermentation ended. Anaerobic fermentation is carried to a first racking.

5. Anaerobic fermentation, i.e. in a fermenter protected from air, is managed until the wine is clear. It is matured according to its character, stabilized, and bottled.

6. Bottles are aged for a period that is determined by tasting.

7. These steps, with some modifications based on ingredients, are the paradigm for 99% of all non-grape winemaking. If you have never made wine before, they may still seem a bit mysterious. We will now try to demystify the process.

Selecting Ingredients

Good wine is made in the vineyard, orchard, briar patch, garden, or wherever the base ingredients originate. You cannot make them better than they are, except if you allow fruit to continue ripening for a few days on the kitchen counter.

Berry and fruit bases should be uniformly ripe. A few underripe berries will change the character of the whole, and not for the better. Don't hesitate to cull anything suspect. Of course, such berries are still good for eating (I usually do this on the spot).

If you don't have enough base material for a batch of wine, and it's perishable, freeze whatever you have in freezer-grade Ziploc bags until you have enough. A way to save space in the freezer is to crush things that yield juice readily, like berries, in the bags so the bags lay flatter than they would have. Label the bags with the material, weight, and date frozen.

Buying from Grocery Stores

If you have to buy your ingredients in a produce or supermarket, the produce manager is often a good source of information. Comice pears, when fully ripe, are one of the sweetest and juiciest pear varieties around. I always ask my produce manager when to expect them, and he always knows within a week or two.

Farmers' Markets and Local Producers Are Better

When I buy carrots for Carrot Whiskey (page 238), I always buy them at a local farmer's roadside stand. They are never more than a day out of the ground and are many times sweeter, fresher, and tastier than those found in my local supermarkets. This is also my source for Sugar Pie Pumpkins and watermelons (for both wines, see Chapter 11). If you live in a city and don't have farmers' roadside stands, look for an area farmers market. There usually is one, although it may be between you and an outlying small town.

Straining Bags

Most winemakers I know call them nylon straining bags because that describes them well. But I can always tell the winemakers with beer-making backgrounds; they call them grain bags. They also call winemaking "brewing," which it's not, but back to the bags.

Nylon straining bags are indispensable to home winemaking because they save you from a lot of work. My first containment bags were cotton. They worked well at containment but could not stand up to the pressures of pressing and often burst. When not used for pressing duties, they only lasted a dozen or so fermentations before they eventually burst. Nylon was a Godsend. It was strong enough to survive the press, and yeast didn't weaken it.

If you've never made wine, you'll be surprised just what yeast can do to berries and soft-fleshed fruit. Even hard fruit, like apples and cooking pears, will be reduced tremendously after chopping and crushing because the yeast can get into them better in that condition. Very fine suspended matter will still find its way into the must when the base, or what is left of it, is eventually pressed or drip-drained. Still, you'll come to love fine mesh.

The bags come in various sizes, both physically and in terms of the mesh. Over the years, I've discovered that the two finest mesh sizes are the most useful. For the majority of bases, we'll be using the fine-meshed bag, which does the best job at containment and, when allowed, pressing.

Preparing the must

Mashing Fruit

The recipes for most fruit and vegetables say to put them into nylon straining bags and mash them. Really soft fruit, like apricots,

peaches, and plums (page 179) can easily be mashed with the bottom of a flat-bottomed wine bottle or certain potato mashers.

When mashing dark berries (page 127), by hand or otherwise, it is smart to wear rubber gloves. Many dark berries can stain hands for several days. Also, be careful to mash them deep inside the primary to contain juice splatters. Some can stain clothing permanently.

Adding Ingredients

In all recipes in this book, ingredients are added in sequences that are based on tradition and science. Winemakers have a certain leeway with some additives but not in others.

Sugar

Sugar, for example, can be added in stages—so much upfront and the rest later. This is usually the preferred method when making high-alcohol wines (14% ABV and higher) wines. Too much sugar upfront can create too much density in the juice itself. Excessive density may impede flow of substances in and out of yeast, and prevent yeast from expelling their waste products, ethanol and CO_2.

Sulfites

We will not be adding sulfites in stages because this would require you to conduct a test for free SO_2 at each racking. Instead, only two additions are required, an initial one, and one at stabilization.

Sulfites can also be added incrementally, and, in fact, this is the preferred method—add them as needed. When making wine from traditional wine grapes, adding excessive sulfites before pitching the yeast, especially in reds, can prevent malolactic fermentation (MLF) from occurring when it is desired. In this book, because we consider MLF a more advanced technique beyond our actual needs, we will use sulfites to prevent it altogether.

Yeast Starter Solution

While every recipe in this book except Watermelon Wine (page 334) uses the same words to describe hydrating and pitching the yeast, it is nonetheless hoped that one will get in the habit of making a yeast starter solution (page 74). This ensures that a viable yeast culture will be introduced, it also adds a vastly increased yeast population to the must. This vast population guarantees a vigorous fermentation with a fraction of the lag time the-more general hydration method stated in the recipe requires. Add a well-made, extended starter, and a vigorous fermentation is often evident within an hour or two.

Pectic Enzyme

Although not carved in stone, it is nonetheless a convention in country wines not to add pectic enzyme before adding sulfites. As the recipes in this book don't depend on malolactic fermentation (MLF), we don't have to load the pectic enzyme upfront and wait until fermentation concludes before adding sulfites. Both can be added before the yeast is introduced. For that reason, when the recipes in this book (with two exceptions) direct you to add sulfites, wait 12 hours, and then add the pectic enzyme. The 12-hour waiting period after adding sulfites and SO_2 is the minimum. Most winemaking manuals request 24 hours. In my experience, anywhere from 12–24 hours is sufficient.

Clearing the Wine

At what point does must become wine? The answer is probably around the first racking, but I always think of it as must until it begins to clear, when it obviously becomes wine. A fermenting must will be opaque. It will look like some form of whey or milk of magnesia, usually tinted with a hue associated with the color of the base. That is often an illusion. The colors we see in a base aren't often incorporated into the wine. They end up as a very fine dusting among the lees, and the wine we are left with has a slight hue (if any) integrated into an otherwise clear liquid. We call it white wine.

Seeing a wine "fall clear" for the first time is a magical experience. The milky substance we've been husbanding suddenly starts clearing toward the top. The milkiness begins to fall, slowly but steadily, like a curtain, leaving above it a liquid that is clear, or at least absent the cloudiness we've grown used to. Reds and dark bases like blackberries, red grapes, and beets assume their inherent colors, but they are clear. It is wonderful to watch. It may take a half-hour or three hours to complete, but it is a magical sight.

Upon seeing this, our first impression is that the wine is actually clear. Relative to what it was before, the wine is clear, but it's not clear enough to be a finished wine. It is still a bit hazy, cloudy, or simply unclear. We want a wine that is absolutely brilliant—crystal clear, like a diamond.

Improving Clarity

So back to our somewhat-clear wine. We'd like to improve its clarity. If it doesn't have a starch or pectin haze and isn't cloudy because of some errant bacteria, it will most likely clear on its own. It just might take a long time. Most often, tiny suspended (often microscopic) particles prevent the wine from clearing. Even though they are small, they reflect and refract light, making their presence known. The vast majority eventually obey the laws of gravity and end up on the bottom of the secondary. We don't want to disturb them, but we do need to very carefully rack the wine, leaving them forever behind. With that said, you need to realize it is very easy to disturb the lees and send those microscopic particles floating back up into the wine. It is also very easy to approach the bottom of the secondary with a racking cane and inadvertently suck the very fine lees up into the newly racked wine.

Fining

Suppose we don't want to wait months for these particulates to settle out or we don't want to risk disturbing the lees when moving the jug to rack it. We can speed things along by fining the wine. Fining is the introduction of an ingredient containing an abundance of either positively or negatively charged ions. These attract whatever oppositely charged particles might be suspended in the wine. The combined weight of the fining agent and the captured suspended matter is enough to cause them to settle out within a few days, and then the clarified wine can be racked off them.

It is more than likely we will not know whether the particulates in suspension are positive or negative in charge. In that case, we can use a 2-part fining regime, where one part is positively charged and the other is negatively charged, just to make sure we capture all the particulates. The only caveat is that if we do not wait long enough for the first agent to settle before adding the second, the two agents will simply attract each other, and we have wasted our time and money. It is essential we follow the instructions for the agents exactly.

Checking the Free SO_2

It was my initial inclination to ask you to do what I try to do, check the free SO_2 whenever the wine is exposed to oxygen. This means almost every racking. But then I lamented over the fact that I was trying to make the recipes simple, and that would complicate them considerably. Besides, that is not what I did as a beginner and had I been required to do it I may have never made more than a few wines. Would I rather you check the free SO_2 from time to time? Yes, but you need not do so. Follow the recipes here and the wine will turn out fine regardless.

There is another reason I didn't ask you to check free SO_2 periodically. That is money. Each test costs you money as consumables are used up and need to be replaced. I do not want you to spend money you don't need to spend. I want you to save your money for necessities, like that pH meter.

I felt uneasy requiring you to purchase a pH meter right upfront. I made wine for

19 years before I purchased a pH meter, and yet once I did I wished I had done so 19 years earlier. But I will say this about pH meters. They are far less expensive today than they were when I purchased mine. I have seen decent ones on eBay for about $40, but much better ones are to be had for $50-$70. This brings up another item I require you to purchase—the gram scale.

When I first decided I needed to measure additives using a gram scale, they cost over $120. I happened to be blessed at the time to work in a medical research lab, and we had gram scales all over the place. And these weren't the cheap $120 ones either.

It was impractical for me to halt my winemaking until the next day when I could measure my additive (usually potassium metabisulfite), so I bought a case of 144 small screw-cap glass vials and filled most of them with specific amounts of potassium metabisulfite. I thought accurate measures were that important. I still do, and so I ask you to bite the bullet and spend around $10 on a digital gram scale. Accurate measurements of potassium metabisulfite are that important. And isn't it wonderful that technological and manufacturing advances have brought the digital gram scale down from $120 for a cheapie to around $10?

A TA test kit is optional. They aren't that expensive—around $20—but I believe pH is more important than TA, so I place the expenditures in that direction. I did not always feel that way. For almost two decades, I fought off the pH enthusiasts. I started in the TA camp and saw no reason to change. But slowly, over the years, I came to recognize that pH could offer so much more insight into what is happening inside the wine and where it needed to go than could TA.

If you read in Chapter 2, under **Acid**, subtopic ***Testing for TA with a pH Meter***, that your pH meter picked up the tab for the TA test kit, I apologetically correct that impression. You'll still need to buy a minimum quantity of sodium hydroxide, a graduated beaker, and a syringe. These individual items cost about as much as just buying the test kit.

After years of measuring TA and tasting the results, I went almost three years measuring TA by taste alone (not recommended that beginners attempt this). I wasn't always right, but I was never far from wrong. I couldn't do that with pH. For pH, I needed a meter. You will too.

Maturation

All of the rests that we give the must and the wine allow gravity to take hold of the must and wine, letting it clear and drop the suspended solids in it. The yeast itself takes the longest to drop. It is during this period when we are waiting for those very fine lees to form, sometimes no more than a light dusting, that the wine is undergoing maturation or bulk aging.

Maturation means coming into maturity. Maturation is one of two critical periods in the life of the wine, the other being bottle aging, for it is when the subtle chemical changes occur that build the character and style of our wine. Maturation creates the basis of the wine, and bottle aging takes it to its potential. During maturation, the two major components of change, the acids, and phenols (especially tannins) undergo their most significant interactions and evolutions.

Maturation is actually an indefinite period. The periods specified in the recipes are based on my experience, and your wine may take slightly less time to mature or quite possibly more. But one thing is certain: one day the wine will taste just right and be ready to bottle. You will know it when you taste it: the rough edges are gone, the wine is smoother, and the major taste components are in balance. If the wine is ready to age for the long haul, the tannins and acidity will say so. It is a wonderful feeling to taste your wine and just know the wine is ready to bottle. I wish I could be there when it first happens to you.

Bottle Aging

Some wines can, and should, be consumed fairly young. Others need to age a few months to reach their potential. Others need a long sleep before they are ready. The hardest part is waiting.

It is legitimate to wonder why "mature" wine, and bottled, at that, needs to age. Well, it is one thing to be ready to leave home and another to be ready for marriage. We have all gone through these stages, and every parent has watched his or her children go through them as well. It is a stretch to compare that with a wine's journey, but it is the first of the two best analogies I could come up with. Being ready to bottle and being ready to drink are simply two different milestones.

Here's another analogy: I love to make spaghetti sauce. I follow no recipe. I just know what essentials are required and start with them: stock, meat, tomato sauce, onions and garlic, salt, and pepper. Then I start adding whatever else I want in there, black olives, chunky mushrooms,

a little thinly sliced celery, and so forth. I allow a certain amount of time to pass for the components to cook, and I taste, make what adjustments might be required, add a little red wine, reduce the heat to a barely perceptible simmer, put on the lid, and walk away. I allow the flavors to mingle, mix, and finally meld together. A half-hour, hour, however long it takes, I'll know it's ready when I taste it. Perfect. I turn off the heat and make the spaghetti, pop the garlic bread under the broiler, and it all comes together at once.

Did you follow that analogy? The base, the additives, the cooking (maturation), and then the aging, and when everything blends into a magnificent sauce, you just know it. Wine goes through similar stages. We just need faith and patience.

Back in the late 1970s, Orson Welles was the advertising voice for Paul Masson wines, with their signature slogan, "We will sell no wine before its time." Modify the slogan from "sell" to "drink" and you've got perfect advice for every home winemaker.

If you're interested in making wine out of a particular type of base or material, I've outlined some advice about issues to look forward to—and look out for—when making wine from each. I've also shared a number of stories about making wine from such materials. Some are funny, some may be surprising, but all, I hope are instructive.

Wine From Berries

Berry wines are flavorful, colorful, and often unique. They have long been a favorite of home winemakers for those reasons, and they can often be gathered in the wild for free. The wines bode well at 12% ABV, but at 13% and higher, they often require too much added sugar to balance and rarely can be presented dry. They can, however, be made into commendable port-style wines, with ABV reaching 18%.

Making wine from berries is both easy and challenging. It is easy because most berries readily ferment. It is challenging because most berries, not all, but most, have low a pH and high TA.

TA is fairly easy to correct. Adding an equal volume of water to a volume of juice will reduce the TA by half. Unfortunately, this has very little effect on pH, requiring other strategies to raise the pH.

Our friendly yeast, Lalvin 71B, can help when malic acid is present. Sweetening to counter the acidity is also possible and often will pull the wine together, although the resulting wine can be too sweet for many palates.

Preparing the must differs from berry to berry. It is sometimes advantageous to use a prepared juice rather than the actual berry. This is especially true if the berry isn't widely cultivated or found in nature.

When Buying Juice, Beware of Preservatives

If you're buying juice for winemaking at a supermarket, always inspect the label carefully. The ingredients must not contain any preservatives that will prevent fermentation. These include examples such as

sorbic acid (E200), sodium sorbate (E201), potassium sorbate (E202), calcium sorbate (E203), benzoic acid (E210), sodium benzoate (E211), potassium benzoate (E212), calcium benzoate (E213), sulfur dioxide (E220), sodium sulfite (E221), sodium bisulfite (E222) sodium metabisulfite (E223), potassium metabisulfite (E224), and potassium sulfite (E225).

Ascorbic acid, often listed as a preservative, is an antioxidant and will not subdue an active fermentation.

Of course, preservatives are not an issue when obtaining concentrates and juices from a winemaking/home brew shop. Concentrates are convenient for making larger batches of wine.

With other categories of wine, I sort of review them here before moving on. Not so with berry wines. The introduction of each wine in the chapter is more than sufficient, and anything I say here would be plagiarizing my own work.

and supplies, and so I set about collecting them. I didn't have any secondaries, so I went to my local supermarket and bought three 1-gallon glass jugs of apple juice, which I fermented into my first solo wines and was left with three secondaries.

Back then, there were no plastic jugs. Now, it seems, there are no glass jugs. But I have recently found them in certain large chain stores catering to the healthy-minded. You just have to look. I also discovered that many roadside fruit stands present their fruit juices in glass. So if you're looking for secondaries, look harder.

You can also buy jug wines in glass. They are usually 4 liters, just a few shot glasses more than a US gallon. They work just fine, and you have wine to drink.

Wine From Fruit

Here we limit our selections to fruits grown in temperate regions. It is readily available in markets, roadside stands, U-Pick orchards, and even trees in your yard.

The common fruits are pomes (apples, pears, quince) and stone fruit (apricots, peaches, nectarines, plums, cherries), but figs and persimmons also make good wine. Each fruit is prepared according to its composition and character. None are especially challenging, even when it comes to getting acidity levels under control, and therefore all are well-suited for the beginning winemaker.

My first winemaking experience was assisting in making a dandelion wine. I enjoyed it, but I wanted to do it myself. The dandelions had disappeared, but I hoped they'd come back (not for another year), and I knew I needed certain equipment

Fruit Wines Are Perfect for Experimenting

Fruit wines beg to be played with. Adding herbs and spices to the fermentation yields a variety of flavors that make the wine more interesting. Blending wines does the same thing.

I know a fellow in Tennessee who has made over 200 variations of pear wine just by playing around with herbs, spices, bark, roots, flowers, other fruit, and blends. He once broke out a bottle that contained 18 different flavors, mostly herbs, and barks, but also anise, clove, and nutmeg.

As a self-appointed project, I once set out to make an apple wine that tasted like apple pie. I made three batches before I was satisfied. The only thing it lacked was the crust. I now know how to get that flavor, too, but have not married it all together. Some day . . .

Peach

Peach wines, like those of apple and pear, are perfect canvases for nuance, and in wine, nuance is what we're looking for. For your first peach wine(s), it is best just to try to capture the full flavor of your fruit. Add a little premium honey at the end, but easy on the additions, especially at first. If you add too much cinnamon, say, it will not taste like peach wine. Wait to unleash your creative additions/ingredients until you've captured the essence of the peach variety you're working with. Remember, your result won't taste like the fresh fruit, but of the wine from that fruit. You'll know when you capture it.

For any given fruit, there are likely hundreds of varieties and cultivars, each with its own character. Take peaches, for example. In the United States, more than 300 varieties are grown. Globally, there are more than 2,000 varieties.

Years ago I bought some early white-fleshed peaches and discovered a virtual treasure trove of flavor. At home, after eating just one, I drove back to the supermarket I purchased them from and talked to the produce manager. He could not tell me off-hand what variety it was, but after a few minutes of pleading, he got on the phone and called his distributor. It turns out the peach is a variety called Champion, a tender, juicy freestone peach with a sweet, delicate flavor. I bought enough for a gallon of wine, and a year later was so rewarded that I didn't want to part with even a bottle to see how it fared in competition. I just mentally awarded myself a Best of Show and drank it all. Don't squander your treasures.

When you find what you really like, stay with it. Every year when the first white-flesh peaches arrive, I buy just one and eat it in the parking lot. If it is Champion, I know it right away and go back in and buy more, with juice still dribbling from my beard.

Wine From Tropical Fruit

Tropical fruits are, well, fruits from the tropics, and the subtropics. In Chapter 7, we look at 12 tropical fruits that make excellent wines. Five of them are citrus. I could have added 3–4 more citrus and they would all make different wines, but I didn't want the chapter to reflect just the *Citrus* genus of the *Rutaceae* family.

With the exception of the banana, with a TA of about 3 g/L, almost all tropical fruit is tangy and acidic. Lemons and limes can have a TA of 50 g/L, a daunting thought. That isn't a TA you're likely to run into, but it's a possibility.

Every time I make lemon wine, which is nothing like hard lemonade, they make great wine. It is always a bit tart, like all lemon beverages, but it's good. My favorite lemon is the Meyer lemon. You can actually eat them without making a face the whole time. I did not include it here, but plan to do so in my next book; it is a good foundation for unusual wine blends. But then so are regular lemon wines.

There are 24 lemon varieties I could reference, but three popular varieties represent most of what we buy at the super-market: Lisbon, Eureka, and Bearss.

The vast majority of winemakers who have mastered lemon wine have done so because they have one or more lemon trees. We had a lemon tree years ago when I was growing up, and it produced so many lemons we could not drink lemonade fast enough to keep up with it.

Mango

Mango is one of my favorite tropicals. It, too, has multiple varieties. I just buy what the market carries, but when my wife and I land in Hawaii it is a different matter altogether. When you visit a large farmer's market, you can see physical differences in the mangoes, and by asking a few vendors who are *not* selling mangoes you can gather several opinions of which are the best. (If you ask a vendor selling them the answer will always be the variety he or she is selling.)

Mangoes make great wine. I had an acquaintance in Honduras who made a couple of batches of mango wine, consulted with me to negotiate a minor problem he was having, and before I knew it, he had established a mango winery. He said he was surrounded by mango trees, everyone had one or more, but very few people knew how easy it was to convert all that fruit into wine.

Passionfruit

The passionfruit is avoided by many simply because they are unfamiliar. Big mistake. They are a different fruit, to be sure, but flavorful and satisfying. Native to Brazil, they can only be grown in the South or in states like Florida or California, although a wild vine was discovered in Maryland of all places in the 1980s. Go figure.

I have never tasted it, but I was told by a reliable horticulturist that one variety of passionfruit (Scarlet Flame) tastes like strawberries, and another (Maypop) has a distinct apricot flavor. The most common commercial variety in the United States is the Purple Granadilla. Its purple skin hides an orangish flesh with delicious, sweet, aromatic, subacidic flavor. It's good eaten out of hand, made into jelly, mixed with ice cream, but also good in beverages, including wine.

Pineapple

If you don't think of Hawaii when you see a pineapple then you haven't lived. There is no sweeter, more fragrant and flavorful pineapple than one harvested the morning of the day you encounter it. They simply lose much of that freshness within 24

Pomegranate

The pomegranate is a truly magnificent fruit. As the thick rind dries on the tree, it locks in the hundreds of small juice sacs, called arils, keeping the seeds viable. That juice is sweet and flavorful, inviting all manner of wildlife to seek them out, spreading the seeds in the process.

Eventually the outer rind of fruit still on the tree finally splits, exposing the aril to the elements. Breezes spread the sweet scent as a calling card, and the winged seed-dispensers come in for a meal.

The flavor of pomegranate depends almost entirely on the variety and the nutrients and moisture the tree can extract from the soil. In bad years, the sweetness and flavor can be thin, so the tree drops some fruit and the remainder stays small, concentrating all that is to give in the waiting arils. In good years, the tree cannot produce enough fruit, and the fruit it does produce is huge, some with as many as 1,000 arils and packed with rich, sweet, flavorful juice.

Only a lack of imagination would pass this fruit by as a source of good wine. Besides the grape, it is the only fruit mentioned by name in the Bible as a wine source (Song of Solomon 8:2). The wine can be thin, especially if consumed too young, but as it ages it gains body, structure, and texture.

I once had a 5-gallon carboy of 3-year-old pomegranate wine, the longest my patience would wait, which, when I finally bottled it, was already better than most grape wines littering the shelves of stores everywhere. There was a woman I met at a nearby winery who had just purchased a premium bottle of strawberry reserve, back-sweetened with pure, clarified strawberry juice. During our chit-chat, I mentioned I had just bottled a pomegranate wine. She immediately offered to trade me the $30 bottle of the strawberry reserve, which I knew to be ambrosia, for a bottle of the pomegranate. I drove home, only 11 or 12 miles away, and

fetched her a bottle of the pomegranate. Upon later drinking the strawberry, as good and rich as it was, I realized that she got the better end of the trade.

Get hold of some pomegranates and make some wine, and then practice patience for as long as you can. If you practice long enough, you'll be richly rewarded.

hours, so most of the pineapple we eat on the mainland is past its peak before it's ever delivered to our market.

I've been convinced a long time that the only way to make the very best pineapple wine is to make it in Hawaii. And then I slowly began to realize something. Canned pineapple is closer to the fresh flavor of a newly harvested one than the ones we can buy in our supermarkets. I began reading the history of the pineapple industry in Hawaii. It is both fascinating and intricate. James Dole is given credit by almost everyone as the driving force and innovator in the Hawaiian pineapple industry. His work in mechanizing the processing and canning of fresh pineapples and planting the dominant variety largely contributed to the industry's growth. He was not alone, nor was he key to every innovation, but he was ever-present and more than willing to reap the rewards of pioneering work done by others. Why am I telling you this? Because he was largely responsible for ensuring that canned pineapple tastes almost as good as the fresh fruit. So I tip my hat to him as I open the cans of pineapple that will give birth to my wine.

Starfruit

If you live in the tropics and know of someone with a carambola tree, try to become good friends. Its fruit, the starfruit, is a culinary and winemaking delight. It makes a wonderful dry white but is probably most often bottled semi-sweet.

The starfruit has considerable amounts of oxalic acid, making it an acquired taste for those who haven't tried one before. But since the wine is made lightly spiced with cinnamon, you shouldn't even notice the oxalic acid in the wine.

This wine comes with a health warning. If you have kidney stones or have suffered kidney failure, you should regretfully not consume this wine or fruit. A small sip to see what it tastes like should be okay, but not a glass.

Tangerine

Tangerines are a favorite citrus snack. Easy to peel, reliably sweet, they are just a good snack food. As one of my aunts said at a family reunion, "You can eat tangerines and smile the whole time." In other words, their acidity level isn't as grimace-inducing as lemons, say.

When fermented along with Valencia, Blood, or Cara-Cara oranges, tangerines make for a very nice wine with a unique flavor profile. Better yet, all one has to do is assemble and prepare the ingredients. The wine makes itself.

Oddly, tangerine is not a wine seen that often in competitions. When entered, a well-made tangerine wine will always do well. That doesn't mean there won't be better wines it has to compete against, but that is true for every wine, period.

Wine From Roots

As unlikely as it seems, some roots can yield really good wines. In Chapter 8, we explore only six, but there are many we passed by, simply for space concerns. My most regretted omission was the sassafras root. The root is stripped of its bark, the bark tenderized and boiled, and the water used to make an aromatic root beer-flavored wine. But no matter, the root vegetables covered in Chapter 8 are more than enough to keep us busy for a while.

Beetroots

Front and center is the beetroot, what I consider to be the best among the lot. Like the pomegranate that spent three years in maturation, I once made a beetroot wine that refused to shed its earthy origins and so sat in a carboy for several years. It came to pass that we had some special guests from Louisiana stay with us. My wife cooked a killer of a meal, and afterward, we sat, totally stuffed and satiated, but we needed something to drink. My friend Luke Clark pointed to the carboy of beetroot and remarked that it has been sitting in that one spot for all the years he's been coming to visit. I apologized up front that it never shed its earthiness, but tilted the carboy and poured some into a carafe anyway so he could see for himself that the wine was just stubborn.

The color was the first surprise. It was even redder than a beetroot itself, clear and just beautiful. As I poured some into a waiting glass, I noticed I did not smell the dirt the roots had grown in. Luke did all the right things. He tilted the glass to examine the edge of the wine against the glass. He remarked on its color. He smelled it, then he swirled it a bit and sniffed again. He remarked on the aromatics of the wine, noting no trace of earthiness. Finally, he took a swig—not a sip, but a swig—played with it in his mouth and finally swallowed. Then he smiled, looked at the ¾ empty carafe and said, "We're going to need more."

Not every batch of beetroot wine takes forever to reach its potential. That particular batch was an exception. Everything about it was slow. It took longer to ferment to dryness—and that was only to 1.014—than most wines. It slowly degassed itself for almost two years. And then it just sat in the carboy year after year, giving no indication it would ever be ready to bottle. And by happenstance, Luke and Lynette Clark drove 350 miles to visit us and the wine responded. There's no explaining it.

An acquaintance from Paris, Texas tried explaining. His theory was that I had not cooked the beetroot long enough, the sugar had not inverted, and the enzymes in the starches had not been released to break the starch into sugar. Because of this, the wine contained all the ingredients, but none were optimized to finish the fermentation quickly. I might buy this explanation, but it would require the yeast, or at least some of them, to hang around for years, slowly fermenting sugars as they were released from the improperly cooked beetroot stew. It's possible, I suppose, but is it probable?

Whatever the reason, that batch was an anomaly. Make some beetroot wine. It won't take anywhere near this long to finish, and you'll be glad you did.

Carrot Wine (Carrot Whiskey)

Carrot wine, named Carrot Whiskey by Noel Whitcomb back in the 1940s, is a special wine everyone should make. It isn't whiskey, doesn't have an outrageous ABV, and only has a slight taste suggestive of the stronger spirit. But it is pleasant to drink, especially chilled, and will leave you feeling warm and cuddly despite going down cold.

The orange color of the carrots is transformed, first by cooking and then by fermentation and aging, into a whiskeyish golden brown. When clear and polished, it does indeed look like the hard stuff. And the aroma is mellower than one would expect, although it's difficult to predict what one would actually expect. It just doesn't smell like carrots, and it isn't earthy. It's a nice wine you'll take pride in.

Parsnips

Parsnip wine, when the vegetables are ripe with a slightly nutty flavor, is another wine that is good but can be exceptional.

According to my wine log, I've made five parsnip wines. Two were exceptional. You can credit the roots for those exceptions. They just tasted fresh and wholesome. Yes, I taste most of my bases when chopping, slicing, or grating them. You need to know what you're working with. Those not good enough for wine go into soups or stews, or as veggies on the dinner plate.

The very first parsnip wine I made used loose roots from a roadside stand; they looked like they had just been washed. I didn't make any inquiries but just bought the roots. In hindsight, I'll bet they had run out of parsnips and ran to the garden to pull some more. They naturally would have washed them to rid them of clinging soil. Or, they may have washed them every 15 minutes all day to keep them looking fresh. I just don't know but want to believe the first possibility.

They smelled fresh when I chopped them, slightly nutty and ever so suggestive of cream soda, and hey, I wrote it down! Like all root wines, the fermentation did not come out of the gate full throttle, but it went quickly enough. At that time I had 17 1-gallon batches going and so was not as focused on any one batch in particular.

It went through a decent maturation and finished off-dry, so it got ⅓ cup of nice tupelo honey before bottling. I may have waited longer than necessary to bottle it, but my plate was full. And it was a root wine, so there was no hurry.

It was spectacular! And it jinxed me. After it, I expected all parsnip wines to match it, but they didn't. Good wines all, but not like that first one. Until I made my fifth batch. It was another show-stopper, a bit higher in alcohol than usual, but a wine you couldn't stop at just one glass. The moral here is to keep at it. There are great wines in your future, but there's no reason why the future can't be the wine waiting in the secondary fermenter.

Potatoes

Potato wine sounds downright pedestrian. It reminds me of the proletariat during the Russian Revolution of 1917, starving but hopeful those Bolsheviks were going to deliver. Meanwhile, they had their potato wine . . .

Nothing could be further from the truth. Potato wine is not spectacular, but it isn't rotgut vodka either. It can be dressed up a bit with herbs, anything that goes with potatoes. The recipe we use includes ginger root for a little zing and white grape juice concentrate for body. You could also add a tablespoon of chives.

Whereas parsnip wine takes a little over two years to uncork, potato wine takes nine months. There are two routes to take, both taking the same amount of time. You can use russet potatoes, which have more starches convertible into sugar, or you can use more flavorful potatoes and add more sugar. Sugar is cheap but not as cheap as potatoes. You will also be retaining the potatoes for your food needs, so you have to ask yourself which potato you want to cook with after they are boiled for the wine.

The recipe uses Muscovado sugar, a molasses-coated sugar. This gives the wine a specific flavor profile, but if you don't particularly care for the taste of molasses, you can use another sugar.

Rutabagas

Rutabaga wine, like most root wines, uses citrus fruit and tartaric acid to raise the TA and lower the pH. The amount of tartaric is based on my experience. The amount could conceivably change with each batch, so be sure to keep an eye on the acidity. The least expensive way to do this is to monitor the pH by measurement and TA by taste.

Some people don't care for rutabaga. The taste is not as familiar as carrots or potatoes and, therefore, somewhat foreign. Others have never tasted it but aren't fond of its name. It conjures up images of some strange far-flung root, which it isn't. These are cultural biases and should not influence the wine we make.

The peppercorns add a nice touch, a little spiciness to brighten up the glass. They are a nice counterpunch to the orange and lemon, all of which shine through. This recipe was sent to me by a woman in Illinois. She really likes this wine, and so I had to try it. The wine finished out in a little over a year and was consumed during a cold spell in about a week. I only wished I had made more.

Sweet Potatoes

Sweet potato wine is a natural marriage of sweet potatoes, raisins, and brown sugar. The color of the wine is light golden-brown but could change depending on the variety of sweet potatoes used. I used the rose-skinned, orange-fleshed Beauregard variety, a long-time favorite of this household.

The must was acidified with raisins and tartaric acid. Not actually shown in the recipe and method was a little citric acid I added near the end, ¾ teaspoon, according to my wine log. I adjusted the acidity by taste. The citric added a little acid while at the same time rounded out the corners of the tartaric, especially after bottle aging. This also demonstrates that balance is in the taste buds.

Sweet potato wine tastes closer to sweet potatoes than russet potato wine does to russet potatoes. It simply is an entirely different root, very yielding when cooked and eager to share its flavor. The light brown sugar melds with the root's flavor and in my opinion is a perfect choice. I made this wine previously using Demerara sugar.  Its unique flavor also made a tasty wine, but when I started making a later batch I was out of Demerara and used light brown instead. Despite my love of Demerara sugar in my wines, I concluded that the light brown made a tastier sweet potato wine.

Wine From Flowers

Flower wines are one of my favorite types of wine to make. It is especially enjoyable—almost adventurous—to make wine with a new flower. You aren't sure what to expect but trust the flowers to tell you what to do. And believe it or not, that is exactly how I make a new flower wine.

There is no shortage of flowers to use. A dozen years ago, I compiled a list of edible flowers suitable for making wine. The list may seem exhaustive but really isn't. If I were to compile such a list today I'm sure it would grow by at least 25–50 percent. There is just so much more information available today. I removed a few flowers from that list during the years and added a few others. I came up with 231 flowers, and include it in this book on page 353.

So what is it about flower wines that attract me to them so strongly? I like big, bold wines. Of all the native grapes of North America, the Mustang Grape is the boldest, so much so that it is edible only as a survival food. But in my opinion, it makes the best wild grape wine. Nothing else really compares. Flower wines occupy a place at the other end of the taste spectrum. Flower wines are, for the most part, delicate, suggestive, fragrant, delicious. I have only made one I didn't really care for, and I have made about two-and-a-half dozen, not a very big dent in my list but a start.

I approach every new flower with the utmost respect for its character, its beauty, or its plainness, its fragrance, its color, its place in the ecology of the field, meadow or garden. I have sought out the flowers of common weeds because they are either neglected or abused and deserve a chance to express themselves. Besides, I like being the first person to ever make wine with a particular base, and it is unlikely that anyone has bothered to harvest these little flowers for wine.

The problem with weeds is that their flowers are so small and it takes a lot to make a gallon batch. So I had a system. I would pick until my back ached, put the flowers in a Ziploc freezer bag and freeze them until I thought I had enough additions. Even weeds flower seasonally. I ended up throwing out a bag of flowers because I realized it would be another year until I saw them again.

The two weeds whose flowers are relatively easy to harvest and make great wine are chicory and dandelion, and both have found their way into Chapter 9.

Cactus Blossom

Cactus blossom wine was something I'd never seen documented, so when the idea of making it struck me, I jumped at the chance to be the first. I now know I certainly wasn't the first—those big flowers are just too obvious to ignore—but I may have been the first to post a recipe for them.

My wife and I were out on a day trip through the vastness of Texas when we found ourselves on a dirt ranch road lined on either side by miles and miles of prickly pear cactus growing along the fencelines. They were all in bloom, and the idea of cactus blossom wine struck me.

The flower petals are fairly large and thick, suggesting they may contain decent flavor and probably a little sugar and acid. I picked a lot that day, not knowing how many I might need. It was enough for two 1-gallon batches.

Because I had plenty of petals, I used a lot in the two batches, in differing amounts as I searched to hone a recipe. The best batch used 2½ quarts, which may seem like a lot but only took a half-hour or less to harvest. The resulting wine was a delight. I used white grape juice concentrate for body, and the flowers filled in the edges with everything you'd want in a flower wine. Flavor in spades, delightful aroma, good mouthfeel, nice balance, great color, and clarity. I've made it several times since that first time, and it always is a wonderful wine. Serve chilled.

Chicory

Chicory is a beautiful roadside weed when in bloom *en masse*. The flower stems reach high, and the fragrant light-blue petals paint the backroads a nice pastel. I remember when the idea of making wine from them first crossed my mind, but I was in a hurry to put miles behind me, and it was a couple of weeks before I again found myself among the chicory of East Texas. This time I was in no hurry to get anywhere, so I took time to harvest the flowers. There were plenty, I was eager, and in no time I had two plastic bags of flowers. Always carry some empty plastic bags for unexpected harvests and a cutting instrument (I carry a fillet knife).

Not having a recipe hasn't stopped me before. I plucked the petals from the flower heads and kept asking the blue beauties how they'd like to be vinified. When finished, I had two quarts of petals, and the flowers spoke to me. I used a tried and true method for making dandelion wine, slipping in my favorite winemaking sugar, Demerara.

This is a very good wine and I encourage anyone who lives in chicory country to make it. No, it is not a blue wine. The color drops out as the wine clears. There are additives I could use to try and capture the anthocyanins responsible for the color, but I'm not sure a blue wine would be that appealing.

Dandelion

Dandelion has to be the queen of flower wines. No other flower wine has been so intensely admired, studied, and written about (although the Brits think the elderflower claims that title). When polished in clarity, its color is vibrant, golden, enchanting.

I have a decanter surrounded with facets that do wonderful things to a wine's presentation, even in a dimly lit room. I once filled it with dandelion wine and took it outside in the sun. It was a dazzling display of brilliance, like a finely cut yellow topaz, full of radiance and photons being reflected every which way.

Dandelion wine's bouquet can be sublime or uplifting, its aroma reserved but inspiring. It has a flavor all its own. When properly aged, it is magnificent. When consumed too soon it is a disappointment. This is one wine you'll want to bottle some in splits to taste during the outer months of aging.

The only difficult thing about making dandelion wine is harvesting the dandelions and plucking the petals from the flower heads (a short, 4-year old granddaughter helps, as she is so much closer to the flowers that her back never seems to ache). Once the ingredients are added, in their correct order, the wine makes itself. But then there is a 7-month maturation and two years of bottle aging. Playing the waiting game may be as difficult as harvesting and preparing the flowers.

Dandelion wine should be reserved for special guests or occasions, like when royalty pays a cordial visit. Cellar it under lock and key, lest an errant offspring sneak in and drink it. When you serve it, have Beethoven's "Ode to Joy" playing in the background. Give it respect. Wear a tuxedo.

Elderflower

Elderflower wine is perhaps the third-most celebrated flower wine, losing second place to rose petal. Elderflower wine is everything dandelion isn't. Its color is of a lesser hue. Its bouquet is anything but reserved, its fragrance intense. Its flavor is unique and at once recognizable. Its finish stays with you a while. In short, it is perhaps the most aggressive and recognizable flower wines. It's like a 3-year old running around hollering, "Look at me. Look at me." Only with elderflower wine, you look.

I've made this wine in several ways. I expected a batch I made using Demerara sugar would be the best, but it was one of those rare times when that wonderful sugar was just too much. It competed with those delicate flowers and only served to detract with an off-flavor that surprised me.

Give this flower wine a chance. It is aggressive, yes, but will delight you on a warm summer day when served chilled on the patio or garden. You harvest the flowers in early summer, and the wine is ready 11 months later. Make two batches.

The flowers are plentiful and the wine easily made. If the first bottle has an off-taste, a bit of minerality, cellar it another 2–3 months.

Hibiscus

Hibiscus wine is always a surprising delight. I don't know why that is. I know it will be a good wine, but it is always better than I remembered. There are several methods for making this wine. I employ the easiest, yielding fine wine in only seven months.

The only challenge you might face is obtaining the dried flowers. If there is a Mexican food market in your town, look there. The flowers are often sold in bulk and are usually red or purple. The wine will inherit the color. In Mexico, the flowers are the base for tea or flavoring in casseroles, soups, salads, or other fares. South of the border, the dried flowers are called Jamaica.

When imbued with more body, this wine really shines. I accomplish this by adding another 50% of the grape concentrate used, and I may add a ripe banana or two during fermentation. I made a fuller-bodied version after receiving a judging sheet that contained the comment, "Almost there. Needs body." I did not use that particular recipe in this chapter because I think the presented version makes a delightful wine. And if you want more body, all it takes is a straining bag and a banana or two.

Honeysuckle

Honeysuckle wine has always disappointed me until I tasted an exquisite one at a county fair wine competition I was judging and elicited the secrets to this wine. The recipe in Chapter 9 captures and exposes the winemaker's secrets. Even when the recipe fails, it still makes a very good wine.

The easiest way to screw up this recipe is to cut short the long maturation and aging times. Don't do that. While the wine develops, get on with your life and forget about the wine until it comes up on your calendar: Rack honeysuckle wine.

There are many species and varieties of honeysuckle. Pass on the ornamentals and select the plain old common honeysuckle found growing on a fence nearly everywhere. But confirm that the species you're foraging for is edible; there are some varieties with inedible flowers.

There is a park in San Antonio with an entire border fence thick with honeysuckle. I assume there is a chain-link fence hidden in their mass somewhere, but I have never really seen it. That's how thick the honeysuckle is. Pick the flowers where you find them, but don't bother a neighbor's vines if you don't have to.

If you have honeysuckle at home, it'll take weeks to deliver enough flowers for a

Lavender

Lavender wine is a special treat. Its fragrance is true to its fresh flowers, but perhaps not quite as strong. Nonetheless, it is legendary. The flavor of the wine can be a bit strong if the flowers are all alphas, so feel free to tweak the amount accordingly. Too many flowers are not necessarily better with this one as they can leave an almost metallic aftertaste.

There are many different varieties of lavender. I made this wine using English Lavender, common enough in nurseries and gardens, but any variety should work. If you have different varieties to choose from, you might collect flowers from them all and make separate batches using a different variety in each and compare them. That is the fun of winemaking. There are so many possibilities.

I have never made this wine with Demerara sugar as the flower does not suggest it. If you listen, the flowers will tell you what to do. I know that sounds strange, but it works for me. Maybe after a few batches of different flowers, you will understand. Perhaps it is just me.

Other than getting the number of flowers right, there is nothing difficult about this wine. Watch the acid, add more if need be. Stay on track with the maturation and bottle aging. There are  no shortcuts here. I have tried a shortcut and it ended up taking me longer to make the wine than it should have.

When everything comes together properly, the wine is refreshing as an afternoon beverage, served chilled, on the patio, or a bench in the garden. To avoid the need for a nap, limit it to two glasses.

batch of wine. Luckily, they can be stored in the freezer while obtaining the quota, and they have a long flowering season. Still, if you can find a stand of honeysuckle like the one in San Antonio you can collect enough flowers in a single harvest. It's worth it.

Orange Blossoms

Orange blossom wine is an old wine. It was especially popular by the Moors during their occupation of the Iberian Peninsula where orange trees were everywhere. They made a low-alcohol version that could be drank or used for washing the hands before meals. We'll be making

a stronger version, around 12% ABV, for drinking only. If you want to wash your hands, I suggest making an orange water concoction, which is not difficult to do. No need to waste a fermentation.

This is a refreshing wine and easy to make once you've collected the flowers. I have but one tree and would completely strip it if used to make this wine. Fortunately, I have a friend only three blocks away who has three trees and doesn't care if the trees produce oranges or not. I can pick all I want and do need a ladder to get to most of them.

The wine is fragrant with a refreshing but subdued taste. I have used more blossoms to increase the flavor but returned to this recipe because it was easier to balance. Keep an eye on the acid. Check the pH with a pH meter and taste for TA. If you need acid in the end, I suggest citric. The wine is finished in only seven months.

Rose Petals

Rose petal wine is both romantic and a nice social wine. I've made many versions and never made a bad one. Some were better than others, but they were all good wines.

It can be made with any fragrant variety of rose, including wild roses. It has traditionally been made with the petals as they wilted. They somehow retain their fragrance for a long time. I make it with the petals when they are fresh. It just seems to make a more fragrant wine that way, although wilted petals retain most of their fragrance, which dwindles slowly with time. It's your call.

Also, most recipes say to cut the flowers and remove the petals later. I want my roses to develop rose hips. I not only make wine from them but also a healthy tea. I suggest you do the same, simply harvest the petals where they form. The petals are easily removed.

The wine has a flavor of its own. The flavor changes slightly with different rose varieties, but not much. The more fragrant the petals, the better the wine tastes. This is true of all wines. The aroma enhances the flavor.

There may be things more romantic than rose petal wine, but not many, for a special occasion, birthday, anniversary, Valentine Day. No, it isn't an aphrodisiac, but don't be surprised if it contributes to romance.

Tulips

Tulip wine was a wine made by circumstance. When an unseasonal hail storm stripped every tulip of its petals, I decided not to let them go to waste. It might be another thing altogether to have to remove the petals from perfectly healthy and showy tulips. If the latter, I would wait until the flowers are in slight decline and harvest the petals then.

Having no references to this wine, I had no way of knowing what to expect. I was pleasantly surprised when it fermented much as my cactus blossom wine and produced a wonderful wine that goes down well and satisfies. It reinforced my belief that most flowers can be made into wine.

Tulip petals are edible. Not only can they be used to adorn salads, but they cook well in soups, chicken stews, other dishes, and casseroles. They even can be used in several desserts, layered in fruit strudels, for example. In other words, they are flavorful. This reinforces their appropriateness for wine.

Except that some tulips, especially the whites, have little or no flavor. Choose your petals wisely.

Wine From Herbs and Spices

Wines from herbs and spices have been around from pre-Roman times. There are almost endless candidates. In Chapter 10, we examine just four, but they should serve as a guide for the inclusion of other herbs and spices.

The most expensive spice wine I have read about is saffron wine, and here we are talking about the freshly dried, bright red stigmas and styles of the *Crocus sativus* flower. Since the flowers only produce three such filaments, saffron is widely accepted as the most expensive spice there is. The color of the wine is true to saffron, bright golden yellow, but the wine's flavor is a huge disappointment, suggestive of the taste of freshly cut hay. At a very large open market in Tangiers, my wife and I bought some fresh saffron threads. I'm not positive about this, but I think we paid the equivalent of $10 for about 15 filaments. They were so valuable to us that we didn't use them for years. We ended up making a saffron chicken-rice casserole, an inglorious end to a noble spice.

Aside from saffron, there are hundreds of other candidates for wine, some in combination. I once decided to make wine from Herbs of Provence. It was somewhat expensive for an herbal wine but worth it. I actually made it a bit too strong and had to dilute with some wine from white grape juice frozen concentrate, which we know

is Niagara grape wine. It was a very nice wine. I used about half of it in cooking, but the rest was consumed traditionally.

Basil

Basil wine is made for cooking and blending with other wines to give them complexity. It can be drunk as a novelty white wine—very warming on a chilly night—but its real value is in the kitchen. I've used it in marinades (chicken, Cornish hens, and fish), braising, sautéing, and in soups and stews in combination with stock.

Basil wine, like garlic wine, ginger wine, and jalapeño wine, can is used whenever a specific flavor is desired. When reduced in the skillet, its sugars caramelize and can be deglazed for richer sauces and gravies. When making bread from scratch, it can be added to the flour in place of plain water to subtly flavor the loaf. If you cook, you've got to make this wine.

There are no issues making it. You simply have to add enough acid and a little tannin, and the sugar and alcohol should balance out. You must use fresh basil leaves, and it really makes no matter which basil variety you use, although Spicy Bush Basil or Sweet Thai Basil are favored.

Ginger

Ginger wine is another classic cooking and blending wine. On a chilly night, it outshines basil by a mile. Ginger is a pungent flavor, spicy and hot, and it has endless

uses in the kitchen. It can do everything basil can and do it with greater flavor. Basil has a greater underlying richness, but ginger is sitting in the front row, waiting to be noticed and appreciated.

There are varieties of ginger, but unless you grow them yourself you'll probably never encounter them. Go with what you have, and by all means grate it. Thin slices work fine, but grated ginger offers the yeast more surface area to attack. Give them the surface area.

I know a winemaker who adds his ginger to the must incrementally. His rationale is that ginger is so strong a flavor that adding it all at once might stunt the development of the yeast. I've never experienced that problem, so I am not recommending it. Besides, I'm not convinced the yeasts have an appreciation for the flavor of ginger.

This wine has a strong flavor and an excellent body. The body is attributed to using two cans of the white grape juice frozen concentrate. This also adds half the required sugar and a good part of the acid. I bottle six 375-mL bottles for cooking and dilute what would be two remaining bottles with white grape juice frozen concentrate wine (Niagara grape). I dilute to taste as a drinking and blending wine and grow the two remaining bottles into three. The beauty is the drinking wine can still be used in the kitchen. It just won't have as potent a flavor.

For this wine, I needed to add a little more acid. I used both tartaric and citric acid as a blend of 60% tartaric and 40% citric. It kicked the acidity up while mellowing the harshness of the tartaric. I felt sure that if I needed to add more acid at the end of maturation, I could use this blend or either component and acidify with precision. I didn't need to add any.

Rose Hip

Rose hip wine is one of the classics. It is easy to make but takes time. It has a wonderful flavor, almost legendary, nothing like rosehip tea. It has an unpredictable color, ranging from a tinted white to a slight orange to a light, golden brown. These variations are likely due to the variety of rose the hips came from, but can also be due to the age and oxidation of the hips themselves. It makes no difference. The color is always beautiful.

With a tip of the hat to the flower wines, rosehip wine is considered by some to be the second-best wine, after grape wine. There is, of course, a caveat to this claim, and that is a well-made rosehip wine. Well-made means not only using fresh rose hips when making the wine but waiting for two long years for it to bottle-age sufficiently. There are no shortcuts. You either wait or you might as well not make it.

Rosemary

Rosemary wine is always a flavor made with another wine. You cannot make it directly. Thus, the winemaker must select a wine,

usually white, that he can make with confidence while infusing it with fresh rosemary.

Rosemary has a potent flavor that can easily get away from the winemaker and make wine too strong to drink but ideal for cooking. Unless you intend to make a cooking wine exclusively, then it is important to monitor the flavor profile closely during a 2–3-day critical period.

The recipe uses white grape juice frozen concentrate to create a wine the rosemary can join. The grape juice wine can be made with a greater body by using two cans of the concentrate. In that case, the sugar would be reduced (to 1 pound) as well as the acid (calculate from actual measurements). Tannin can be halved. The amount of rosemary used does not change.

The instructions say to age the wine at least a year, but it will improve to 2 years. It is strongly advised to sit it out for the long term. Wines are not worth making if not made to their potential. Rosemary is a wine that is easy to make short of its potential by shaving months from the aging time, but this would be a mistake.

Novelty Wines

These are wines that did not easily fit in any of the previous categories. This will become obvious as we briefly leaf through them.

Jalapeño

Jalapeño wine is primarily a cooking wine but goes down well as a versatile sipping or blending wine. In any of those roles, this wine delivers.

The biggest issue with making Jalapeño Wine is the jalapeños themselves. Back in the not-so-ancient past, Pace Picante Sauce funded Texas A&M to develop a milder jalapeño for their use. What resulted from this effort is the TAM (Texas A&M) jalapeño. In the intervening years, TAM jalapeños have increasingly invaded the supermarkets, making it more and more difficult to make a pungent jalapeño wine.

It is necessary to taste the raw fruit to gauge the heat and number of jalapeños you'll need. Since we all have different tolerances for pungency, even before the TAM jalapeño appeared, we had to judge the amount we need for this wine. The difference is that if the jalapeños are TAMs and we want wine with heat, it will take so many more to deliver the same piquancy. It makes it difficult to outline a reliable wine recipe.

In one sense, the need for more TAM jalapeños in our wine is a good thing. Surprising to some, jalapeños have a very good, underlying flavor. Putting more of them in the must gives us a better chance of tasting that flavor without increasing the heat. Many dark clouds have silver linings. The wine is drinkable in 9 months.

Nettle

Nettles in your wine may seem truly bizarre, but nettle tips have long been a staple in certain diets and regions. Even the least

well-off amongst us have grown too affluent to gather portions of our meals from the forests, fields, and meadows. Or, even if we are predisposed to do so, there is somehow a stigma attached to those who do.

There is nothing wrong with the tender, young tips of nettles—stinging or otherwise—in our soups, casseroles, or wine. Before I made nettle tips wine I was just as apprehensive about it as I was about jalapeño. My only problem was in finding the nettles. But I eventually did, while collecting wild grapes near an old Spanish mission in south San Antonio. The wine itself was simple to make, but you need to find this out for yourself.

Pawpaw

Pawpaws are a fruit with a wide distribution and yet are virtually unknown by most people who live among it. The pawpaw, a relatively small forest tree, produces

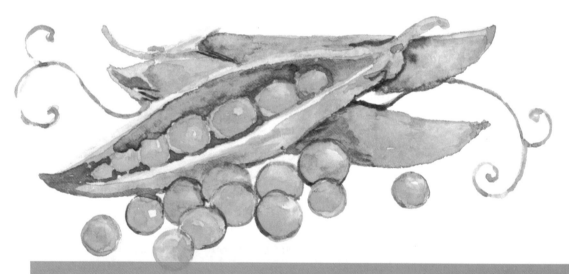

Pea Pods

Pea pod wine is simply a nice, white wine. One doesn't expect much from pea pods, so even being acceptable would be a plus, but it really is a nice white wine. It does take a lot of pea pods to make, but a family-size garden will probably work.

I did not enter it in competition but I am confident it would have at least placed. I made mine from bags of frozen pea pods given to me by a friend who admitted she was just too put off by the thought of it to make it but was fairly confident I'd be up for the challenge. It was drinkable in 10 months, quicker than many grape wines, and my friend enjoyed her gift bottle.

the largest edible, native, tree-born fruit in North America. Its soft, custard-like flesh combines the flavors most associated with mangoes, bananas, and pineapple. It's a versatile fruit and can be used in any recipe using any of the three flavors mentioned, but I think it's best eaten fresh, slightly chilled.

When I first made this wine, I thought the recipe must be in error. It just did not seem like it ought to take this long to make, so I carved two months out of the recipe I found on the internet. It was not that bad, but not that spectacular either. The second time I played it smart and was very pleased with the result. I still don't know why it takes so long to make Pawpaw wine, but it just does. It can be consumed in 13 months.

Pumpkin

Pumpkin wine is less a novelty than a wine needing a chapter to fit into. It is a fairly standard holiday wine, made during the holidays one year and served during the holidays the next. I've probably received more communications about good pumpkin wine than any other type.

The standard pumpkin pie pumpkin, those smaller ones that pack the flavor, are the standard pumpkins for this wine. If presented with a choice, the Sugar Pie Pumpkin is by far superior, with Baby Pam coming in as second choice. There is also a sweet white pumpkin called Lumina with orange flesh and smooth texture, which is said to be superior to Baby Pam. I have seen them in the supermarket but have not tried them yet. The best thing about these little gems is that you do not need to be in a hurry to process them into wine. In cool, dry storage, they will easily keep 6–8 months if healthy when purchased.

Rhubarb

Every winemaker comes to appreciate rhubarb wine if they've ever made it. You will read this over and over again in this book: rhubarb tends to adopt the flavor of whatever it is blended with, and therein lies its greatest value in winemaking. It is almost the perfect wine for topping up and for stretching out a batch of almost anything when you come up short.

Rhubarb is also a nice tasting wine by itself. I have only tasted one I considered exquisite, but I have also only tasted one I thought was a waste of good rhubarb. It's a fairly fast wine, drinkable in 8 months.

Tomato

When I mention tomato wine to an audience, I always hear a few shouts of, "Yuck!"

This, of course, is from people who have never before heard of tomato wine let alone tasted one. In a blind tasting, I'll bet those same people would think it a decent if not an outright good wine.

Like rhubarb, I've only tasted one tomato wine I considered exquisite. I've tasted a few that were not well made. One had been made with dark raisins for body instead of white (my recipe uses 100% white grape juice frozen concentrate), undoubtedly too many, and the raisins could be tasted. The rest, and I'm only guessing, used under-ripe or over-ripe tomatoes. As in any other wine, you simply must start with a ripe, flavorful base.

I use Demerara sugar in my recipe. Sugar-in-the-Raw would be my second choice, although it lacks the unique flavor of Demerara. I know my favorite sugar is costly. I have no control over that and own no interest in its production, distribution, or marketing. I just like the taste of the stuff. This wine is drinkable in 8 months.

Walnut Leaf

Walnut leaf wine is a very old stand-by when there is nothing else to make wine with. Now I'll let you in on a secret. Even if there are plenty of things to make wine with, if there is a Black Walnut tree nearby and you can reach eight growing branch tips, pick yourself the 40 newest leaves and make a batch of this wine for the future (it takes 26 months to reach its prime). You'll be ever so glad you did.

Just as someone did, I'm sure, hundreds of years ago, I made wine from the leaves of probably a dozen trees before I had access to a Black Walnut tree with branches close enough to the ground to harvest some leaves. Of all the leaves I made into wine, only three were worth repeating. Black Walnut was by far the best, required fewer leaves, and didn't taste like it was made from tree leaves.

Let me tell you how this recipe came to be developed. I long ago came across two competing recipes for this wine, each claiming to make the very best Black Walnut leaf wine. One used brown sugar. The other used honey. Both used raisins. I largely switched from raisins to frozen grape juice concentrate between 20 and 22 years ago, so that was my first modification of each recipe. But I still had to choose brown sugar or honey. I knew honey would deliver a richness brown sugar couldn't match, but I knew I would substitute Demerara sugar for the brown. In the end, I couldn't decide, so I combined the two modified recipes and used a pound of Demerara and a pound of honey, without raisins. It worked out better than I ever anticipated.

Watermelon

One of the most difficult wines to make is Watermelon Wine, a delicate beverage that neither smells nor tastes like actual watermelon but is unique. That is, it comes close when the wine actually ferments to dryness without incident.

Like all melons, watermelon juice spoils very fast once liberated from the fruit. There is, therefore, a race to ferment the juice faster than it can spoil. Ideally, this would be done in temperature-controlled vats with a fast yeast capable of coping with low temperatures. I know of fast yeasts and I know of yeasts capable of low-temperature fermentation, but as juice gets colder, even fast yeasts necessarily slow down.

Plan B is a multi-pronged attack. First, we need to find a melon with outstanding flavor large enough for our purposes. Once the melon is cut, we protect the flesh and refrigerate it. Then we make a yeast starter solution using a very fast yeast. As the starter grows, we begin exposing it to short periods of refrigeration to try to bring it close to the temperature of the melon. We also begin exposing the starter to the watermelon juice, so the yeast culture grows used to its future environment and snack bar. Then we extract the juice from the melon and join it and the yeast. And, of course, we pray to the God or Goddess of Wine and Winemaking of your choice (there are several to choose from). If everything works, you'll be drinking it in less than a year.

Zucchini

Zucchini makes a fast wine; it's drinkable in 7 months. It might not be your first choice, but it makes a good wine. It has more than zucchini in it, including ingredients to perk up the blandness many people associate with the green squash. Besides my old standbys, grape juice frozen concentrate, and Demerara sugar, it also includes ginger root to give it a little zing. The combination was a hit with family and friends, gone before I could enter it into a competition.

Smaller, young zucchinis make far better wine than the larger, older ones, but if you have to use the older ones consider using the optional peppercorns to give it a little more spiciness.

GRAPE WINES

❖

Traditional Wine Grapes

There are literally thousands of grape varieties, but less than a couple hundred contribute to the commercial wines of the world. These are the traditional wine grapes, which vary from region to region. In the U.S. and Canada, the most familiar traditional wine grapes are largely the "noble" grapes of Europe, varieties developed over many centuries from wild grapes by carefully breeding and selecting grapes with desired characteristics (acidity, sugar, flavor, color, seasonality, vigor, etc.). Examples include grapes with names you already know: Cabernet Sauvignon, Cabernet Franc, Chardonnay, Chenin Blanc, Pinot Blanc, Pinot Noir, Merlot, Riesling, Sauvignon Blanc, and so on. About 80 of these varieties represent about 99% of the commercial wines we consume.

In my experience, it is unlikely that the average beginning winemaker will have access to these grapes, or recognize it if they do. If your situation is different, I apologize for including you in a generalization. Because noble grapes are a relative rarity for beginning home winemakers, I won't discuss recipes for them here. This actually solves one dilemma, as there are dozens of methods for making wine from these grapes, each devised for a particular variety.

It is far more likely that most beginning home winemakers will have access to grapes purchased from supermarket or perhaps a roadside stand or farmers market. Some of you likely also have grapes growing at home. You may or may not know what kind they are, but chances are, they are not noble grapes.

This leaves us with describing a method for making wine from generic grapes. Red and white grape wines are usually made by different methods, and so I will be describing a method for each. I will also describe a generic method for making red wine from wild grapes (species native to the U.S.). Wild grapes do not include hybrids with European varieties.

Cabernet Sauvignon grapes

Red Wine ❖

Most backyard grapes have the following characteristics: The grapes ripen in medium-size bunches of bluish-purple to purplish-black grapes of decent size in late August to mid-September (depending on location).

The vines are usually on an arbor, trellis structure, or a fence, were definitely planted by someone, were untrimmed when the current owner acquired them, exhibited vigorous growth after being pruned, and are winter hardy, even in the Great Lakes regions, and no one has a clue as to what kind of grapes they might be. Finally, the grapes have seeds, are very sweet, and are good to eat. If you have similar grapes, this recipe is for you.

Unless you know otherwise, I'd assume your grapes are Concord grapes or a hybrid of this variety, which is the most common yard grape in America. The Concord grape was first cultivated in 1849 and introduced to the market in 1853 by Ephraim Wales Bull of Concord, Massachusetts. Virtually everyone in America has tasted this grape, as it is the "red" grape that Thomas Bramwell Welch made famous in juice, jelly, and soda. It has a distinct flavor, grows well almost everywhere, and is resistant to most (but not all) diseases that affect European grapes.

Of course, your grapes may *not* be Concord, but that won't be a problem, as this recipe will work for most cultivated grapes. **Note:** By "cultivated," I mean a grape that was planted in a yard (not a wild grape species.)

About 12 pounds of grapes are usually required to produce a gallon of wine, but this could vary by one, or several, pounds (especially if the grapes are pressed by hand). Destem the grapes, cull out any unripe or unsound ones, crush the healthy ones by hand, with the flat bottom of a wine bottle, or with the masher of your choice, transfer them to as many nylon straining bags as required, and either squeeze out the juice by hand or use a grape or fruit press to extract the juice. Alternatively, the juice can be extracted with a juicer, although be wary of juicers that grind away at the seeds, as this will produce a bitter wine.

If topping up with water, this recipe makes a wine with 12% alcohol by volume. If topping up with finished red wine, only adjust the starting specific gravity to 1.088. Most people like this wine best with a little sweetness, but it also makes a very good dry wine.

As we want to avoid malolactic fermentation (see page 58), our free SO_2 must stay above 20 mg/L throughout the fermentation process. We will start high enough to allow for much of it to be bound and still leave enough to last until we stabilize.

> Unless you know otherwise, I'd assume your grapes are Concord grapes or a hybrid of this variety.

JACK'S TIP

MANY YEARS AGO, tired of wringing bags, I devised a simple press made of two pieces of ½-inch oak plywood, 2 feet by 2 feet square. I had a carpenter use a router to cut a ¾-inch wide shallow channel all the way around it about an inch from the edges with an exit channel from that. That was the bottom of my press. The spillway was extended over the edge of a work-counter over a collection bucket. Grapes were placed in nylon straining bags, which were then placed in the center of the bottom piece of the press. The top piece of plywood was then placed on the grapes, and the whole upper surface was covered with a layer of bricks, then a second, third, and fourth layer. The gradual weight being applied was enough to press the grapes gradually more and more. I typically placed six to eight layers of bricks before I was satisfied the grapes had been adequately pressed. Alternatively, one could use weights, big bags of animal feed, or anything that's heavy that can be stacked. About 120 to 180 pounds of weight are required for adequate pressing. As weight is added, the stack is allowed to settle for 5-15 minutes for the juice to work its way out of the grapes. The most expensive part of the press was the oak plywood and routering. I had the bricks already, but I suppose if I had to buy them, they would exceed the total cost of the routered plywood. When all grapes have been pressed, transfer the juice to a secondary and attach an airlock. Wait until all fermentation ceases and the airlock is still for two weeks, then rack into another sanitized secondary, top-up and refit the airlock.

Juice falling from a wine press

Red Wine Recipe

from Generic Backyard Grapes

WINE IS READY IN: **9 months**

YOU'LL NEED: **12 pounds grapes per gallon of wine**

ADDITIONAL EQUIPMENT: **nylon straining bags and a press**

MAKES: **1 gallon, but can be scaled up**

INGREDIENTS

12 lb. red grapes

granulated sugar to raise the specific gravity to 1.095

1 tsp pectic enzyme

potassium metabisulfite, as needed

½ tsp potassium sorbate

1 tsp yeast nutrient

1 sachet Lalvin 71B (if high acidity) or EC1118 wine yeast

DIRECTIONS

Prepare must: Wash grapes and cull injured or unhealthy ones. Divide into manageable masses and put one group at a time into nylon straining bags, tie off, put in your primary, and crush by hand or masher. Leave bags in the primary fermenter but collect about a cup of juice.

Use your hydrometer to check the specific gravity of juice and adjust to 1.090 by adding sugar (if too low) or water (if too high) or additional juice (if just right). Check the pH of the juice. Add 0.2 g potassium metabisulfite to protect the grapes and juice, and stir it well. If not stirred, the potassium metabisulfite can bleach the juice, not permanently, but bothersome just the same. Cover the primary and set it aside for at least 12 hours. Then stir in the pectic enzyme, always after the potassium metabisulfite, re-cover the primary, and wait another 12 hours. Stir in the yeast nutrient.

Add yeast: To 1 cup of warm water (not to exceed 102 degrees F.) add a pinch of yeast nutrient, 1 teaspoon of sugar, and stir to dissolve. Add the yeast to water, stir, and cover the mixture for 30 minutes. Add the mixture to the primary, stir, and cover the primary.

Fermentation: Fermentation should be evident within the day or the next. The CO_2 will push the bag to the surface where it should be punched beneath the surface at least twice daily and squeezed to expel the CO_2. Failure to do so will allow the floating grapes to dry out and could allow spoilage organisms to grow in the drying grapes. When the wine's SG drops to 1.020, or lower if the fermentation is still vigorous, remove the bags one at a time and press the grapes, returning pressed juice to the primary.

Press each bag of crushed grapes in a wine or fruit press, although it is unlikely the beginner will have such equipment. Most people take one bag at a time and wring the bag out several times by hand. Fluffing the bag between wringings actually allows more juice to be extracted.

Post-Fermentation: Wait an additional six weeks and add 0.2 g potassium metabisulfite and ½ teaspoon potassium sorbate to a sanitized secondary, rack the wine onto it, top-up, and refit the airlock.

Wait 30 days and taste the wine. If too tart, sweeten to balance—acid should be as evident as sugar, with neither hiding the other—and bottle the wine. Wait six months to allow the wine to gain some age before tasting. If tannic astringency is evident, wait an additional six months or until tannins smooth out.

Options: Many red wines respond well to oak. Light, medium, or dark toasted oak chips, dust, cubes, beans, spirals, or other forms can be inserted in the secondary during the 6-week maturation period. When racking off the oak, topping-up will be necessary. Top up with a similar red wine in the variety and style you are making.

Red grape wine blends well with blackberry, blackcurrant, and elderberry. Do not allow the blended wine to overpower the grape flavor; it should instead add an underlying suggestion that it is there. Blending trials are essential to get it right.

Similar fruit: This recipe, with sugar modifications as necessary, will work with any red grape and many native-noble grape hybrids, such as Concord, Norton (Cynthiana), Frontenac, Marechal Foch, Baco Noir, Marquette, etc.

White Wine ❖

This recipe begins with the pressed juice of the grapes rather than the grapes themselves. For a how-to, see the discussion prior to the red grape recipe (page 113). Although it may seem obvious that white wine is made from white grapes, this is not necessarily a requirement. Many red-skinned grapes have white or clear pulp, their color confined to the skins only. When these grapes are crushed and immediately pressed, the resulting juice is clear and makes white or light blush wine (think White Zinfandel). When crushed, macerated, and fermented with their skins, they produce a rosé or red wine.

About 12 pounds of grapes are usually enough to produce the amount of juice required, but this could vary by one, or several, pounds (especially if pressing by hand-wringing). Destem the grapes, cull out any unripe or unsound ones, crush the healthy ones by hand or with the flat bottom of a wine bottle, transfer them to a nylon straining bag, and either squeeze out the juice by hand or use a grape or fruit press to extract the juice. Alternatively, the juice can be steam-extracted or extracted with a juicer, although be wary of juicers that grind away at the seeds, as this will produce a bitter wine. Steam extraction could set the pectin, making clarification difficult, if not impossible.

If topping up with water, this recipe makes a wine with 12% alcohol by volume. If topping up with finished white wine, only adjust starting specific gravity to 1.088. Most people like this wine best with a little sweetness, but it also makes an excellent dry wine.

We are not allowing malolactic fermentation, so our sulfites must stay above 20 mg/L throughout the alcohol fermentation.

White Wine Recipe

from Generic Grapes

WINE IS READY IN: **6 months**

YOU'LL NEED: **grapes to produce 7½ pints freshly pressed grape juice per gallon of wine**

ADDITIONAL EQUIPMENT: **nylon straining bags and a press**

MAKES: **1 gallon, but can be scaled up**

INGREDIENTS

7½ pt. freshly pressed grape juice

granulated sugar to raise the specific gravity to 1.095

1 tsp pectic enzyme

potassium metabisulfite, as needed

½ tsp potassium sorbate

1 tsp yeast nutrient

1 sachet Lalvin 71B (if high acidity) or EC1118 wine yeast

DIRECTIONS

Prepare must: Use your hydrometer to check the specific gravity of juice and adjust to 1.088 by adding sugar (if too low) or water (if too high) or additional juice (if balanced). Put the juice in the primary. Add 0.2 g potassium metabisulfite to protect the juice and stir it well. Cover the primary and set it aside for at least 12 hours. Then stir in the pectic enzyme, always after the potassium metabisulfite, re-cover the primary, and wait another 12 hours. Stir in the yeast nutrient.

Add yeast: To 1 cup of warm water (not to exceed 102 degrees F.) add a pinch of yeast nutrient, 1 teaspoon of sugar, and stir to dissolve. Add the yeast to water, stir, and cover the mixture for 30 minutes. Add the mixture to the primary, stir well, and cover the primary.

Fermentation: When specific gravity drops to 1.020, or lower if the fermentation is still vigorous, transfer to a secondary and attach an airlock. Wait until all fermentation ceases and the airlock is still for two weeks, then rack into a sanitized secondary, top up, and refit the airlock.

Post-Fermentation: Wait an additional 4–6 weeks of maturation and add 0.2 g potassium metabisulfite and ½ teaspoon potassium sorbate to a sanitized secondary, rack the wine onto it, top-up, and refit the airlock. Wait 30 days, sweeten to taste or to balance, and bottle the wine. If sweetened, wait three months after bottling to allow the wine to recover from the agitation of bottling before tasting.

Options: None.   **Similar fruit:** Any white grape.

Wine from Wild Grapes ❖

Except in the frigid north of the tundra, no matter where you live on this vast continent of North America, there are probably wild grapes growing not far from your home. Even in the deserts, there are wild grape species that have adapted to that climate and conditions. Depending on which taxonomy you chose to follow, there are between 19 and 34 species of wild grapes inhabiting the United States alone (I have seen this number reduced to 6 by one blogger and expanded to 60 by another, but neither agrees with accepted taxonomy, which is largely DNA sorted). In my immediate area, there is just one wild grape species that I know of, but within 60 miles, there are at least six species from which I have collected grapes. If I lived 150 miles further east, four more species would be available.

Wild grapes are often difficult to identify by species without experience. Certain ones are unmistakable if you have experience or a field guide to consult. In my opinion, it makes no difference, as long as you're certain it's a wild grape (and not a toxic lookalike, such as Canada moonseed). Always confirm your finds with an expert or multiple guides before making wine from foraged materials. All wild grapes possess similar traits of high acidity and low sugar. Some are more tannic, some ferment with better color, and some certainly have better flavor, but the approach to making wine from them is about the same.

The traditional way of making wine from wild grapes uses fewer grapes than "pure" grape wines, and requires amelioration with sugar and water to tame the acid and raise the sugar content enough to get at least a 12% alcohol by volume (ABV) wine. To make a pure grape wine from any of them requires between 12 and 18 pounds of grapes. I know of only two species I would attempt this with, although there may be more if the growing conditions are right.

Because the grapes differ so much in taste and chemistry, it is important for the winemaker to quantify, at a minimum, the acidity, the sugar, and the potential flavor of the wine. We must know where we are starting in order to proceed. The flavor of the finished wine is often difficult at best to predict. The vilest tasting of the North American natives is the Mustang Grape, and yet it makes a very good wine at its worst, and a glorious wine with skill. In one year, 65,000 gallons of this grape's wine were produced by one winery in the early days of Texas statehood.

The following guidance is based on starting with a safe four pounds of grapes. For certain species, this may be the upper limit of what can be prudently used. Other species could use another 2 to even 4 pounds without presenting challenges but will do fine with 4 pounds for all species. If we use this number as a starting point, you'll be able to adjust future batches from experience. When I have happened upon a stand of wild grapes, not from my area, I picked as many as I could, destemmed 4 pounds for immediate use, and froze the rest for later use, fully expecting that I would adjust subsequent batches. When you have a finished wine that has aged well, use the knowledge gained to decide if next year you'll increase the poundage. In my own experience, I have reduced the poundage for one quirky grape found in the Texas Hill Country and increased it for two other species. But in all cases, I started with 4 pounds for my first batch.

Native grapes require more maturation to reach their potential. You'll also need to test the wines more often. Obtain a case or two of 187-mL splits (with screw caps) and fill four of them with each wine you expect will have an extended aging period. These smaller bottles will allow you to taste a wine at different points in time, preventing you from wasting a full, 750-mL bottle on every sampling not yet at its potential.

Wild grapes

Wine Recipe
from Wild Grapes

WINE IS READY IN: **16 months**

YOU'LL NEED: **4 pounds wild grapes per gallon of wine**

ADDITIONAL EQUIPMENT: **1 nylon straining bag**

MAKES: **1 gallon, but can be scaled up**

INGREDIENTS

4 lb. wild grapes

1 lb., 12 oz. very fine white granulated sugar

water to make 1 gal.

1 tsp pectic enzyme

potassium metabisulfite, as needed

½ tsp potassium sorbate

1¼ tsp (4 g) yeast nutrient

Lalvin 71B yeast (5 g)

calcium carbonate, as needed

DIRECTIONS

Prepare must: Wash the grapes thoroughly to get rid of insects, and destem by hand. Wear gloves, as the acid can really burn your hands. Put the grapes in a nylon straining bag, tie it off, and crush them by hand or a masher in your primary.

Collect ¼ cup of the grape juice and mix with ¾ cup of water. Use this to load your hydrometer's chimney and measure the specific gravity (SG). Determine how much sugar you'll need to add to the primary to bring that number up to 1.090 by consulting the hydrometer chart (page 57). Write down that amount for reference, as you're essentially creating a recipe for your specific grape type. Now wring the straining bag by hand as well as you can and set the bag in a bowl. Pour the grape juice you extracted into a container temporarily and measure the juice, one cup at a time. Let's pretend it is 1½ pints. You need a gallon of liquid, so you'll be adding 104 fluid ounces or 6½ pints of water. Write that number down, and while you have the juice handy, check the pH, and write it down too.

Return the straining bag of grapes to the primary with the juice. Put three pints of water on to boil. As soon as it boils, remove it from the heat and stir the sugar into it. Stir really well, so it dissolves completely. This could take five minutes, so relax and stir. Pour the hot sugar-water over the grapes. Add the remainder of the water (3½ pints). Stir the yeast nutrient into the primary.

Take a look at the pH you wrote down. If the pH is below 3.1, you'll want to reduce the acid and get that number up. Review **_Acid_** in Chapter 2 (page 45, specifically) and its subsections on acid reduction. Determine how much you need to reduce the acid to get the pH into a healthy range (3.1 or higher). Do not worry about the TA for now. You'll be using calcium carbonate to reduce the acid and that will take some time, so settle in and begin the acid reduction. When you add calcium carbonate to the must, it will explode in a foaming growth, which is why the primary should be at least twice the volume of the must. I use a 3-gallon primary for 1-gallon batches. Only add 1 gram at a time and wait the several hours it takes for the must to settle down, then add another gram. When done, if you have added 4 grams of calcium carbonate, 1 gram at a time when the must settles down, taste it. If the must tastes a bit chalky, you should not reduce it more. If it doesn't taste chalky and you still need to reduce the acid, add another gram of calcium carbonate and taste the must again when the must comes to rest. Continue doing this until the pH is 3.1 or higher or the must tastes a little chalky. If it still tastes acidic, you may want to test your TA just to see where it is.

Add 0.2 g potassium metabisulfite and stir the must well. Cover the primary and set it aside for at least 12 hours. Then stir in the pectic enzyme, re-cover the primary, and wait another 12 hours.

Add yeast: To 1 cup warm water (not to exceed 102 degrees F.) add a pinch of yeast nutrient, 1 teaspoon of sugar, and stir to dissolve. Add yeast to water, stir, and cover mixture for 30 minutes. Add mixture to primary, stir, and cover primary.

The yeast we are using is Lalvin 71B. It can metabolize a higher percentage of malic acid than other wine yeasts and therefore will assist us in correcting the pH and TA.

Fermentation: Ferment five days, squeezing the straining bag twice daily. Remove straining bag to a press, extract the juice, discard the pressed grapes, and return the pressed juice to the primary. If you do not have a way to press the grapes, suspend the bag over a large bowl so it can drip-drain. Squeeze the bag really well every 15 minutes for an hour. Discard the grape pulp and add extracted juice to the primary. When SG drops to 1.020, or lower if the fermentation is still vigorous, transfer juice to a secondary and affix an airlock. Wait 30 days and carefully rack.

Post-Fermentation: Move wine to a dark, cool place, and rack every 30 days until wine clears. Wait another 30 days after clearing and check for continued sedimentation and improved clarity. If the wine is hazy, aid clarity by adding ½ teaspoon of pectic enzyme, stirring, and let the wine rest 3-4 hours. If haze disappears, but the wine isn't crystal clear, use a 2-part fining (such as **Super-Kleer KC™**). If fined, wait four days and rack.

Add 0.2 g potassium metabisulfite and ½ teaspoon dissolved potassium sorbate. Stir. Check pH and taste the wine. If pH and TA are not totally where we want them, sweetening the wine may correct the imbalance. Sweeten to taste or to balance. If sweetened, wait 30 days to ensure no renewed fermentation and carefully rack into bottles. This wine can be consumed in 6 months, but the usual aging in bottles is 9–12 months.

Options: When sweetening at the end, try using Demerara sugar for more complexity.

Similar fruit: This recipe, with sugar modifications as necessary, will work with any wild grape and many native-noble grape hybrids (e.g. Frontenac, Concord, etc.).

Preservative-free fruit juices are an option for wine-making.

Wine from Concentrates, Juices, and Kits

Concentrates and juices have long been an important part of the home winemaker's pantry. Nicolas Appert first bottled juices in the 1790s, and canned juices followed later, but until then, juice had to be obtained directly from a grower with a fruit press. If you don't live where certain fruit grows, or where you're unable to buy it bulk, juices offer the home winemaker a way to expand their winemaking repertoire.

Grape and other fruit juices were, and still are remain, an important source of winemaking material. The downside to many juices is that they are shelf-stable because preservatives have been added. A few years ago, processors found means of stabilizing the juice without the use of preservatives, but you never know if a small processor can afford the upgrade, so always check the label. You also want to check the label to make sure it's not actually a blend of juices or has flavors added. If you can buy specific juices directly from a grower, it's even better, as it will fill a niche not available at your local supermarket.

Juices are very convenient. You just put a measured amount in your fermentation container, dissolve enough sugar to make a wine of the strength you desire, balance the acids and tannins, stir in some yeast nutrient, add a cultured yeast strain, and wait. After a couple or more rackings and intervening waiting periods, you fuss a bit over its clarity and bottle it. That is a lot easier than making wine from scratch.

Concentrates

A growing food and beverage industry has always been the main driver behind the popularity of fruit juices. Because juice is both heavy and somewhat bulky, shipping it is expensive. This compelled the industry to develop a process for concentrating grape and other fruit juices, streamlining the process of shipping juice. Concentrates for the consumer market were a by-product of this development.

Home winemakers became fans of these products early-on, recognizing that concentrates on the shelf had no seasons. Early concentrates were not even close to as pure as those we take for granted today. Re-constituted juices were often cloudy and occasionally subject to biological contamination. As improvements in processing technology largely eliminated these faults, and concentrates became more popular and accepted. Both concentrated grape and major fruit juices became available year-round and sold in an assortment of volumes convenient for use in the kitchen and for home winemaking.

The development of frozen concentrates eliminated the need for preservatives. Originally limited to grape juice, apple juice, orange juice, and lemonade, their acceptance led to a widening product-line that today encompasses dozens of fruits, cocktails, and other mixes.

Today, pure frozen fruit juice concentrates play an increasing role in home winemaking, and they are becoming more popular than raisins when building body in otherwise thin, watery wines. Concentrates can also be used exclusively to make wines, as many winemakers have discovered. This led to the next leap in home winemaking convenience.

Wine Kits Are Born

It wasn't until the popularization of grape varietals in the 1970s and '80s that the seeds of a new industry were planted. While it was recognized that it would be relatively easy to develop varietal concentrates, there was no practical market for them. Supermarket shoppers would have little interest in grapes that were developed for the wine industry, and possessed flavors the average consumer would find foreign or even objectionable. The real market opportunity was in the home winemaking realm, but selling varietal juice by itself didn't lead to much demand.

One of the strengths of capitalism is that when a readily available product exists, but the market for it is fledgling, product development, reengineering, and repackaging can create demand. That's what happened with wine kits; rather than distributing cans of varietal concentrates, some of which were already on the shelves of home brew shops with only marginal demand, the re-development of the winemaking process was undertaken. Concentrate was just a major part of it. The winemaking process for each variety was essentially reduced and simplified to concentrates and packets of additives specific to each variety.

It was, in hindsight, a logically ambitious development effort. It was largely a chemical engineering challenge, and then a marketing effort. The result, of course, was the winemaking kit. The very first kits were, predictably, not perfect. But the problems were sorted out, and the kit wine business took off.

I recently read that more kit wine is now made by home winemakers than wine from scratch. I don't know if this is actually true, but I do know that a lot of kit wines are entered in competitions. Yet, when I look at the entries of the competitions I sometimes judge, the number of entries of wines from scratch greatly outweigh those from kits. If there is any truth to the claim that more wine is made from kits than from scratch, it's likely an issue of volume. Many non-grape entries are made in 1–3 gallon batches, while probably 90% of kit wine is made in 6 gallon batches.

I am not a big fan of kit wines. There is no mystique involved in their wines, no gamble as to whether or not the winemaker got it right. In short, there is no art, no craft. For the average Joe, it's like making a German Chocolate Cake using a cake mix. You really can't go wrong if you follow the instructions, but can you really claim credit for the result? The real work was done by the manufacturer's chemists, cooks, and winemakers.

Of course, in kit winemaking, as in all winemaking, you can screw it up. You absolutely have to sanitize your equipment if you want good results. The only kit wines

I've tasted that had major faults were probably biologically contaminated. When you taste and smell acetic acid, be suspicious. This goes for wines from scratch, too.

Nonetheless, I welcome all kit winemakers into the hobby of winemaking. I know that sooner or later, a good many of them will try their hand at making wines from scratch. That's when they will either become real winemakers or go back to kits.

There is a competition I judge whenever I am available. Two particular kit winemakers invariably fight it out for the sweepstakes while the other kit makers fight for third place—or second place if one of the two titans didn't show up. After one competition I asked one of the titans how he won so often when theoretically all kits should be equal. Then he stated the obvious. "They aren't. The more expensive the kit, the better the grapes." But of course!

5

BERRY WINES

Berry wine instantly brings to mind blackberries, blueberries, raspberries, strawberries, and elderberries. Red and black currants, mulberries, and gooseberries also come to mind. The berries above range in color, but all are juicy, acidic, tart-sweet to tart, with varying degrees of tannin and pectin. All are good in pies, jams, and jellies, but they are something special when fermented into wine.

When making berry wines, you need to monitor many of the same characteristics as in grape wine, especially ripeness, sugar, TA, pH, and tannins. In berry wines, you also need to add pectin, and of course the above characteristics need to be adjusted, sometimes considerably, to levels supporting good wine.

I did not mention alcohol. Because many wine yeast strains are capable of fermenting to 16% ABV or higher, there is a very bad tendency to make higher alcohol wines that are out of balance. There is perhaps no easier way to make an out-of-balance wine than to push the alcohol higher than the style of wine requires. For berry wines, unless you are making a port or another style of dessert wine, the best alcohol levels are between 11–14 percent ABV, with 12–13 percent being the better range. Remember, you control the alcohol level by controlling the amount of fermentable sugar in the must, and this is measured with a hydrometer (page 55).

There is a magic number when it comes to alcohol, and that number is 12% ABV. This is the level at which the wine is mostly biologically stable. "Mostly" is a keyword. When we add sulfites to 12% ABV wine, we close the gap considerably, as there are few microbes that can exist in 12% ABV wine with 50 mg/L of free SO_2. An ABV of 12% is also the number that pretty much assures you that the wine will last at least 24 months before heading south.

A Note About Acidity

Berry wines are generally a tad more difficult to make than grape wines, if for no other reason than the conundrum of acidity. One major difference is that phenolics can also present a challenge.

Commercial US wineries are allowed to ameliorate the musts of domestic nongrape berries by adding up to 60% water. This should make it clear that the acidity of certain berries is excessive, their sugar content is deficient, and both require considerable correction to make a balanced wine. The same is often true of other fruit as well.

Table 7. Acid and Sugar Characteristics of Some Domestic Berries

NAME	PH	TA RANGE (g/L)	PERCENT SUGAR	MAJOR ORGANIC ACID	MINOR ORGANIC ACID
Blackberry	2.85–3.35	6.00–15.00	4.80–10.10	Malic	Citric
Blackcurrant	2.65–3.10	6.70–21.00	4.80–18.20	Malic	Citric
Blueberry	2.80–3.40	3.80–10.20	5.10–11.50	Citric	Quinic, Malic
Elderberry	4.57–5.20	9.00–23.00	6.60–12.00	Citric-Malic	Succinic, Tartaric
Gooseberry	2.80–3.10	16.00–23.0	8.00–15.80	Citric-Malic	Shikimic
Mulberry	3.30–5.30	3.20–6.40	5.30–8.40	Citric-Malic	Tartaric, Succinic
Raspberry	3.20–3.80	6.50–15.40	6.30–14.70	Citric	Malic, Succinic
Strawberry	3.20–3.40	5.20–11.80	5.35–10.60	Citric	Malic, Quinnic

Data for Table 7. were collected from a wide variety of sources, on the internet and from print. Since many of these berries are cultivated throughout the Northern Hemisphere, care was taken to seek values representative of American harvests. Some harvests included foraged berries. Citric-Malic means the values of each are close, but citric is predominant.

In this chapter, we'll be examining methods for making wine from the eight berries presented in Table 7. The recipes are only guidelines. For greatest accuracy, test for actual acidity and sugar (SG) and adjust according to the values you obtain. As you can see from Table 7, there is a great deal of variability in the actual values that can be expected.

When I say recipes are only guidelines, I mean just that. The timelines that these recipes are based on my experience. Yours may differ for no other reason than you and the author are not using the same batch of berries, even though they may be the same variety (blackberries, say). Even after correcting acidity and sugar, the individual berries themselves will vary—they will certainly contain different phenolics, amino acids, pectin, trace vitamins and minerals, and other soluble solid compounds, which affect color, aroma, astringency, density,

flavor, and fermentation. They will reflect the soil they grew in, the climate they adapted to, the joy of rain and the agony of drought, the cloud cover, sunshine, and wildlife they knew. Make the best of them. They struggled and grew for you.

Because your blackberries will not be the same as mine, it is entirely probable that the doses I prescribe in the recipe are not exactly accurate for your berries. That need not matter. They will be close enough, and your measurement for the final free SO_2 adjustment will correct any deviations in chemistry. If you choose not to make a measurement for the final adjustment, use my numbers and it will probably be close.

For this and all recipes in this book, you will need a hydrometer, a gram scale, a pH meter, and (optional) an SO_2 test kit. An acid titration kit is optional, but worth the investment.

Blackberry Wine ❖

Blackberry wine is a favorite because of the rich and wholesome flavor of the berry. With over 120 species and many more cultivars in the United States alone, it goes without saying that some are more flavorful than others. Cultivars bred for flavor and aromatics are exceptional, with deep layers of subtlety and richness.

When it comes to foraged blackberries, the fully ripened wild berry can reach flavor heights almost as good as the cultivars. It is worth noting that many cultivated blackberries escape the farm and are planted by birds in the usual places: along fence lines, hedgerows, ditches, the edges of forested areas, under power lines, and among other brambles. Good blackberries almost scream, "Make me into wine." No wonder so many winemakers answer the call.

JACK'S TIPS

BLACKBERRIES are acidic, specifically they are low in pH and high in TA. Because their range of acidity, for both pH and TA, can be wide (2.85–3.35 and 6–15 respectively), it is essential that pH, at a minimum, be tested during maceration—before any yeast is added. Actual numbers should be your guide. When adding sugar, blackberry wine should not exceed 13% ABV unless balance demands it.

Dilution with up to 60% water can bring down the TA but will raise the pH far less dramatically. Do not blindly add water. A bench trial with three 100-mL samples of the juice, one undiluted, one diluted with 25% water, the other with 50% water, and each then tested for TA, will reveal the expected results from each.

If making wine from pure juice, without dilution, choose the right yeast and use calcium carbonate exclusively to reduce acid. Under no circumstances allow MLF. Maintain free SO_2 at least 20 mg/L to discourage MLF.

Because I know that half my SO_2 addition will become bound within minutes, if I initially want 20 mg/L, I add 40 mg/L, but some of that will become bound before I make another addition, dipping the level below 20 mg/L. To allow for that and buy some insurance, I initially add 50 mg/L. Did you follow that? If not, read it again. It's really important.

THE AUTHOR has made dozens of batches of blackberry wine. Referring back to my log entries I find a wide range of chemistry for blackberries—pH, TA, and sugar are all over the place. One thing stands out: TA is never a problem. Amelioration with sweetened water always brings it within reason and occasionally requires a post-fermentation addition of acid to balance the wine (judged by testing TA).

Notice I said, "amelioration with **sweetened** water" (emphasis added). Although not always followed in these recipes, it is highly recommended that the sugar be added and water brought up to the target level (1 gallon or whatever the batch size) before measuring pH and free SO_2. Sugar does have an effect on acid measurements, however slight that may be.

Blackberry Wine Recipe

WINE IS READY IN: **19 months**

YOU'LL NEED: **6 pounds of ripe blackberries per gallon of wine**

ADDITIONAL EQUIPMENT: **Ziploc bags, nylon straining bags, 3–5 gallon primary**

MAKES: **1 gallon, but can be scaled up**

INGREDIENTS

6 lb. fully ripe blackberries

1 lb., 10 oz. very fine granulated sugar

water to make 1 gal.

½ tsp pectic enzyme

⅓ tsp powdered grape tannin

calcium carbonate to bring acid to pH 3.2 or above

potassium metabisulfite, as needed

½ tsp potassium sorbate

1 tsp (3 g) yeast nutrient

1 g Fermaid-K

Lalvin 71B yeast (5 g)

DIRECTIONS

Prepare must: Place berries in Ziploc bags and freeze for at least five days to break down cell walls and liberate juice before starting wine. Thaw berries completely (1–2 days). Working inside your primary or in a sanitized plastic bucket, transfer berries into a small-mesh nylon straining bag and tie the bag closed. Mash and squeeze berries to liberate juice. Leave the bag in primary. Add water and sugar to make 1-gallon total volume, stirring until sugar is completely dissolved (about 5 minutes). Use pH meter to determine pH. If very low (3.1 or below), add 1 gram of calcium carbonate, wait 2–3 hours and add second gram. If higher than 3.1 (3.2 or above), taste to decide if you need to raise to pH 3.3. If 3.3 or higher, do not add calcium carbonate. Wait 4 hours and add 0.2 g potassium metabisulfite and stir well. Cover the primary and wait 12 hours. Add pectic enzymes and yeast nutrients, stirring until completely dissolved. Set aside 12 hours.

Add yeast: To 1 cup warm water (not to exceed 102 degrees F.) add a pinch of yeast nutrients and stir to dissolve. Add yeast to water, stir, and cover mixture for 30 minutes. Add mixture to primary, stir well, and cover primary.

Fermentation: Squeeze nylon straining bag 4–6 times a day. Check SG daily. When SG drops to 1.060, remove nylon straining bag and press or squeeze thoroughly to expel juice. Discard blackberry pulp. Dissolve 1 gram of Fermaid-K™ in 2 cups juice and stir well to thoroughly dissolve. Add to primary and stir again. Continue checking SG daily and when at 1.020, or lower if the fermentation is still vigorous, gently transfer to secondary, then affix airlock. Carefully rack in 30 days.

Post-Fermentation: Move wine to a dark, cool place for 60 days and carefully rack. Return to dark for six months, checking airlock periodically; then add 0.2 g potassium metabisulfite, ½ teaspoon dissolved potassium sorbate, and stir well. Polish clarity with an additional ½ teaspoon pectic enzyme if needed. Sweeten to off-dry (SG 1.002) or to balance. If sweetened, wait 30 days to ensure no renewed fermentation and carefully rack into bottles. Allow 9 months or more in bottles before tasting.

Options: To add body, add one or two very ripe bananas, cut crosswise into ½-inch slices, before pitching yeast. To make it easier to remove, place it in a separate straining bag.

Sweeten at the end with purified honey or Demerara sugar to add complexity.

This wine responds to oak very well. One cup of oak cubes in the wine for 6–8 weeks during maturation is usually enough. Let taste be your guide, but don't overdo it.

As with all berry wines, because tasting can consume all your wine, it is wise to bottle four 187-mL splits to use for that purpose.

Similar berries: The following berries can be substituted for blackberries in this recipe. Acidity and sugar levels will require adjustment: dewberries, boysenberries, loganberries, Marionberries, ollalieberries, tayberries, youngberries.

Author's Note: I last made this wine in 2002. Additives and adjustments are from my wine log. The last bottle of this wine was consumed in 2005 and was excellent: well-balanced with a good body, smooth tannins, and an excellent flavor.

Blackcurrant Wine ❖

Blackcurrant wine can be the toughest wine of all to make if the acidity level in your berries is on the extreme of what these berries are capable of producing. But don't be intimidated. When augmented by higher-end sugars, they taste absolutely divine, even when highly acidic. Taste the berries, test them, and decide if you are up to the challenge.

At their best, blackcurrants are an absolute delight to eat, so they are terrific in pies, jams, jellies, syrup, culinary uses, and wine. They possess a unique, and complex, flavor profile, with layers of fruit and floral hints in their aroma when they are at their best behavior.

The berries can be found in the wild, but once the sugar levels rise in the maturing berries they are favorite targets of wildlife. It is far easier to obtain farm-grown berries, and this gives you some say in the flavor and balance of the berries you choose to ferment. Canned blackcurrant, either as berries, puree, concentrate, or juice, is a good choice for those not living in the relatively few states in which they are currently cultivated.

Blackcurrant wine is worth making because of the wealth of flavor it conceals. With aromatic floral notes, good structure and complexity worthy of any noble grape, blackcurrant is simply the Cabernet of berry wines.

The good thing about canned blackcurrant products, whether berries, puree, concentrate, or juice, is that its sometimes nightmarish acidity will almost certainly be manageable when canned. This goes a long way to simplifying the winemaking effort. Follow good winemaking procedures and this will be a wine to show off your skills. This recipe requires blackcurrant juice. I recommend Knudsen Just Black Currant juice; it comes in 32 oz. bottles; a case of 12 makes 3 gallons.

JACK'S TIP

THE MUST will almost certainly require dilution, but how much depends on the berries themselves. Test, taste, and test again. If the acid appears manageable, a minimum amelioration may be required. I have made blackcurrant wine with as little as 20% and as much as about 60% water added, the latter only because I didn't have enough canned berries. Just be cognizant of lurking tannins.

Since the berry's minor acid is malic, Lalvin 71B yeast can eliminate most or all of it. The problem is it is difficult to test for malic acid in the home, so you don't know how much the yeast will reduce TA. However, sugar will go a long way toward balancing the wine, so higher acidity can be dealt with if the pH can be raised to at least 3.2 to give the yeast a less-hostile environment in which to work.

For both amelioration and chaptalization, bench trials are in order. Once you have ballpark numbers to work with, less water may be sufficient if the added sugar is dissolved in the water to be added.

Blackcurrant
Wine Recipe

WINE IS READY IN: **11 months**

YOU'LL NEED: **1 gallon of juice per gallon of wine**

ADDITIONAL EQUIPMENT: **3–5 gallon primary**

MAKES: **1 gallon, but can be scaled up**

INGREDIENTS

1 gal. blackcurrant juice (I recommend Knudsen Just Black Currant)

1 lb., 10 oz. very fine granulated sugar

calcium carbonate, to raise pH to 3.2–3.3

potassium metabisulfite, as needed

½ tsp potassium sorbate

1 tsp (3 g) yeast nutrient

1 g Fermaid-K™

Lalvin 71B yeast (5 g)

DIRECTIONS

Prepare must: Add juice to primary and use pH meter to determine its pH. If very low (3.1 or below), add 1 gram of calcium carbonate, wait 2–3 hours, and add the second gram; wait an additional 2–3 hours and add a third gram. If higher than 3.1 (3.2 or above) taste to decide if you need to raise to pH 3.3. If 3.3. or higher, do not add calcium carbonate. Wait 4 hours and add sugar and yeast nutrient, stirring until completely dissolved. Wait 4 hours and add 0.2 g potassium metabisulfite and stir well. Cover the primary and set aside 12 hours.

Add yeast: To 1 cup warm water (not to exceed 102 degrees F.) add a pinch of yeast nutrient and stir to dissolve. Add yeast to water, stir, and cover mixture for 30 minutes. Add mixture to primary and cover primary.

Fermentation: Check SG daily. When SG drops to 1.060, stir in Fermaid-K. When SG drops to 1.020, or lower, if the fermentation is still vigorous, transfer to secondary, and affix airlock. In 30 days, carefully rack.

Post-Fermentation: Move wine to a dark, cool place and allow to sit untouched 60 days while lees settle. Carefully rack. The wine must now sit an additional three months. Rack and add 0.2 g potassium metabisulfite and ½ teaspoon dissolved potassium sorbate and stir well. Check clarity and correct if necessary with pectic enzyme. Sweeten to taste or to balance. If sweetened, wait 30 days to ensure no renewed fermentation and carefully rack into bottles. Allow six months or more in bottles before tasting.

Options: To add body, add one or two very ripe bananas, cut crosswise into ½-inch slices, before pitching yeast. For ease of removal, place in a separate straining bag.

This wine responds to oak very well. One cup of oak cubes in the wine for 4–6 weeks during maturation is usually enough. Let taste be your guide, but don't overdo it.

As with all berry wines, because tasting can consume all of your wine, it is wise to bottle four 187-mL splits to use for that purpose.

Similar berries: The following berries are more tart than the blackcurrant and require additional processing, but the basic recipe shown above is still relevant: Red Currant, White Currant.

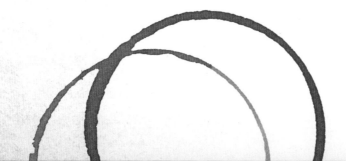

Blueberry Wine ❖

After blackberry and strawberry wines, blueberry wine is the third-most common berry wine in America. This is because blueberries grow through much of the country and are available commercially nationwide. And let's face it, blueberries have a wonderful flavor. They are sweet when mature, with variable acidity.

JACK'S TIP

THE EXPECTATION with blueberry wine is that their wonderful flavor will be transferred to the wine, but this is not necessarily the case. Relatively few people in the general population have tasted Cabernet Sauvignon grapes, but the truth is their wine doesn't taste like the grapes. Flavors are transformed by fermentation. This also happens with blueberries. But the aim here will be to capture as much of that fresh berry flavor as possible. Why else make the wine? My recipe tries to do that.

Blueberry wine can be made from fresh berries, puree, concentrate, juice, or dried berries. While making it from juice is the most convenient method, some of their flavor and nutritional value is lost in the juicing process. For the best wine, fresh berries are the best option.

One thing cannot be stressed enough. Use uniformly fully ripe berries. Just a few green-to-less-than-mature berries will affect the flavor and chemistry of the entire batch. It is not unusual to cull 5–10 percent of the berries, so start with more than enough.

Although wild blueberries can have wide swings in acidity, this actually is rare in commercial berries. The berry's acid is largely masked during eating by its sweetness. Average acidity is nonetheless usually high enough to require correction for winemaking. Test TA, then pH if deemed necessary.

Blueberry Wine Recipe

WINE IS READY IN: **16 months**

YOU'LL NEED: **4 pounds of berries, 1 can frozen 100 percent red grape juice concentrate per gallon of wine**

ADDITIONAL EQUIPMENT: **1 nylon straining bag and a 3–5 gallon primary**

MAKES: **1 gallon, but can be scaled up**

INGREDIENTS

4 lb. blueberries

1 can 100 percent red grape juice frozen concentrate, thawed (Welch's, Old Orchard, etc.)

1 lb., 8 oz. very fine granulated sugar

1 tsp powdered pectic enzyme

calcium carbonate, to raise pH to 3.2–3.4

potassium metabisulfite, as needed

½ tsp potassium sorbate

1 tsp (3 g) yeast nutrient

½ tsp yeast energizer (split)

1 g Fermaid-K

Lalvin RC212 yeast (5 g)

DIRECTIONS

Prepare must: Cull, wash, and place berries in nylon straining bag, and tie bag closed in the primary. Put 1 liter water on the stove and bring it to boil. Meanwhile, crush berries thoroughly in the primary. When water boils, remove from heat and add sugar, yeast nutrient, and half the yeast energizer (¼ teaspoon) to the water. Stir until sugar is completely dissolved. Pour over nylon straining bag, cover the primary, and wait until water cools. Add thawed red grape juice concentrate and water to make 1 gallon must. Use pH meter to determine pH. If very low (3.1 or below), calcium carbonate additions apply. If higher than 3.1 (3.2. or above), taste to decide if you need to raise to pH 3.3. If 3.3 or higher, do not add calcium carbonate. If adding calcium carbonate, add 1 gram of calcium carbonate, wait 2–3 hours and add second gram, wait 2–3 hours and add a third gram, and wait 2–3 hours and add a fourth gram. Wait 8–10 hours and add 0.2 g potassium metabisulfite and stir well. Cover the primary and wait 12 hours. Add pectic enzyme, stirring until completely dissolved. Set aside 12 hours.

Add yeast: To 1 cup warm water (not to exceed 102 degrees F.) add 1 teaspoon sugar, half the yeast energizer (¼ teaspoon), a pinch of yeast nutrient and stir to dissolve. Add yeast to water, stir, and cover mixture for 30 minutes. Add mixture to primary and cover primary.

Fermentation: Squeeze nylon straining bag 4–6 times a day. Check SG daily. When SG drops to 1.060, remove the nylon straining bag and squeeze well to expel juice. Discard blueberry pulp. Dissolve Fermaid-K and remaining ¼ teaspoon yeast energizer in 2 cups juice, stir well to dissolve, add to primary, and stir again. Re-cover primary. Continue checking SG daily and when at 1.020, or lower if the fermentation is still vigorous, transfer to secondary, and affix airlock. In 30 days, carefully rack.

Post-Fermentation: Move wine to a dark, cool place for 60 days and carefully rack. After additional 60 days add 0.2 g potassium metabisulfite and ½ teaspoon dissolved potassium sorbate. Stir well, check clarity, and correct as necessary with pectic enzyme. Sweeten to taste or to balance. If sweetened, wait 30 days to ensure no renewed fermentation and carefully rack into bottles. Blueberry wine should age in bottles one year before tasting.

Options: To add body, add one or two very ripe bananas, cut crosswise into ½-inch slices, before pitching yeast. For ease of removal, place in a separate straining bag.

This wine responds well to light oak. One cup of oak cubes in the wine for 3–5 weeks during maturation is usually enough. Let taste be your guide, but don't overdo it.

As with all berry wines, because tasting can consume all of your wine, it is wise to bottle four 187-mL splits to use for that purpose.

Similar berries: The following berries can be substituted for blueberries in this recipe. Acidity and sugar levels will vary, of course: bilberries, huckleberries, whortleberries.

Elderberry Wine ❖

As a kid, I'd eat wild elderberries every chance I got. They grew all over the place in rural Louisiana and East Texas. I quickly learned how to spot the really ripe ones, the darkest berries on drooping clusters. Then I spent many years in areas where no elderberries grew. So I was overjoyed when I discovered elderberries growing alongside the road after moving back to Texas. When I first started making wine with them, I forgot to look for drooping clusters and just picked berries with abandon. Big mistake!

JACK'S TIP

ELDERBERRIES are high in tannins, TA, and tend to be higher in pH than one would want. They also pack more sugar than one might guess, which does its best to balance that acid and tannin. Berries that aren't fully ripe throw off those numbers even more than they naturally are. And so my first batch of elderberry wine was a disaster I could not fix because my berries were, for the most part, not fully ripe. But it was a learning experience, as all failures should be. So choose elderberries with drooping clusters, and only those with fully mature berries.

High tannin levels and TA suggest a wine that can age for years. Indeed, I made an elderberry wine that was nine years old before it was ready to drink, but what a wine it was! Five gallons of sheer bliss! But you don't need to make one that takes so long. I did it to see how far I could push these little berries. Most of my elderberries were drinkable after only a year, none less than that.

Some people don't like the taste of elderberry wine. I suspect they have not sampled a really good one. The recipe on page 140 will make a really good one.

The acidity in elderberries presents two problems. First, they tend to be high in TA. Second, they tend to be high in pH but still have a lot of acid (high TA), but it's mostly citric acid, with a trailing amount of malic and some other organic acids. The high pH means that the acid isn't very strong. That gives us enough information to plan a strategy for getting the acidity where we want it.

We must remember that acidity is inversely proportional to the volume of the must/wine. If we double the volume, the TA is halved, but pH will only be affected slightly because the strength of the acid has not changed all that much. So for practical purposes, we'll pretend there is no change in pH.

With elderberry, we will be adding a great deal of water, approximately 75% of the total volume, so the TA may correct itself. Lowering the pH is another matter. To do this we need to add acid, the stronger the better, and that means tartaric acid. That will then raise the TA again, so we ought to reduce the unknown amount of malic acid, which we will do by using 71B yeast.

Elderberry Wine Recipe

WINE IS READY IN: **18 months**

YOU'LL NEED: **3 pounds of berries per gallon of wine**

ADDITIONAL EQUIPMENT: **1 nylon straining bag, 1 large bowl, and rubber gloves**

MAKES: **1 gallon, but can be scaled up**

INGREDIENTS

3 lb. elderberries

water to make 1 gal.

1 lb., 14 oz. very fine granulated sugar

1 tsp powdered pectic enzyme

potassium metabisulfite, as needed

tartaric acid, as needed

½ tsp potassium sorbate

1 tsp (3 g) yeast nutrient

½ tsp yeast energizer (split)

1 g Fermaid-K

Lalvin 71B yeast (5 g)

DIRECTIONS

Prepare must: Bring 2 quarts water to a boil and stir in sugar until dissolved. Then, while wearing rubber gloves, put berries in nylon straining bag, tie closed, and put in primary. Mash the berries and cover with boiling sugar-water. Cover primary and set aside to cool to room temperature. Add water to make 1 gallon. Measure pH. If pH is above 3.5, add tartaric acid in 3.785 g/gal. increments until pH is at or below 3.5. Wait 4 hours and add 0.2 g potassium metabisulfite and stir well. Cover the primary and wait 12 hours. Add pectic enzyme and yeast nutrient, stirring until completely dissolved. Set aside 12 hours.

Add yeast: To 1 cup warm water (not to exceed 102 degrees F.) add 1 teaspoon sugar and a pinch of yeast nutrient and stir to dissolve. Add yeast to water, stir, and cover mixture for 30 minutes. Add mixture to primary and cover primary.

Fermentation: Wearing rubber gloves, squeeze berries 2–3 times a day when the bag is at the surface. After the third day of fermentation, remove bag and hang it over large bowl. Squeeze very gently every 15 minutes, for one hour, to expel free-flowing juice. Do not squeeze hard. Discard berry pomace and add drippings to the primary. Check SG daily until at 1.060. Add Fermaid-K, yeast energizer, and stir well. When SG is at 1.020, or lower if the fermentation is still vigorous, transfer to secondary and affix airlock. After 30 days, carefully rack.

Post-Fermentation: Put in a dark place for 60 days. Rack and return to a dark place. After additional 60 days, add 0.2 g potassium metabisulfite and ½ teaspoon potassium sorbate, stir well, wait 24 hours, and rack. After 48 hours, check clarity and intervene if necessary with pectic enzyme and/or two-part fining agents. If fined, wait four days and rack. Sweeten to taste or to balance. If sweetened, wait 30 days to ensure no renewed fermentation and carefully rack into bottles. Allow one year in bottles before tasting. Age longer if needed.

Options: To add body, add one or two very ripe bananas, cut crosswise into ½-inch slices, before pitching yeast. For ease of removal, place in a separate straining bag.

This wine responds very well to oak. One cup of oak cubes in the wine for 6–8 weeks during maturation may be enough. Let taste be your guide, but don't overdo it.

As with all berry wines, because tasting can consume all of your wine, it is wise to bottle four 187-mL splits to use for that purpose.

Similar berries: While there are numerous similar-looking berries, none share the characteristics of the elderberry enough to be named here.

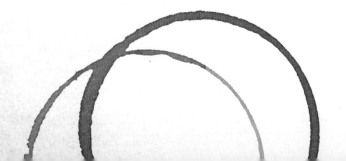

Gooseberry Wine ❖

Wild gooseberries: I've only eaten them once and they were a chore, with thick leathery skins and small hairs all over. The taste was unexceptional and I was not impressed. Some months later I was at a diner and the guy next to me was served a generous portion of some kind of pie. He dug into it with gusto and sounds of pleasure, so I ordered, "what he's having." It turned out it was gooseberry pie, and it was delicious. I decided to give the berry another chance. Maybe the ones I ate were underripe or the wrong variety. But then I moved from the Pacific Northwest, and I've never been in gooseberry country for an extended period since.

While at a local home brew shop some years ago, I came upon a large can of processed gooseberries, enough for 3–5 gallons of wine. I had to try them, and so I made a 3-gallon batch and a pie. Both the wine and pie were very good. I've wanted to make it again but just haven't gotten around to it.

There are hundreds of established varieties of gooseberry. One source says thousands. It seems they are so easy to cross that anyone with two or more differentiated bushes and patience can do it. Well, perhaps not that easy, but there's no doubt there are many varieties and cultivars out there. Commercially, not as many.

Growers want bushes they can machine harvest, with lots of big, juicy-sweet berries. They grow bushes just like that, but no one cultivar has all the attributes desired, at least not yet. But they're working on it.

I mashed my berries using my old "masher," a 4-foot piece of hardwood 4 x 4 which had a lathed baseball bat-like handle and a smooth, flat business end with a nicely rounded bevel. It served me well until I got in a hurry and forgot to clean and sanitize it after mashing two fresh pineapples. A flat-ended wine bottle works almost as well.

The must will be slightly astringent, due to high tannins in the skins. The red grape juice concentrate will smooth it out a bit, and any residual astringency will be dealt with by fining the wine.

JACK'S TIP

GOOSEBERRIES vary a great deal in terms of size, taste, and color. Some have thick, tough skins or almost spiny hairs, while others have skin that's thin and yielding, and smooth, and they occur in almost every color of the rainbow. They run the range of tastes, from tart to sweet, bland to rich, complex, and almost blueberry in flavor. But unless you have access to the fresh berries and love chopping hairy berries with tough skins, the best way to make gooseberry wine is purchasing canned, processed berries. Most winemaking or home brew shops carry them or can get them.

Is it worth it? Those cans are pricey, but the two batches of gooseberry wine I've tasted (my own and that of an acquaintance) were such a tasty novelty that I can say yes, it is worth it. And the best part is that the wild acidity levels in foraged gooseberries—they have freakish acidity ranges—are much more manageable when using canned fruit.

Gooseberry Wine Recipe

WINE IS READY IN: **18 months**

YOU'LL NEED: **3 pounds of berries, 1 can frozen 100 percent red grape juice concentrate per gallon of wine**

ADDITIONAL EQUIPMENT: **1 nylon straining bag**

MAKES: **1 gallon, but can be scaled up**

INGREDIENTS

3 lb. gooseberries

1 can 100 percent red grape juice frozen concentrate, thawed (Welch's, Old Orchard, etc.)

water to make 1 gal.

1 lb., 8 oz. very fine granulated sugar

1¼ tsp powdered pectic enzyme

potassium metabisulfite, as needed

½ tsp potassium sorbate

1 tsp (3 g) yeast nutrient

1 g Fermaid-K

Lalvin DV10 yeast (5 g)

DIRECTIONS

Prepare must: Bring 2 quarts water to a boil and stir in 1 pound of sugar until dissolved. Then put berries in nylon straining bag, tie closed, and put in primary. Mash the berries well and cover with boiling sugar-water. Cover and set aside to cool. When lukewarm, dissolve yeast nutrient in 1 cup of juice and stir into the primary. Add thawed grape concentrate and water to make 1 gallon; stir well. Wait 4 hours and add 0.2 g potassium metabisulfite and stir well. Cover the primary and wait 12 hours. Add pectic enzyme, stirring until completely dissolved. Set aside 12 hours.

Add yeast: To 1 cup warm water (not to exceed 102 degrees F.) add a pinch of yeast nutrient and stir to dissolve. Add yeast to water, stir, and cover mixture for 30 minutes. Add mixture to primary and cover primary.

Fermentation: Stir must, measure SG, and gently squeeze berry bag 2–4 times daily. When SG drops to 1.060, draw off 1 liter of juice, add remaining sugar to the liter and stir until dissolved. Add to this the Fermaid-K, stir well to dissolve and add to primary, stirring to integrate. When SG drops to 1.020, or lower if the fermentation is still vigorous, remove berry bag and hang it over a large bowl for 1 hour, but do not squeeze. Discard berry pulp, add juice from bag to primary, transfer to secondary, and affix airlock. Ferment to dryness and stir well.

Post-Fermentation: Carefully rack every 30 days until wine clears. When clear, polish wine with a two-part fining agent. Add 0.2 g potassium metabisulfite, dissolved potassium sorbate, and sweeten to taste or to balance. If sweetened, wait 30 days to ensure no renewed fermentation and carefully rack into bottles. Allow one year in bottles before tasting.

Options: To add body, add one or two very ripe bananas, cut crosswise into ½-inch slices, before pitching yeast. For ease of removal, place in a separate straining bag.

As with all berry wines, because tasting can consume all of your wine, it is wise to bottle four 187-mL splits to use for that purpose.

Similar berries: The following berries can be substituted for gooseberries in this recipe: Tasti Berry, Jostaberry. Acidity and sugar amounts will need to be adjusted.

Mulberry Wine ❖

Native to the United States, the mulberry is found all over the United States, but especially in the South. It should not be confused with the flowering mulberry, an ornamental tree, and is only a distant cousin to the Chinese or Asian mulberry (which have fruit approaching 2 inches in length). It naturally inhabits stream beds or areas with high runoff or rainfall because of its appetite for water.

If not planted near patios, driveways, parking areas, or sidewalks (where they can make a mess), they are wonderful shade trees, and their fruit is delicious raw, cooked into cobbler or made into jelly, syrup, or wine. The fruit can be messy, especially after passing through the digestive system of any number of birds that feed on them. Leave the upper branches for the birds and harvest the ones you can reach easily or with a stepladder. The average 30-foot high tree with a 40-foot spread will easily yield enough fruit for several gallons of wine and a few cobblers.

JACK'S TIP

MULBERRIES generally have acceptable pH—it can be out of our desired range, but not by much—and acceptable-to-low TA. These tend to make their sugar more perceptible. Nonetheless, mulberries by themselves tend to make a poor wine unless you go all out and use 100% juice with little or no water. Even then, you'll need a body booster and acid adjustment. The recipe that follows uses grape concentrate to strengthen the wine's body.

Mulberry Wine Recipe

WINE IS READY IN: **18 months**

YOU'LL NEED: **10 pounds of berries, 1 can frozen 100 percent red grape juice concentrate per gallon of wine**

ADDITIONAL EQUIPMENT: **1 nylon straining bag**

MAKES: **1 gallon, but can be scaled up**

INGREDIENTS

10 lb. mulberries

1 can 100 percent red grape juice frozen concentrate, thawed (Welch's, Old Orchard, etc.)

water to make 1 gal.

1 lb. very fine granulated sugar

1¼ tsp powdered pectic enzyme

potassium metabisulfite, as needed

½ tsp potassium sorbate

tartaric acid, as needed

1 tsp (3 g) yeast nutrient

½ tsp yeast energizer (split)

1 g Fermaid-K

Lalvin RC212 yeast (5 g)

DIRECTIONS

Prepare must: Bring 1 pint of water to a boil and thoroughly dissolve 1 pound of sugar in it. Put berries in nylon straining bag, tie closed, and put in primary. Mash the berries well and stir boiling sugar-water into the primary. Dissolve yeast nutrient and half (¼ teaspoon) of the yeast energizer in 1 cup of juice and stir into a primary. Add thawed grape concentrate and water to make 1 gallon and stir well. Add 1 gram tartaric acid and stir well. Check pH. If pH is above 3.4, add another gram of tartaric acid and stir well until the acidity is correct (below 3.4). Wait 12 hours and add 0.2 g potassium metabisulfite and stir well. Cover the primary and wait 12 hours. Add pectic enzyme, stirring until completely dissolved. Set aside 12 hours.

Add yeast: To 1 cup warm water (not to exceed 102 degrees F.) add a pinch of yeast nutrient, a pinch of yeast energizer, and stir to dissolve. Add yeast to water, stir, and cover mixture for 30 minutes. Add mixture to primary, stir and cover primary.

Fermentation: Stir must and gently squeeze berry bag 2–4 times daily. When SG drops to 1.060, remove the straining bag, and hang it over a large bowl. Squeeze bag gently every 15 minutes for 1 hour, then discard berry pulp and add extracted juice to the primary. Draw off 1 liter of juice, add remaining yeast energizer, and 1 gram Fermaid-K to liter and stir well. Stir into the must. When SG drops to 1.020, or lower if the fermentation is still vigorous, transfer to secondary and affix airlock. Ferment to dryness.

Post-Fermentation: Carefully rack, wait 30 days and rack again. After 60 days, check the clarity of the wine and correct it if needed with pectic enzyme. Wait 12 hours and add 0.2 g potassium metabisulfite and potassium sorbate. Stir well and taste the wine. If acid is low, add acid until the taste is right. Sweeten to taste, but try to obtain and maintain a balance between acid and sugar. The wine will taste sweeter in one year. If sweetened, wait four days and carefully rack. If sweetened, wait 30 days to ensure no renewed fermentation and carefully rack into bottles. This wine must bottle age one year but really shines after two years.

Options: To add body, add one or two very ripe bananas, cut crosswise into ½-inch slices, before pitching yeast. For ease of removal, place in a separate straining bag.

This wine responds well to light oak. One cup of oak cubes in the wine for 3–5 weeks during maturation may be enough. Let taste be your guide. Don't overdo it.

As with all berry wines, because tasting can consume all of your wine, it is wise to bottle four 187-mL splits to use for that purpose.

Similar berries: None.

Red Raspberry Wine ❖

A dear friend and I went to the annual wine competition in Paris, Arkansas. In the parking lot, we were approached by a gentleman who pulled the cork on a bottle of red wine. Within seconds of the cork being pulled, I was hit by a wave of the most intense raspberry fragrance. The wine was as wonderful as its aromatics.

The red-fruited raspberry is one of about a dozen or so varieties of the raspberry species native to the United States and Canada. It is found throughout the Rocky Mountain states, the Midwest, New England, and throughout Canada south of the Arctic Circle. The berries are globular in shape, or nearly so, and a half-inch to nearly an inch in size. They form in June and July and turn from light-green to rose, then to bright red, ripening from July to September. When ripe, the berries are juicy with an underbelly of light but crisp tartness.

It is no wonder this berry is a favorite for vinification. Loaded with a unique, signature flavor and imbued with an astounding aroma, the berry fights a battle between sweetness and tartness. Raspberries typically have a low pH, so tartness usually dominates, and yet its sweetness lingers. It is a wonderful thing to drink.

JACK'S TIP

RED RASPBERRIES make a fragrant, subtle wine, but with a bold flavor. It's subtle because of a delicate interplay between tartness, astringency, and sweetness, even when the wine is made dry; it's bold because its flavor is just that. And it should be dry so that a hint of tartness carries its distinct flavor to the sides of the tongue as it is sipped, chilled.

The pH of red raspberry is usually within our desired window of 3.3–3.4, while its TA is usually high—when measured as tartaric, as in Table 7 (page 128). But acidity, as with most metrics, fluctuates among cultivars and harvests, the latter a result of numerous soil, climate, and weather variables. In the recipes here, we won't adjust acidity unless, in the end, it needs adjusting.

The natural sugar levels in this berry are difficult to measure because its high amount of soluble solids often produces a false hydrometer reading. Just assume the initial reading is SG 1.018 and you will be close.

The pectin and tannin contents in raspberries are high because each berry is an aggregate of many small berries, each with its own skin and seed. We will address both of these variables in the recipe.

Red Raspberry Wine Recipe

WINE IS READY IN: **18 months**

YOU'LL NEED: **3 pounds of raspberries per gallon of wine**

ADDITIONAL EQUIPMENT: **1 nylon straining bag**

MAKES: **1 gallon, but can be scaled up**

INGREDIENTS

3 lb. red raspberries

1 lb., 11 oz. very fine granulated sugar

water to make 1 gal.

4 tsp powdered pectic enzyme

potassium metabisulfite, as needed

½ tsp potassium sorbate

1 tsp (3 g) yeast nutrient

½ tsp yeast energizer (split)

1 g Fermaid-K

Lalvin RC212 yeast (5 g)

DIRECTIONS

Prepare must: Bring 2 cups of water to a boil, remove from heat and thoroughly dissolve sugar in it. Put berries in nylon straining bag, tie closed, and put in primary. Mash the berries well and pour boiling sugar-water over berries. Dissolve yeast nutrient and half (¼ teaspoon) the yeast energizer in 1 cup of juice and add to the primary. Add water to 1 gallon, stir. Add 0.2 g potassium metabisulfite and stir well. Cover the primary and wait 12 hours. Add pectic enzyme, stirring until completely dissolved. Set aside 12 hours.

Add yeast: To 1 cup warm water (not to exceed 102 degrees F.) add a pinch of yeast nutrient and stir to dissolve. Add yeast to water, stir, and cover mixture for 30 minutes. Add mixture to primary and cover primary.

Fermentation: Stir must and gently squeeze berry bag 2–4 times daily. When SG drops to 1.060, remove the straining bag and hang it over a large bowl. Squeeze bag gently every 15 minutes for 1 hour, then discard berry pulp and add extracted juice to the primary. Draw off 1 liter of juice, add remaining yeast energizer, and 1 gram Fermaid-K to liter and stir well while adding to the must. When SG drops to 1.020, or lower if the fermentation is still vigorous, transfer to secondary and affix airlock. Ferment to dryness.

Post-Fermentation: Carefully rack, wait 60 days and rack again. After another 60 days, check the clarity of wine and correct if needed with pectic enzyme. Add a two-part fining agent. Wait a final 60 days, add 0.2 g potassium metabisulfite and stir well. Wait 12 hours and check pH. If the taste does not reveal appropriate acidity, adjust as required.

Let your taste buds have a say in the matter. Add potassium sorbate and sweeten to taste and to balance. If sweetened, wait four days and carefully rack. Then wait another 30 days to ensure no renewed fermentation, and carefully rack into bottles. This wine must bottle age one year, longer if deemed necessary.

Options: To add body, add one or two very ripe bananas, cut crosswise into ½-inch slices, before pitching yeast. For ease of removal, place in a separate straining bag.

This wine responds well to light oak. One cup of oak cubes in the wine for 3–5 weeks during maturation may be enough. Let taste be your guide, but don't overdo it.

This wine blends well with pear wine. Do not overpower or dilute the raspberry flavor. Instead aim for a balance; conduct bench blending trials to find the right ratio.

Blended with a little elderberry wine, red raspberry can be transformed into a completely different animal. It will add color, structure, and longer life to the raspberry. The danger is blending in too much elderberry. For this reason, bench blending trials are essential.

This wine can be made with 1½ quart of red raspberry juice (no preservatives); this reduces the pectin, tannins, and gross lees. Ferment with one or two ripe bananas, bagged, for extra body.

As with all berry wines, because tasting can consume all of your wine, it is wise to bottle four 187-mL splits to use for that purpose.

Similar berries: The following berries can be substituted for red raspberries in this recipe, though you'll need to adjust acidity and sugar levels: yellow raspberry, apricot raspberry, amber raspberry. Purple raspberry and black raspberry have a slightly different, sweeter flavor, with different acidity and sugar.

Strawberry Wine ❖

Excellent strawberry wine is almost the stuff of legend. The bouquet and aroma are vibrant and captivating, the taste and finish divine. But I have never tasted a bad strawberry wine, whether excellent or not. It's just that some are better than others, and some are better than most. The very best strawberry wine is made from wild strawberries.

A ripe wild strawberry is usually only about the size of a pencil eraser, or the size of your little fingernail, but it packs many times more intense flavor than the very best cultivar. Unlike cultivated berries, which are bred for berries with size that ship well, its flavor has not been bred out of it.

The only downside to wild strawberries is that, as far as I know, you can't buy them. You have to find them. But when you do, the strawberry patch is liable to be quite large. They prefer a semi-dry area; some prefer partial shade. They are found throughout much, if not all, of the U.S. and Canada.

But not everyone lives in the right environment or can afford the time it takes to happen upon them. For these folks, aside from growing your own, there are three alternatives: fresh strawberries (visit a U-pick farm if you can), frozen strawberries, or canned strawberries. Most local home brew shops carry the 96 oz. cans of strawberries intended for the wine.

Like most berries, strawberries are usually more acidic than they appear. Their sugars largely keep the acid in check, producing a flavorful treat with just a hint of citrus in the finish. But the acid will be diluted with water, and we'll be adding more acid to account for that.

Did I mention that they taste pretty terrific, too? Rarely, a bland one may sneak in like an uninvited guest, but the next one will make up for the intrusion. They come in, invited or not, with more than enough pectin but not quite enough tannin. These are easy things to correct.

JACK'S TIP

THE RECIPE calls for 3½ pounds of fruit. You can push that up to 5 pounds or even 6, but you'll have to work out your own numbers for everything else—just let the pH, TA, and SG tell you what to do.

Amelioration will drop the TA, so acid must be added to get the numbers back on track.

We can add tartaric or citric acid, but citric acid will preserve the natural taste of the strawberries.

Strawberry Wine Recipe

WINE IS READY IN: **9 months**

YOU'LL NEED: **3½ pounds of strawberries per gallon of wine**

ADDITIONAL EQUIPMENT: **1 nylon straining bag**

MAKES: **1 gallon, but can be scaled up**

INGREDIENTS

3½ lb. strawberries

1 lb., 12 oz. very fine granulated sugar

water to make 1 gal.

½ tsp powdered pectic enzyme

potassium metabisulfite, as needed

citric acid

½ tsp potassium sorbate

1 tsp (3 g) yeast nutrient

1 g Fermaid-K

Lalvin EC-1118 yeast (5 g)

DIRECTIONS

Prepare must: Bring 2 quarts of water to a boil and thoroughly dissolve sugar in it. Chop berries and put in a fine-mesh nylon straining bag, tie closed, and put in primary. Mash the berries well and pour boiling sugar-water over them. Dissolve yeast nutrient in 1 cup of juice and add to the primary. Add water to make 1 gallon, stir. Add 0.2 g potassium metabisulfite and stir well. Cover the primary and wait 12 hours. Add pectic enzyme, stirring until completely dissolved. Set aside 12 hours.

Add yeast: To 1 cup warm water (not to exceed 102 degrees F.) add a pinch of yeast nutrient and stir to dissolve. Add yeast to water, stir, and cover mixture for 30 minutes. Add mixture to primary and cover primary.

Fermentation: Cover primary and gently squeeze bag several times daily. When SG drops to 1.060, draw off 1 liter of juice and dissolve 1 g Fermaid-K. Stir into the must. When SG drops to 1.020, or lower if the fermentation is still vigorous, transfer to secondary and affix airlock. Ferment to dryness.

Post-Fermentation: Rack, move to a dark place, wait 30 days, and rack again. After another 30 days, check the clarity of wine and correct if needed with pectic enzyme. Test the TA and correct it with citric acid. Add 0.2 g potassium metabisulfite, potassium sorbate, or sweeten to taste and to balance. Stir very well. If sweetened, wait 4 days and carefully rack. Then wait 30 more days to ensure no renewed fermentation and carefully rack into bottles. Taste in 6 months, longer if deemed necessary.

Options: To add body, add one or two very ripe bananas, cut crosswise into ½-inch slices, before pitching yeast. For ease of removal, place in a separate straining bag.

This wine blends well with rhubarb, peach, and kiwi wines. Conduct bench blending trials to find the right ratio.

As with all fruit wines, because tasting can consume all of your wine, it is wise to bottle four 187-mL splits to use for that purpose.

Similar berries: The following berry can be substituted for strawberries in this recipe. Acidity and sugar are not quite the same: Pineberry, Mock Strawberry.

CHAPTER SIX
FRUIT WINES

❖

The subject of fruit wines spurs the imagination. The only limitation is your definition of fruit. The problem is that there is a plethora of fruit, and it comes in all sorts of varieties. To make things more manageable, this book puts berries in its own chapter (page 127), and the same is true for tropical fruits (page 191). Then there's the trouble of chili peppers and tomatoes (technically fruits too), so we have to make some tough calls. Even after separating berries and tropicals, there are more than enough fruits from which to make wine.

In this chapter, we'll be examining methods for making wine from the ten fruit presented in Table 8. As always, the recipes are only guidelines. You're encouraged to test for actual acidity and adjust according to the values you obtain. While this is not actually necessary to complete the recipe, it will give you control of the acid and help you become a better winemaker. As can be seen from Table 8, there is a great

deal of variability in actual values obtained in the references consulted, but your average commercial fresh fruit should not see such extremes.

For some fruit, the range of acidity is too great to accurately predict a probable pH and TA, so you'll be asked to measure the actual pH, as a minimum, and adjust acid accordingly to bring the wine within a pH 3.2–3.5 window.

Table 8. Acid and Sugar Characteristics of Some Domestic Fruit

FRUIT	PH	TA RANGE (g/L)	PERCENT SUGAR	MAJOR ORGANIC ACID	MINOR ORGANIC ACID
Apple (page 157)	3.00–4.00	2.90-10.60	13.30	Malic	Quinnic
Apricot (page 160)	3.30–4.80	8.40–20.00	9.30	Malic	
Cherry, Sour (page 163)	3.20–3.80	5.10–19.80	8.10	Malic	Citric, Quinnic
Fig (page 166)	5.00–5.90	3.90–4.10	6.90	Malic	
Nectarine (page 169)	3.90–4.20	2.40–9.50	8.50	Malic	
Peach (page 172)	3.30–4.00	3.30–4.00	8.70	Malic	Citric, Quinnic
Pear (page 175)	3.50–4.60	3.50–4.60	10.50	Malic	Citric
Persimmon (page 179)	4.40–4.70	4.40–4.70	12.50	Malic	Citric
Pluot (page 182)	3.60–4.20	3.60–4.20	9.60	Malic	Quinnic
Plum (page 185)	2.80–3.40	2.80–3.40	9.50	Malic	Quinnic, Skikimic
Quince (page 188)	3.10–4.10	3.10–4.10	8.90	Malic	

Data for Table 8 were collected from a wide variety of sources, on the internet and from print. Since many of these fruits are cultivated throughout the Northern Hemisphere, care was taken to seek values representative of American harvests.

Apple Wine ❖

There are thousands of apple varieties grown worldwide, with more than 2,000 grown in the U.S. alone. Apple trees grow in every state, but only 100 or so are grown commercially, and most commercial production occurs in just a handful of states. Around 15 varieties account for about 90% of U.S. production.

Interestingly, only the crab apple is native to America. Cultivated apples trace their lineage back to Central Asia, though European crab apples played an important genetic role as well. Seeds from cultivated apples, when grown in the wild, tend to devolve into the lowly crab apple, which are prized as the rootstock for most cultivars.

Archaeological evidence suggests that apples are among the first agricultural products. Our love of apples is very old, and for as almost as long as we've loved apples, we've made apple cider and wine.

JACK'S TIP

THIS RECIPE will produce a pure juice product after the apples are pressed. Apples consist of about 85% water. If all of this water could be extracted, far fewer apples would be required to create an end product of pure juice. But the average home winemaker won't have a press capable of extracting this much juice.

The acidity of apples varies, but even mild acid can seem pronounced if there's little sugar. In this recipe, I opt for more acidic varieties, while Delicious and other predominately sweet varieties are avoided. The reason for this is two-fold. First, the tarter varieties add more structure to the wine, and second, we are going to be adding sugar anyway, so a shortfall here will be fixed.

This recipe calls for mixed apple varieties. This creates a wine with more texture and structure. You should include at least three varieties from the following list: Granny Smith, Pink Lady, Braeburn, McIntosh, Jonathan, Empire, Cortland, Winesap, any Cripps variety, and any cider apples available to you. Crab apples can also be included.

You'll probably still be adding acid to achieve pH 3.3. Add tartaric, and don't worry about the TA. That can be balanced with additional sugar after fermentation. Because malic acid is predominant in apples, we'll be discouraging MLF with free SO_2 maintained well above 20 g/L— at least half of the sulfites added will be bound, so in order to maintain free SO_2 above 20 mg/L, the additions will necessarily exceed 40 mg/L unless the existing free SO_2 in the must/wine is high enough to allow a lower number.

This recipe seems a little labor-intensive for the first 7–8 days but needs minimal intervention after that. A fruit or wine press is very helpful to obtain the required amount of juice.

Apple Wine Recipe

WINE IS READY IN: **12 months**

YOU'LL NEED: **18–20 pounds apples per gallon of wine**

ADDITIONAL EQUIPMENT: **3 nylon straining bags**

MAKES: **1 gallon, but can be scaled up**

INGREDIENTS

18–20 lb. apples, mixed varieties

1 lb., 10 oz. very finely granulated sugar

3 tsp pectic enzyme

⅛ tsp grape tannin

acid correction, as needed

potassium metabisulfite, as needed

½ tsp potassium sorbate

1 tsp (3 g) yeast nutrient

Lalvin BA11 or
    Red Star Côte des Blancs yeast

DIRECTIONS

Prepare must: Chop apples into small pieces (discard any cut seeds) in a primary. Sprinkle apples with pectin enzyme, tossing to distribute. Mist apples with distilled water and cover primary with lid, linen, or sanitized towel. Toss apples and mist every 2–3 hours for at least 12 hours.

Add yeast: To 1 cup warm water (not to exceed 102 degrees F.) add a pinch of yeast nutrient, 1 teaspoon of sugar, and stir to dissolve. Add yeast to water, stir, and cover mixture for 30 minutes. Drizzle mixture over apples in primary, stir and cover the primary.

Fermentation: Continue stirring and misting apples several times a day. After 7 days, transfer apples into nylon straining bags and tie securely closed. Forcefully crush apples enough to release some juice. Squeeze and turn bags 3–4 times a day for three days. Remove one bag at a time and press apples, returning juice to the primary. Discard apple pulp and, if needed, add water to make 1 gallon. Remove 1 liter of juice and to it add sugar and yeast nutrient, stirring to dissolve thoroughly. Add to primary, stirring well. Test juice for pH. Begin acid correction, if needed, to bring pH to pH 3.3 if feasible. When SG drops to 1.020, or lower if the fermentation is still vigorous, transfer to secondary and affix airlock. In 30 days add 0.2 g potassium metabisulfite, stir well, let lees settle for 24 hours, and carefully rack.

Post-Fermentation: Move wine to a dark, cool place for 30 days. Carefully rack. Wine must now sit an additional 60 days. Add 0.2 g potassium metabisulfite, ½ teaspoon dissolved potassium sorbate, and ⅛ teaspoon grape tannins. Wait 24 hours and rack. After 30 days, check clarity and correct as necessary with pectic enzyme—use 2-part fining only if necessary. If fined, wait four days and rack. Sweeten to taste or to balance. If sweetened, wait 30 days to ensure no renewed fermentation and carefully rack into bottles. Allow six months before tasting, one year for the best results.

Options: To add body, add one or two very ripe bananas, cut crosswise into ½-inch slices, before pitching yeast. For ease of removal, place in a separate straining bag.

As with all fruit wines, because tasting can consume all of your wine, it is wise to bottle four 187-mL splits to use for that purpose.

Similar fruit: The following fruit can be substituted for apples using this recipe: crab apples.

Apricot Wine ❖

Fresh, ripe apricots are a treat to savor. Owning an apricot tree elevates you to the aristocracy, in my mind. Apricots off the tree are the apex of apricot enjoyment. The notion that they make great wine is an afterthought when you're standing next to the tree, stuffing the very ripest ones into your mouth while trying not to look gluttonous. Unfortunately, I last had access to an apricot tree more than two decades ago. But I am always on the lookout for a neighborhood tree.

There are many varieties of apricot. Flavor varies as does the number of chill-hours (a certain number of hours exposed to 32–45 degrees) to bear fruit, but that simply means due diligence is required when selecting a variety to plant. Most are self-fertile, so a single tree can still be fruitful. Dwarf varieties exist, as do ultra-dwarf cultivars perfect for patio planters.

If you don't have or don't know anyone who has an apricot tree, you are in good company. Most of us have to buy our apricots fresh, and they can be pricey, and even then you don't know if you're buying a highly flavored or somewhat bland variety. But that's easy to test: just buy one, eat it outside the market, and return for more if the flavor warrants.

JACK'S TIP

THIS RECIPE uses white grape juice concentrate to add body to the wine. Before frozen concentrates came onto the market, we had to chop or mince white raisins to accomplish the same thing—or use bananas. Concentrate gives a better fermentation and helps with the balance of the wine.

We can expect the pH to be near where we want it, but TA will usually be a little high (or sometimes far too high). The high TA is noticeable in a few varieties as a mild tartness, but usually, it is masked by the apricot's sweetness. The TA will be dropped by amelioration—to the point where acid will have to be added.

Resist the urge to make this more than a dry to semi-sweet wine, low-alcohol wine (anything more than 11-12% ABV). Served chilled on a hot afternoon, this is a satisfying sipper. This is also a great wine to share with an afternoon salad, sushi, or crabcakes, or paired with salmon, shrimp, or other seafood at dinner. My favorite pairing was with baked trout and roasted asparagus with Béarnaise sauce, although grilled wild salmon with creamy chanterelles was a close second. You have to make the most of those annual splurges.

Apricot Wine Recipe

WINE IS READY IN: **12 months**

YOU'LL NEED: **4–6 pounds fresh apricots, 1 can frozen 100 percent white grape juice concentrate per gallon of wine**

ADDITIONAL EQUIPMENT: **3 nylon straining bags**

MAKES: **1 gallon, but can be scaled up**

INGREDIENTS

4–6 lb. apricots

1 can 100 percent white grape juice frozen concentrate, thawed

1 tsp powdered pectic enzyme

⅛ tsp grape tannins

1 lb., 10 oz. very finely granulated sugar

acid correction, as needed

sulfite, as necessary

½ tsp potassium sorbate

1 tsp (3 g) yeast nutrient

Lalvin EC-1118 yeast

DIRECTIONS

Prepare must: Wash, pit, dice apricots, and tie closed in nylon straining bag. In the primary, squeeze apricots thoroughly to release as much juice as possible. Leave the apricot bag in the primary. To primary, add grape concentrate and yeast nutrient. Add water to make 1 gallon and wait 12 hours. Remove 1 liter of juice and thoroughly dissolve sugar into it. Add to primary and stir. Test juice for pH. Begin acid correction, if needed, to bring pH to pH 3.3. Add 0.2 g potassium metabisulfite, stir well and wait 12 hours. Add pectic enzyme, stirring until completely dissolved. Set aside 12 hours.

Add yeast: To 1 cup warm water (not to exceed 102 degrees F.) add a pinch of yeast nutrient, 1 teaspoon of sugar, and stir to dissolve. Add yeast to water, stir, and cover mixture for 30 minutes. Add mixture to primary, stir, and cover primary.

Fermentation: Gently squeeze bag several times daily for five days. Remove bag to a large bowl and squeeze firmly but not excessively (do not allow the pulp to ooze through mesh) to expel juice. Hang the bag over the bowl for 30 minutes and squeeze again. Add juice to primary and discard apricot pulp. When SG drops to 1.020, or lower if the fermentation is still vigorous, transfer to secondary and affix airlock. Ferment to dryness.

Post-Fermentation: Move wine to a dark, cool place for 60 days. Check clarity. Correct with pectic enzyme and, if necessary, two-part fining. If fined, wait four days and rack. Add 0.2 g potassium metabisulfite, ½ teaspoon dissolved potassium sorbate, and ⅛ teaspoon grape tannins. Sweeten to taste or to balance. If sweetened, wait 30 days to ensure no renewed fermentation and carefully rack into bottles. Allow to age one year or longer.

Options: This wine blends well with peach, plum, or pineapple wine. Do not overpower the apricot. Bench blending trials are essential to get it right.

If sweetening, try using honey instead of sugar. At the end of the final 30-day waiting period (after stabilization), carefully check to see if pollen has precipitated out of the honey. Do not disturb any fine lees when bottling. If in doubt, rack again, wait three days, and then bottle.

As with all berry wines, because tasting can consume all of your wine, it is wise to bottle four 187-mL splits to use for that purpose.

Similar fruit: The following relatives can be substituted for apricots in this recipe: Tibetan Apricot, Marmot Plum, Manchurian Apricot, Chinese Plum, Siberian Apricot.

Cherry (Sour) Wine ❖

Some of the best wines I have enjoyed were cherry wines. The San Antonio Regional Wine Guild had a member who entered a cherry wine every competition. His wines always made it to the run-off for Best of Show and even claimed that title twice. At my urging, he brought some fresh cherries for us to taste. They were so tart they were almost inedible. The amazing thing is that he could grow cherries this far south.

Cherries can be sweet, sour (tart) or in-between—either sweet-tart or tart-sweet. Sweet cherries are slightly more difficult to make into a solid, balanced wine than are sour cherries. The tartness of sour cherries comes from their ancestry, and who are we to argue with that?

The Sour Cherry, *Prunus cerasus,* is native to Europe and Asia; it's a close relative of the Sweet Cherry, *Prunus avium,* but it's more acidic. *Prunus cerasus* (Sour Cherry) is native to Central-to-Eastern Europe and Southwest Asia. While closely related to the sweet cherry (Prunus avium), it has a fruit that is more acidic.

There are two kinds of sour cherries: Amarelle cherries, which have pale skin, and juice and flesh that are light to clear. Morello cherries have darker skin (usually red to black) and have red flesh and juice. Remember, both are sour cherries.

The best-known tart cherry in the U.S. is the Montmorency (Amarelle-type). The Montmorency has light red skin and soft, yellow flesh. It is juicy and tart, excellent in cobblers, pies, and jellies, and makes a very good wine. Morello-type cherries come in many varieties and generally have better flavor than Amarelle-types.

You make wine out of fresh, frozen, or canned cherries, or juice, but fresh is best if you can get them. Unfortunately, fresh cherries can be hard to come by except at a produce market. If you can't find them near you, you need to choose between frozen cherries, canned cherries, or juice. For many reasons, I recommend using juice.

The cherry of choice is the Morello. Most Morello-type cherries grown in America are sold for processing into cherry flavoring. It's that good. So let's look at tart cherry juice—in other words, read the label. The most important thing to look for is preservatives. If it mentions preservatives or lists a preservative, pass. If it mentions anything artificial (color, flavor, and so on), pass. "Natural flavor added" is okay. If it mentions any other fruit juice—typically apple, pear, grape—pass. We want nothing but water and cherry juice, either cold-pressed or reconstituted from concentrate.

JACK'S TIP

SOUR CHERRIES are tart because they have much more acid than sugar, but that acid is mostly malic. Malic is not all that strong compared to tartaric acid, for example, and, therefore, is easily corrected with amelioration and tweaking. Since we will be making our wine from juice, the acid (and sugar) corrections have already been made for us, but the juice will still be acidic.

Please note: This is a tart cherry wine and should be tart. Do not adjust TA lower than 6.0 g/L. It's supposed to taste tart. If you can drink lemonade, you can drink this.

Sour Cherry
Wine Recipe

WINE IS READY IN: **12 months**

YOU'LL NEED: **½ gallon tart cherry juice per gallon of wine**

ADDITIONAL EQUIPMENT: **nothing beyond the typical gear**

MAKES: **1 gallon, but can be scaled up**

INGREDIENTS

½ gal. tart cherry juice

1 lb., 2 oz. very finely granulated sugar

acid correction, as needed

potassium metabisulfite, as needed

½ tsp potassium sorbate

1 tsp (3 g) yeast nutrient

Red Star Côte des Blancs yeast

DIRECTIONS

Prepare must: In your primary, add water to cherry juice to make approximately 1 cup less than 1 gallon. Test for pH. Draw off 1 liter of juice, add sugar and yeast nutrient and stir well to dissolve thoroughly. Add sugar-juice to primary and stir. Add 0.2 g potassium metabisulfite, stir well, and set aside 12 hours.

Add yeast: To 1 cup warm water (not to exceed 102 degrees F.) add ¼ teaspoon sugar and a pinch of yeast nutrient and stir to dissolve. Add yeast to water, stir, and cover mixture for 30 minutes. Add mixture to primary and cover primary.

Fermentation: Stir and check SG daily. When SG drops to 1.020, or lower if the fermentation is still vigorous, transfer to secondary, and affix airlock. In 30 days, carefully rack.

Post-Fermentation: Move wine to a dark, cool place for 60 days and carefully rack. Set aside an additional 60 days or until the wine is perfectly clear for at least 30 days. Carefully rack. Add 0.2 g potassium metabisulfite and ½ teaspoon dissolved potassium sorbate. Stir well. In 1 week check clarity and correct as necessary with pectic enzyme and, if necessary, two-part fining. If fined, wait four days and rack. Sweeten to taste or to balance. If sweetened, wait 30 days to ensure no renewed fermentation and carefully rack into bottles. Allow one year in bottles before tasting. Age longer if deemed necessary.

Options: To add body, add one or two very ripe bananas, cut crosswise into ½-inch slices, before pitching yeast. For ease of removal, place in a separate straining bag.

This wine responds well to light oak. One cup of oak cubes in the wine for 3–5 weeks during maturation is usually enough. Let taste be your guide, but don't overdo it.

As with all fruit wines, because tasting can consume all of your wine, it is wise to bottle four 187-mL splits to use for that purpose.

Similar berries: The following fruit can be substituted for tart cherry in this recipe, although Black Cherry is the one available as a juice. Acidity and sugar levels will vary: black cherry, chokecherry, bird cherry, pin cherry, wild cherry.

Fig Wine ❖

Figs are a strange fruit. In wild figs, the skin is a container for the flower, which is entirely internal. A small opening at the growing end of the female fig allows a female fig wasp to enter, lay her eggs, and die. Without the wasp, the trees do not bear fruit.

Fortunately, there is a species of fig (*Ficus carica*), the common fig, which is self-pollinating and does not require wasps to produce fruit. This is the fig from which we will make our wine. Some of the common cultivars of this fig are Kadota, Black Mission, Brown Turkey, Brunswick, and Celeste. They are not only the garden varieties of the home and conservatory but are cultivated commercially for large harvests. Thus, if you don't have a fig tree or know someone who does, they are usually available in produce markets but they are seasonal—August to early October. They freeze well for winemaking purposes, and all make good wine.

Fig color varies between cultivars due to various amounts of anthocyanins. This affects the color of the fermenting wine, but not the end result, as all fig wines tend to end up as white or slightly tinted wines.

I have made very good fig wines from two pounds of fruit per gallon but also from four pounds per gallon. The higher concentration of fruit yields a more flavorful and viscous wine, but regardless of the amount, the wine does not taste like the fruit. This is a letdown for many people and tends to create an unfair bias against the wine.

So if you think you might not like something because it doesn't taste like what you expected, perhaps you shouldn't make this wine. On the other hand, if you can accept new flavors, then, by all means, make it. This wine doesn't have to "grow on you," you have to grow on it.

I have heard of wines made from pure fig juice that are in another league altogether, but I have never been so rich in figs that I could even contemplate making it. But I do wonder how it tastes. I mention it here to plant the seed if anyone out there wants to try making it. And if you do, please contact me and tell me about it—and save me a bottle.

JACK'S TIP

WE ARE GOING TO USE 3½ pounds of fruit per gallon. I arrived at that number because it is the amount I used when I made my best fig wine. The fruit are about 80% water, but you will never extract that much from them without a hydraulic press. Figs also have decent sugar but are low in acid, but no worry. We can fix that.

A word of caution. Do not attempt to chop the figs with a food processor or juicer. This will only cause off-flavors to be released from the skins and seeds. Instead, let the yeast do the processing and extracting.

Fig Wine Recipe

WINE IS READY IN: **12 months**

YOU'LL NEED: **3½ pounds fresh figs per gallon of wine**

ADDITIONAL EQUIPMENT: **1 nylon straining bag**

MAKES: **1 gallon, but can be scaled up**

INGREDIENTS

3½ lb. common figs

1 lb., 12 oz. very finely granulated sugar

water to make 1 gal.

½ tsp powdered pectic enzyme

⅛ tsp grape tannin

acid correction, tartaric, as needed

potassium metabisulfite, as needed

½ tsp potassium sorbate

1 tsp (3 g) yeast nutrient

1 g Fermaid-K

Lalvin K1 yeast

DIRECTIONS

Prepare must: Bring 2 quarts water to a boil, remove from heat, and stir in sugar until dissolved. Concurrently, wash, destem, chop figs, and tie closed in a nylon straining bag. In the primary, mash figs to release as much juice as possible. Pour sugar-water over figs. Cover and set aside to cool. When lukewarm, dissolve yeast nutrient and tannin in 1 cup of juice and stir into the primary. Add water to make 1 gallon. When the water is at room temperature, test juice for pH. Adjust acidity as necessary to bring pH to 3.3. Add 0.2 g potassium metabisulfite, stir well, cover the primary, and set aside for 12 hours. Add pectic enzyme, stirring until completely dissolved. Set aside 12 hours.

Add yeast: To 1 cup warm water (not to exceed 102 degrees F.) add a pinch of yeast nutrient, 1 teaspoon of sugar, and stir to dissolve. Add yeast to water, stir, and cover mixture for 30 minutes. Add mixture to primary, stir, and cover primary.

Fermentation: Gently squeeze bag daily for five days. Remove bag to large bowl and squeeze firmly but not excessively (do not allow pulp to ooze through mesh) to expel remaining juice. Hang the bag over a large bowl and squeeze bag every 15 minutes for 1 hour. Add juice to primary and discard fig pulp. When SG drops to 1.060, dissolve 1 gram of Fermaid-K in 1 cup juice, stir to dissolve, and then stir into the primary. When SG drops to 1.020, or lower if the fermentation is still vigorous, transfer to secondary and affix airlock. Ferment to dryness.

Post-Fermentation: Move wine to a dark, cool place for 60 days. Check clarity. Correct with pectic enzyme and, if necessary, two-part fining. If fined, wait four days and rack. Add 0.2 g potassium metabisulfite and ½ teaspoon dissolved potassium sorbate. Sweeten to taste or to balance. If sweetened, wait 30 days to ensure no renewed fermentation and carefully rack into bottles. This wine can be consumed young (3 months) but will improve immensely with age (and improve your opinion of fig wine).

Options: This wine blends well with blackberry wine, but don't overpower the fig. Bench blending trials will assist you greatly.

When sweetening this wine at the end, honey or dark brown sugar adds complexity.

As with all fruit wines, because tasting can consume all of your wine, it is wise to bottle four 187-mL splits to use for that purpose.

Similar fruit: None.

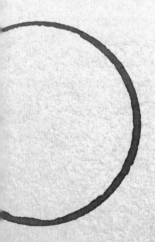

Nectarine Wine ❖

Genetically, nectarines are essentially peaches; the difference between them is a single recessive gene. At least that is what the botanists say. The gene in question stops producing the fuzz on the skin of the fruit.

This would be believable if they had the same texture in their flesh, the same taste, the same aroma. But they don't share these characteristics. Each has its own distinct character. In a blind tasting, it is easy to distinguish them apart.

On average, nectarines have higher pH and lower TA than peaches. Their sugar content is similar, with peaches being slightly sweeter. Nectarines appear to have a more complex mix of natural organic acids than peaches, which makes them a bit zestier and spicier than peaches.

JACK'S TIP

THE NAME of the fruit suggests nectar, a sure sign that this is a special fruit, with juice that is almost ambrosia-like. That is a good way to approach it, and we will be doing all we can to make a wine that lives up to that notion. To those who insist the nectarine is just a fuzzless peach, we will prove them wrong.

To extract that nectar this wine will use lots of fruit. The challenge will come in adjusting the acidity. The pH will usually be a bit high, and the TA will be close to where we want it but perhaps a tad low. The natural acid in nectarines is malic acid with perhaps a bit of citric, although I have found no confirmation of the latter. We will lower the pH with tartaric acid, trying to get as close to pH 3.3 as possible without sending the TA too high—a TA of 7 g/L might be acceptable, but let your taste buds be the arbiter.

This should be a 10–11% ABV wine that will be consumed within 18 months. I like this wine off-dry; a little sweetener at the end will enhance the nectar quality of the base.

Nectarine
Wine Recipe

WINE IS READY IN: **10 months**

YOU'LL NEED: **10–11 pounds nectarines per gallon of wine**

ADDITIONAL EQUIPMENT: **2 nylon straining bags**

MAKES: **1 gallon, but can be scaled up**

INGREDIENTS

10–11 lb. nectarines, unpeeled

1 lb., 4 oz. very finely granulated sugar

water to make 1 gal.

1½ tsp powdered pectic enzyme

⅛ tsp grape tannin

acid correction, tartaric, as needed

potassium metabisulfite, as needed

½ tsp potassium sorbate

1 tsp (3 g) yeast nutrient

1 g Fermaid-K™

Lalvin EC-1116 yeast

DIRECTIONS

Prepare must: Wash, destem, and chop nectarines rather finely, discarding their stones (pits). At the same time, bring 1 pint water to a boil, place chopped nectarines in nylon straining bags and tie closed. In the primary, mash fruit to release as much juice as possible. Add sugar to boiling water, stirring to dissolve. Pour sugar water over bags and stir well. When lukewarm, dissolve yeast nutrient in 1 cup of juice and stir into the primary. Add water to make a total of 1 gallon and test juice for pH. Adjust acidity as necessary. Add 0.2 g potassium metabisulfite, stir well, cover primary, and set aside for 12 hours. Add pectic enzyme, stirring until completely dissolved. Set aside 12 hours.

Add yeast: To 1 cup warm water (not to exceed 102 degrees F.) add a pinch of sugar and yeast nutrient and stir to dissolve. Add yeast to water, stir, and cover mixture for 30 minutes. Add to primary and stir well.

Fermentation: Gently squeeze bags twice daily for five days. Remove bags to large bowl and squeeze firmly to expel remaining juice. Hang the bags over the bowl and squeeze every 15 minutes for 1 hour. Add juice to primary and discard pulp. When SG drops to 1.020, or lower if the fermentation is still vigorous, transfer to secondary and affix airlock. If the wine does not fill secondary, do not top up at this time. Ferment to dryness.

Post-Fermentation: Move wine to a dark, cool place for 60 days, stirring every 15 days. Check clarity. Correct with pectic enzyme and, if necessary, two-part fining. If fined, wait four days and rack. Return to dark place and allow to mature for 4–6 months, tasting to determine length of maturation. Add 0.2 g potassium metabisulfite, ½ teaspoon dissolved potassium sorbate, and ⅛ teaspoon tannins. Sweeten to taste or to balance. If sweetened, wait 30 days to ensure no renewed fermentation and carefully rack into bottles. Taste after four months, but it will improve immensely in one year.

Options: To add body, add one or two very ripe bananas, cut crosswise into ½-inch slices, before pitching yeast. For ease of removal, place in a separate straining bag.

This wine blends well with apricot, peach, and plum wines, or a combination of these. Do not overpower the nectarine. The blended wine(s) should offer complexity and hints of flavor—no more than hints. Bench blending trials are essential.

When sweetening this wine at the end, honey or Demerara sugar both add for sweetness and complexity. Honey adds a little length to the finish.

Similar fruit: The following fruit are similar to nectarine and can be substituted in this recipe: Peach, Apricot.

Peach
Wine ❖

Years ago, I made the best peach wine I've ever tasted. My wife had talked a grower out of two bushels of blemished peaches. That's about 18–20 gallons of peaches. When we got home we both went through them, cutting out all the brown spots and underlying rotting flesh, reducing the usable produce by about ⅓, but that is still a lot of fruit to deal with immediately.

My wife got a large pot of water boiling, and I prepared an ice water bath. She put three peaches at a time in the boiling water, and after 30 seconds, I transferred them to the ice water. After 30 seconds in the bath, I then twisted each fruit and removed the skin whole, which I placed in a bowl. The peaches then were placed on cooling racks, which quickly filled up. We then took time out to cut the peaches into wedges and secure them in freezer-grade gallon Ziploc bags that went straight into the freezer when full, destined for peach cobblers. We then repeated the process with new peaches until we had processed them all in the wee hours of the morning.

I claimed every other peach for wine, which I chopped up without peeling and also froze. When we were done, I put all the skins I had removed from my wife's peaches into another Ziploc bag. When I made my wine, I made a 3 gallon batch, and just for the hell of it, put the peach skins in one of the nylon mesh bags. The resulting wine had the best flavor I've ever tasted in a peach wine, and I'm convinced it is because the must contained at least twice the amount of skins as it should have.

Most peach wine recipes call for 3–4 pounds of peaches per gallon, which is what I used in my 3 gallon batch. But, as in the nectarine wine recipe, we will depart from that to make a fragrant, full-bodied wine that brings forward the essence of peaches. This wine is delightful on a warm afternoon—chilled, of course.

JACK'S TIP

THE PEACH WINE we will be making will be fragrant and full-bodied. The acidity of peaches can be all over the place, but by using only ripe fruit from different trees and of varying varieties, the acid should level out with an elevated TA and slightly high pH. We'll correct the pH, and amelioration should take care of the TA.

Ripe peaches should be slightly yielding when gently squeezed. They can be left at room temperature for a few days to ripen if not ripe when obtained. There are also hard peaches that never really yield when squeezed when ripe. I always leave these out a few days just to make sure they are riper than when I obtained them.

Peach Wine Recipe

WINE IS READY IN: **12 months**

YOU'LL NEED: **8–10 pounds peaches per gallon of wine**

ADDITIONAL EQUIPMENT: **2 nylon straining bags**

MAKES: **1 gallon, but can be scaled up**

INGREDIENTS

8–10 lb. peaches

1 lb., 4 oz. very fine granulated sugar

1½ tsp powdered pectic enzyme

⅛ tsp grape tannins

water to make 1 gal.

acid correction, tartaric, as needed

potassium metabisulfite, as needed

½ tsp potassium sorbate

1 tsp (3 g) yeast nutrient

Lalvin EC-1116 yeast

DIRECTIONS

Prepare must: Wash, destem, and chop peaches rather finely, discarding their stones (pits). Place chopped peaches in nylon straining bags and tie closed. In the primary, mash fruit completely to release as much juice as possible. Put 1 pint water on to boil. Remove from heat when water boils, add sugar, stirring well to dissolve. Pour sugar water over bags and stir well. Add water to make 1 gallon and test juice for pH. Adjust acidity as necessary. Add 0.2 g potassium metabisulfite, stir well, cover primary, and set aside for 12 hours. Add pectic enzyme, stirring until completely dissolved. Re-cover primary and set aside 12 hours.

Add yeast: To 1 cup warm water (not to exceed 102 degrees F.) add a pinch of sugar and yeast nutrient and stir to dissolve. Add yeast to water, stir, and cover mixture for 30 minutes. Add to primary and stir well.

Fermentation: Gently squeeze bags twice daily for five days. Remove bags to a large bowl and squeeze firmly to expel remaining juice. Hang the bags over the bowl and squeeze every 15 minutes for one hour. Add juice to primary and discard pulp. When SG drops to 1.020, or lower if the fermentation is still vigorous, transfer to secondary and affix airlock. Ferment to dryness.

Post-Fermentation: Move wine to a dark, cool place, and rack every 30 days until the wine clears. Correct clarity with pectic enzyme and, if required, two-part fining. If fined, wait four days and rack. Return to dark another 60 days and carefully rack. Add 0.2 g potassium metabisulfite, ½ teaspoon dissolved potassium sorbate, and ⅛ teaspoon grape tannin. Stir well and sweeten to taste or to balance. If sweetened, wait 30 days to ensure no renewed fermentation and carefully rack into bottles. Taste after four months, but it will improve immensely in 9 months.

Options: To add body, add one or two very ripe bananas, cut crosswise into ½-inch slices, before pitching yeast. For ease of removal, place in a separate straining bag.

This wine blends well with apricot, nectarine, and plum wines, or a combination of these. Do not overpower the peach. The blended wine(s) should offer complexity and hints of flavor—no more than hints. Bench blending trials are essential.

When sweetening this wine at the end, honey or Demerara sugar adds complexity. Honey adds a little length to the finish.

As with all fruit wines, because tasting can consume all of your wine, it is wise to bottle four 187-mL splits to use for that purpose.

Similar fruit: The following fruit are similar to peach and can be substituted in this recipe: nectarine, apricot.

Pear Wine ❖

With around 20 species, 3,000 varieties and thousands of cultivars, it is obvious the pear has been cultivated for a very long time with plenty of natural variety to breed. It is almost a shame, then, to walk into a large supermarket and find 6 or 8 varieties, at most, to select from. That is probably more the fault of the growers than the market.

On the other hand, my wife and I stopped at several large, open-air produce markets in Spain, and there were probably 50–60 varieties to choose from—some small, some very large, some elongated, some round, and many in between. The vendors were anxious to cut a slice for you to try, and because of that, we bought just two each of four different and unusual tasting varieties we would never have experienced. I can only imagine what their wines would have tasted like.

Most people who make pear wine have one or more pear trees or know someone who does. An adult tree will produce more pears than a person can possibly consume. We used to have three pear trees until a blight killed them. I can say from experience that three adult trees produce an overwhelming crop. You can't eat, preserve, make wine, or give them away fast enough to use them, and we had no livestock to feed the leftovers to.

But I did learn quite a bit about making pear wine. For one thing, it is as easy to make a good pear wine as it is to make a poor one. Making a poor one is just as instructive as making a good one. In either case, you learn what to do and what not to do. With a little more focus on balance, that good pear wine can be an excellent one.

Balance in pear wine, as in most wines, is the counterplay between acidity, tannin, alcohol, and sugar. Get any one of these too high or too low, and the wine will express the fault. We are making a still (non sparkling) wine around 12% ABV. That is the magic number among wines. It is the number where alcohol's biological stabilizing quality is assured. It is also the number at which the wine is expected to age at least 18 months before declining in quality. Generally, still wines below 12% have less ability to age.

An unusual thing happens to some pear wines as they age. The color begins to shift from clear to a slight pink to purple. The only explanation I have ever run across for this is it is probably due to the enzymatic oxidation of certain unidentified phenolic compounds. It is quite natural and such wines don't suffer as a result.

JACK'S TIP

THIS RECIPE uses a lot of pears. If you have a pear tree, you will thank me. If you have to buy them, maybe not so much. You must take the extra time to remove the core and seeds from each pear. I guarantee you the seeds will impart an off-taste that will spoil the wine. Yes, this is time-consuming, but you can do it while watching the news or a mindless sitcom.

It is important that once you start de-seeding the pears you immediately move to the next steps. If you don't, they will begin to oxidize and turn brown. A light browning is acceptable, but not a dark one. You don't want your wine to oxidize before you even make it. You can prevent this by putting your cut pears in a non-aluminum stockpot half-filled with water and the juice of 3 lemons.

Once you've de-seeded the pears, it makes no difference how you chop them. I obtained as good a result from coarsely chopping and then mashing them into a juicy pulp as I did finely chopping them in a food processor. I did not like the result when carrying the food processor a bit too far and making a puree, as it was a bit too difficult to contain in a nylon straining bag and resulted in a thick layer of gross lees.

Pears have decent sugar but poor acidity. Get the pH down to at least 3.5, 3.3 if you can without sending the TA too high. However, let your taste buds help determine if the TA is too high.

Pear Wine Recipe

WINE IS READY IN: **13 months**

YOU'LL NEED: **5 pounds pears per gallon of wine**

ADDITIONAL EQUIPMENT: **1–2 nylon straining bags**

MAKES: **1 gallon, but can be scaled up**

INGREDIENTS

5 lb. pears

1 lb., 6 oz. very fine granulated sugar

water to make 1 gal.

1¼ tsp powdered pectic enzyme

⅛ tsp grape tannins

acid correction, tartaric, as needed

potassium metabisulfite, as needed

½ tsp potassium sorbate

1 tsp (3 g) yeast nutrient

Lalvin EC-1116 yeast

DIRECTIONS

Prepare must: Wash, de-seed, and chop pears rather finely, discarding their seeds. Place chopped pears in nylon straining bags and tie closed. In the primary, mash fruit completely to release as much juice as possible. Put 1 liter of water on to boil and add sugar, stirring well to dissolve. Pour sugar water over bags and stir well. When lukewarm, dissolve yeast nutrient in 1 cup of juice and stir into the primary. Add water to make 1 gallon and test juice for pH. Adjust acidity as necessary. Add 0.2 g potassium metabisulfite, stir well, cover primary, and set aside for 12 hours. Add pectic enzyme, stirring until completely dissolved. Re-cover primary and set aside 12 hours.

Add yeast: To 1 cup warm water (not to exceed 102 degrees F.) add a pinch of sugar and yeast nutrient and stir to dissolve. Add yeast to water, stir, and cover mixture for 30 minutes. Add to primary and stir well.

Fermentation: Gently squeeze bags at least twice daily for five days. Remove bags to a large bowl and squeeze firmly to expel remaining juice. Hang the bags over the bowl and squeeze firmly after 30 minutes. Add juice to primary and discard pulp. When SG drops to 1.020, or lower if the fermentation is still vigorous, transfer to secondary and affix airlock. Ferment to dryness.

Post-Fermentation: Move wine to a dark, cool place for 60 days, stirring every 15 days. Rack off of sediment and set aside another 60 days without stirring. If the wine is not clear, rack and set aside until wine clears. Carefully rack, check clarity, and correct with pectic enzyme and, if required, two-part fining. If fined, wait four days and rack. Add 0.2 g potassium metabisulfite, ½ teaspoon dissolved potassium sorbate, and ⅛ teaspoon grape tannin. Stir well and sweeten to taste or to balance. If sweetened, wait 30 days to ensure no renewed fermentation and carefully rack into bottles. Taste after six months, but it will improve considerably at one year.

Options: To add body, add one or two very ripe bananas, cut crosswise into ½-inch slices, before pitching yeast. For ease of removal, place in a separate straining bag.

This wine blends well with many different wines, most boringly with apple, but any fruit will do. Experiment, but do not overpower the pear. The blended wine(s) should offer complexity and hints of flavor—no more than hints. Bench blending trials are essential.

When sweetening this wine at the end, honey or raw sugar adds both sweetness and complexity. Honey adds a little length to the finish.

As with all fruit wines, because tasting can consume all of your wine, it is wise to bottle four 187-mL splits to use for that purpose.

Similar fruit: The following fruit are similar to pear and can be substituted in this recipe: Quince, Apple.

Persimmon Wine ❖

Usually a favorite among family and friends, a well-made persimmon wine also does well at competitions. The fruit is very sweet, low in acids, and can be quite strong in tannins, especially underripe fruit of the American persimmon and Hachiya varieties of Asian (Japanese) persimmons. The tannins soften and almost disappear when the fruit is fully ripe, leaving a soft, often jelly-like interior. Some are sweet with a honey-like quality, while others have a soft, sweet, fibrous interior with a mildly acidic tanginess.

The Fuyu varieties are considered non-astringent because their tannins are so slight. They can be eaten fresh before they completely ripen, although their flavors improve when allowed to mature. The ripe interior of both types of persimmon darkens and in some cases browns, but this does not affect their flavor.

Most persimmons have a few seeds, but seedless cultivars have been developed.

With rare exceptions, persimmon trees are either male or female, and botanically the fruit is a berry. The color of the ripe fruit differs from variety to variety, from a light yellow to soft orange, from bright orange-red to brilliant red. Both native Texas persimmons and Mexican Black Sapote are black when ripe. Persimmons generally hang on the tree until fully ripe in early winter, after which they drop naturally or when the tree is shaken.

Persimmon harvest can begin slowly, and within a few days scores of fruit will drop daily. Staking claim to a wild tree can grow ugly when several people rush in to gather the fallen harvest. But pragmatic minds can easily see that a mature tree (35–40 feet) can drop enough fruit for everyone to make a few dozen cookies, several bread loaves, a few pies, some jelly and jam, and several gallons of wine. The trees simply get that big and drop as many as hundreds of fruit varying from ¾ to 3½ inches in diameter. Smaller trees (15–20 feet) with smaller harvests are perfect for the garden.

We are interested in gathering at least three pounds of fruit per gallon-batch—3½ pounds is better. It makes a very good wine.

JACK'S TIP

WE'LL MAKE our wine from the whole fruit, fermenting everything but the large, hard, 4-petal calyx, which is easily removed if the fruit is truly ripe. The leathery skin yields when ripe, releasing the calyx and is easily chopped up. Remove the seeds.

It is from the skin that we will try to extract the last of the tannin and as much color as remains. We will almost certainly have to add a little tannin. Regardless of the persimmon's skin color, we should expect a wine that is yellow-orange to golden-orange. Extraction will be easier if, after removing the calyxes, we freeze the fruit for at least five days and then thaw it out completely. If it is not thoroughly thawed, the yeast might withdraw and fail.

Persimmon Wine Recipe

WINE IS READY IN: **16 months**

YOU'LL NEED: **3½ pounds persimmons per gallon of wine**

ADDITIONAL EQUIPMENT: **1 nylon straining bag**

MAKES: **1 gallon, but can be scaled up**

INGREDIENTS

3½ lb. persimmons

1 lb., 8 oz. very fine granulated sugar

water to make 1 gal.

½ tsp powdered pectic enzyme

⅛ to ¼ tsp powdered grape tannins

acid correction, tartaric, as needed to
   reach pH 3.5–3.3

potassium metabisulfite, as needed

½ tsp potassium sorbate

1 tsp (3 g) yeast nutrient

Lalvin EC-1116 yeast

DIRECTIONS

Prepare must: Wash, de-seed, and chop persimmons rather finely, discarding seeds. Place chopped persimmons in nylon straining bag, tie closed, and place in primary. Put 2 quarts of water on to boil, add sugar and stir well to dissolve. Pour sugar water over bags and stir well. When lukewarm, dissolve yeast nutrient in 1 cup of juice and stir into the primary. Add water to make 1 gallon and test juice for pH. Adjust acidity as necessary. Add 0.2 g potassium metabisulfite, stir well, cover primary, and set aside for 12 hours. Add pectic enzyme, stirring until completely dissolved. Re-cover primary and set aside 12 hours.

Add yeast: To 1 cup warm water (not to exceed 102 degrees F.) add a pinch of sugar and yeast nutrient and stir to dissolve. Add yeast to water, stir, and cover mixture for 30 minutes. Add to primary and stir well.

Fermentation: Gently squeeze bags twice daily for five days. Remove bag to a large bowl and squeeze firmly to expel remaining juice. Hang the bag over the bowl and squeeze firmly after 30 minutes. Add juice to primary and discard pulp. When SG drops to 1.020, or lower if the fermentation is still vigorous, transfer to secondary and affix airlock. Ferment to dryness, top up and replace airlock.

Post-Fermentation: Move wine to a dark, cool place until clear, then another 15 days. Correct clarity with pectic enzyme and, if required, two-part fining. If fined, wait four days and rack. Add 0.2 g potassium metabisulfite, ½ teaspoon dissolved potassium sorbate, and ⅛ teaspoon grape tannin. Sweeten to taste or to balance. If sweetened, wait 30 days to ensure no renewed fermentation and carefully rack into bottles. If you can stand the suspense, age this wine in the bottle for one year.

Options: To add body, add one or two very ripe bananas, cut crosswise into ½-inch slices, before pitching yeast. For ease of removal, place in a separate straining bag.

When sweetening this wine at the end, honey or raw sugar adds both sweetness and complexity. Honey adds a little length to the finish.

As with all fruit wines, because tasting can consume all of your wine, it is wise to bottle four 187-mL splits to use for that purpose.

Similar fruit: There are fruit similar in appearance to the persimmon, but none that work as a substitute in this recipe.

Pluot Wine ❖

The pluot's story began in areas where apricots and plums were either indigenous or long cultivated. A natural hybrid would occasionally be produced, resulting in either the apricot (Apriplums) or the plum (Plumcots) parent. Pluots are a later generation hybrid, completely engineered by man to cross the Japanese Plum with the apricot. Pure breeds of the parents are essential. The result is a fruit closely resembling the plum, with smooth skin and a flavorful, juicy, yielding flesh, usually borrowing colors from the plum parent.

For a fruit that was developed and introduced in the late twentieth century, there sure are many cultivars. Many people have no idea what cultivar they are buying.

I have two supermarkets in town with decent produce sections. One displays the fruit with a sign that says, "Pluots, $2.95 lb." There may be six varieties on display, but the buyer has no idea which cultivars they are. The other market displays the fruit with signs that say, "Pluots, Flavor Finale, $3.49 lb.," "Pluots, Flavor King, $3.29 lb.," etc. I prefer to know what I am buying. There is plenty of background information on the cultivars, so you can know what flavors to expect before you take a bite.

The pluot season is moderately long, with different fruit hitting the produce shelves every two or so weeks, ranging from moderately early ripening and early ripening types to early midseason, midseason, late midseason, and so on. If you missed the one you wanted there's always next year.

JACK'S TIP

THIS RECIPE uses white grape juice concentrate to add body to the wine. Before the convenience of the frozen concentrates, we had to chop or mince white raisins to accomplish the same thing—or use bananas, dates, or other body-builders. The concentrate gives a better fermentation, eliminates any competing flavors, and helps with the balance of the wine.

We can expect the pH to be near where we want it, albeit a little high. On the other hand, TA is all over the place but should be expected to be just a tad low. Since we'll have to add acid to drop the pH, the TA will necessarily climb. If it wanders out of our comfort zone, do not worry. Amelioration will drop it back where it should be or perhaps even a bit low. Just keep an eye on it and be prepared to intervene with malic acid to fine-tune it. Let your taste buds help in the judging.

There are some interesting flavors in those pluots. To better capture what we can of them, we'll be using Lalvin BA11 yeast because it is a moderate-to-fast fermenter that should create a complex wine retaining the characteristics we desire.

Finally, we must keep in mind that pluots, like all of the fruit in this chapter, is a malic fruit. We absolutely must keep the free SO_2 level well above 20 mg/L to prevent MLF, which is why I try to keep it above 50 mg/L until the end, where it is kicked up to 100 mg/L for bottle aging. Remember, at least half of what we add will become bound very quickly.

Pluot Wine Recipe

WINE IS READY IN: **9 months**

YOU'LL NEED: **4 pounds fresh pluots, 1 can frozen 100 percent white grape juice concentrate per gallon of wine**

ADDITIONAL EQUIPMENT: **2 nylon straining bags**

MAKES: **1 gallon, but can be scaled up**

INGREDIENTS

4 lb. pluots

1 can 100 percent white grape juice frozen concentrate, thawed

1 lb., 8 oz. very fine granulated sugar

water to make 1 gal.

1 tsp powdered pectic enzyme

⅛ tsp grape tannins

acid correction, as needed

potassium metabisulfite, as needed

½ tsp potassium sorbate

1 tsp (3 g) yeast nutrient

Lalvin BA11 yeast

DIRECTIONS

Prepare must: Wash, pit, dice pluots, and tie closed in nylon straining bag. In the primary, squeeze pluots thoroughly to release as much juice as possible. Leave the pluot bag in the primary. To primary, add grape concentrate, sugar, and stir until completely dissolved. Add water to make 1 gallon. Wait 4 hours and test juice for pH. Begin acid correction if needed to bring pH to 3.3–3.4. Add 0.2 g potassium metabisulfite, stir well, cover primary, and set aside for 12 hours. Add pectic enzyme, stirring until completely dissolved. Re-cover primary and set aside 12 hours.

Add yeast: To 1 cup warm water (not to exceed 102 degrees F.) add a pinch of yeast nutrient and stir to dissolve. Add yeast to water, stir, and cover mixture for 30 minutes. Add to primary and stir well.

Fermentation: Gently squeeze bag at least twice daily for five days. Remove bag to large bowl and squeeze firmly to expel juice. Hang the bag over the bowl for 30 minutes and squeeze again. Add juice to primary and discard pluot pulp. When SG drops to 1.020, or lower if the fermentation is still vigorous, transfer to secondary and affix airlock. Ferment to dryness.

Post-Fermentation: Move wine to a dark, cool place until clear. Correct clarity with pectic enzyme and, if required, two-part fining. If fined, wait four days and rack. Add 0.2 g potassium metabisulfite, ½ teaspoon dissolved potassium sorbate, and ⅛ teaspoon grape tannin. Sweeten to taste or to balance. If sweetened, wait 30 days to ensure no renewed fermentation and carefully rack into bottles. Allow to age six months or longer.

Options: To add body, add one or two very ripe bananas, cut crosswise into ½-inch slices, before pitching yeast. For ease of removal, place in a separate straining bag.

This wine blends well with peach, plum, apricot, or pineapple wine. Do not overpower pluot. Bench blending trials are essential to get it right.

If sweetening, try using honey instead of sugar. At the end of the final 30-day wait period (after stabilization), carefully check to see if pollen has precipitated out of the honey. Do not disturb any fine lees when bottling. If in doubt, rack again, wait three days, and then bottle.

As with all fruit wines, because tasting can consume all of your wine, it is wise to bottle four 187-mL splits to use for that purpose.

Similar fruit: The following relatives can be substituted for pluots in this recipe: apriplum, aprium, plucot, plumcot.

Plum Wine ❖

The plum may be one of the first fruits ever cultivated. Three of the most abundant and significant cultivars are only found around human settlements, not in the wild, and plum pits have been found in Neolithic villages along with grapes, figs, and olives.

Plum wine and other fermented drinks are found worldwide wherever plums are cultivated, often adjacent to stands of wild plums. There are 13 separate species of wild plums native to the United States. Their fruit range from cherry size to as large as those of average cultivars. I once had a stand of 11 wild plum trees near my pear trees. They were about the size of cherries, were yellow-green-skinned that turned lightly blushed when ripe, and made the best plum wine I have ever made or tasted. The blight that took out my pear trees also took out the plum trees.

Worldwide, there are about 40 species of plum, with many varieties and cultivars. Interestingly, only three varieties account for the majority of the world's plum production. China produces about 55% of the world's total tonnage.

Plums vary in taste from sweet to tart, from bland to astringent, from juicy and yielding to those with compact, hard flesh. The best-tasting plums combine juicy sweetness with crisp acidity. The tannins responsible for astringency are confined to the skin, but only in certain species. When making plum wine, the skin is almost always included in the fermentation. Without it, even plums with red flesh would produce a white or, at most, a blush wine. Even with the skin, colored plum wines are the exception rather than the norm.

Distilling plum wine to make plum brandy or other spirits probably began as soon as distilling was invented. I have the last bottle of a plum brandy I made 25 years ago. I only bring it out for special guests or when I want to feel its warm glow inside.

JACK'S TIP

THIS RECIPE uses white grape juice concentrate to add body. Before the convenience of the frozen concentrates, we had to chop or mince white raisins to accomplish the same thing—or use bananas, dates, or other body-builders. The concentrate gives a better fermentation and helps with the balance of the wine. Depending on the plum variety and color of its skin and flesh, either red or white grape concentrate might be used.

We can expect the pH to be near where we want it, albeit possibly a little low. On the other hand, TA is generally where we want it. But, since we will be ameliorating the must, the TA will drop and needs to be raised. Raising the TA without seriously affecting an already low pH is a tricky business. We'll raise the pH with calcium carbonate, then add a weak acid such as citric acid to raise the TA. Because its concentration is weak, it will have some but not much of an effect on the pH. While this adjustment is crucial to the balance of the wine, we should not rely on numbers alone. Let your taste buds have a say. We're making this to drink, not just to satisfy some formula.

Because we will likely have a low pH must, we'll use Lalvin DV10 yeast, a strain known to do well in low pH conditions. It is also a good choice for fruit wines and will ferment to dryness.

As with other stone fruit, we must keep in mind that plums are a malic fruit. We absolutely must keep the free SO_2 level well above 20 mg/L to prevent MLF, which is why we try to maintain it at 50 mg/L, then raise it for bottling and aging. Remember, up to half of what we add will become bound very quickly.

Plum Wine Recipe

WINE IS READY IN: **9 months**

YOU'LL NEED: **6 pounds fresh plums, 1 can frozen 100 percent white grape juice concentrate per gallon of wine**

ADDITIONAL EQUIPMENT: **1 nylon straining bag**

MAKES: **1 gallon, but can be scaled up**

INGREDIENTS

6 lb. plums

1 can 100 percent white grape juice frozen concentrate, thawed

1 lb., 10 oz. very fine granulated sugar

water to make 1 gal.

1 tsp powdered pectic enzyme

⅛ tsp grape tannins

acid correction, as needed

potassium metabisulfite, as needed

½ tsp potassium sorbate

1 tsp (3 g) yeast nutrient

1 g Fermaid-K

Lalvin DV10 yeast

DIRECTIONS

Prepare must: Bring 2 quarts water to a boil, remove from heat, and stir in sugar until dissolved. Concurrently, wash, destem, pit, chop plums and tie closed in nylon straining bag. In the primary, mash plums to release as much juice as possible. Pour sugar-water over plums. Cover and set aside to cool. When lukewarm, dissolve yeast nutrient and tannin in 1 cup of juice and stir into the primary. Add water to make 1 gallon. Test juice for pH. Adjust acidity as necessary to bring pH to 3.1–3.3. Wait 4 hours and add 0.2 g potassium metabisulfite, stir well, cover primary, and set aside for 12 hours. Add pectic enzyme, stirring until completely dissolved. Re-cover primary and set aside 12 hours.

Add yeast: To 1 cup warm water (not to exceed 102 degrees F.) add a pinch of yeast nutrient and stir to dissolve. Add yeast to water, stir, and cover mixture for 30 minutes. Add to primary and stir well.

Fermentation: Gently squeeze bag several times daily for five days. Remove bag to a large bowl and squeeze firmly to expel remaining juice. Suspend the bag over the bowl and squeeze every 15 minutes for 1 hour. Add juice to primary and discard plum pulp. Meanwhile, when SG drops to 1.060 dissolve 1 gram Fermaid-K in 1 cup of juice and add to primary, stirring well. When SG drops to 1.020, or lower if the fermentation is still vigorous, transfer to secondary and affix airlock. Ferment to dryness.

Post-Fermentation: Move wine to a dark, cool place for 30 days and rack. Repeat this every 30 days until wine clears. Correct imperfect clarity with pectic enzyme and, if necessary, two-part fining. If fined, wait four days and rack again. Add 0.2 g potassium metabisulfite and ½ teaspoon dissolved potassium sorbate. Stir well to integrate additives. Sweeten to taste or to balance. If sweetened, wait 30 days to ensure there's no renewed fermentation and carefully rack into bottles. This wine can be consumed after six months, but if not up to expectations age it another six months. It will improve immensely with age.

Options: To add body, add one or two very ripe bananas, cut crosswise into ½-inch slices, before pitching yeast. For ease of removal, place in a separate straining bag.

This wine blends well with blackberry wine. Do not overpower the plum. Bench blending trials will assist you greatly.

When sweetening this wine at the end, honey or Demerara sugar will add complexity.

As with all fruit wines, because tasting can consume all of your wine, it is wise to bottle four 187-mL splits to use for that purpose.

Similar fruit: The following relatives can be substituted for plums in this recipe: apriplum, aprium, pluot, plucot, plumcot, wild plum.

Quince Wine ❖

The lowly quince looks much like a pear on the outside and resembles an apple on the inside, only with more seeds. It tastes like neither. At a local wine competition several years ago, a judge had to evaluate a quince wine. Unfamiliar with the fruit, he asked the other judges what a quince tasted like. One replied, "Like an unripe apple with acid on steroids."

Of the dozen or so species of quince, only two produce fruit, which, when fully ripe, can be eaten raw. All others require that the flesh be boiled, broiled, stewed, or peeled and roasted before it can be considered edible. Even the two edible species improve in flavor when cooked.

But wherever the quince grows, there are fermented quince drinks, some quite ancient in origin and similar to beer in alcohol and others quite remarkable. Double distillation of quince wine produces several locally popular spirits.

JACK'S TIP

THE QUINCE has a pH that ranges from marginally low to high. Their TA is generally where we want it, although it can be low. This seems paradoxical for a fruit known for its searing acidity, but the acidity drops as the fruit ripens. Usually, the TA is correct for this wine, but will be diluted with amelioration and need correction.

Quince wine possesses a strong, individualistic bouquet. The fruit itself is quite aromatic. A bowl of the fruit was once placed in gathering or social rooms to take advantage of the aromas.

Quince wine can be quite problematic in several ways. If the fruit's pulp is over-cooked, the wine will resist clarifying as its high pectin will set. If the cooked pulp is squeezed rather than drip drained, the wine will resist clarifying as even more pectin is driven from the pulp.

If any yeast but Montrachet is used, the wine can take an extraordinarily long time to ferment to dryness, and even Montrachet, a legendary fast fermenter, will be slowed by the quince.

Finally, the wine will not impress the drinker until it has aged from 18 to 24 months. It is still drinkable, although unremarkable, when young. Like some flower and root wines, this is one for the future. Bottle it, cellar it, and forget it. I aged my quince wine 2½ years before it began to show promise. After another six months, I was quite proud of it.

Quince Wine Recipe

WINE IS READY IN: **21 months**

YOU'LL NEED: **20 quinces, 1 can frozen 100 percent white grape juice concentrate per gallon of wine**

ADDITIONAL EQUIPMENT: **1 nylon straining bag**

MAKES: **1 gallon, but can be scaled up**

INGREDIENTS

20 quinces

1 can 100 percent white grape juice frozen concentrate, thawed

1 lb., 10 oz. very fine granulated sugar

water to make 1 gal.

1½ tsp powdered pectic enzyme

⅛ tsp grape tannins

acid correction, as needed

potassium metabisulfite, as needed

½ tsp potassium sorbate

1 tsp (3 g) yeast nutrient

Red Star Montrachet yeast

DIRECTIONS

Prepare must: Wash, destem, and grate the skin and fruit as close to their cores without including any seeds. Place grated pulp in sufficient boiling water to cover and boil for 15 minutes and no longer. Pour into nylon straining bag in primary and drip drain (do not squeeze!) about an hour or until no more liquid is evident. You can save the pulp for marmalade or discard it. Cover the primary and allow it to cool to room temperature. Meanwhile, add the grape concentrate and water to make 1 gallon. Stir in yeast nutrient and tannin. Test for pH. Correct as needed. Add 0.2 g potassium metabisulfite, stir well, cover primary, and set aside for 12 hours. Add pectic enzyme, stirring until completely dissolved. Re-cover primary and set aside 12 hours.

Add yeast: To 1 cup warm water (not to exceed 102 degrees F.) add a pinch of yeast nutrient and stir to dissolve. Add yeast to juice, stir, and cover mixture for 30 minutes. Add to primary and stir well.

Fermentation: Set aside in a warm place for three days. Strain into secondary and affix airlock. Do not rack until wine clears, then rack every 60 days until SG registers dryness.

Post-Fermentation: Rack, add 0.2 g potassium metabisulfite, stir in ½ tsp dissolved potassium sorbate, and sweeten to taste (although the taste at this point will not be impressive). Move wine to a dark, cool place for 30 days. Carefully rack into bottles.

Similar fruit: None.

CHAPTER SEVEN
TROPICAL FRUIT WINES

By definition, tropical fruit are fruit that are native to the tropics. There are thousands of tropical fruits, but just because a plant is native to the tropics doesn't mean it also isn't native elsewhere. Most citrus species are considered tropical even though some are native to both the tropics and the subtropics. Olives, figs, persimmons, and avocados are both tropical and subtropical.

In this book, we treat citrus species as tropical fruits, while figs and persimmons were treated as temperate fruit. This decision was based on the very wide distribution of native figs and persimmons while citrus species had rather limited native distributions until man intervened. Through DNA analysis, we now know that all commercial citrus we know today were derived by natural and assisted hybridization from a handful of original wild species—including the citron (possibly the oldest), the pomelo and mandarin—and to a lesser extent the papedas and kumquat (also possibly the oldest).

As with all country wines, we are reminded that there is a magic number when it comes to alcohol, and that number is 12% ABV. This is the level at which the wine is mostly biologically stable. "Mostly" is a key word. When we add sulfites to the 12% ABV wine, we close the gap considerably, as there are few microbes that can exist in 12% ABV wine with 50 mg/L of free SO_2. 12% ABV is also the number that pretty much assures you that the wine will last at least 18 months before heading south. A 10–11 percent ABV wine should be consumed within a year.

So if 12% ABV is good, then 14% ought to be better, right? No! Wine is much easier to balance at 12% ABV than at 14%. And in the end, it's all about balance—the counterplay between acid, tannins, alcohol, and sugar. White grape wines, because they lack tannin, rely on higher acidity levels to achieve balance. In our white wines, we add a little tannin to assist in balancing the wine.

Unless we are making a very high alcohol wine, what would be a fortified wine in traditional grape wines, country wines should never exceed 13.5% ABV. Above that, you're likely to have balance problems. Play it safe and stay within the guidelines of the recipes. This is especially applicable with tropical fruit wines, where you'll often have your hands full when adjusting acidity. Don't complicate things unnecessarily.

While all fruit in the previous chapter were predominately malic in acidity, most of the fruit in this chapter will have mostly citric acid and possibly great amounts of it. As such, the TA of these fruits may be quite high while the pH is not necessarily very low. Reducing the TA will be done through amelioration, but lowering the pH should be done with tartaric acid. If the resulting TA still seems quite high, let your taste buds help determine if this is actually the case. If so, then the wine will have to be sweetened at the end to counter the acidity. In cases where the pH is low, the wine should be deacidified using calcium carbonate, and the resulting TA raised with citric acid.

Citric acid is inherently unstable. That doesn't mean it's going to disappear, but a bit of it will along the way. The result is a softer, rounder wine. Just keep the sulfites up to protect the wine and the citric acid.

Table 9. Acid and Sugar Characteristics of Some Tropical Fruit

FRUIT	PH	TA RANGE (g/L)	PERCENT SUGAR	MAJOR ORGANIC ACID	MINOR ORGANIC ACID
Banana	5.00–5.30	3.00	15.60	Malic	Oxalic, Citric
Grapefruit	3.00–3.80	20.00	6.20	Citric	Malic
Lemon	2.00–2.60	7.00–50.00	2.50	Citric	Malic
Lime	2.00–2.80	5.00–50.00	0.40	Citric	Malic, Fumaric
Loquat	3.80	9.00–14.00	3.50	Malic	Citric, Succinic
Mango	3.40–4.80	4.20	14.80	Citric	Malic, Tartaric
Orange	3.70–4.30	12.00–15.00	8.90	Citric	Malic
Passionfruit	2.70–3.30	23.00	11.20	Citric	Malic, Lactic
Pineapple	3.20–4.00	11.00	11.90–15.00	Citric	Malic
Pomegranate	3.00–3.20	12.00	8.90	Citric	Malic, Tartaric
Star Fruit	3.40	12.50	0.60-9.40	Oxalic	Tartaric, Citric
Tangerine	3.30–4.50	4.00–6.50	8.70	Citric	Malic, Fumaric

Data for Table 9 were collected from a wide variety of sources, on the internet, and from print. Since many of these fruits are cultivated throughout the Northern Hemisphere, care was taken to seek values representative of American harvests.

In this chapter, we'll be examining methods for making wine from the twelve fruit presented in Table 9. The recipes are only guidelines. Since many of these fruits are very acidic, test for actual pH and TA and adjust according to the values you obtain. As can be seen from Table 9, there is a great deal of variability in actual values that were measured, but the fruit you obtain should be consumer-oriented and not out in the extremes.

Again, I say recipes are only guidelines and mean just that. The timelines they present are based on those experienced by the recipe's author. Your timelines may differ for no other reason than your fermentation is faster or slower, or your wine clears faster or slower than the author's. No two batches are ever the same. I know several winemakers whose wine has completely fermented to dryness in 24–36 hours. That's not supposed to happen, but it has.

When possible, I have provided recipe measurements in common fractions of teaspoons that correspond with the fractions of a gram actually required for the additives. The only exception to this is the amount of potassium metabisulfite needed to maintain free SO_2 at 50 mg/L or above. The last sulfite addition will only be accurate if you test the wine's sulfite level with your SO_2 test kit and adjust the free SO_2 to 100 mg/L for bottling. This should even out any deviations and ensure your wine is prepared for a 2- to 3-year cellar-life expectancy. The formula for calculating this final addition is in Chapter 2 (page 71). However, there are many online sulfite calculators that will compute the result for you if you are not confident of your math skills. You'll still have to use your SO_2 test kit to obtain the numbers needed for the calculator.

For some fruit, the range of acidity is too great to accurately predict a probable pH and TA, so in the recipe you'll be asked to measure the actual pH, as a minimum, and adjust acid accordingly to bring the wine within a pH 3.2–3.5 window.

If you have made any of the wines in the previous chapters, by now you should be comfortable with the testing and adjustment routines—routines are all they are. The more wine you make, the more routine it will become. So get out there and get used to the routine. My advice, as always, is to keep those yeast working.

Banana Wine ❖

Banana wine is usually made for blending but it was (and is) a wine in and of itself. It is made in varying quantities, both commercially and privately, in many islands and countries in the tropics, with larger productions in Africa and India. It is also popular as a base wine for various herbs, spices, juices, or extracts.

Banana wines can be made to have high alcohol content, but it drinks better (and sooner) at 12–13 percent ABV.

JACK'S TIP

WE ARE GOING TO MAKE a heavy-bodied banana wine. This recipe can be the jumping-off point for any number of flavored wines, but I suggest you make it "pure" the first time just to experience its color and flavor. It can also be blended with any wine that lacks body.

If you are blessed enough to have a market nearby that offers a variety of bananas, it is advisable that around one-fourth of your total vary from the common table or dessert varieties Big Banana pushes on us. Bananas to choose from include different species, such as red bananas, dwarf bananas, fig bananas, etc.—but not plantains—as well as different varieties of what are known as dessert bananas (probably the only banana in your local market, but we can hope), usually referred to in the marketing world as Cavendish bananas.

Avoid buying green or green-tinted bananas or even the brightest yellow ones. For making wine, we want ripe to very ripe fruit (technically, bananas are berries). These are bananas that have begun developing brown spots on the skins. This is when they are approaching their sweetest and it's a good time to buy them. In another day or two, the market will replace them with new bananas. Actually, you might ask the produce manager if he will give you a reduced price on five pounds of brown-spotted bananas. Very often, they will accommodate you, so it's worth a shot.

Bananas are mostly water and starch, with a small amount of acid, natural sugars, some vitamins and minerals, and pectin. That starch is naturally broken down by enzymes as the fruit ripens and is converted into additional sugars. You cannot coax them out of the fruit as juice because no matter how ripe the flesh gets: when you press it, you get mush. In order to bring that additional sugar out, we'll supplement the two major enzymes a bit and then rely on the yeast to find them for us, along with major flavor and aroma compounds. For this, we'll add pectinase (pectic enzyme) and amylase (starch enzyme). Of course, we'll also add acid and sugar

Surprisingly, we'll also be fermenting the banana peels. They contain some of the sugar, some acid, a small amount of tannin, but also a lot of the aroma and flavor compounds we associate with the banana. We want all of that in our wine.

This recipe calls for procedures different than for other wines. At first reading, they sound really complicated, but if you follow them closely you will be rewarded.

Banana Wine Recipe

WINE IS READY IN: **16 months**

YOU'LL NEED: **4½ pounds bananas per gallon of wine**

ADDITIONAL EQUIPMENT: **1–2 nylon straining bags**

MAKES: **1 gallon, but can be scaled up**

INGREDIENTS

4½ lb. bananas

1 lb., 14 oz. sugar

½ tsp pectic enzyme

½ tsp amylase

⅛ tsp grape tannin

acid correction, as needed

potassium metabisulfite, as needed

½ tsp potassium sorbate

1 g Fermaid-K

1 tsp (3 g) yeast nutrient

Lalvin ICV-D47 (Côtes du Rhône) yeast

DIRECTIONS

Prepare must: Put 1 quart water on to boil. Meanwhile, slice bananas cross-wise through peel and flesh, about ½-inch slices. Put banana slices in fine-meshed, nylon straining bag and set in your primary. Mash with your hands or a masher. When water boils, remove from heat and add sugar, stirring well to dissolve. When completely dissolved, pour over bananas. Cover the primary and set aside 30 minutes, then add water to make 1 gallon. Stir in amylase, grape tannins, and yeast nutrient.

Add yeast: Make a yeast starter solution (see Chapter 2), maintaining it at least 8 hours. Pour yeast starter over bananas.

Fermentation: Add 2 grams tartaric acid, stir well, and test juice for pH. Begin acid correction, if needed, to bring pH to 3.3. Squeeze bananas 3–4 times a day for ten days. Remove the bag of banana pulp to a large bowl and squeeze to extract as much juice as possible without forcing banana through the mesh. Discard banana pulp. When SG drops to 1.060 (may occur before removing bananas), remove 1 cup of juice and into it dissolve 1 g Fermaid-K, then stir into the primary. When SG drops to 1.020, or lower if the fermentation is still vigorous, carefully rack to secondary and affix airlock. Add pectic enzyme, stirring until completely dissolved. Re-cover primary and set aside 12 hours.

Post-Fermentation: After 60 days, carefully rack again. Repeat every 60 days until wine clears. If wine is dry when clear, add 0.2 g potassium metabisulfite and ½ teaspoon dissolved potassium sorbate, wait 24 hours, and rack. Sweeten to taste or to balance. After 30 days, correct clarity with pectic enzyme, amylase, or two-part fining only if necessary. If fined, wait four days and carefully rack into bottles. Allow one year before tasting, two years for the best results.

Options: To add complexity, put one tablespoon toasted bitter almond slivers or slices, one tablespoon unsweetened coconut flakes, and one split vanilla bean into a jelly bag until first racking. You might make a gallon of this wine for drinking and a gallon without the additions for blending.

This wine can be sweetened with honey for greater complexity. Most honey contains pollen, so check the bottom of secondary after 30 days for signs of a very light dusting of pollen. If present, very carefully rack and immediately rack again into bottles.

As with all fruit wines, because tasting can consume all of your wine, it is wise to bottle four 187-mL splits to use for that purpose.

Similar fruit: Except for other species of bananas, there really is no similar fruit.

Grapefruit Wine ❖

The grapefruit is a rather modern hybrid species; it originated in Barbados in the seventeenth century. It was almost certainly an accidental cross between the introduced pomelo and the sweet orange. Both parent species originated in Asia.

The flavor of subsequent varieties and cultivars can be sour to semi-sweet and somewhat bitter. The color of the pulp is either white (light yellowish-green), yellow, pink, or red. A few purple varieties have been bred, but they aren't commercially available yet.

Almost as soon as the grapefruit was widely harvested the practice of making wine from the fruit appeared. Since the only acid correction at the time was amelioration, the wine was often sweetened at the end to achieve balance. It was sometimes made very sweet and served as a dessert wine. Sweetening was usually with raw sugar or molasses, both of which produced hues of light brown—today considered unsightly. Tannin was added in the form of a cup of black tea, further browning the wine. Today, molasses is either a cultural or an acquired taste. Adding refined sugar or honey is far more common, as is adding powdered grape tannin.

Among households with two or more grapefruit trees, grapefruit wine is often a staple, made in quantity to utilize the crop. When 5, 10, or 15 or more gallons are made annually, batches can easily be divided and various blends with other fruit done experimentally. This is how several successful blends became popularized.

Blends with wines from wild grapes, rhubarb, dark berries, pears, apples, and even peaches have been seen at competitions. The most novel blend this author has seen was grapefruit and nettle-tips. The maker of that wine, which was quite good, explained that he purposely made his nettle-tip wine with low acidity just to blend it with his grapefruit. He said he had similarly blended nettle-tip wine with lemon wine.

Right up front, I have to warn anyone taking prescription medication(s) of any kind to check with your doctor or pharmacist to determine if grapefruit juice interacts negatively with any of your medications. Negative reactions can be quite severe, so play it safe and check.

JACK'S TIP

WE WILL BE MAKING a dry wine and sweetening it at the end. It can be made with white, pink, or red grapefruit.

We will be adding 100% White Grape Juice Frozen Concentrate for body. We also encourage you to use the sweetest grapefruit you can find, if you're buying them.

Any Texas Red cultivar will do (there are several, some sweet and others sweeter). If you are using fruit from your own tree, use what you have and buy more sugar.

We will also thinly grate the outer skin of 2 or 3 grapefruit, depending on their size, and add this to the peeled, mashed pulp. This necessitates that you first wash the fruit very thoroughly. On store-bought citrus fruit destined for wine, I use a soapy bath and a scrub brush, then rinse completely.

Grapefruit may be frozen (optional) 5 days, then thawed completely before using (about one day).

Grapefruit Wine Recipe

WINE IS READY IN: **19 months**

YOU'LL NEED: **6 large grapefruit, 1 can frozen 100 percent white grape juice concentrate per gallon of wine**

ADDITIONAL EQUIPMENT: **1 nylon straining bag**

MAKES: **1 gallon, but can be scaled up**

INGREDIENTS

6 large grapefruit

1 can 100 percent white grape juice frozen concentrate, thawed

1 lb., 12 oz. very fine granulated sugar

water to make 1 gal.

1 tsp pectic enzyme

½ tsp grape tannin powder

calcium carbonate to bring acid to pH 3.3–3.4

potassium metabisulfite, as needed

½ tsp potassium sorbate

1 tsp (3 g) yeast nutrient

Lalvin R2 yeast (5 g)

DIRECTIONS

Prepare must: Scrub grapefruit clean. Put ½ gallon water on to boil while thinly grating peelings of 2–3 grapefruit. Put gratings in nylon straining bags. Peel grapefruit and remove all pith. Section all fruit and place in bag with zest, tie closed. Put the bag in a primary. Squeeze the segments to liberate juice. Add tannin, yeast nutrient, and grape juice concentrate to the primary. Remove boiling water from heat and stir in 1 pound sugar until completely dissolved. Pour over grapefruit, add additional water to increase the liquid to 1 gallon, cover primary, and set aside to cool. Test juice for pH. Begin acid correction, as needed, to bring pH to 3.3. Add 0.2 g potassium metabisulfite and stir well. Cover the primary and wait 12 hours. Add pectic enzyme, stirring until completely dissolved. Set aside 12 hours.

Add yeast: To 1 cup warm water (not to exceed 102 degrees F.) add a pinch of yeast nutrient and stir to dissolve. Add yeast to water, stir, and cover mixture for 30 minutes. Add mixture to primary and cover primary.

Fermentation: Squeeze nylon straining bag 4–6 times a day. Check SG daily. When SG drops to 1.060, remove nylon straining bag and drip drain (do not squeeze) over a large bowl for 1 hour. Discard grapefruit pulp and pour juice into the primary. Re-cover primary. Continue checking SG daily and when at 1.020, or lower if the fermentation is still vigorous, carefully transfer to secondary, then affix airlock. In 30 days, carefully rack.

Post-Fermentation: Move wine to a dark, cool place for 60 days and carefully rack. Rack again when wine clears. Correct clarity as necessary with pectic enzyme and 2-part fining. If fined, wait four days and rack. Add 0.2 g potassium metabisulfite and ½ teaspoon dissolved potassium sorbate. Stir well and sweeten to taste or to balance. If sweetened, wait 30 days to ensure no renewed fermentation and carefully rack into bottles. Allow nine months or more in bottles before tasting.

Options: This wine can be sweetened with honey for greater complexity. Most honey contains pollen, so check the bottom of secondary after 30 days for signs of a very light dusting of pollen. If present, very carefully rack and immediately rack again into bottles.

   If you want to add some color to your wine, adding 15 dried elderberries can permanently color the wine, impart a hint of flavor, and add needed tannin. This addition is totally optional and not part of the recipe, but if elderberries are added, then eliminate the powdered grape tannin.

Similar fruit: The following fruit can be substituted for grapefruit in this recipe: pomelo, oroblanco, ugli.

Lemon Wine ❖

The lemon is a natural hybrid of the citron and bitter orange. It is slightly more acidic than the lime, nearly twice as acidic as the grapefruit, and about five times as acidic as the Valencia orange. Despite this acidity, it was enjoyed as lemon wine long before it was enjoyed as lemon pie.

JACK'S TIP

LEMONS are typically fermented with other fruit or sometimes ginger and spices to make it more drinkable.

Because a great deal of water is required to dilute the lemon's acidity to palatability, the finished wine is thin and lacks character. We will correct both by adding grape juice concentrate for body and lemon zest for character.

Lemon Wine Recipe

WINE IS READY IN: **13 months**

YOU'LL NEED: **8 medium-size lemons, 1 can frozen 100 percent white grape juice concentrate per gallon of wine**

ADDITIONAL EQUIPMENT: **1 nylon straining bag**

MAKES: **1 gallon, but can be scaled up**

INGREDIENTS

8 medium-size lemons

1 can 100 percent white grape juice frozen concentrate, thawed

1 lb., 10 oz. sugar

water to make 1 gal.

1 tsp pectic enzyme

¼ tsp grape tannin powder

calcium carbonate as necessary

potassium metabisulfite, as needed

½ tsp potassium sorbate

1 tsp (3 g) yeast nutrient

Lalvin R2 yeast (5 g)

DIRECTIONS

Prepare must: Scrub lemons clean. Put ½ gallon water on to boil while thinly grating peelings of 2 lemons. Put gratings in a nylon straining bag. Peel lemons and remove all pith. Section all fruit and place in the bag, tie closed. Put the bag in a primary. Squeeze the segments to expel juice. Add tannins, yeast nutrient, and thawed grape juice concentrate to the primary. Remove boiling water from heat and stir in sugar until completely dissolved. Pour over lemons, add additional water to increase the liquid to 1 gallon, cover primary, and set aside to cool. When cooled, test juice for pH. Begin acid correction as needed (see calcium carbonate, page 45). Add 0.2 g potassium metabisulfite, stir well, cover primary, and set aside for 12 hours. Add pectic enzyme, stirring until completely dissolved. Re-cover primary and set aside 12 hours.

Add yeast: To 1 cup warm water (not to exceed 102 degrees F.) add a pinch of yeast nutrient, 1 teaspoon of sugar, and stir to dissolve. Add yeast to water, stir, and cover mixture for 30 minutes. Add mixture to primary, stir, and cover primary.

Fermentation: Squeeze nylon straining bag 4–6 times a day. When SG drops to 1.060, remove nylon straining bag and drip drain (squeeze gently every 15 minutes) over a large bowl for 1 hour. Discard lemon pulp and pour juice into the primary. Re-cover primary. When SG is at 1.020, or lower if the fermentation is still vigorous, transfer to secondary and affix airlock. In 30 days, carefully rack.

Post-Fermentation: Move wine to a dark, cool place for 60 days and carefully rack. Rack again when wine clears. Correct clarity with pectic enzyme and, if necessary, two-part fining. If fined, wait four days and rack. Add 0.2 g potassium metabisulfite and ½ teaspoon dissolved potassium sorbate, stirring well. Sweeten to taste or to balance. If sweetened, wait 30 days to ensure no renewed fermentation and carefully rack into bottles. Allow nine months (one year is better) in bottles before tasting.

Options: This wine can be sweetened with honey for greater complexity. Most honey contains pollen, so check the bottom of secondary after 30 days for signs of a very light dusting of pollen. If present, very carefully rack and immediately rack again into bottles.

This wine blends very well with lime wine. Running bench tasting trials is essential to getting it right.

As with all fruit wines, because tasting can consume all of your wine, it is wise to bottle four 187-mL splits to use for that purpose.

Similar fruit: The following fruit can be substituted for lemons in this recipe: Meyer lemon, lime, kaffir lime, Key lime, Sorrento lemon, citron, bitter orange.

Lime Wine ❖

For some reason, it seems like I've seen more lime wines at competitions than lemon. I could be wrong. But either way, it tells me a lot of people are making lime wines, including key lime and novelty wines. I learned from Martin Benke how to make a margarita-style wine he calls Lime-A-Rita and I call Key-Lime-A-Rita.

I have not yet found historical information on when lime wines first appeared in the literature. However, I have no doubt they were made soon after limes became a steady harvest.

There are several species, varieties, and cultivars of lime. With the exception of the key lime, their names are seldom revealed at large supermarkets. The Key Lime is the smallest and also known as the Mexican Lime. This tiny wonder is the least juicy of the limes, with only 40 percent by weight being juice, and yet they are often cited as the best, most "limey" tasting of the limes. The Bearss Seedless, also known as the Tahitian and the Persian Lime, is about the size of a small-to-medium lemon and packed with juice but not as flavorful as the Key Lime. The Sweet Lime is seedy but juicy and only relatively sweet.

JACK'S TIP

LIME WINES are a challenge because of their high acidity, but no more so than lemon wines. The key is raising the pH so as not to stress the yeast into inactivity. At the same time, TA is already high, and raising the pH drives it higher. Water dilution can only go so far, and so lime wines, like lemon wines, tend to finish with high TA, but you can sweeten to taste or balance at the end.

This recipe assumes the Persian Lime will be used because it is by far the most commercially available lime. The limes should be juiced and the hollowed skins discarded. Fermenting the skins extracts too much something-or-other from the exposed pith inside the hollowed leftovers and ruins the wine—there is nothing you can do to correct it.

The recipe calls for the zest of 3–4 limes—4 if smaller limes, 3 if larger. The limes should be washed well and dried before zesting. The zest is easier to make if the limes are first frozen and zested while frozen. When thawed, they will give up their juice easier, and you might have a slight increase in volume.

I cannot predict how much juice you will get from a given number of limes. It all depends on their size, whether or not they have seeds, and how ripe they are when juiced. If the skin is still lime green when juiced, they were underripe. Limes turn yellow as they ripen and, when fully ripe, can resemble a lemon. Whether the number is 10 limes or 12, you will need 2 cups of juice, so buy a couple more than you think you might need just in case. The juice from leftovers can be effectively used on roasted or grilled chicken and salmon, trout, catfish, or other swimmers.

Finally, remove all seeds from the juice. Their phenolic signature will only taint the wine. Even the seedless limes have an occasional seed, so take nothing for granted.

Lime Wine Recipe

WINE IS READY IN: **18 months**

YOU'LL NEED: **10–12 medium-size limes, 1 can frozen 100 percent white grape juice concentrate per gallon of wine**

ADDITIONAL EQUIPMENT: **nothing beyond the basics**

MAKES: **1 gallon, but can be scaled up**

INGREDIENTS

10–12 medium-size limes

1 can 100 percent white grape juice frozen concentrate, thawed

1 lb., 12 oz. very finely granulated sugar

water to make 1 gal.

1 tsp pectic enzyme

½ tsp grape tannin powder

calcium carbonate as necessary

potassium metabisulfite, as needed

½ tsp potassium sorbate

1 tsp (3 g) yeast nutrient

Lalvin R2 yeast (5 g)

DIRECTIONS

Prepare must: Scrub limes clean. Put ½ gallon water on to boil while thinly grating peelings of 3 limes. Put gratings in nylon straining bags. Peel limes and remove all pith. Section all fruit and place in the bag, tie closed and put in primary. Squeeze the segments to free juice. Add tannin, yeast nutrient, and thawed grape juice concentrate to the primary. Remove boiling water from heat and stir in sugar until completely dissolved. Pour over limes, add additional water to make 1 gallon, cover primary, and set aside to cool. When cool, test juice for pH. Begin acid correction as needed (see calcium carbonate, page 45). Add 0.2 g potassium metabisulfite, stir well, cover primary, and set aside for 12 hours. Add pectic enzyme, stirring until completely dissolved. Re-cover primary and set aside 12 hours.

Add yeast: To 1 cup warm water (not to exceed 102 degrees F.) add a pinch of yeast nutrient, 1 teaspoon of sugar, and stir to dissolve. Add yeast to water, stir, and cover mixture for 30 minutes. Add mixture to primary, stir, and cover primary.

Fermentation: Squeeze nylon straining bag 4–6 times a day until SG drops to 1.060, remove nylon straining bag and drip drain (squeeze gently every 15 minutes) over a large bowl for 1 hour. Discard lime pulp and pour juice into primary. Re-cover primary. When SG drops to 1.020, or lower if the fermentation is still vigorous, transfer to secondary and affix airlock. In 30 days, carefully rack.

Post-Fermentation: Move wine to a dark, cool place for 60 days and carefully rack. Rack again in 60 days or when wine clears. Correct clarity with pectic enzyme and, if necessary, two-part fining. If fined, wait four days and rack. Add 0.2 g potassium metabisulfite and ½ teaspoon dissolved potassium sorbate. Stir well. Sweeten to taste or to balance. If sweetened, wait 30 days to ensure no renewed fermentation and carefully rack into bottles. Do not taste or sample this wine for 12 months. Doing so will only disappoint you, and you will have opened a bottle for no good reason.

Options: This wine can be sweetened with honey for greater complexity. Most honey contains pollen, so check the bottom of secondary after 30 days for signs of a very light dusting of pollen. If present, very carefully rack and immediately rack again into bottles.

Adding a few basil leaves to the maturation phase for 30 days adds a unique freshness to this wine. It also makes a good base for margaritas.

Adding a few sprigs of cilantro to the maturation phase for 10–15 days (no longer) turns the wine into a South-of-the-Border treat, especially served chilled on a hot afternoon with tortilla chips and salsa.

This wine blends very well with other wines such as banana or coconut. Running bench tasting trials is essential to getting it right.

Since there is no recipe for coconut wine in this book, adding three tablespoons of coconut flakes (not shredded) to the must before fermentation begins adds an interesting flavor to the wine. Using lightly toasted flakes makes it easier to clear the wine.

Similar fruit: The following fruit can be substituted for limes in this recipe. Kusai Lime, Key lime, sweet lime, citron, bitter orange.

Loquat Wine ❖

Often called the Japanese or Chinese Plum, the loquat is actually more closely related to the apple and pear than the plum, yet remains as the lone species in its own genus. Cultivated for more than 1,000 years, many varieties exist and over 200 cultivars have been developed.

The tree is unusual in that it flowers in the late fall or early winter and begins fruiting in the spring through early summer. The fruit develop several large seeds that can easily be germinated in pots but need to be transplanted after 4–5 months.

The mature fruit are yellow to gold to golden-orange, often with a light rose blush, somewhat resembling the apricot. They are moderately juicy, sweet to slightly tart, and are easily processed into jams, jellies and are used in various cuisines and as pastry fillings and pies. They are sometimes substituted for apricots in cooking. Finally, they make very good wine.

Although native to China, the loquat spread east, southeast, south, and into southwestern Asia. It wasn't widely used in winemaking until the plant was exported to the Mediterranean basin and north into the Balkans, although it may have been so utilized in India, Iran, and elsewhere without being recorded.

This recipe calls for fresh fruit. Fresh means no more than two days after being picked. If you cannot make the wine in that timetable, freeze the fruit for later use. It deteriorates in quality quickly after being picked. This recipe also uses white grape juice concentrate to add body to the wine. Golden raisins or sultanas, chopped or minced, can be substituted for the grape juice.

JACK'S TIP

WE CAN EXPECT the pH to be near where we want it, but TA will usually be a little (or quite) high. The high TA is noticeable in a few varieties as a mild tartness, but usually, it is masked by the loquat's sweetness, which is remarkable for a fruit with relatively low natural sugar. Despite adding tartaric acid to adjust pH, additional acid will have to be added after amelioration.

The recipe calls for 4½ pounds of fresh loquats. Do not exceed this amount or the wine may be difficult to balance. I have made this wine with 4, 4½, 5, and 6 pounds of fruit, and 4 is the easiest to balance, while 4½ just requires you to tweak the acids carefully when you make it.

The recipe says to chop the fruit. Do not, under any circumstances, mash the fruit or put it in a food processor, blender, or juicer. If you do, the wine may take as long as a year to clear.

Toss out any damaged or bruised fruit. To chop the fruit correctly, first destem it and then cut it lengthwise, remove the seeds. Then cut each half, with the skin-side on the cutting board and the pulp-side up, crosswise into thirds or fourths (depending on size). It takes time, but it is worth it.

Loquat wine only expresses the fruit's natural character when served semi-sweet to sweet. We will be fermenting the wine to absolute dryness, stabilize it, mature it, and then sweeten it to taste or to balance. This is different than most methods we have followed thus far. Just follow the recipe and you'll be rewarded.

Loquat Wine Recipe

WINE IS READY IN: 12 months

YOU'LL NEED: 4½ pounds fresh loquats, ½ can frozen 100 percent white grape juice concentrate per gallon of wine

ADDITIONAL EQUIPMENT: 1–2 nylon straining bags

MAKES: 1 gallon, but can be scaled up

INGREDIENTS

4½ lb. loquats

½ can 100 percent white grape juice frozen concentrate, thawed

1 tsp powdered pectic enzyme

⅛ tsp grape tannins

1 lb., 14 oz. very finely granulated sugar

acid correction, as needed

potassium metabisulfite, as needed

½ tsp potassium sorbate

1 tsp (3 g) yeast nutrient

Lalvin EC-1118 yeast

DIRECTIONS

Prepare must: Add sugar to 1 quart of hot water and stir to dissolve completely. Destem, wash, de-seed, and chop loquats as described above and tie closed in nylon straining bag in a primary. To the primary, add sugar-water, grape concentrate, tannin, and yeast nutrient. Test juice for pH and begin acid correction if needed. Add water to make 1 gallon and stir to integrate. Add 0.2 g potassium metabisulfite, stir well, cover primary, and set aside for 12 hours. Add pectic enzyme, stirring until completely dissolved. Re-cover primary and set aside 12 hours.

Add yeast: To 1 cup warm water (not to exceed 102 degrees F.) add 1 teaspoon sugar and a pinch of yeast nutrient and stir to dissolve. Add yeast to water, stir, and cover mixture for 30 minutes.

Fermentation: Very gently squeeze bag 3–4 times daily for seven days. Remove the bag and hang over a large bowl to drip drain for 1 hour, squeezing very gently every 15 minutes. Add juice to primary and discard loquat pulp. When SG drops to 1.020, or lower if the fermentation is still vigorous, transfer to secondary and affix airlock. After 30 days, add 0.2 g potassium metabisulfite and stir well.

Post-Fermentation: Move wine to a dark, cool place, and rack every 30 days until wine clears. Correct clarity with pectic enzyme and, if necessary, 2-part fining. If fined, wait four days and rack. Add 0.2 g potassium metabisulfite and ½ teaspoon dissolved potassium sorbate. Set aside for 60 days. Sweeten to taste or to balance. If sweetened, wait 30 days to ensure no renewed fermentation and carefully rack into bottles. You can drink this wine after two months, but it will be much improved after six months. Consume within 18 months.

Options: This wine blends well with apricot, peach, or plum wine. Do not overpower the loquat. Bench blending trials are essential to get it right.

You can sweeten using honey instead of sugar. At the end of the final 30-day wait period (after sweetening), carefully check to see if pollen has precipitated out of the honey. If present, rack again, wait three days, and then bottle.

As with all fruit wines, because tasting can consume all of your wine, it is wise to bottle four 187-mL splits to use for that purpose.

Similar fruit: The following fruit can be substituted for loquats in this recipe: common apricot, Tibetan apricot, Manchurian apricot, Siberian apricot.

Mango Wine ❖

Mangoes are related to the cashew, pistachio, poison oak, and poison sumac, however unlikely that seems. Mango cultivation was referenced over 4,000 years ago in India and possibly began even earlier. Many varieties and over 500 cultivars exist, and more are being evaluated all the time.

A well-stocked, large produce department in an American supermarket will typically offer two or three cultivars of mango, although this is not always apparent. If you see an orangish-red mango, it is probably a Haden. If green with uneven ripening colors of yellow to red, it may well be a Kent. If it ripens to yellow, red, and purple, it is almost certainly a Tommie Atkins, the most commonly sold mango in the world. If it is long, thin and yellow, it is probably an Ataulfo and usually the only variety named except in markets carrying several varieties, in which case they may all be named. I have made wine from all of these cultivars, plus a couple of unusual ones I found in South Florida and hauled back to Texas in the trunk of my car.

Mangoes are appreciated for their distinctive aromatic flavor and delicious taste, in which acidity and sweetness are well-balanced. They have been described as a delicate blend of peach, pineapple, and apricot flavors, with the ripe flesh possessing a buttery texture, although it can sometimes be a bit fibrous. Immature fruits are usually dominated by citric acid, with malic, oxalic, succinic, and tartaric acids in that order. As the fruit ripens, malic emerges and in some varieties is dominant with citric a close second and tartaric a distant third. In most "New World" cultivars, citric still prevails, with malic, tartaric and succinic trailing.

There are several ways to make mango wine, a lusciously rich, fragrant, golden wine as unmistakably unique as dandelion or strawberry wine. The peels are never fermented as they contains a mouth and throat irritant. Fermenting the seed only produces off-notes that detract from the purity of flavors in the flesh.

The best flavor is obtained from fermenting the freshly juiced flesh. Fermenting the diced flesh is just a little less flavorful than fermenting the freshly made juice. Please notice that I've twice said fresh juice, not canned, and not reconstituted from concentrate. I would go with the recipe using freshly made juice, but not everyone has a centrifugal juicer. So here we will use diced mango flesh.

JACK'S TIP

MANGOES tend to have a pH that is a little high for wine, while concurrently having a TA that is decidedly low. Lowering the pH will raise the TA. Of course, when we ameliorate, the TA will drop again, so we need to think this through.

So our tactic will be to prepare the must and measure the actual pH and TA, then get the pH into a region you can fine-tune. The TA may be high by then, but perhaps not. But if it is, that is less important than an outside-the-window pH. In other words, we can counterbalance high TA with sugar, but only acid can affect pH.

Mango Wine Recipe

WINE IS READY IN: **12 months**

YOU'LL NEED: **4 pounds fresh mangoes, ½ can frozen 100 percent white grape juice concentrate per gallon of wine**

ADDITIONAL EQUIPMENT: **1 nylon straining bag**

MAKES: **1 gallon, but can be scaled up**

INGREDIENTS

4 lb. fresh, ripe mangoes

½ can 100 percent white grape juice frozen concentrate, thawed

1 tsp powdered pectic enzyme

⅛ tsp grape tannin

3–4 cups of sugar

acid correction, as needed

potassium metabisulfite, as needed

½ tsp potassium sorbate

1 tsp (3 g) yeast nutrient

Lalvin BA11 yeast

DIRECTIONS

Prepare must: Dissolve 3 cups of sugar thoroughly in 1 quart of hot water. Destem, peel, and cut up the mango flesh. Place flesh in a nylon straining bag and tie closed, Place bag in primary, and mash the fruit. Be careful, however, as the juice will stain clothing. To the primary, add sugar-water, grape concentrate, grape tannin, and yeast nutrient. Add additional water to make 1 gallon and stir to integrate. Measure SG and add more sugar to no higher than SG 1.090. Test juice for pH. Begin acid correction, as needed. Add 0.2 g potassium metabisulfite, stir well, cover primary, and set aside for 12 hours. Add pectic enzyme, stirring until completely dissolved. Re-cover primary and set aside 12 hours.

Add yeast: To 1 cup warm water (not to exceed 102 degrees F.) add 1 teaspoon sugar and a pinch of yeast nutrient and stir to dissolve. Add yeast to water, stir, and cover mixture for 30 minutes. Add mixture to primary, stir, and cover primary.

Fermentation: Gently squeeze bag 3–4 times daily for seven days. Remove the bag and hang over a large bowl to drip drain for 1 hour, squeezing every 15 minutes. Add juice to primary and discard mango pulp or save for mango bread. When SG drops to 1.020, or lower if the fermentation is still vigorous, transfer to secondary and affix airlock.

Post-Fermentation: Move wine to a dark, cool place and rack every 30 days until the wine clears. Correct clarity with pectic enzyme and, if necessary, 2-part fining. If fined, wait four days and rack. Add 0.2 g potassium metabisulfite and ½ teaspoon dissolved potassium sorbate. Set aside for 60 days. Sweeten to taste or to balance. If sweetened, wait 30 days to ensure no renewed fermentation and carefully rack into bottles. Mango wine simply has to age a year to reach its potential.

Options: This wine blends well with apricot, peach, coconut, strawberry, or pineapple wine. Do not overpower the mango. Bench blending trials are essential to get it right.

This wine can be sweetened with honey for greater complexity. Most honey contains pollen, so check the bottom of secondary after 30 days for signs of a very light dusting of pollen. If present, very carefully rack and immediately rack again into bottles.

As with all fruit wines, because tasting can consume all of your wine, it is wise to bottle four 187-mL splits to use for that purpose.

Similar fruit: The following fruit can be substituted for mangoes in this recipe: common (wild) mango, horse mango, white mango.

Orange Wine ❖

Orange wines are great for sipping, for blending into Sangria, cocktails, or other beverages, and for culinary uses too numerous to mention. Whether you like your wine dry, off-dry, semi-sweet, or sweet, you can make an orange wine to suit. With care, it can be made into a dessert wine and co-produced with chocolate for a real treat.

Orange refers to the citrus tree and its fruit. It is a hybrid of ancient origin, but only one or two hybrids distant away from the original three main citrus species—citron, pomelo, and tangerine. It quite possibly is a natural hybrid of the pomelo and tangerine, making it very ancient indeed and nothing like the oranges we enjoy today. Its fruits were small, bitter to bitter-sweet, and the tree was protected by long thorns.

Early cultivation of the orange in India and southern China led to the selection of hybrids that were thornless and either sweet or bitter, varied in size, shape, pulp color, and thickness of peel. The first sweet orange tree was brought to Europe from China in the early 16th century by Portuguese explorer Vasco de Gama. It is from that single tree, which still stands in the courtyard of the Lisbon home of the Count of Saint-Laurent, that almost all sweet oranges of Portugal, Spain, France, and the Middle East are descended.

Ultimately, the tree found its way to North and South America. Around 1820, in a garden at a monastery in Bahia, Brazil, a sweet orange tree developed a bud-sport, a mutation that developed into a branch with essentially infertile flowers. These flowers did not need pollination to produce fruit (actually, berries) but no seeds developed, and the flower's ovary became a second, albeit rudimentary, berry within the orange at the end where the flower was attached—the "navel" of the orange. Grafting has enabled more of these plants to be produced. But, I digress.

Orange wine was made in Lisbon as soon as there was a harvest ample enough to allow it. Its history in Asia is less certain, but both ancient Indian and Chinese writings mention fermented beverages made from the fruit.

Today, we are blessed to have oranges in the market year-round. Therefore, orange wine can be made anytime one decides to make it.

JACK'S TIP

ORANGES possess a high TA composed almost entirely of citric acid, and their pH can sometimes be somewhat high as well. Bringing the pH down to an acceptable level for wine will raise the TA even higher. The TA can be brought down considerably with amelioration, but the wine will still initially be acidic. This can be smoothed out a bit by aging, especially since it is citric acid.

This is a fairly simple wine to make. It is best when made from a mix of Valencia and tart oranges (blood oranges will do), but these are not always available. If made from navel oranges, it will be necessary to zest half the oranges thinly. Otherwise, the zest of two of the oranges will do.

Orange Wine Recipe

WINE IS READY IN: **16 months**

YOU'LL NEED: **8 medium-size oranges, 1 can frozen 100 percent white grape juice concentrate per gallon of wine**

ADDITIONAL EQUIPMENT: **1 nylon straining bag**

MAKES: **1 gallon, but can be scaled up**

INGREDIENTS

8 medium-size oranges

zest of 2 oranges

1 can 100 percent white grape juice frozen concentrate, thawed

1 lb., 10 oz. finely granulated sugar

water to make 1 gal.

1 tsp pectic enzyme

½ tsp grape tannin powder

tartaric acid, as needed

potassium metabisulfite, as needed

½ tsp potassium sorbate

1 tsp (3 g) yeast nutrient

Lalvin BA11 yeast (5 g)

DIRECTIONS

Prepare must: Scrub oranges clean. Put ½ gallon water on to boil while thinly grating peelings of 2 oranges. Put gratings in a nylon straining bag. Peel oranges and remove all pith. Section all fruit and place in bag with zest, tie closed. Put bag in primary and squeeze the segments. Add tannin, yeast nutrient, and thawed grape juice concentrate to primary. Remove boiling water from heat and stir in sugar until completely dissolved. Pour over oranges, add additional water to increase the liquid to 1 gallon, cover the primary and set aside to cool. When cool, test juice for pH. Begin acid correction if necessary. Add 0.2 g potassium metabisulfite, stir well, cover primary, and set aside for 12 hours. Add pectic enzyme, stirring until completely dissolved and set aside 12 hours.

Add yeast: To 1 cup warm water (not to exceed 102 degrees F.) add a pinch of yeast nutrient, 1 teaspoon of sugar, and stir to dissolve. Add yeast to water, stir, and cover mixture for 30 minutes. Add mixture to primary, stir, and cover primary.

Fermentation: Squeeze nylon straining bag 4–6 times a day. When SG drops to 1.060, remove nylon straining bag and drip drain (squeeze gently every 15 minutes) over large bowl for 1 hour. Discard orange pulp and pour juice into the primary. When SG drops to 1.020, or lower if the fermentation is still vigorous, transfer to secondary and affix airlock. In 30 days, carefully rack.

Post-Fermentation: Move wine to a dark, cool place for 30 days and carefully rack. Repeat every 30 days until wine clears. Correct clarity with pectic enzyme and, if necessary, two-part fining. If fined, wait four days and rack. Add 0.2 g potassium metabisulfite and ½ teaspoon dissolved potassium sorbate. Stir well. Sweeten to taste or to balance. If sweetened, wait 30 days to ensure no renewed fermentation and carefully rack into bottles. Allow to age one year in bottles for acid to smooth out before tasting.

Options: This wine can be sweetened with honey for greater complexity. Most honey contains pollen, so check the bottom of secondary after 30 days for signs of a very light dusting of pollen. If present, very carefully rack and immediately rack again into bottles.

This wine blends very well with many wines. Running bench tasting trials is essential to getting it right.

As with all fruit wines, because tasting can consume all of your wine, it is wise to bottle four 187-mL splits to use for that purpose.

Similar fruit: The following fruit can be substituted for oranges in this recipe: tangerine, clementine, satsuma, cara cara navel, bitter orange, and citron.

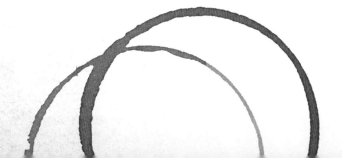

Passionfruit Wine ❖

Native to Mexico and Central and South America, Passionfruit is a member of the *Passiflora* genus. The present name was given to it by Spanish missionaries and refers to the "Passion of Christ" rather than to other human emotive states.

I can find no references to fermented passionfruit beverages prior to the sixteenth century, possibly because the indigenous peoples' writings were largely destroyed by their European subjugators.

There are many varieties of passionfruit, but not all are edible. All are filled with seeds surrounded by a juicy, acidic, aromatic pulp. *Passiflora edulis* is the primary edible variety, known as the Purple Granadilla in Central America and some Latino produce markets in the United States. Except in Hawaii, where it is called Lilikoi. The fruit is round or ovoid, and the outer rind may be purple, red, yellow, or green when ripe. When in doubt, ask the grocer or grower, as there is great variation.

North America's has a number of native species; *P. incarnata*, *P. lutea*, and *P. pailens* all have edible fruit, which is smaller and less flavorful than *P. edulis*. The acidity, sweetness, and aroma vary greatly among the species. The rind and white pith just under it are not used in winemaking.

JACK'S TIP

THERE ARE MANY RECIPES for this wine. I have collected over 20 but have only made wine using two recipes in addition to my own recipe.

Wine can be made from the pure juice concentrate if you can find it. It can also be made from the fruit juice if you can find it preservative-free. Canned passionfruit pulp has been available in home brew shops and may still be in stock or available on order.

This recipe assumes the use of fresh fruit—fresh ripe fruit. Only the seeds and juicy pulp are fermented. The seeds impart some tannin, so no grape tannins are added. However, if the wine lacks the familiar wine "bite" at the pre-bottling sweetening step, add powdered grape tannins in ⅛ teaspoon increments until satisfied. On the other hand, if the wine is overly tannic from seed contact, consider fining with egg white to smooth out the bite and preserve or improve mouthfeel. Rack carefully 21–30 days after fining with egg white.

Expect the pH to be low and the TA to be high. The must will have to be deacidified to at least pH 3.2, although pH 3.4 is better. The TA will come down with deacidification and amelioration.

Passionfruit Wine Recipe

WINE IS READY IN: **16 months**

YOU'LL NEED: **4 pounds passionfruit, 1 can frozen 100 percent red or white grape juice concentrate per gallon of wine**

ADDITIONAL EQUIPMENT: **1 nylon straining bag**

MAKES: **1 gallon, but can be scaled up**

INGREDIENTS

4 lb. fresh, ripe passionfruit

1 can 100 percent red or white grape juice frozen concentrate, thawed

1 lb. 10 oz. very finely granulated sugar

water to make 1 gal.

1 tsp pectic enzyme

calcium carbonate, as needed

potassium metabisulfite, as needed

½ tsp potassium sorbate

1 tsp (3 g) yeast nutrient

Lalvin BA11 yeast (5 g)

DIRECTIONS

Prepare must: Wash fruit and cut in half. Scoop seeds and juicy pulp from each half and save, discarding the rinds and white pith. Over primary, pour juice and saved seed-pulp into a nylon straining bag, then tie the bag closed and leave in primary. Add yeast nutrient and thawed grape juice concentrate to the primary. Dissolve sugar in 1 liter of hot water and pour over pulp, add cold water to make 1 gallon liquid. Test juice for pH. Begin acid correction as needed. Add 0.2 g potassium metabisulfite, stir well, cover primary, and set aside for 12 hours. Add pectic enzyme, stirring until completely dissolved and set aside 12 hours.

Add yeast: To 1 cup warm water (not to exceed 102 degrees F.) add a pinch of yeast nutrient, 1 teaspoon of sugar, and stir to dissolve. Add yeast to water, stir, and cover mixture for 30 minutes. Add mixture to primary, stir, and cover primary.

Fermentation: Squeeze nylon straining bag 3–4 times a day. When SG drops to 1.060, remove nylon straining bag, squeeze to extract all juice possible, and discard spent pulp. When SG drops to 1.020, or lower if the fermentation is still vigorous, transfer to secondary and affix airlock. In 30 days, carefully rack.

Post-Fermentation: Move wine to a dark, cool place for 30 days and rack. Wait until clear, then wait another week. Correct clarity with pectic enzyme and, if necessary, two-part fining. If fined, wait four days and rack. Add 0.2 g potassium metabisulfite and ½ teaspoon dissolved potassium sorbate. Sweeten to taste or to balance. If sweetened, wait 30 days to ensure no renewed fermentation and carefully rack into bottles. Some people drink this wine almost immediately and never taste the wine when it is actually ready to be tasted. Allow one year in bottles for acid to smooth out before tasting, although it may take two. Be patient, and you'll be rewarded.

Options: This wine can be sweetened with honey for greater complexity. Most honey contains pollen, so check the bottom of secondary after 30 days for signs of a very light dusting of pollen. If present, very carefully rack and immediately rack again into bottles.

This wine blends very well with a few other wines, including lime, guava, pineapple, and Lychee wines. Running bench tasting trials is essential to getting it right.

As with all fruit wines, because tasting can consume all of your wine, it is wise to bottle four 187-mL splits to use for that purpose.

Similar fruit: None.

Pineapple Wine ❖

Pineapples are native to South America and have been cultivated for perhaps 4000 years. Wild pineapples still exist, but they are small and inferior to garden and commercial varieties. While there are over a hundred varieties of pineapple, only a half-dozen are economically important. The variety we are most familiar with is the Smooth Cayenne pineapple, selected and cultivated by the indigenous peoples of Venezuela long ago. It is one of the most popular varieties because its firm flesh and sweet-acidic flavor are well suited for canning.

Fermented pineapple beverages have been present in native pineapple regions for centuries, but most are non-chaptalized low-alcohol drinks. It wasn't until the 1920s that Jim Dole successfully transformed the introduction of canned pineapples from Hawaii to mainland America and beyond, and that is when home wine enthusiasts began making proper pineapple wines.

Besides making the wine from the juicy flesh of the fruit, there is another kind of pineapple wine that is popular in certain cultures. That wine is made from the shavings, or peelings, of the fruit and perhaps the top and bottom when dressed for cutting. Having never made such a wine, I cannot judge it but am nonetheless skeptical of its quality until proven otherwise.

JACK'S TIP

THE PINEAPPLE progressively loses a great deal of flavor after being harvested. After only 24 hours, it has lost its freshness, some of its more delicate aromas, and much of the distinct uniqueness that made it a prized delicacy over the millennia. The canning industry preserved the essential character of the fruit. It's not exactly the same thing, but pretty close. Some vitamin degradation occurs, but it's better than a day-old pineapple.

The pineapples in supermarkets in the Lower 48 states were harvested at least three days ago and probably longer. So the saying goes, "If you want to taste a fresh Hawaiian pineapple, either buy one at midday in Hawaii or open a can of Dole pineapples."

So yes, this recipe uses canned crushed pineapples in 100% pineapple juice. A caution here. Buy the premium label—Dole, Del Monte, etc., not store brand. The pH should be around 3.7 and TA varies from 6–12 g/L, with roughly 87% citric and 13% malic. A minimum pH correction is in order, using 2 g/L tartaric, or 7.57 g/gal. (2 g/L x 3.785 L/gal.)—you can round it up to 8 for insurance. The rise in TA will be negated by amelioration.

In its 20-ounce can, Dole claims its crushed pineapple in 100% juice contains 185 grams of sugar. Two cans equal 370 grams. Add to that the 32 grams of sugar in Welch's 100% White Grape Juice Frozen Concentrate and we have 402 grams of sugar, or 14 ounces rounded down.

Pineapple Wine

WINE IS READY IN: **11 months**

YOU'LL NEED: **2, 20-oz. cans Dole crushed pineapple, 1 can frozen 100 percent white grape juice concentrate per gallon of wine**

ADDITIONAL EQUIPMENT: **1 nylon straining bag**

MAKES: **1 gallon, but can be scaled up**

INGREDIENTS

2 20-oz cans Dole crushed pineapple in 100 percent pineapple juice

1 can Welch's 100 percent white grape juice frozen concentrate, thawed

1 lb., 4 oz. sugar

water to make 1 gal.

1 tsp pectic enzyme

8 g tartaric acid

potassium metabisulfite, as needed

½ tsp potassium sorbate

1 tsp (3 g) yeast nutrient

Lalvin EC1118 yeast

DIRECTIONS

Prepare must: Bring 1 liter water to boil, remove from heat, and dissolve sugar in water, stirring until dissolution is complete. In primary, pour crushed pineapple and juice into a nylon straining bag, then tie bag closed and leave in primary. Add grape juice concentrate, half the tartaric acid (use other half only as needed), and yeast nutrient to the primary. Pour sugar-water over fruit and stir to dissolve additives. Add water to make 1 gallon. Measure pH and correct it as needed. Add 0.2 g potassium metabisulfite, stir well, cover primary, and set aside for 12 hours. Add pectic enzyme, stirring until completely dissolved and set aside 12 hours.

Add yeast: To 1 cup warm water (not to exceed 102 degrees F.) add a pinch of yeast nutrient, 1 teaspoon of sugar, and stir to dissolve. Add yeast to water, stir, and cover mixture for 30 minutes. Add mixture to primary, stir, and cover primary.

Fermentation: Squeeze nylon straining bag 3–4 times a day. When SG drops to 1.040, remove nylon straining bag, squeeze to extract all juice possible, and discard spent pulp. Re-cover primary. When SG drops to 1.020, or lower if the fermentation is still vigorous, transfer to secondary and affix airlock. In 30 days carefully rack.

Post-Fermentation: Move wine to a dark, cool place for 60 days and rack. Wait until wine is clear, then wait another two weeks. Correct clarity with pectic enzyme and, if necessary, two-part fining. If fined, wait four days and rack. Add 0.2 g potassium metabisulfite and ½ teaspoon dissolved potassium sorbate. Sweeten to taste or to balance. If sweetened, wait 30 days to ensure no renewed fermentation and carefully rack into bottles. This wine can be consumed at six months.

Options: This wine can be sweetened with honey for greater complexity. Most honey contains pollen, so check the bottom of secondary after 30 days for signs of a very light dusting of pollen. If present, very carefully rack and immediately rack again into bottles.

This wine blends very well with other tropical wines. Running bench tasting trials is essential to getting it right.

As with all fruit wines, because tasting can consume all of your wine, it is wise to bottle four 187-mL splits to use for that purpose.

Similar fruit: None.

Pomegranate Wine ❖

The pomegranate originated in southwestern Asia, in the area extending from Iran to northern India. It is an ancient genus, but very tightly speciated. Indeed, only two species seem to exist with few true varieties, although there are over 500 named cultivars of just the single species we know best. *Punica granatum* is a shrub or small tree which can live a very long time—200-year old trees exist in France.

Pomegranate cultivation is nearly as old as civilization itself, with cultivation dating back to at least 3000 B.C. It has been widely cultivated since ancient times throughout the Mediterranean basin and the Middle East. It soon became cultivated in suitable areas along land and shipping trade routes.

Historically speaking, its introduction into the Americas by Spanish, Portuguese, and English colonialists and missionaries is rather recent. In the United States, it grows best in the South and Southwest, preferring drier climates without habitual harsh winters.

Grown both as a garden ornamental and a food source, the pomegranate varies in terms of the color of its flower, the color of the fruit's rind, juice, and seed sacs (called arils), as well as in terms of size and how hard the seeds are. The acidity, sweetness, and astringency of its juice can vary greatly too.

Technically a berry, the pomegranate is unusual in that its arils, which house the juice surrounding the seeds, form in irregular chambers without attachment. Once the rind is breached and chambers are opened, the arils are easily collected by giving the hard rind a thump. But opening each section should be done carefully because the arils are fragile, and released juice will quickly stain hands and clothing. Indeed, the juice has long been used to dye thread, yarn, and fabric. It has also long been used in the making of fermented beverages, most notably wine.

The Bible is full of references to wine from grapes, often referred to as the fruit of the vine, but the only other named wine within it is spiced pomegranate wine (Song of Solomon 8:2), a wine made throughout the ancient world.

JACK'S TIP

POMEGRANATES are acidic. The pH falls at or just below the desired pH range. The TA is a bit high. Because the dominant acid is malic, both measures of acidity can be corrected by selecting Lalvin 71B yeast and allowing it to metabolize some of the malic acid. If, by chance, it metabolizes too much, a simple tartaric addition can fix that.

Pomegranate wine tends to be a bit thin. Adding 100% Red Grape Juice Concentrate will boost the body, contribute sugar, and round out the acids present.

This is an easy wine to make, once the arils are separated from the fruit. When separating the arils, it is helpful to eject them into a large bowl of 2 liters of cool water. Be sure to wear rubber gloves. The arils will sink, and any white pith will float, where it can easily be skimmed off. The water, which will contain some juice, can be used in the recipe.

Pomegranate Wine Recipe

WINE IS READY IN: **10 months**

YOU'LL NEED: **8–18 ripe pomegranates, depending on their size, 1 can frozen 100 percent red grape juice concentrate per gallon of wine**

ADDITIONAL EQUIPMENT: **1 nylon straining bag**

MAKES: **1 gallon, but can be scaled up**

INGREDIENTS

8–18 ripe pomegranates, depending on their size

1 can Welch's 100 percent red grape juice frozen concentrate, thawed

1 lb., 8 oz. finely granulated sugar

water to make 1 gal.

1 tsp pectic enzyme

¼ tsp powdered grape tannin powder

tartaric acid, if necessary

potassium metabisulfite, as needed

½ tsp potassium sorbate

1 tsp (3 g) yeast nutrient

Lalvin 71B yeast

DIRECTIONS

Prepare must: Bring ½ liter water to boil, remove from heat, and dissolve sugar in water, stirring until completely dissolved. In primary, pour arils and water into a nylon straining bag, then tie the bag closed and leave in the primary. Add grape juice concentrate, tannin, and yeast nutrient to primary. Pour sugar-water over fruit and stir to dissolve additives. Add water to make 1 gallon. Measure pH and correct it if needed. Add 0.2 g potassium metabisulfite, stir well, cover primary, and set aside for 12 hours. Add pectic enzyme, stirring until completely dissolved and set aside 12 hours.

Add yeast: To 1 cup warm water (not to exceed 102 degrees F.) add a pinch of yeast nutrient, 1 teaspoon of sugar, and stir to dissolve. Add yeast to water, stir, and cover mixture for 30 minutes. Add mixture to primary, stir, and cover primary.

Fermentation: Squeeze nylon straining bag 3–4 times a day. It is not necessary to crush arils (but you can if you want to—it's kind of fun, like stepping on bubble-wrap), as yeast will do that. Squeezing bruises the membranes, which assists the yeast. When fermentation is vigorous, check SG daily. When SG drops to 1.020, or lower if the fermentation is still vigorous, remove nylon straining bag, squeeze to extract all juice possible, and discard spent pulp and seeds. Carefully transfer to secondary and affix airlock. In 30 days carefully rack.

Post-Fermentation: Move wine to a dark, cool place until wine clears. Correct clarity with pectic enzyme and, if necessary, two-part fining. If fined, wait four days and rack. Add 0.2 g potassium metabisulfite and ½ teaspoon dissolved potassium sorbate. Stir well and sweeten to taste or to balance. If sweetened, wait 30 days to ensure no renewed fermentation and carefully rack into bottles. This wine can be consumed at six months but greatly improves at one year.

Options: When opening the pomegranates, the arils can be strained from the water and blotted dry with paper towels, then placed in freezer-grade Ziploc bags and frozen.

This wine is very good as is, or lightly spiced. To spice, add three whole cloves and a 4-inch stick of cinnamon (crushed) to nylon staining bag. Remove cloves after two weeks.

This wine can be sweetened with honey for greater complexity. Most honey contains pollen, so check the bottom of secondary after 30 days for signs of a very light dusting of pollen. If present, very carefully rack and immediately rack again into bottles.

This wine blends very well with blackberry, black raspberry, black cherry, and black-currant. Running bench tasting trials is essential to getting it right and not allowing the blended wine to overpower the pomegranate.

As with all fruit wines, because tasting can consume all of your wine, it is wise to bottle four 187-mL splits to use for that purpose.

Similar fruit: None.

Starfruit (Carambola) Wine ❖

These amazing fruit are sweet-sour until fully ripe when the fruit soften somewhat turning from green to light-to-dark yellow. There are two types of starfruit, a small, very tart one, and a larger one that is very sweet with a lingering tartness when ripe. Oxalic acid is the major acid in starfruit, which is unusual in the plant world.

Native to Sri Lanka or Indonesia, the carambola tree has been distributed throughout the tropics, and its fruit is very popular as fresh fruit in most areas where cultivated. Besides eaten fresh, they have many culinary uses; they are made into jams and jellies, as well as fermented into low-alcohol local beverages and wine.

The fruit typically has five longitudinal ridges, which, when the fruit is sliced crosswise, resemble a star. Occasionally, they may have from four to eight ridges. Select fruit that have no traces of green remaining but have not yet developed brown spots, as the latter are overripe and inferior in taste.

When not augmented with sugar, the fermented fruit make a very low-alcohol beverage. Only with chaptalization can they be made into wine. The wine is often spiced lightly with cinnamon.

WARNING: The fruit poses a health risk to persons suffering from kidney failure or stones and for those taking medications with which grapefruit is prohibited. Both the oxalic acid and caramboxin are strong antagonists to kidney failure patients. Caramboxin is a neurotoxin.

To healthy individuals, the fruit poses no health risk.

JACK'S TIP

IT IS ASSUMED you will select the sweeter type of starfruit. Fresh fruit are preferred, but they are also available canned. The recipe is somewhat forgiving, yielding acceptable wine from a small amount of fruit to a very full wine from more fruit. There is, however, a limit at which the acidity cannot be easily tamed.

When sliced, the fruit should be somewhat crunchy, firm, and yet extremely juicy. When the fruit ripen, they must be consumed or otherwise utilized within a few days. Underripe fruit will turn yellow at room temperature but will not increase in sweetness.

The pH is usually spot on, but TA can be high. The TA can be corrected via amelioration.

Starfruit (Carambola) Wine Recipe

WINE IS READY IN: **10 months**

YOU'LL NEED: **2½ to 4 pounds fresh, ripe starfruit, depending on their size, 1 can frozen 100 percent white grape juice concentrate per gallon of wine**

ADDITIONAL EQUIPMENT: **1 nylon straining bag**

MAKES: **1 gallon, but can be scaled up**

INGREDIENTS

2½ to 4 lb. fresh, ripe starfruit

1 can Welch's 100 percent white grape juice frozen concentrate, thawed

1 lb., 12 oz. very finely granulated sugar

2 3-inch sticks of cinnamon bark, not crushed

water to make 1 gal.

½ tsp pectic enzyme

⅛ tsp powdered grape tannin powder

citric acid, if necessary

potassium metabisulfite, as needed

½ tsp potassium sorbate

1 tsp (3 g) yeast nutrient

Lalvin R2 yeast

DIRECTIONS

Prepare must: Cut fruit crosswise into thin slices. Meanwhile, bring 1 liter water to boil, remove from heat, and dissolve sugar in water, stirring until completely dissolved. In the primary, pour fruit into a nylon straining bag, tie bag closed, and leave in primary. Add grape juice concentrate, tannin, and yeast nutrient to primary. Pour sugar-water over fruit and stir to dissolve additives. Add water to make 1 gallon. Measure pH and correct it as needed. Add 0.2 g potassium metabisulfite, stir well, cover primary, and set aside for 12 hours. Add pectic enzyme, stirring until completely dissolved and set aside 12 hours.

Add yeast: To 1 cup warm water (not to exceed 102 degrees F.) add a pinch of yeast nutrient, 1 teaspoon of sugar, and stir to dissolve. Add yeast to water, stir, and cover mixture for 30 minutes. Add mixture to primary, stir, and cover primary.

Fermentation: Squeeze nylon straining bag 3–4 times a day for the first five days. It is not necessary to mash or aggressively crush the fruit. When SG drops to 1.020, or lower if the fermentation is still vigorous, remove nylon straining bag, squeeze firmly to extract all juice possible, and discard spent pulp and seeds. Carefully transfer to secondary and affix airlock. In one week, add the cinnamon sticks to wine and carefully rack in 3 additional weeks.

Post-Fermentation: Move wine to a dark, cool place until wine clears. Correct clarity with pectic enzyme and, if necessary, 2-part fining. If fined, wait four days and rack. Add 0.2 g potassium metabisulfite and ½ teaspoon dissolved potassium sorbate. Stir well and sweeten to taste or to balance. If sweetened, wait 30 days to ensure no renewed fermentation and carefully rack into bottles. This wine should mature at six months and should be consumed within 18 months.

Options: This wine is very good as is or with 3–4 cloves added with the cinnamon.

This wine can be sweetened with honey for greater complexity. Most honey contains pollen, so check the bottom of secondary after 30 days for signs of a very light dusting of pollen. If present, very carefully rack and immediately rack again into bottles.

This wine blends very well with strawberry and kiwi, being careful not to get ahead of the flavor of the starfruit. Conduct bench trials to get it right.

As with all fruit wines, because tasting can consume all of your wine, it is wise to bottle four 187-mL splits to use for that purpose.

Similar fruit: None.

Tangerine Wine ❖

Tangerines are a cross between the mandarin and pomelo, which was crossed back onto the mandarin several generations. In other words, the pomelo was there in the beginning, and then its influence was diluted with cross-breeding with mandarins repeatedly.

Tangerines are noted for three traits. One, the skin is less firmly attached to the pulp than oranges or most other mandarins. Two, their pulp is more reddish than oranges or most mandarins. Three, they are sweeter and less acidic than oranges or most mandarins. The third trait has the most influence on tangerines as a wine base.

JACK'S TIP

TANGERINES are seldom made into wine by themselves as their wines lack complexity and tend to be one-dimensional. They are almost always co-fermented with another citrus, and that is the case here. This recipe specifically calls for Valencia oranges, but you can substitute any tart orange—blood oranges are a good candidate—or other citric fruit, such as grapefruit, pomelos, Meyer lemons, etc. Regular lemons, limes, and citron are less commonly co-fermenters as they tend to overpower the tangerines.

Tangerine Wine Recipe

WINE IS READY IN: **14 months**

YOU'LL NEED: **16–24 tangerines and 8–10 small oranges per gallon of wine**

ADDITIONAL EQUIPMENT: **1–2 nylon straining bags**

MAKES: **1 gallon, but can be scaled up**

INGREDIENTS

16–24 tangerines (sweet and sour varieties, equally mixed, is ideal)

8–10 small Valencia oranges

zest of 5 oranges

1 lb., 8 oz. finely granulated sugar

water to make 1 gal.

1 tsp pectic enzyme

¼ tsp grape tannin powder

potassium metabisulfite, as needed

½ tsp potassium sorbate

1 tsp (3 g) yeast nutrient

Lalvin DV10 yeast (5 g)

DIRECTIONS

Prepare must: Scrub tangerines and oranges clean. Put 2 liters water on to boil while thinly grating peelings of 5 oranges. Put gratings in a nylon straining bag. Peel tangerines and oranges and remove all pith. Section all fruit and place in bags, tie closed, and put bags in primary. Squeeze or mash the segments to extract the juice. Add tannin and yeast nutrient to primary. Remove boiling water from heat and stir in sugar until completely dissolved. Pour over fruit, add additional water to increase the liquid to 1 gallon, cover primary, and set aside to cool. When cool, test juice for pH and correct it as necessary. Add 0.2 g potassium metabisulfite, stir well, cover primary, and set aside for 12 hours. Add pectic enzyme, stirring until completely dissolved and set aside 12 hours.

Add yeast: To 1 cup warm water (not to exceed 102 degrees F.) add a pinch of yeast nutrient, 1 teaspoon of sugar, and stir to dissolve. Add yeast to water, stir, and cover mixture for 30 minutes. Add mixture to primary, stir, and cover primary.

Fermentation: Squeeze nylon straining bags 4–6 times a day. When SG drops to 1.020, or lower if the fermentation is still vigorous, remove nylon straining bags and drip drain (do not squeeze) over a large bowl for 30 minutes. Discard tangerine and orange pulp and pour juice into primary. Transfer to secondary and affix airlock. In 30 days, carefully rack.

Post-Fermentation: Move wine to a dark, cool place for 60 days and carefully rack. Repeat every 60 days for six months (total of 3 60-day periods). Correct clarity as necessary with pectic enzyme and, if absolutely required, 2-part fining. If fined, wait four days and rack. Add 0.2 g potassium metabisulfite and ½ teaspoon dissolved potassium sorbate. Stir well and sweeten to taste or to balance. If sweetened, wait 30 days to ensure no renewed fermentation and carefully rack into bottles. Age 6 months to 1 year in bottles for acid to smooth out before tasting.

Options: This wine can be sweetened with honey for greater complexity. Most honey contains pollen, so check the bottom of secondary after 30 days for signs of a very light dusting of pollen. If present, very carefully rack and immediately rack again into bottles.

This wine blends very well with many wines, but mostly citrus, pineapple, guava, and mango. Running bench tasting trials is essential to getting it right.

As with all fruit wines, because tasting can consume all of your wine, it is wise to bottle four 187-mL splits to use for that purpose.

Similar fruit: The following fruit can be substituted for tangerines in this recipe: clementine, Satsuma, Cara-Cara navel, blood orange.

Multiple wine batches in secondary fermenters

CHAPTER EIGHT
ROOT WINES

When someone brings up making country wines, roots aren't the first thing that probably come to mind. The truth is, there are many roots that make perfectly good wines. Beetroots, for example, make one of the better non-grape wines around. It just takes a long time to age it to perfection.

What does a root have to have to make it a good candidate for a wine?

First and foremost, it has to be palatable. Dandelion roots qualify for a few weeks at most, and then they turn bitter. We could leech the bitterness out of the roots, but that is quite involved and it's not guaranteed it'll work.

Second, it must have sugar, either directly or stored as readily available starch. The potato comes to mind, full of starch which can be broken down into sugars. But it is quite bland, and it takes minor feats of magic to manipulate it into a delicious wine—but it can be done. And why bother when carrots, providing they are not too old and large, are an inviting root crop, with a decent amount of sugar and flavor but sadly deficient in acidity. And speaking of sugar, there is the sugar beet, also quite bland but easily augmented to produce a good wine.

Third, they must have an inviting flavor. Think of sweet potatoes, parsnips, or turnips (an acquired taste). There are others we will not get into because their fermentation odors are downright torturous—onions, scallions, garlic, and others. Ginger is generally considered a spice, so we will visit it in another chapter.

All of these root vegetables are available in most supermarket produce departments, although a couple may be seasonal if your market isn't a decent importer. Do look for quality and freshness. An oversized root usually means it'll be tough. Just try to choose well and you probably will.

In this and all chapters of this book, when possible, measurements are given in common fractions of teaspoons in the recipes to correspond with the fractions of a gram actually required for the additives. The exception is the amount of potassium metabisulfite to maintain free SO_2 at 50 mg/L or above. However, these are approximations based on the author's experience with these wines. It is almost certain they are not accurate for every making of these wines. There are simply too many variables. Therefore, the last sulfite addition will only be accurate if you test the wine's sulfite level with your SO_2 test kit and adjust the free SO_2 to 100 mg/L for bottling. This should even out any deviations and ensure your wine is prepared for a 2- to 3-year cellar-life expectancy. The formula for calculating this final addition is in Chapter 2 in "Sulfites" (see page 71). However, there are many online sulfite calculators that will compute the result for you if you are not confident of your math skills. You'll still have to use your SO_2 test kit to obtain the numbers needed for the calculator.

At a minimum, it is suggested you measure the actual pH and adjust acid accordingly to bring the wine within a pH 3.2–3.5 window.

So let's get to the recipes.

Beetroot Wine ❖

According to friends and relatives, one of the best wines I ever made was a beetroot wine that aged for four years in the carboy. There is a story behind that, but just because the stars were aligned just right for me does not mean that I'm recommending that you age your wines for four years in carboys.

Beet wines taste earthy when young, a taste that can last for a long time. In my case, it was at least three years because I racked the wine at that point and then stowed it away for further aging, without much hope it would improve. A year later some dear friends from Louisiana came to spend a few days with us, and somehow the beet wine entered the conversation. When we tasted it, we all nearly fainted. It was so good it was sinful not to drink it. I had 3 gallons, so why not?

Beetroots are alkaline, with a pH of 7.5 to 8.0. Beetroot's TA is 1.4 g/L. In other words, they need a large infusion of acid to get to winemaking standards. The challenge is to not change the character and flavors of the beet into something we won't recognize.

JACK'S TIP

THE RECIPE that follows is the result of fine-tuning a recipe that worked well for me. You will note that a total of 2½ pounds of sugar is used. The yeast selected should reach alcohol toxicity and die out at 14% alcohol, leaving some residual sugar for an off-dry to sweet wine. You will have to check the alcohol content with a hydrometer. I cannot predict this because every fermentation is a bit different. I also recommend you check the pH post-fermentation and bring it under 3.55 if necessary.

Beetroot Wine Recipe

WINE IS READY IN: **16 months**

YOU'LL NEED: **5 pounds red beetroots, 4 oranges, 1 lemon per gallon of wine**

ADDITIONAL EQUIPMENT: **1–2 nylon straining bags**

MAKES: **1 gallon, but can be scaled up**

INGREDIENTS

5 lb. red beetroots

4 medium oranges, juiced

1 lemon, juiced

2 lb. very fine white granulated sugar

⅛ tsp grape tannin powder

1 tsp (3 g) yeast nutrient

potassium metabisulfite, as needed

½ tsp amylase

1 tsp pectic enzyme

5 g Lalvin 71B yeast

½ lb. light brown sugar

½ tsp potassium sorbate

water to make 1 gal.

DIRECTIONS

Prepare must: Scrub beets and citrus clean. Slice beets thinly—with a food processor slicing disc if you have one—and remove peeling from slices (they add an earthy taste to the wine). Put all sliced beets in a large pot, add 2 quarts water and bring to a boil. Reduce the heat to low boil, put a lid on the pot, and cook an additional 20–30 minutes. Meanwhile, juice the oranges and lemon, save the juice and toss the rest. Place a second pot with 1¼ quarts water on to boil. Remove water from heat when it boils and thoroughly dissolve 2 pounds of white sugar in it. Strain beets while transferring beet juice to a primary. Set beet slices aside for culinary use. Pour the sugar water, orange juice, tannins, and yeast nutrient in the primary. Cover primary and set aside to cool. Add 0.2 g potassium metabisulfite, stir well, cover primary, and set aside for 12 hours. Stir in amylase and set aside for 6 hours. Add pectic enzyme, stirring until completely dissolved and set aside 12 hours.

Add yeast: To 1 cup warm water (not to exceed 102 degrees F.) add a pinch of yeast nutrient, 1 teaspoon of sugar, and stir to dissolve. Add yeast to water, stir, and cover mixture for 30 minutes. Add mixture to primary, stir, and cover primary.

Fermentation: Stir primary daily for seven days. Remove 1 quart of liquid from the primary and add to it the brown sugar. Stir until completely dissolved. Return the quart to the primary. Re-cover the primary and ferment an additional 14 days. Carefully rack into a secondary and top up.

Post-Fermentation: Move wine to a dark, cool place for 45 days and carefully rack. Repeat racking every 60 days for six months. Add 0.2 g potassium metabisulfite and ½ teaspoon dissolved potassium sorbate, and sweeten to taste or to balance. The wine will not taste agreeable at this time, so it is best to sweeten to balance. If sweetened, wait 30 days to ensure re-fermentation does not begin, and carefully rack into bottles. Store in dark place for 18 months. Do not taste until the 18 months have passed. If not to your liking, put away another year and taste again. When the wine is fully aged it will be wonderful, so if it isn't, put it away another six months.

Options: Don't mess with it. This wine will be perfect when it is ready.

As with all fruit wines, because tasting can consume all of your wine, it is wise to bottle four 187-mL splits to use for that purpose.

Similar fruit: There are no other root vegetables that can be substituted for beets in this recipe—not even sugar beets.

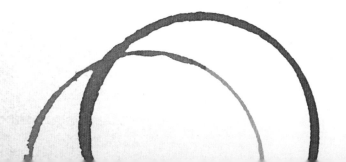

Carrot Wine (Carrot Whiskey) ❖

I once tracked this recipe back to its earliest publication, in a column by Noel Whitcomb in the *London Daily Mirror* in the 1940s, just to learn why it was called Carrot Whiskey. Noel said it wasn't because it tasted like whiskey, but rather that its richness in taste and color reminded him of whiskey. To be fair, the British spell it whisky and I (and Whitcomb) have Americanized it.

This recipe is quite famous. I have found it in most of the books I have on country winemaking. The problem is that there are many versions of this recipe out there. Try as I did, I was not able to obtain a copy of Noel's original column with the recipe in it. I went through my books and references and found one that was consistently the same the most often and deduced it was probably the original. I then changed it by adding sulfites and pectic enzyme into the equation. I really wanted to add amylase but risked straying too far from the path Whitcomb had charted. I had it handy should it be needed.

JACK'S TIP

THE RECIPE corrects the biggest deficiency of carrots—acidity. The pH is high, ranging from 5.6–6.4, and the TA is around 3 g/L. The citrus and raisins should settle this where we want it nicely. The wheat is a surprise but simply another source of starch. I used red wheat (because we had a 25-pound can of it), but any kind will do—available at home brew shops and all health food stores.

Carrot Wine (Carrot Whiskey) Recipe

WINE IS READY IN: **16 months**

YOU'LL NEED: **6 pounds carrots, 2 oranges, 2 lemons, 1 pound wheat, 1 pound raisins per gallon of wine**

ADDITIONAL EQUIPMENT: **1 nylon straining bag**

MAKES: **1 gallon, but can be scaled up**

INGREDIENTS

6 lb. carrots

2 oranges

2 lemons

2½ lb. very fine white granulated sugar

1 lb. white or golden raisins (Sultanas)

1 lb. wheat

water to make 1 gal.

1 tsp pectic enzyme

potassium metabisulfite, as needed

½ tsp potassium sorbate

1 tsp (3 g) yeast nutrient

Lalvin 71B yeast (5 g)

DIRECTIONS

Prepare must: Scrub carrots and citrus. Cut carrots into 1-inch pieces and put in 3 quarts of water. Bring to boil, then reduce heat to simmer until tender (about 25–30 minutes). Meanwhile, put half the sugar (1¼ lb.) into a primary. Slice citrus thinly, remove any seeds and place slices on top of sugar, peeling on. When carrots are done, strain them, pouring water over sugar and citrus. Stir until sugar is completely dissolved. Cover the primary and set aside to cool to lukewarm. Add chopped raisins, wheat, and yeast nutrient. Cover the primary and set aside until room temperature. Add 0.2 g potassium metabisulfite, stir well, cover primary, and set aside for 12 hours. Add pectic enzyme, stirring until completely dissolved and set aside 12 hours.

Add yeast: To 1 cup warm water (not to exceed 102 degrees F.) add a pinch of yeast nutrient, one teaspoon of sugar, and stir to dissolve. Add yeast to water, stir, and cover mixture for 30 minutes. Add mixture to primary, stir, and cover primary.

Fermentation: Stir primary daily for six days. Add roughly half of the remaining sugar and stir well to dissolve. Ferment another eight days and add the remainder of the sugar. Ferment an additional ten days, stirring daily. Carefully rack and top up.

Post-Fermentation: Move wine to a dark, cool place for 30 days. Measure acidity and make corrections if warranted. Wait four hours and carefully rack. Repeat racking in 30 days. If wine is clear, add 0.2 g potassium metabisulfite and ½ teaspoon dissolved potassium sorbate, correct clarity as necessary with pectic enzyme, and, if necessary, amylase and/or two-part fining. If fined, wait four days and carefully rack into bottles. Store in a dark place for one year. Do not taste earlier.

Options: This wine responds to oak very well. One cup of dark roast oak cubes in the wine for 30 days during maturation is usually enough. Let taste be your guide, but don't overdo it.

As with all root wines, because tasting can consume all of your wine, it is wise to bottle four 187-mL splits to use for that purpose.

Similar fruit: None.

Parsnip Wine ❖

Parsnip wines have a legacy across northern Eurasia. When left in the ground until after the first frost, some of the starch in the root, which is naturally sweet, is converted to sugar. Before the introduction of cane and beet sugars, parsnips were often used as a sweetener.

With sweetness comes wine. It just seems natural. There are fermentations that only use the sugar in the roots, which results in a low-alcohol drink more like a beer. When supplemented with sugar or honey, a magnificent wine can be crafted with a subtle savory, nutty flavor.

JACK'S TIP

THERE ARE MANY RECIPES for parsnip wine. Of all the root bases, it perhaps yields the best-tasting wine. But, like all root crops, parsnip wine takes a long time to make and needs to age for a long time before it is ready to drink. I've seen several recipes to select from, but the one I'm providing is the richest in complexity and body.

The pH of the parsnip is between 5.3 and 5.7. The recipe corrects for that and pushes the TA to respectable heights, knowing they will diminish during amelioration. The recipe also adds plenty of body by using banana and complexity by adding elderflowers or rose petals. Because parsnips are a winter crop, they remain in the soil plenty long enough to cross paths with those flower blossoms. If you don't grow them, they are usually still in the produce departments as the flowers open.

Parsnip Wine Recipe

WINE IS READY IN: **27 months**

YOU'LL NEED: **4 pounds parsnips, 1 pound bananas,
½ cup elderflowers or citrus blossoms, 1 can frozen 100 percent white
grape juice concentrate per gallon of wine**

ADDITIONAL EQUIPMENT: **1 nylon straining bag and 1 jelly bag (for flowers)**

MAKES: **1 gallon, but can be scaled up**

INGREDIENTS

4 lb. parsnips

1 lb. ripe bananas

1 can Welch's 100 percent white grape juice
frozen concentrate, thawed

½ cup (packed) fresh elderflowers or
citrus blossoms

1¾ lb. Demerara sugar

1½ tsp tartaric acid

¼ tsp grape tannin powder

water to make 1 gal.

1 tsp pectic enzyme

potassium metabisulfite, as needed

½ tsp potassium sorbate

1 tsp (3 g) yeast nutrient

Lalvin R2 yeast (5 g)

simple syrup, as needed

DIRECTIONS

Prepare must: Wash and scrub parsnips. Slice thinly, peel and slice the bananas, and place
all in a pan with 3 quarts of water. Bring to a low boil for 30 minutes, skimming off any
scum that forms on the surface. Strain off liquid into primary and leave to settle. After
24 hours, siphon the clear liquid into a 4-liter secondary. Add white grape juice concentrate, tartaric acid, grape tannins, and yeast nutrient. Stir to mix and cover secondary
with a paper napkin held in place with a rubber band or other breathable covering. Bring
1 pint water to boil, remove from heat, add sugar, stirring until completely dissolved.
Add to secondary and re-cover secondary. Set aside until cool. Add 0.2 g potassium
metabisulfite, stir well, cover primary, and set aside for 12 hours. Add pectic enzyme,
stirring until completely dissolved and set aside 12 hours.

Add yeast: To 1 cup warm water (not to exceed 102 degrees F.) add a pinch of yeast nutrient, 1 teaspoon of sugar, and stir to dissolve. Add yeast to water, stir, and cover mixture
for 30 minutes. Add mixture to secondary, stir, and cover.

Fermentation: When fermentation is vigorous, add sugar water and flowers and fit airlock. After 1 week, strain off flowers and rack. Refit airlock and ferment until wine is clear. Carefully rack and top up.

Post-Fermentation: Move wine to a dark, cool place. Measure pH and make adjustments if warranted, then carefully rack. In 60 days add 0.2 g potassium metabisulfite, ½ teaspoon potassium sorbate dissolved in ½ cup water, and carefully rack again. Sweeten with simple syrup to SG 1.008 or to balance, top up and refit airlock. Periodically check airlock for liquid and rack every six months for 18 months. Correct clarity if necessary and carefully rack into bottles. Store in dark place for six months. Do not taste earlier.

Options: This wine may blend well with other wines, but the author simply has never tried that yet.

As with all root wines, because tasting can consume all of your wine, it is wise to bottle four 187-mL splits to use for that purpose.

Similar fruit: The following may be substituted for parsnips (but with a different flavor) using this recipe: turnips.

Potato Wine ❖

Possibly domesticated as far back as 10,000 years ago, the potato is native to South America. Of approximately 5,000 cultivated varieties worldwide, some 3,000 of them are located in the Andes alone. There are still about 200 wild species and subspecies, many of which can be crossbred with cultivars to transfer specific traits or disease resistance. By itself, potato wine is thin and bland. Think of straight vodka, a product of the potato—thin and bland (but hot). Potatoes lack acidity, tannins, and the enzymes necessary for the conversion of their starch into simple sugars. Yes, the yeast have some of the latter, but not nearly enough to tackle that starch wall in front of them. In many Old World countries, the tuber is used to make potato beer, but it cannot naturally be made into wine. We can open our winemaker's chemistry set to help it out, or we can choose another route. We choose the latter.

But first, let's start with the potato itself. The green part that grows above the ground is quite toxic, as are green potatoes. As the tubers ripen underground, they lose their toxicity while becoming starches and they gain density. The peelings are quite edible but yield an unsightly but harmless scum when boiled, so it is recommended that you peel them. Also, as the potato ages, it will wrinkle slightly and begin pushing small buds, which will eventually become sprouts. This "small bud" stage is the best for making wine from the potato because the starches change somewhat as they prepare sugar and other nutrients for the growth of sprouts. Cut out the buds before they swell and then peel the potato. Discard any potato that actually develops sprouts as it will rot under fermentation and ruin the wine.

JACK'S TIP

THERE ARE DOZENS of ways to make potato wine. Of all the recipes out there, this one seems the most sound to me and makes a pretty good wine.

There are a couple of additions you might find of value. Russet potatoes have a very high starch content which will convert into more sugar. Yukon Gold and Yellow Finn have less starch but greater flavor.

In the recipe, it says to cut up the potatoes. Thought should be given beforehand what you will use the potatoes for besides wine. They are only going to be boiled and then removed, so they will be adaptable for use in many culinary recipes afterward. How you anticipate using then may well influence the way you cut them up. Personally, I get the most use out of them if I dice them into ½-inch cubes or thin slices.

Potato Wine Recipe

WINE IS READY IN: **9 months**

YOU'LL NEED: **5 pounds potatoes, 4 medium oranges,
½ oz. ginger root, 1 can frozen 100 percent white grape
juice concentrate per gallon of wine**

ADDITIONAL EQUIPMENT: **1 jelly bag**

MAKES: **1 gallon, but can be scaled up**

INGREDIENTS

5 lb. potatoes (russet, white, gold, red, etc.)

1 can Welch's 100 percent white grape juice
frozen concentrate, thawed

4 medium oranges

zest of 2 oranges

½ oz. ginger root

2 lb. Muscovado (or dark brown) sugar

water to make 1 gal.

1 tsp amylase (divided)

1 tsp pectic enzyme

¼ tsp grape tannin powder

potassium metabisulfite, as needed

½ tsp potassium sorbate

1 tsp (3 g) yeast nutrient

Lalvin BA11 or EC1118 yeast (5 g)

DIRECTIONS

Prepare must: Scrub potatoes, peel, and cut up. Put 3 liters water on to boil while scrubbing and zesting two oranges. Peel and juice all. Put the zest in a jelly bag in the primary and cut-up potatoes and thinly sliced ginger root in boiling water. Boil potatoes until tender and strain into primary, setting potatoes aside for culinary use. Add sugar to primary and stir until completely dissolved. Add white grape juice concentrate and juice of oranges to primary. Stir in tannin and yeast nutrient. Add water to make 1 gallon, cover primary, and set aside to cool. Add 0.2 g potassium metabisulfite, stir well, cover primary, and set aside for 12 hours. Stir in half the amylase and set aside for 6 hours. Add pectic enzyme, stirring until completely dissolved and set aside 12 hours.

Add yeast: To 1 cup warm water (not to exceed 102 degrees F.) add a pinch of yeast nutrient, 1 teaspoon of sugar, and stir to dissolve. Add yeast to water, stir, and cover mixture for 30 minutes. Add mixture and remaining amylase to primary, stir, and cover primary.

Fermentation: Stir must 2–3 times a day. After five days add remaining amylase and stir well. When SG drops to 1.020, or lower if the fermentation is still vigorous, remove the jelly bag and discard the zest. Transfer to secondary and affix airlock. In 30 days, carefully rack.

Post-Fermentation: Move wine to a dark, cool place for 30 days. Measure pH and make corrections if warranted. Carefully rack. Rack every 30 days until wine clears. Correct clarity with pectic enzyme, amylase, and, if necessary, two-part fining. If fined, wait four days and rack. Add 0.2 g potassium metabisulfite and ½ teaspoon dissolved potassium sorbate. Stir well. Sweeten to taste or to balance. If sweetened, wait 30 days to ensure no renewed fermentation and carefully rack into bottles. This wine can be consumed in 4 months, but that is considered young. It usually needs to age in bottles for 6–9 months for the flavor to mature and acid to smooth out.

Options: This wine does not blend well in quantity but is sometimes used for topping up other wines after racking.

As with all root wines, because tasting can consume all of your wine, it is wise to bottle four 187-mL splits to use for that purpose.

Similar fruit: None.

Rutabaga Wine ❖

The cultivated history of this plant is not known, except that it is believed to have originated in Scandinavia or Russia as a natural cross between the wild turnip and wild cabbage. The plant has many names, even within in the same country, and this can be confusing since some of the aliases are legitimate names for other plants.

The rutabaga is a winter crop in that it sweetens after the first frost and this delays harvest; it can then be cellared over the winter with little adverse effect. Like the parsnip, it trades starch for sugar following a frost, and this makes it is a natural candidate for wine. The root itself will naturally only produce enough sugar to make a low-alcohol beverage similar to beer, but when chaptalized, it makes a good wine.

I have not run across any early Old World records of this wine. However, due to the vast number of names for this root vegetable, many of which are legitimate names for other plants, it would be easy to miss references.

However, owing to the root becoming sweeter after first and successive frosts, it is unthinkable it would not be a natural candidate for wine. The earliest record I can find of making this wine is 1831 in Ohio.

JACK'S TIP

THE PH of rutabaga is 5.5–5.85. The dominant acid is malic, and the TA is low, as usual for root vegetables. The recipe handles the acid deficiency nicely.

Rutabaga Wine Recipe

WINE IS READY IN: **14 months**

YOU'LL NEED: **6 pounds rutabagas, 3 oranges, 2 lemons,
  10 peppercorns per gallon of wine**

ADDITIONAL EQUIPMENT: **1 nylon straining bag**

MAKES: **1 gallon, but can be scaled up**

INGREDIENTS

6 lb. rutabagas

3 oranges, zest and juice

2 lemons, zest and juice

10 bruised black peppercorns

2½ lb. very fine white granulated sugar

½ tsp tartaric acid

½ tsp grape tannin powder

1 tsp pectic enzyme

water to make 1 gal.

potassium metabisulfite, as needed

½ tsp potassium sorbate

1 tsp (3 g) yeast nutrient

Lalvin R2 yeast (5 g)

DIRECTIONS

Prepare must: Trim tops at root shoulders and wash and scrub rutabagas well. Dice roots and put in a pot with peppercorns and water to just cover. Simmer (do not boil) for 45 minutes. Meanwhile, zest the citrus and put zest in a jelly bag with a dozen glass marbles for weight, tied closed, and set in your primary. Strain rutabagas and peppercorns into primary and discard solids or retain for culinary uses. Add sugar, yeast nutrient and tannin to primary and stir until completely dissolved. Add juice from citrus, cover primary and set aside to cool. Add 0.2 g potassium metabisulfite, stir well, cover primary, and set aside for 12 hours. Add pectic enzyme, stirring until completely dissolved and set aside 12 hours.

Add yeast: To 1 cup warm water (not to exceed 102 degrees F.) add a pinch of yeast nutrient, 1 teaspoon of sugar, and stir to dissolve. Add yeast to water, stir, and cover mixture for 30 minutes. Add mixture to primary, stir, and cover.

Fermentation: Stir daily. After ten days, remove the jelly bag and discard the zest. Carefully rack into secondary and affix airlock.

Post-Fermentation: Move wine to a dark, cool place, and rack every two months for six months. If wine is clear, add 0.2 g potassium metabisulfite and ½ teaspoon potassium sorbate, stirring well. Sweeten to taste or to balance and set aside for 30 days before carefully racking into bottles. Age six months before tasting.

Options: This wine may blend well with other wines, but the author simply has never tried that.

As with all root wines, because tasting can consume all of your wine, it is wise to bottle four 187-mL splits to use for that purpose.

Similar fruit: None.

Sweet Potato Wine ❖

Sweet potatoes are native to the Americas, believed to have become a separate species somewhere between the Yucatan in Mexico and northeast Venezuela. Its actual parents are not yet known. It was domesticated at least 5,000 years ago and spread into the Caribbean and South America by 2,500 BC. It was brought to Spain by Columbus and spread throughout the world by post-Columbian exploration and trade.

Little is known about its use in winemaking before the eighteenth century. But it's difficult to believe its natural sweetness was not put to use much earlier than that. In any event, it has been a staple in the South since at least the Civil War.

The recipe that follows probably dates back no earlier than the 1920s-30s, but this is just an educated guess based on its ingredients. I have updated the recipe, and I made a significant change to it two decades ago.

JACK'S TIP

AS IS USUAL for root vegetables, the pH of the sweet potato is high—pH 5.3 to 5.6. I never recorded its TA, but know it was not very high. The recipe that follows takes care of the acid, but you should check it at least once, preferably before fermentation begins, to make sure things are on track.

Sweet Potato Wine Recipe

WINE IS READY IN: **12 months**

YOU'LL NEED: **6 pounds sweet potatoes per gallon of wine**

ADDITIONAL EQUIPMENT: **1–2 nylon straining bags**

MAKES: **1 gallon, but can be scaled up**

INGREDIENTS

6 lb. sweet potatoes

1 lb. white or golden raisins

2 lb. light brown sugar

water to make 1 gal.

1½ tsp tartaric acid

1 tsp pectic enzyme

⅛ tsp grape tannin powder

potassium metabisulfite, as needed

½ tsp potassium sorbate

1 tsp (3 g) yeast nutrient

Lalvin EC1118 yeast (5 g)

DIRECTIONS

Prepare must: Scrub sweet potatoes and dice finely, skin on. Put diced potatoes in a pot and just cover with water. Bring to boil, cover the pot, reduce to simmer for 25 minutes. Meanwhile, mince or chop raisins and put in primary with half the sugar. Strain the potatoes over the primary, setting potatoes aside for later culinary use. Stir to dissolve sugar and add tartaric acid, and yeast nutrient. Add enough water to make up 1 gallon and wait 1 hour. Add 0.2 g potassium metabisulfite, stir well, cover primary, and set aside for 12 hours. Add pectic enzyme, stirring until completely dissolved and set aside 12 hours.

Add yeast: To 1 cup warm water (not to exceed 102 degrees F.) add a pinch of yeast nutrient, 1 teaspoon of sugar, and stir to dissolve. Add yeast to water, stir, and cover mixture for 30 minutes. Add mixture to primary, stir, and cover primary.

Fermentation: Ferment 7 days, stirring twice daily. Strain through nylon and discard strained raisins. Add remainder of sugar, stir well to dissolve, transfer to a secondary, and affix airlock. Wait 30 days and carefully rack.

Post-Fermentation: Move wine to a dark, cool place for 30 days and rack. Rack every 30 days until wine clears (may take 4–5 months). Wait another 30 days after clearing and check for continued sedimentation and improved clarity. Aid clarity as necessary with amylase, pectic enzyme, or two-part fining. If fined, wait four days and rack. Add 0.2 g potassium metabisulfite and ½ teaspoon dissolved potassium sorbate. Stir. Sweeten to taste or to balance. If sweetened, wait 30 days to ensure no renewed fermentation and carefully rack into bottles. This wine can be consumed in six months, but the usual aging in bottles is nine months.

Options: When sweetening at the end, try using Barbados, Muscovado, or dark brown sugar for more complexity.

This wine may blend well, but this author simply has never tried it.

As with all root wines, because tasting can consume all of your wine, it is wise to bottle four 187-mL splits to use for that purpose.

Similar fruit: The African yam looks similar, but shouldn't be used in this recipe. There are no substitutes for the sweet potato using this recipe.

CHAPTER NINE
FLOWER WINES

Flower wines are a bit of work to make but can be terribly rewarding. They can be subtle, light wines, often delicate on the palate, or they can offer up bold, in-your-face flavors. Too much of a good thing—lavender, for instance—can result in off-flavors or odors with an almost metallic underpinning. But get it right and the wine is simply enchanting.

Flowers have some acid, some sugar, but the amounts are so small as to be negligible, so we'll treat them as having none. Thus, whatever is fermented is completely in our hands. This is technically true of every wine but more so for flower wines.

A crockpot full of elderberries, if simply left alone, has a chance to simply start fermenting on its own yeast and produce some sort of wine, albeit probably undrinkable. But a crockpot full of elderflowers has nothing to ferment. The flowers will either grow mold or they will dry up. They possess no natural potential for making wine.

We must engineer their future. The tools and the methods employed for flower wines are often common among them or nearly so. The path from flower petals to wine is not that wide, but there is room enough for both craftsmanship and artistic expression.

These wines begin with the flowers' innate qualities. Some flowers have a subtle hint of licorice. Others suggest anise, or garlic, or mint, or lemons. Still others offer reminiscences of spices—pepper, clove, oregano, mustard. There are hundreds of edible flowers, each with a unique character.

To gain a glimpse of that character, it is advisable to both eat a few of the flowers and to make a cup of tea from them. The flavor we taste in a flower is only a tantalizing clue as to what lies within, not a guarantee of what will be extracted. There is no direct roadmap.

A flower's flavor will undoubtedly change during fermentation, both because the esters and essential oils responsible

for the flavor will be cooked in a chemical stew and because of the numerous variables that contribute to that stew. And there is also the yeast. Different yeasts metabolize different qualities, and here the path widens considerably. If you have enough flowers and time you can experiment with different acids, different sugars, different yeasts.

Finally, like any wine, flower wines need to age. Dandelion wine can be made in many different ways, but all of them require at least a year of bottle aging—some 18 months. Rose petal wines come into their own after 6–12 months. Hibiscus can be consumed almost immediately after bottling but will improve considerably in 6 months. It is best to put away several small bottles for tasting at 6, 9, and 12 months. If you don't have a collection of small wine bottles, you can use beer bottles—they accept corks.

In this and all chapters of this book, when possible, measurements are given in common fractions of teaspoons in the recipes to correspond with the fractions of a gram actually required for the additives. The exception is the amount of potassium metabisulfite to maintain free SO_2 at 50 mg/L or above. However, these are approximations based on the author's experience with these wines. It is almost certain they are not accurate for every making of these wines. There are simply too many variables. It is suggested you test the wine's sulfite level with your SO_2 test kit and adjust the free SO_2 to 100 mg/L for bottling. This should even out any deviations and ensure your wine is prepared for a 2- to 3-year cellar-life expectancy. The formula for calculating this final addition is in Chapter 2 in "Sulfites." However, there are many online sulfite calculators that will compute the result for you if you are not confident of your math skills. You'll still have to use your SO_2 test kit to obtain the numbers needed for the calculator.

Cactus Blossom Wine ❖

One day, many years ago my wife and I were driving the Texas backroads, enjoying the wildflowers, with Longhorns and Black Angus sprinkled across miles and miles of fenced-off range. Growing along the barbed wire fences on either side of the road were thousands of prickly pear cactus—mile after mile of them—planted by birds.

On this day, the cactus were in bloom, covered in large yellow, orange or red flowers. After a while, a question formed in my mind. "Why not?" I always travel with a number of plastic bags, rawhide gloves, and a sharp fillet knife, so I was equipped to harvest the cactus blossoms.

I quickly discovered it is wise to look inside the flowers before harvesting them. I found a bee in almost every flower, laden down with pollen, but they left without incident when I disturbed them. I quickly discovered the best technique for harvesting these flowers. I held the fingers of one hand underneath the blossom, gathering the petals together and with the other hand, I cut them free from the cactus with the fillet knife.

JACK'S TIP

THE GLOVES were essential because immediately below each flower grew a protective ring of short spines that released from the cactus when they made contact with the glove. When I was finished with my harvest, I had thousands of tiny, almost invisible spines covering the glove. Cleaning them from the glove was simple once I got home. I used a small propane torch to burn them off.

I had so many cactus petals—mostly yellow but some orange and some red—that I made two batches of wine, each by a different list of ingredients and method. The recipe that follows was the best, and I made this wine annually for many years.

Cactus Blossom Wine Recipe

WINE IS READY IN: **17 months**

YOU'LL NEED: **2½ quarts cactus petals, 1 can frozen 100 percent white grape juice concentrate per gallon of wine**

ADDITIONAL EQUIPMENT: **1 nylon straining bag**

MAKES: **1 gallon, but can be scaled up**

INGREDIENTS

2½ qt. cactus petals

1 can 100 percent white grape juice frozen concentrate, thawed

2 lb. granulated sugar

1½ tsp tartaric acid

⅛ tsp grape tannin powder

potassium metabisulfite, as needed

½ tsp potassium sorbate

1 tsp (3 g) yeast nutrient

Lalvin EC-1118 yeast

DIRECTIONS

Prepare must: Wash the flowers and put in nylon straining bag with a dozen glass marbles for weight, tie closed, and put in primary. Add grape juice concentrate. Heat 1 quart water and dissolve sugar, tartaric acid, grape tannin, and yeast nutrient. Pour over the bag of petals. Add water to make 1 gallon. Add 0.2 g potassium metabisulfite and stir well. Cover the primary and wait 12 hours. Add pectic enzyme, stirring until completely dissolved. Re-cover primary and set aside 12 hours.

Add yeast: To 1 cup warm water (not to exceed 102 degrees F.) add a pinch of yeast nutrient, 1 teaspoon of sugar, and stir to dissolve. Add yeast to water, stir, and cover mixture for 30 minutes. Add mixture to primary, stir, and cover primary.

Fermentation: Gently squeeze bag daily until SG drops to 1.020, or lower if the fermentation is still vigorous. Remove the bag and hang it over a large bowl to drip-drain for 30 minutes (do not squeeze). Add drippings to primary and discard cactus blossoms. Transfer to secondary and affix airlock.

Post-Fermentation: Put in a dark place for 45 days and carefully rack. Rack again when clear. Wait 60 days and rack again. Return to the dark for 90 days. Very carefully rack off the dusting of fine pollen, and return to dark another 90 days. Add 0.2 g potassium metabisulfite and ½ teaspoon dissolved potassium sorbate. Wait 6 hours, add 2-part fining, wait four days, and carefully rack. Sweeten to SG 1.002 or to balance. If sweetened, wait 30 days to ensure no renewed fermentation and carefully rack into bottles. Allow to age six months before tasting.

Options: To add body, add one very ripe banana, cut crosswise into ½-inch slices, before pitching yeast. For ease of removal, place it its own straining bag.

When sweetening at the end, try using honey instead of sugar. At the end of the final 30-day wait period (after stabilization), carefully check to see if pollen has precipitated out of the honey. Do not disturb any fine lees when bottling. If in doubt, rack again, wait three days and then bottle.

As with all flower wines, because tasting can consume all of your wine, it is wise to bottle four 187-mL splits to use for that purpose.

Similar flower: The following can be substituted for prickly pear cactus blossoms: any cactus flowers.

Chicory Flower Wine ❖

Chicory (*Cichorium intybus*) is a common roadside weed with a wide range in the Americas. It is related to the common dandelion and sends up flowering stalks in the summer, up to a meter high, which branch and sport numerous blue flowers similar in appearance to dandelion flowers except for the color. The petals are wider than the dandelions and toothed at their terminus. Their spring leaves are eaten in salads, and their dried taproot is used to make a brew somewhat stronger than coffee. The roots aren't of interest in winemaking, although their flowers are collected and used to make a very nice wine.

JACK'S TIP

CHICORY FLOWER wine is typically a light wine that lacks body. Thus many recipes use raisins, sultanas or white grape juice (or concentrate) as body-builders, but you could use dates or figs or rhubarb instead. Whatever you use will affect the color, so white or golden raisins or sultanas, or golden figs, are usually used with chicory flowers (some of these are usually available in bulk at grocery stores). For convenience, we will use 100% white grape juice frozen concentrate. Although the recipe specifies Welch's, you can use Old Orchard or any brand as long as it contains no preservatives and is 100% white grape juice concentrate.

Chicory flowers are prepared by plucking the petals from the flower head. There are several methods for doing this. The easiest, in my opinion, is to reach underneath the flower head, lift up and gather the petals in a bunch, and slowly keeping pulling them upward while working them from side to side in a circular motion. The petals will pull clear of the flower head without any waste once the technique is mastered.

This recipe calls for Demerara sugar, which is a variety of cane sugar with a fairly large grain size and a pale tan color. It is less refined than white sugar and therefore is colored by retaining a small amount of molasses. Its flavor is pleasant and often described as toffee-like. It can be used in place of brown sugar. However, brown sugar cannot really be used in place of Demerara sugar.

Chicory Flower Wine Recipe

WINE IS READY IN: **16 months**

YOU'LL NEED: **2 quarts chicory petals, 1 can frozen 100 percent white grape juice concentrate, 2 lemons, 2 oranges per gallon of wine**

ADDITIONAL EQUIPMENT: **1 nylon straining bag**

MAKES: **1 gallon, but can be scaled up**

INGREDIENTS

2 qt. chicory flower petals

1 can Welch's 100 percent white grape juice frozen concentrate, thawed

1 lb., 10 oz. Demerara sugar

2 lemons, juice and zest

2 oranges, juice and zest

½ tsp pectic enzyme

⅛ tsp powdered grape tannin

water to make 1 gal.

potassium metabisulfite, as needed

½ tsp potassium sorbate

1 tsp yeast nutrient

1 g Fermaid-K

Lalvin K1 yeast

DIRECTIONS

Prepare must: Remove all petals and place in nylon straining bag with 20 glass marbles for weight. Add the zest of lemons and oranges, tie closed, and put in primary. Add grape juice concentrate and juice from citrus. Heat 1 quart of water and dissolve sugar, grape tannin, and yeast nutrient. Pour over the bag of petals and heads. Add water to make 1 gallon. Add 0.2 g potassium metabisulfite and stir well. Cover the primary and wait 12 hours. Add pectic enzyme, stirring until completely dissolved. Re-cover primary and set aside 12 hours.

Add yeast: To 1 cup warm water (not to exceed 102 degrees F.) add a pinch of yeast nutrient, one teaspoon of sugar, and stir to dissolve. Add yeast to water, stir, and cover mixture for 30 minutes. Add mixture to primary, stir, and cover primary.

Fermentation: Squeeze bag daily until SG drops to 1.060. Remove the bag and squeeze the daylights out of it over the primary, then discard flower petals and zest. Stir in 1 gram Fermaid-K, transfer to secondary and affix airlock. Put in a dark place until wine falls clear and carefully rack.

Post-Fermentation: Move wine back to a dark place for 60 days and rack again. Rack again in 90 days and again in another 90 days. Add 0.2 g potassium metabisulfite and ½ teaspoon dissolved potassium sorbate. Add 2-part fining, wait four days, and carefully rack. Sweeten to SG 1.002 or to balance. If sweetened, wait 30 days to ensure no renewed fermentation and carefully rack into bottles. Cellar 6 months and enjoy a bottle. Cellar another six months and enjoy it all.

Options: To add body, add one or two very ripe bananas, cut crosswise into ½-inch slices, before pitching yeast. For ease of removal, place it in a separate straining bag.

When sweetening at the end, try using honey instead of sugar. At the end of the final 30-day wait period (after stabilization), carefully check to see if pollen has precipitated out of the honey. Do not disturb any fine lees when bottling. If in doubt, rack again, wait three days and then bottle. Honey adds a little length to the finish.

As with all flower wines, because tasting can consume all of your wine, it is wise to bottle four 187-mL splits to use for that purpose.

Similar flowers: There are approximately 85 flowers that could be substituted for chicory in this recipe, but none can duplicate the flavor of the chicory flower. It is safer to say "none."

Dandelion Flower Wine ❖

When living in Colorado during my first marriage, I was trying to sleep in late one Saturday when I was awakened by the sound of women speaking Vietnamese. After three tours in "the Nam" I was well-acquainted with the sound of the language. I peeked through the blinds, and there were three women squatting in our front yard harvesting what must have seemed like a treasure trove of young dandelion leaves. The yard was blanketed with them, although they hadn't yet pushed up any flowers. I grabbed some trousers and ran into the kitchen. From our trash, I fished out the empty spray bottle of Roundup and then hurried out into the lawn, waving it and shouting, "Dùng lại! Poison!" I didn't know the Vietnamese word for poison, but I well remembered the Vietnamese for "Stop!" They recognized the bottle I was holding up, looked at me with disdain and dumped their baskets of greens on my lawn. I looked at the three piles. It must have taken them an hour to collect that many leaves.

The many-toothed leaves are almost as recognizable to home-owners as the bright yellow flower. Most don't realize the leaves are great in green salads or steamed until the flowers appear, at which time they turn bitter.

Dandelion wine is the classic flower wine. More has been written about it than any other flower wine. When made well, it is absolutely exquisite. When made poorly, it can still be pretty darned good. But too much greenery in with the flower petals will make the wine bitter—a waste of many, many hours of work.

I don't know anyone who doesn't recognize the bright yellow, many rayed flowers of *Taraxacum officinale* at first glance. Most think of it as a weed, but others look upon them differently. My wife actually *planted* dandelions in one of our flower beds, and the result was quite stunning when they bloomed *en masse*. Others, like the three Vietnamese ladies, look upon their leaves as salad or greens for steaming or cooking into casseroles, omelets, and other dishes. But for the winemaker, the dandelion is simply the king of flowers.

Though the two most widespread species of dandelion were brought by Europe to the Americas, native North American species of dandelions exist, and indigenous peoples used dandelions as both food and medicine long before Columbus ever sailed.

JACK'S TIP

THE APPROACHES to making dandelion wine differ enormously. Some use the whole flower heads trimmed only of the stalks. Still others use the flowerheads trimmed of all greenery. Others will use only the petals. I used to use only the petals until I happened upon the recipe that follows, which leaves the calyx (the green cuplike sepals enclosing the lower portion of the flower) on about 1 in 5 flowers—no more than that.

Pick the flower heads as soon as the sun burns the dew off the petals, but not too late. Around noonish, the flower senses the sun's progress and begins turning all those beautiful petals into those parachute seeds that can ride a good breeze for miles. As soon as you've picked your allotment for the day (usually determined by the aching in your back), wash your hands (they get sticky while picking the flowers), sit in the shade and pull the petals off the flowers.

It helps considerably if you have a couple of grandkids in the 3–5-year age group. Being shorter, they are a lot closer to the flowers than we grown-ups are. For about two years, my granddaughter would fill a small bucket with flower heads for a quarter a bucket. Pretty good deal for each of us.

While the stems are bitter, a little greenery from the calyx ("calyces" is the plural) actually adds a little *je ne sais quoi* to the wine if not overdone. This little something is actually engineered into the wine in this recipe, and wines made this way will keep for many, many years if acid and SO_2 are correct.

This wine takes a long time to mature to its potential, which is why it is worth it to gather dandelions daily, put the prepared petals in freezer-grade Ziploc bags, and freeze them until you have enough to make 3 to 5 gallons. Once you taste the finished wine, you'll want to make it every year.

Dandelion Flower Wine Recipe

WINE IS READY IN: **33 months**

YOU'LL NEED: **2½ quarts dandelion petals and heads, 1 can frozen 100 percent white grape juice concentrate, 2 oranges, 2 lemons per gallon of wine**

ADDITIONAL EQUIPMENT: **2 nylon straining bag**

MAKES: **1 gallon, but can be scaled up**

INGREDIENTS

2 qt. dandelion petals

½ qt. dandelion heads with calyces and petals only

1 can Welch's 100 percent white grape juice frozen concentrate, thawed

1 lb., 10 oz. Demerara sugar

2 lemons, juice only

2 oranges, juice only

½ tsp pectic enzyme

⅛ tsp grape tannin powder

water to make 1 gal.

potassium metabisulfite, as needed

½ tsp potassium sorbate

1 tsp yeast nutrient

1 g Fermaid-K

Lalvin K1 yeast

DIRECTIONS

Prepare must: Prepare the flowers and put in nylon straining bag with 20 glass marbles for weight, tie closed, and put in primary. Add grape juice concentrate and juice from citrus. Heat 1 quart water and dissolve sugar, grape tannin, and yeast nutrient. Pour over the bag of petals. Add water to make 1 gallon. Add 0.2 g potassium metabisulfite and stir well. Cover the primary and wait 12 hours. Add pectic enzyme, stirring until completely dissolved. Re-cover primary and set aside 12 hours.

Add yeast: To 1 cup warm water (not to exceed 102 degrees F.) add a pinch of yeast nutrient, 1 teaspoon of sugar, and stir to dissolve. Add yeast to water, stir, and cover mixture for 30 minutes. Add mixture to primary, stir, and cover primary.

Fermentation: Squeeze the bag several times daily until SG drops to 1.060. Stir in 1 gram Fermaid-K. When SG falls to 1.020, or lower if the fermentation is still vigorous, remove the bag of dandelion petals, squeeze lightly only, discard flower matter, transfer liquid to secondary, affix airlock, and set aside in a dark place until wine falls clear (1–2 months). Carefully rack and reattach airlock.

Post-Fermentation: Move wine back to a dark place for 30 days and carefully rack. Return to the dark for 60 days. Carefully rack and return to dark another 60 days. Rack again, reattach airlock and return to the dark a final 60 days. Add 0.2 g potassium metabisulfite and ½ teaspoon dissolved potassium sorbate. Add two-part fining, wait four days, and carefully rack. Sweeten to SG 1.002 or to balance. If sweetened, wait 30 days to ensure no renewed fermentation and carefully rack into bottles. This wine is for the long term and for winning competitions, so cellar it for two years before tasting. Don't waste a bottle by tasting early. It's best to make a 3–5-gallon batch.

Options: To add body, add one or two very ripe bananas, cut crosswise into ½-inch slices, before pitching yeast. For ease of removal, place it in a separate straining bag.

When sweetening at the end, use quality honey instead of sugar. At the end of the final 30-day wait period (after stabilization), carefully check to see if pollen has precipitated out of the honey. If present, rack again, wait three days and then bottle.

As with all flower wines, because tasting can consume all of your wine, it is wise to bottle four 187-mL splits to use for that purpose.

Similar flowers: The false dandelion could be fermented using this recipe, but it is an inferior flower and not worth the time and effort. The appropriate answer is "none."

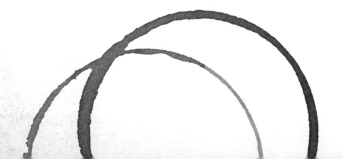

Elderflower Wine ❖

An acquired taste for some, for many others, elderflower wine is simply the one flower wine that can define you as a wine-maker. Unlike the delicate, suggestive, and elusive dandelion wine, elderflowers are bold, spicy, and demanding—the "look-at-me, look-at-me" child who wants your full attention and approval.

The fruit of all varieties of elderberries are slightly bitter when eaten fresh. Three varieties are toxic and can put you in the hospital, but universally their flowers are toxin-free, as boldly fragrant as jasmine, and enriching as a food source. That they invite you to make them into wine goes without saying.

JACK'S TIP

TOO MUCH of a good thing is still too much. As a wine base, elder-flower begs for moderation. Not enough flowers will leave you guessing, but too many will yield an almost undrinkable vile, soup . And so somewhere between not-enough and too-many is that sweet spot that produces ambrosia.

If you can find that sweet spot, you can coax the flower into greatness. This is the challenge of the flower to every winemaker. It is as if the flower is saying, "Make me into a great wine, and you will have mastered the flower wine tableaux of winemaking."

The recipe that follows has found the sweet spot, the correct quantity of elderflowers for a US gallon using white grape juice concentrate. If you opted not to add the concentrate, the flowers and sugar would need to be increased slightly.

Elderflower Wine Recipe

WINE IS READY IN: **11 months**

YOU'LL NEED: **1 pint fresh elderflowers, 1 can frozen 100 percent white grape juice concentrate per gallon of wine**

ADDITIONAL EQUIPMENT: **1 nylon straining bag**

MAKES: **1 gallon, but can be scaled up**

INGREDIENTS

1 pt. fresh elderflowers

1 can Welch's 100 percent white grape juice frozen concentrate, thawed

2 lb. very fine granulated sugar

1 tsp tartaric acid

1 tsp malic acid

water to make 1 gal.

potassium metabisulfite, as needed

½ tsp potassium sorbate

1 tsp yeast nutrient

Lalvin R2 or Red Star Côte des Blancs yeast

DIRECTIONS

Prepare must: Put 3 liters water on to boil. Meanwhile, destem flowers, wash well, and put in nylon straining bag. Put flower bag with a dozen glass marbles for weight, tie closed, and put with sugar and grape concentrate in primary and pour boiling water over them. Stir well to dissolve sugar, cover with a sanitized cloth, and set aside until cool. Add acids, yeast nutrient, and 0.2 g potassium metabisulfite and stir well. Cover the primary and wait 12 hours.

Add yeast: To 1 cup warm water (not to exceed 102 degrees F.) add a pinch of yeast nutrient, 1 teaspoon of sugar, and stir to dissolve. Add yeast to water, stir, and cover mixture for 30 minutes. Add mixture to primary, stir, and cover primary.

Fermentation: Ferment six days, squeezing the bag several times daily. Remove the bag of flowers, squeeze gently several times and discard flowers. Transfer the wine to secondary, top-up and attach airlock. Set aside in a dark place for 30 days and carefully rack.

Post-Fermentation: Move wine back to a dark place for 30 days and carefully rack. Return to the dark for 60 days. If clear, check and correct clarity. Add 0.2 g potassium metabisulfite and ½ teaspoon potassium sorbate. Stir well. Check pH and correct it as needed. Sweeten to SG 1.002 or to balance. If sweetened, wait 30 days to ensure no renewed fermentation and carefully rack into bottles. Age wine six months before tasting.

Options: To add body, add one or two very ripe bananas, cut crosswise into ½-inch slices, before pitching yeast. For ease of removal, place it in a separate straining bag.

This wine responds to some light oak. Add during the maturation phase for 3–4 weeks. Don't overdo it.

When sweetening at the end, use quality honey instead of sugar. At the end of the final 30-day wait period (after stabilization), carefully check to see if pollen has precipitated out of the honey. If present, rack again, wait three days and then bottle.

As with all flower wines, because tasting can consume all of your wine, it is wise to bottle four 187-mL splits to use for that purpose.

Similar flowers: None.

Hibiscus Wine ❖

The hibiscus belongs to its own genus containing many species. One, in particular, the *Hibiscus sabdariffa*, is considered the most edible of the genus and the basis for this wine. Much more famous as a tea and infusion for numerous beverages, the flower and resulting drinks are known by different names throughout the world. Grown throughout the temperate, sub-tropic and tropic zones, the plant and its tea have a global expanse.

The tea can be made from the dried flower petals or, more traditionally, from the calyces after pollination and the petals fall, but before fruit development. The calyces are dried, chopped and ground to produce the dried powder or granules which are then rehydrated to make the tea.

In Asia and the Indies, as well as in parts of Africa, the calyces are made into wine. The wine can also be made from the tea. When made into wine, the calyces are not dried, but chopped and pressed, to yield the juice that is then made into wine.

JACK'S TIP

FOR THIS WINE, none of the above methods are used. Instead, the wine is made from the dried flower petals or from commercial hibiscus tea, also known as Jamaica, the name of the flower and tea in Mexico.

I buy my flowers from Mexican markets, where they are often found in bulk or at the very least, in containers for tea. They are also available at many health food stores. The Mexican markets are less expensive.

I had a friend who saved the dried flowers for me from his garden, but he has moved, and the commercial ones I buy are of higher quality and produce better color anyway—either red or purple.

Hibiscus Wine Recipe

WINE IS READY IN: **7 months**

YOU'LL NEED: **2 ounces dried hibiscus flowers or hibiscus tea per gallon of wine**

ADDITIONAL EQUIPMENT: **1 jelly bag**

MAKES: **1 gallon, but can be scaled up**

INGREDIENTS

2 oz. dried hibiscus flowers or hibiscus tea

2 lb. very fine granulated sugar

1 tsp tartaric acid

1 tsp citric acid

water to make 1 gal.

potassium metabisulfite, as needed

½ tsp potassium sorbate

1 tsp yeast nutrient

Red Star Côte des Blancs yeast

DIRECTIONS

Prepare must: Bring 3 liters water to boil, remove from heat and dissolve sugar, acids and yeast nutrient into it. Put flowers or tea in a jelly bag with several glass marbles, tie closed, and place in primary. Pour sugar-water over the jelly bag, cover with a sanitized cloth, and set aside until cool. Add 0.2 g potassium metabisulfite and stir well. Cover the primary and wait 12 hours.

Add yeast: To 1 cup warm water (not to exceed 102 degrees F.) add a pinch of yeast nutrient, 1 teaspoon of sugar, and stir to dissolve. Add yeast to water, stir, and cover mixture for 30 minutes. Add mixture to primary, stir, and cover primary.

Fermentation: Squeeze jelly bag 2–3 times daily until SG drops to 1.020, or lower if the fermentation is still vigorous. Remove the jelly bag, squeeze well, and discard flowers. Transfer the wine to secondary and attach airlock. Set aside in a dark place for 30 days and carefully rack.

Post-Fermentation: Move wine back to the dark for 30 days and carefully rack and reattach airlock. Keep in the dark another 60 days. Check and correct clarity. Carefully rack. Add 0.2 g potassium metabisulfite and ½ teaspoon dissolved potassium sorbate Check pH and correct as needed. Sweeten to SG 1.002 or to balance. If sweetened, wait 30 days to ensure no renewed fermentation and carefully rack into bottles. May taste in 2 months, but six months is better.

Options: To add body, add one or two very ripe bananas, cut crosswise into ½-inch slices, before pitching yeast. For ease of removal, place it in a separate straining bag.

This wine responds to a very light oak. Add during the maturation phase for 3–4 weeks. Don't overdo it.

When sweetening at the end, use quality honey instead of sugar. At the end of the final 30-day wait period (after stabilization), carefully check to see if pollen has precipitated out of the honey. If present, rack again, wait three days and then bottle.

As with all root wines, because tasting can consume all of your wine, it is wise to bottle four 187-mL splits to use for that purpose.

Similar flowers: None.

Honeysuckle Wine ❖

For years I tried, without success, to make a good honeysuckle wine, mainly following the recipes of those who went before me. Well, "without success" is perhaps a bit dramatic. I made wine. Most people liked it. But I didn't. Then one day I was judging a county fair wine competition and tasted the perfect honeysuckle wine. I met up with the winemaker after the competition and we talked about his wine. I finally had to ask him outright how many flowers he used. He told me and I knew what I had been doing wrong.

Honeysuckle wine has been around at least two thousand years, so it amazes me that all the recipe references I've read make a weak wine. True, for the most part, honeysuckle wine was a "homestead wine," generally made by the woman of the house, and it was a quality wine, no doubt, but they did not often write books on winemaking. So those recipes seemingly have been lost, but perhaps there are many recipes that simply haven't been discovered. I can only wonder why so many authors have gotten it so wrong throughout the nineteenth and twentieth centuries.

The earliest mention I can find of honeysuckle wine is in ancient Korea. It's a mention, not a recipe. Honeysuckles are found over much of the world, so I assume if they were making it in Korea, they were making it in many other places. It just wasn't mentioned in a way I can retrieve.

What follows is the recipe I managed to elicit from the competition entrant, plus sulfite additions and other essentials. I made the yeast selection myself.

JACK'S TIP

WITH 180 SPECIES of honeysuckle recorded and many imported ones having become naturalized and now invasive, no single species can be cited as "the best" for making wine. My only advice is that if it is fragrant, it can be used with expectations of success. There is a good chance that the common honeysuckle, with white and yellow flowers, is the imported, now naturalized and invasive, *Lonicera japonica*, or a variety thereof, or cultivar. Introduced into the United States in 1806, it became widely naturalized by the 1860s. The native, common honeysuckle, *Lonicera periclymenum*, also known as woodbine, is substantially widespread. Either is a candidate for wine, as is the coral or trumpet honeysuckle (*Lonicera sempervirens*).

Note: Before making honeysuckle wine, confirm the identity of the honeysuckle species you're harvesting and that it's edible. Don't make wine out of honeysuckle berries, as they are often toxic.

Honeysuckle Wine Recipe

WINE IS READY IN: **14 months**

YOU'LL NEED: **2 quarts of honeysuckle flowers per gallon of wine**

ADDITIONAL EQUIPMENT: **1 colander**

MAKES: **1 gallon, but can be scaled up**

INGREDIENTS

2 qt. (packed) honeysuckle flowers

2 lb. very fine granulated sugar

2 tsp tartaric acid

1 tsp citric acid

¼ tsp grape tannin powder

water to make 1 gal.

potassium metabisulfite, as needed

½ tsp potassium sorbate

¼ tsp yeast energizer

1 tsp yeast nutrient

Lalvin DV10 yeast

DIRECTIONS

Prepare must: Wash flowers under cold water. Put in a large pot with a tight-fitting lid and 2½ quarts water. Bring to simmer and place the lid on the pot. Turn off heat and let steep three hours. Meanwhile, bring 1 quart water to boil, remove from heat and dissolve sugar, grape tannin, yeast nutrient, yeast energizer, and acid thoroughly in water. Pour into your primary. Using a colander, strain flower water into primary, pressing flowers well to extract as much essence as possible. Discard flowers. Add 0.2 g potassium metabisulfite, stir well, cover primary, and wait 12 hours.

Add yeast: To 1 cup warm water (not to exceed 102 degrees F.) add a pinch of yeast nutrient, 1 teaspoon of sugar, and stir to dissolve. Add yeast to water, stir, and cover mixture for 30 minutes. Add mixture to primary, stir, and cover primary.

Fermentation: Stir 2–3 times daily until SG drops to 1.020, or lower if the fermentation is still vigorous. Transfer the wine to secondary and attach airlock. Set aside in a dark place for 30 days and carefully rack.

Post-Fermentation: Move wine back into the dark for 90 days and carefully rack. Rack again after another 90 days. Correct clarity if necessary and wait three days. Add 0.2 g potassium metabisulfite, ½ teaspoon dissolved potassium sorbate, check pH, and correct as needed. Sweeten to SG 1.002 or to balance. If sweetened, wait 30 days to ensure no renewed fermentation and carefully rack into bottles. Taste in 6 months.

Options: To add body, add one or two very ripe bananas, cut crosswise into ½-inch slices, before pitching yeast. For ease of removal, place it in a separate straining bag.

When sweetening at the end, use quality honey instead of sugar. At the end of the final 30-day wait period (after stabilization), carefully check to see if pollen has precipitated out of the honey. If present, rack again, wait three days and then bottle.

As with all root wines, because tasting can consume all of your wine, it is wise to bottle four 187-mL splits to use for that purpose.

Similar flowers: None.

Lavender Wine ❖

Lavender is its own genus (*Lavandula*) with 47 known species, followed by numerous varieties, cultivars, and hybrids. The most common garden variety is English Lavender (*L. angustifolia*), which isn't the most fragrant of the genus but still very nice. It has a long history of use for its extracted essential oils, for cut flowers used to freshen up a room, and for culinary uses.

It is referenced in the works of Shakespeare, Chaucer, and Spenser in passing. A contemporary French reference to lavender mead likewise offers no recipe. Perhaps it is because there are so many species of lavender, each with its own character. Any recipe without specificity to species would invariably lead to problems, but then again, maybe I'm overanalyzing this. It could also be that Shakespeare, Chaucer, and Spenser were not known for detailing recipes in their writings.

JACK'S TIP

WINEMAKERS in the twentieth and twenty-first centuries struggle with the exact amount of the flower to use without overwhelming the product. The recipe we shall use offers a range of 1 to 1½ quarts of the fresh flower. This is quite a spread when you think of the percentages involved, so let me elaborate. If you know for certain your lavender is *L. angustifolia*, use 1½ quarts. If another species or enhanced cultivar, use 1-quart. You can taste-test later and add an infusion or tea to increase the flavor if too weak for your taste.

Be warned, however, that if the flavor is too strong the wine will suffer from off-flavors and possibly even odors. The only remedy is to dilute the wine with sweetened water, which could result in a volume for which you have no appropriate secondary fermenter.

Lavender Wine Recipe

WINE IS READY IN: **17 months**

YOU'LL NEED: **1 to 1½ pints of lavender flowers, 1 can frozen 100 percent white grape juice concentrate per gallon of wine**

ADDITIONAL EQUIPMENT: **1 nylon straining bag**

MAKES: **1 gallon, but can be scaled up**

INGREDIENTS

1 to 1½ pt. (packed) lavender flowers (depending on the fullness of scent)

1 can Welch's 100 percent white grape juice frozen concentrate, thawed

1¾ lb. very fine granulated sugar

2 tsp citric acid

¼ tsp grape tannin powder

water to make 1 gal.

potassium metabisulfite, as needed

½ tsp potassium sorbate

⅛ tsp yeast energizer

1 tsp yeast nutrient

Lalvin DV10 yeast

DIRECTIONS

Prepare must: Bring 2½ quarts water to boil. Meanwhile, wash flowers under cold water, place in nylon straining bag, tie closed, and place in your primary. Pour thawed grape juice concentrate over flowers. When water boils, remove from heat and stir in sugar, acid, grape tannin, yeast nutrient, and yeast energizer until dissolved. Pour over flowers in the primary. Cover primary. When the water cools to lukewarm, add the remaining water to make 1 gallon. Check pH and correct it as needed. Add 0.2 g potassium metabisulfite, stir well, cover primary, and wait 12 hours.

Add yeast: To 1 cup warm water (not to exceed 102 degrees F.) add a pinch of yeast nutrient, 1 teaspoon of sugar, and stir to dissolve. Add yeast to water, stir, and cover mixture for 30 minutes. Add mixture to primary, stir, and cover primary.

Fermentation: Stir 2–3 times daily for seven days. Remove nylon straining bag, squeeze flowers firmly, transfer the wine to secondary and attach airlock. Set aside in a dark place for 60 days. Stir in yeast energizer and carefully rack.

Post-Fermentation: Move wine back to the dark place for 60 days and carefully rack. Add 0.2 g potassium metabisulfite and ½ teaspoon dissolved potassium sorbate. Correct clarity if required with pectic enzyme. Sweeten to SG 1.002 or to balance. If sweetened, wait 30 days to ensure no renewed fermentation and carefully rack into bottles. Age one year before tasting.

Options: To add body, add one or two very ripe bananas, cut crosswise into ½-inch slices, before pitching yeast. For ease of removal, place it in a separate straining bag.

When sweetening at the end, use quality honey instead of sugar. At the end of the final 30-day wait period (after stabilization), carefully check to see if pollen has precipitated out of the honey. If present, rack again, wait three days and then bottle.

As with all flower wines, because tasting can consume all of your wine, it is wise to bottle four 187-mL splits to use for that purpose.

Similar flowers: None.

Orange Blossom Wine ❖

Orange blossom (flower) wines have been around a long time and made many different ways. The heaviest have always been made using Seville oranges—peel, pulp, juice, and flowers—and sometimes with lemon added. Seville oranges are sour oranges best suited for marmalade, as they are so acidic as to almost be inedible. The peel was shaved very thinly, a more homogeneous fare than today's grated peel zest. Zest is preferred, as it offers more surface area for the yeast, acids, and alcohol to work on and extract the essential oils and esters.

These were not true orange blossom wines, but rather an orange wine with the flowers added for increased bouquet. The shift was gradual from orange wine to orange blossom wine—just the fermented flowers, please. The latter was favored by the Moors, who inhabited much of the Iberian Peninsula and greatly influenced the beverages and cuisine of Spain and Portugal. The Moors also favored orange flower water, used mainly in two ways—as a refreshing hand and face wash for arriving guests and before meals and refreshments.

A century ago and beyond the wine was made using a spirit such as rum to extract the essential oils and fragrances. This was because fermentation relied on bread or beer yeast and produced low-strength alcohols incapable of good extraction. The isolation and cultivation of wine yeasts made the spirits unnecessary, although some winemakers kept them in because they had grown fond of the taste.

JACK'S TIP

ORANGE BLOSSOM (flower) wine is simplicity itself. It can be made, although not made well without including everything it doesn't have—sugar, acid, a teeny bit of tannin, yeast nutrient, and sulfite.

Orange Blossom Wine Recipe

WINE IS READY IN: **7 months**

YOU'LL NEED: **½ ounce dried orange flowers or 3 ounces fresh per gallon of wine**

ADDITIONAL EQUIPMENT: **1 jelly bag or 1 nylon straining bag**

MAKES: **1 gallon, but can be scaled up**

INGREDIENTS

½ oz. dried orange flowers or 3 oz. fresh

2 lb. very fine granulated sugar or 3 lb. orange blossom honey

2 tsp citric acid

½ tsp tartaric acid

⅛ tsp yeast energizer

⅛ tsp grape tannin powder

water to make 1 gal.

potassium metabisulfite, as needed

½ tsp potassium sorbate

1 tsp yeast nutrient

Lalvin R2 yeast

DIRECTIONS

Prepare must: Put dried flowers in a jelly bag, tie closed, and put in your primary. Meanwhile, bring 3 quarts of water to boil and dissolve the sugar, acid, yeast nutrient, and yeast energizer. Pour over the jelly bag. Cover the primary and set aside to cool to room temperature. Add 0.2 g potassium metabisulfite, 1½ pints water, cover primary, and set aside 12 hours.

Add yeast: To 1 cup warm water (not to exceed 102 degrees F.) add a pinch of yeast nutrient, 1 teaspoon of sugar, and stir to dissolve. Add yeast to water, stir, and cover mixture for 30 minutes. Add mixture to primary, stir, and cover primary.

Fermentation: Stir 2–3 times daily for four days. Remove the jelly bag and drain (do not squeeze), discard flowers, transfer the wine to secondary, and attach airlock. Set aside in a dark place for 30 days and carefully rack.

Post-Fermentation: Move wine back to the dark place until wine clears (30–60 days) and carefully rack. Set in the dark for 60 days and rack. Return to the dark additional 60 days and rack. Add 0.2 g potassium metabisulfite and ½ teaspoon dissolved potassium sorbate. Check pH and correct it as needed. Correct clarity if required and sweeten to SG 1.002 or to balance. If sweetened, wait 30 days to ensure no renewed fermentation and carefully rack into bottles. Age three months before tasting, but is much improved at six months. Serve chilled as an aperitif and appreciate the wonderful bouquet and flavor.

Options: To add body, add one or two very ripe bananas, cut crosswise into ½-inch slices, before pitching yeast. For ease of removal, place it in a separate straining bag.

When sweetening at the end, use quality honey instead of sugar. At the end of the final 30-day wait period (after stabilization), carefully check to see if pollen has precipitated out of the honey. If present, rack again, wait three days and then bottle.

As with all root wines, because tasting can consume all of your wine, it is wise to bottle four 187-mL splits to use for that purpose.

Similar flowers: The following flowers can be substituted for orange blossoms in this recipe: lemon blossoms, lime blossoms, grapefruit blossoms, kumquat blossoms, and tangerine blossoms.

Rose Petal Wine ❖

I have made many rose petal wines and never made a bad one yet. At our house, we are blessed to have a heritage rose that is deep red and extremely fragrant, but we have no idea what variety or cultivar it is. It was here when we bought our property. It puts out long (up to 12 feet!) canes that it then decorates with anywhere from 5–20 4-inch roses on each cane. The canes get so heavy with these red perfume bombs that they usually droop to the ground. We also planted two Lady Banks roses, a climbing vine that puts out about 80–100 dusty yellow 2½-inch roses every spring. We have no shortage of roses.

Rose petal wine predates the Romans, whose elite's households made as much as their rose gardens could supply. Even gardenless common citizens made the wine, buying wilted or dried rose petals from vendors. In the countryside, wild roses filled the bill for whoever collected them.

It seems that wherever roses are grown, rose petal wine appears. And rose petal soup. What could be better than having a bowl of rose petal soup with a large chunk of fresh bread and a glass of rose petal wine?

JACK'S TIP

IF YOU HAVE a variety of rose bushes that bloom at different times, collect the petals from each fragrant variety in turn as they begin to wilt and freeze them until you have enough to make a batch of wine. Even dried petals of fragrant varieties should be collected.

Many recipes instruct the winemaker to cut the roses and pull the petals later. I beg you not to do this unless you are cutting them for flower arrangements. Instead, just pull the petals from the flowers on the plant. Most petals easily detach, and doing it this way leaves the rosehip intact to develop and offer you another wine base at a later date. Rose hips also make a healthy tea, most welcome on chilly winter nights and for winter sniffles.

Rose petal wines tend to be thin on their own, so a body-enhancer is almost always prescribed. I've made it using raisins, pea pods, grape concentrate, dates, barley, and whole wheat to thicken the body. Without a doubt, grape concentrate works best. It works as well as, if not better than, most as a body-builder, but also has the least noticeable aroma and flavor modifiers.

Most rose petal wine recipes use a Champagne yeast. I prefer a Sauternes yeast, but you're welcome to switch yeasts. The following recipe is, in my opinion, the best.

Rose Petal
Wine Recipe

WINE IS READY IN: **13 months**

YOU'LL NEED: **6–7 pints rose petals, 1 can frozen 100 percent red or white grape juice concentrate per gallon of wine**

ADDITIONAL EQUIPMENT: **1 nylon straining bag**

MAKES: **1 gallon, but can be scaled up**

INGREDIENTS

6 pt. wilted rose petals or 7 pt. of fresh

1 can 100 percent red or white grape juice frozen concentrate, thawed

2 lb. very fine granulated sugar

3 tsp citric acid

⅛ tsp grape tannin powder

water to make 1 gal.

potassium metabisulfite, as needed

½ tsp potassium sorbate

⅛ tsp yeast energizer

1 tsp yeast nutrient

Lalvin R2 yeast

DIRECTIONS

Prepare must: Put flowers in a jelly bag, tie closed and put in your primary. Meanwhile, bring 3 quarts of water to boil and dissolve the sugar, acid, yeast nutrient, and yeast energizer. Pour over the jelly bag. Cover the primary and set aside to cool to room temperature. Add 0.2 g potassium metabisulfite, 1½ pints water, cover primary, and set aside 12 hours.

Add yeast: To 1 cup warm water (not to exceed 102 degrees F.) add a pinch of yeast nutrient, 1 teaspoon of sugar, and stir to dissolve. Add yeast to water, stir, and cover mixture for 30 minutes. Add mixture to primary, stir, and cover primary.

Fermentation: Stir 2–3 times daily for four days. Remove the jelly bag and drain (do not squeeze), discard flowers, transfer the wine to secondary, and attach airlock. Set aside in a dark place for 30 days and carefully rack.

Post-Fermentation: Move wine back to the dark place until wine clears (30–60 days) and carefully rack. Set aside in the dark another 60 days and rack. Return to dark additional 60 days. Rack, add 0.2 g potassium metabisulfite and ½ teaspoon dissolved potassium sorbate. Check pH and correct it as needed. Correct clarity if required and sweeten to SG 1.002 or to balance. If sweetened, wait 30 days to ensure no renewed fermentation and carefully rack into bottles. Age three months before tasting, but it is much improved at six months.

Options: To add body, add one or two very ripe bananas, cut crosswise into ½-inch slices, before pitching yeast. For ease of removal, place it in a separate straining bag.

When sweetening at the end, use quality honey instead of sugar. At the end of the final 30-day wait period (after stabilization), carefully check to see if pollen has precipitated out of the honey. If present, rack again, wait three days and then bottle.

As with all flower wines, because tasting can consume all of your wine, it is wise to bottle four 187-mL splits to use for that purpose.

Similar flowers: None.

Tulip Wine ❖

Twenty years ago I stopped at a roadside collection of booths and tailgates selling produce, handicrafts, knockoffs, and junk. I got there at just the right time. The vendors wanted to go home and were offering their best deals. A guy was selling plants, seeds, and bulbs from a pickup truck. A display box, nearly empty, contained some bulbs which were steadily drying out under the hot sun. I paused just long enough to see what kind of bulbs they were. The vendor said, "Yellow tulips. You can have them all for $4." There were several dozen left. I was thinking of a place they would fit in the garden when he said, "Hell, you can have them for $2." Four dollars would have been a good deal but $2 was a steal. I took them.

A long wait later, about 80 tulips were spreading their yellow petals to the heavens when the heavens unleashed a hailstorm. When it ceased I went out to survey the damage to my young grapes and the garden. About half the grapes were on the ground but every tulip petal also shared that fate. I looked at the yellow carnage on the ground that had been my cheerful tulips and wondered if I could make wine from them. I hurried about, collecting them in a bucket, washed them well and made a gallon of wine.

I don't know if anyone else had ever made tulip petal wine before (I'd bet the farm I wasn't the first), but I could not find any mention of it in even the most obscure references in my collection.

I can only report that the wine came out fine, but I didn't know how good it would be at 18 months, so I drank most of it between 6 and 12 months, keeping only one bottle for 18 months—most rewarding.

I have since learned that there is wide variability in the taste of tulip varieties and cultivars. Why I didn't assume this is beyond me. I am told that reddish and orangish petals generally taste better than yellow ones, so if you grow tulips or have the opportunity to harvest the petals keep this in mind. Simply eating a couple of petals should tell you all you need to know.

JACK'S TIP

THERE ARE PROBABLY many ways to make this wine, but I only had one shot at it and this is the recipe I developed back in 1999. A number of people have contacted me since and reported good results using this recipe, so it remains largely unchanged. I do, however, recommend using two rather than three quarts of petals. The wine had a very faint minerality taste when young (using three quarts of petals), but this faded as it aged and was not detected at 18 months.

Tulip Wine Recipe

WINE IS READY IN: **13 months**

YOU'LL NEED: **2–3 quarts tulip petals, 1 can frozen 100 percent white grape juice concentrate per gallon of wine**

ADDITIONAL EQUIPMENT: **1 nylon straining bag**

MAKES: **1 gallon, but can be scaled up**

INGREDIENTS

2–3 qt. tulip petals

1 can 100 percent white grape juice frozen concentrate, thawed

2 lb. very fine granulated sugar

2 tsp citric acid

⅛ tsp grape tannin powder

water to make 1 gal.

potassium metabisulfite, as needed

½ tsp potassium sorbate

⅛ tsp yeast energizer

1 tsp yeast nutrient

Lalvin BA11 yeast

DIRECTIONS

Prepare must: Put flower petals in a nylon straining bag, tie closed and put in your primary. Meanwhile, bring 3 quarts of water to boil and dissolve the sugar, acid, yeast nutrient, and yeast energizer. Pour over straining bag. Cover primary and set aside to cool to room temperature. Add thawed grape concentrate, check pH, and correct as needed. Add 0.2 g potassium metabisulfite, 1½ pints water, cover primary, and set aside 12 hours.

Add yeast: To 1 cup warm water (not to exceed 102 degrees F.) add a pinch of yeast nutrient, 1 teaspoon of sugar, and stir to dissolve. Add yeast to water, stir, and cover mixture for 30 minutes. Add mixture to primary, stir, and cover primary.

Fermentation: Stir and squeeze bag 2–3 times daily for five days. Remove straining bag and squeeze to extract as much flavor as you can, discard flowers, transfer the wine to secondary, and attach airlock. Set aside in a dark place for 30 days and carefully rack.

Post-Fermentation: Move wine back to the dark place until wine clears (30–60 days) and carefully rack. Set back in the dark 60 days and rack. Return to dark additional 60 days. Rack, add 0.2 g potassium metabisulfite and ½ teaspoon dissolved potassium sorbate. Correct clarity if required with pectic enzyme and sweeten to taste or to balance. If sweetened, wait 30 days to ensure no renewed fermentation and carefully rack into bottles. Age six months before tasting, but is much improved at 12 and 18 months.

Options: To add body, add one or two very ripe bananas, cut crosswise into ½-inch slices, before pitching yeast. For ease of removal, place it in a separate straining bag.

When sweetening at the end, use quality honey instead of sugar. At the end of the final 30-day wait period (after stabilization), carefully check to see if pollen has precipitated out of the honey. If present, rack again, add ⅛ teaspoon potassium metabisulfite, wait three days and then bottle.

As with all flower wines, because tasting can consume all of your wine, it is wise to bottle four 187-mL splits to use for that purpose.

Similar flowers: The following flowers can be substituted for cultivated tulip petals in this recipe: wild tulips.

CHAPTER TEN
HERBAL & SPICE WINES

There are almost as many herbal and spice wines as there are herbs and spices. None of the herbs listed here make wines per se but instead are added to other bases and together make the herbal wine. Spices can be treated in the same manner to make individual spice wines or a proven blend of spices used to make a spice blend.

These wines are primarily used in cooking or marinades. Blending these wines is an art, but one well worth learning if you are an adventuresome cook. A few of them can stand on their own as interesting social wines or aperitifs, and those are the ones we'll be making in this chapter.

I'm including two herb wines, basil and rosemary, which are wonderful for use in the kitchen. The only spice wine I'm including here is ginger, a root sometimes treated as a spice, a condiment, substrate for candy, and a flavoring in beverages, baking, brewing. Rose hips are actually a fruit but they are often treated as an herb, spice, and berry in a multitude of uses—and they are often blended with hibiscus.

These wines all use a 100% white grape juice (from concentrate) base, which is easy to work with, predictable in fermentation, and clears easily. The herbs and spices add their own chemistry to the wine and may require extra steps in clarifying. All can also be made with rhubarb instead of grape concentrate, but that will change the acidity and sugar needed. It will also deny the wine phenols and other components advantageous to a well-rounded wine. If you want to make a rhubarb wine, see page 325. Rhubarb is unique in that it tends to adopt the flavor of whatever is fermented or blended with it.

Basil Wine ❖

Basil wines are popular for both cooking and blending. They also hold their own as aperitifs and nice sipping wines on chilly evenings. Both can be also terrible if too much base is used.

Basil offers greater variety than ginger if only because there are over 40 known varieties, each with dozens of cultivars with almost as many aromas and flavors. So, you first have to ask yourself what are your intended uses for the wine and do you have the cultivar that will match that use. If mainly for blending, cooking and sipping, then sweet basil or any of its varieties, cultivars, or even hybrids would be the logical choice.

A woman in a wine guild made a very large batch of lemon basil wine. Her primary use for it was to compose about 25% of the water she used in making her iced tea. She had been making this wine for this use for about 15 years and I assume she still is.

There are many different kinds of basils to choose from when making this wine:

Spice (or spicy) bush basil can be intensely flavored and is often used in cooking as an additive to stews, soups, and sauces. When added to a vegetable or chicken stock, it becomes perfectly paired with any fowl, fish, or seafood.

Sweet Thai Basil is distinct in delivering a spicy aroma and flavor akin to both anise and clove. The licorice component dominates over the clove, but the two are very recognizable and staples in much Asian cuisine.

Lime basil is another that adds a little something to iced tea and many mixed drinks. It is also refreshing served chilled on a warm afternoon.

Holy Basil is another that is revered in both hot and iced tea. It holds a place of reverence in the Hindu religion, where it is known as Tulsi or Sacred Basil.

Cinnamon Basil and Dark Opal Basil are each spicy in their own way and suitable for replacing plain water in cold soups.

JACK'S TIP

WHATEVER BASIL you select, which may be as simple as whatever basil you might be growing, will work fine in this recipe. You may have to use less of it at the outset, so steep it, taste, and adjust according to taste. Having made more than a few basil wines from the same plants (sweet basil), I can attest to the need to start with fewer leaves than the recipe calls for and add a few leaves at a time until you find the right taste. It might turn out to be the exact number called for in the recipe, but then again it may not.

Basil Wine Recipe

WINE IS READY IN: **8 months**

YOU'LL NEED: **1 cup basil leaves, loosely packed, 2 cans frozen 100 percent white grape juice concentrate per gallon of wine**

ADDITIONAL EQUIPMENT: **1 nylon straining bag**

MAKES: **1 gallon, but can be scaled up**

INGREDIENTS

1 cup loosely packed basil leaves

2 cans 100 percent white grape juice frozen concentrate, thawed

14 oz. very fine granulated sugar

2½ tsp tartaric acid

¼ tsp grape tannin powder

water to make 1 gal.

potassium metabisulfite, as needed

½ tsp potassium sorbate

1¼ tsp yeast nutrient

Lalvin EC-1118 yeast

DIRECTIONS

Prepare must: Wash the basil leaves and put in a nylon straining bag with six glass marbles for weight, tie closed, and put aside. Put grape concentrate, sugar, acid, tannin, water, and yeast nutrient in primary and stir well to dissolve thoroughly. Put the bag of basil leaves in the primary. Add 0.2 g potassium metabisulfite, stir well, cover primary, and set aside for 12 hours.

Add yeast: To 1 cup warm water (not to exceed 102 degrees F.) add a pinch of yeast nutrient, 1 teaspoon of sugar, and stir to dissolve. Add yeast to water, stir, and cover mixture for 30 minutes. Add mixture to primary, stir, and cover primary.

Fermentation: Gently squeeze bag daily and taste until the flavor is sufficient (about 5–6 days). Re-cover primary until SG drops to 1.020, or lower if the fermentation is still vigorous. Remove the bag and hang it over a bowl to drip-drain for 30 minutes (do not squeeze). Add drippings to primary and discard basil leaves. Transfer to secondary and affix airlock.

Post-Fermentation: Move wine to a dark place for 30 days and carefully rack. Repeat until wine clears and no new sediments form during the next 30-day period. Add 0.2 g potassium metabisulfite and ½ teaspoon dissolved potassium sorbate. Add 2-part fining if needed, wait four days, and carefully rack. Sweeten to SG 1.002 or to balance. If sweetened, wait 30 days to ensure no renewed fermentation and carefully rack into bottles. Age 3 months before tasting, but improves in 6 months.

Options: To add body, add one or two very ripe bananas, cut crosswise into ½-inch slices, before pitching yeast. For ease of removal, place it in a separate straining bag.

For added complexity, replace ⅛ cup of basil with a second type of basil.

When sweetening at the end, try using premium honey instead of sugar. At the end of the final 30-day wait period (after stabilization), carefully check to see if pollen has precipitated out of the honey. Do not disturb any fine lees when bottling. If in doubt, rack again, wait three days and then bottle.

When sweetening at the end, you can also use Demerara sugar or sugar-in-the-raw instead of honey.

As with all herbal and spice wines, because tasting can consume all of your wine, it is wise to bottle four 187-mL splits to use for that purpose.

Similar herb: None.

Ginger Wine ❖

The root of the ginger plant has long been an important food supplement. Dried and ground, it is a spice. Pickled, it is a relish. Candied, it is a delicacy. Shredded or thinly sliced fresh, it is a condiment. In the condiment form, it is sometimes added to wine recipes which would otherwise yield uninspiring results. But it can also be used to make a wine of its own.

I have always been amazed at how often this wine has placed well in competitions, including my own. The secret, I believe, is because it is just a good wine. Whether made for cooking, blending or drinking, the result is the same.

Ginger wine can be enjoyed in its own right or used as a blend to give life and interest to wines that would otherwise lack them, especially herbal, grain, and vegetable wines. As a separate wine, it should be stabilized and sweetened to a specific gravity of no more than 1.008 (2% residual sugar). It goes well unchilled on a cold day, being both pleasant and warming. On warmer days, it should be served chilled as it offers an inner warmth without warming the outside.

JACK'S TIP

MAKING A THIN WINE by itself, it requires a body-builder to be fully enjoyed. Here we use 100% grape juice concentrate to supply that body without subtracting from its own character. The amount of ginger used is more than sufficient to provide that character. If that proves too much, you can reduce it by half and it will still shine through. Neither amylase nor pectic enzyme are part of the recipe but may be required if the wine does not clear on its own.

Ginger Wine Recipe

WINE IS READY IN: **7 months**

YOU'LL NEED: ½ **pound ginger root, 2 cans frozen 100 percent white grape juice concentrate per gallon of wine**

ADDITIONAL EQUIPMENT: **1 jelly bag**

MAKES: **1 gallon, but can be scaled up**

INGREDIENTS

½ lb. ginger root, grated

2 cans 100 percent white grape juice frozen concentrate, thawed

¼ tsp pectic enzyme

1 lb. very fine granulated sugar

water to make 1 gal.

2½ tsp tartaric-citric acid blend (60:40 ratio, or 1½ tsp: 1 tsp)

¼ tsp grape tannin powder

potassium metabisulfite, as needed

½ tsp potassium sorbate

1¼ tsp (4 g) yeast nutrient

Lalvin EC-1118 yeast

DIRECTIONS

Prepare must: Wash the ginger root, grate it (it makes no difference if you peel the root or not, but I suggest you do not), and put in a jelly bag with 4–5 sanitized glass marbles for weight, tie closed, and put in primary. Put all other ingredients, including 0.2 g potassium metabisulfite, except yeast in primary and stir well to dissolve thoroughly. Cover primary and set aside for 12 hours.

Add yeast: To 1 cup warm water (not to exceed 102 degrees F.) add a pinch of yeast nutrient, 1 teaspoon of sugar, and stir to dissolve. Add yeast to water, stir, and cover mixture for 30 minutes. Add mixture to primary, stir, and cover primary.

Fermentation: Gently squeeze bag twice daily until SG drops to 1.020, or lower if the fermentation is still vigorous. Remove the bag and squeeze firmly. Add drippings to primary and discard ginger root. Transfer to secondary, stir well and affix airlock.

Post-Fermentation: Move wine to a dark place for 30 days and carefully rack. Repeat until absolute dryness and wine clears (2–3 months). If clarity is not pristine, add a small amount of amylase and wait 6 hours. If haze persists, add ¼ teaspoon pectic enzyme. A second addition may be required. Wait 12 hours and add 0.2 g potassium metabisulfite and ½ teaspoon dissolved potassium sorbate. Add two-part fining only if needed, wait four days, and carefully rack. Sweeten to taste or to balance. If sweetened, wait 30 days to ensure no renewed fermentation and carefully rack into bottles. Allow to age three months before tasting but will improve in 6 months.

Options: To add body, add one or two very ripe bananas, cut crosswise into ½-inch slices, before pitching yeast. For ease of removal, place it in a separate straining bag.

When sweetening at the end, try using premium honey instead of sugar. At the end of the final 30-day wait period (after stabilization), carefully check to see if pollen has precipitated out of the honey. Do not disturb any fine lees when bottling. If in doubt, rack again, wait three days and then bottle.

When sweetening at the end, avoid the anxiety of honey and use Demerara sugar or Sugar-in-the-Raw instead.

As with all root wines, because tasting can consume all of your wine, it is wise to bottle four 187-mL splits to use for that purpose.

Similar spice: None.

Rosehip Wine ❖

The rosehip, also known as the rose hep and the rose haw, is the fruit of the rose plant, and begins forming immediately after successful pollination. When ripe, in late summer through mid-autumn, the fruit turns bright orange-to-red, but darker (almost black) rose hips are known, depending on the rose species, variety, or cultivar.

Rose hips have been used for thousands of years in a variety of ways, including in herbal teas, soups, jam, marmalade, jelly, syrups, bread, pies, beverages, mead, wine, and, in time, distilled brandy. Rhodomel (rosehip mead) is especially good.

They are also good eaten raw, but this is an acquired skill. You must avoid at all costs the hairy layer of protection around the seeds. This is not difficult but requires focus until you get the hang of it. Rose hips are ripe when they give a little when being slightly squeezed. Wrinkled ones and hips with dark spots should not even be picked as they will spoil a wine thoroughly.

Rosehip wine is considered by some to be the second-best wine after grape wine to be found. There is, of course, a caveat to this claim, and that one needs to make a well-made rosehip wine. This recipe leads to such a wine, but it must be bottle-aged at least two years to come into its own. If you are not willing to wait, don't make it. You'll simply be wasting perfectly good rose hips.

JACK'S TIP

SELECT THE ROSE HIPS when they are fully mature, fat, bright in color, and before they wrinkle and begin to dry. If you are collecting from several varieties of roses, taste one from each variety. The better they taste, the better the wine will taste. Skip any plant with rose hips that don't taste good.

Do not collect any rose hips past maturity (wrinkled, dark spots, etc.). If the hips of different varieties are ripening at different times, collect what you can and freeze them until you have enough. It takes a lot to make what is required, so if you aren't going to have enough begin contacting friends and neighbors. I have augmented mine from plantings around public buildings and with wild rose hips, collected in the Texas Hill Country.

Rosehip Wine Recipe

WINE IS READY IN: **34 months**

YOU'LL NEED: **5½ pounds rosehips, 2 cans frozen
100 percent white grape juice concentrate per gallon of wine**

ADDITIONAL EQUIPMENT: **1 nylon straining bag**

MAKES: **1 gallon, but can be scaled up**

INGREDIENTS

5½ lb. rosehips

2 cans 100 percent white grape juice frozen
concentrate, thawed

1 lb., 14 oz. very fine granulated sugar

water to make 1 gal.

2 tsp tartaric acid

⅛ tsp grape tannin powder

potassium metabisulfite, as needed

½ tsp potassium sorbate

1¼ tsp yeast nutrient

Lalvin EC-1118 yeast

DIRECTIONS

Prepare must: Wash the rose hips, cut both ends off, and chop coarsely, placing in nylon straining bag with 20 glass marbles for weight, tie closed, and put in primary. Meanwhile, put 1 quart water on to boil, remove from heat, and thoroughly dissolve sugar, acid, and yeast nutrient in water. Pour over rose hips, cover primary and allow to cool to lukewarm.

Add yeast: To 1 cup warm water (not to exceed 102 degrees F.), add a pinch of yeast nutrient, 1 teaspoon of sugar, and stir to dissolve. Add yeast to water, stir, and cover mixture for 30 minutes. Add mixture to primary, stir, and cover primary.

Fermentation: Stir twice daily for 8–9 days, squeezing bag each time. Remove the bag from primary and squeeze well to extract the juice. Transfer to secondary. Add 0.2 g potassium metabisulfite, stir well, fit an airlock, and set aside in a dark place for six weeks.

Post-Fermentation: Rack, top-up, and affix airlock. Return to dark another three months and repeat racking. Add 0.2 g potassium metabisulfite, ½ teaspoon dissolved potassium sorbate, stir well and affix airlock. If the wine has not cleared, fine with a two-part fining agent, wait two weeks and rack again. Sweeten to taste or to balance. If sweetened, wait 30 days to ensure no renewed fermentation and carefully rack into bottles. Allow to age two years. Do not taste before then.

Options: To add body, add one or two very ripe bananas, cut crosswise into ½-inch slices, before pitching yeast. For ease of removal, place it in a separate straining bag.

When sweetening at the end, try using premium honey instead of sugar. At the end of the final 30-day wait period (after stabilization), carefully check to see if pollen has precipitated out of the honey. Do not disturb any fine lees when bottling. If in doubt, rack again, wait three days and then bottle.

When sweetening at the end, you can avoid the anxiety of honey and use Demerara sugar or Sugar-in-the-Raw instead.

Rosehip wine blends especially well with strawberry and kiwi wines, but care must be taken not to allow the blended wine to become too prominent and diminish the flavor of the rosehip. The idea is to add a suggestion of it being there. Taste trials are essential to getting this right.

As with all herbal and spice wines, because tasting can consume all of your wine, it is wise to bottle four 187-mL splits to use for that purpose.

Similar fruit: None.

Rosemary Wine ❖

Rosemary wine can be traced back to the eighteenth century, but probably precedes that by hundreds of years. The plant was used by the Egyptians and later civilizations for its incense and aromatic qualities.

Its use in cooking became almost universal in North Africa and ancient Greece, Babylonia, Rome, and Anatolia, eventually making its way to China. It's hard to believe no one made wine with it, but if they did, it wasn't in any records I could find.

The plant imparts a spicy, piney, and camphor-like flavor that marries well with roasted meats, from goat to pork to beef to poultry to fish. It also makes a strong tea often reputed for its medicinal value.

JACK'S TIP

ROSEMARY cannot be made into wine directly; instead, it flavors another wine such as white grape or rhubarb. It is rarely married to red wine but has been known to do so. Because its flavor is so pronounced, care must be taken in making this wine, or it will quickly become too strongly flavored and distasteful for sipping, but still useful in cooking.

The amount of rosemary in this recipe is the maximum to use. Begin with 1 cup and taste during fermentation. If more is required, bruise the leaves of a second cup and add to fermentation. If still not enough, bruise the leaves of a half to full cup and add to fermentation.

Rosemary Wine Recipe

WINE IS READY IN: **34 months**

YOU'LL NEED: **1–3 cups (see note at left) rosemary, 1 can frozen 100 percent white grape juice concentrate per gallon of wine**

ADDITIONAL EQUIPMENT: **1 jelly bag**

MAKES: **1 gallon, but can be scaled up**

INGREDIENTS

1–3 cups (see note at left) rosemary leaves

1 can 100 percent white grape juice frozen concentrate, thawed

1 lb., 14 oz. very fine granulated sugar

water to make 1 gal.

2 tsp tartaric acid

⅛ tsp grape tannin powder

¾ tsp powdered pectic enzyme

potassium metabisulfite, as needed

½ tsp potassium sorbate

1 tsp yeast nutrient

Lalvin EC-1118 yeast

DIRECTIONS

Prepare must: Wash the rosemary, bruise with the tines of a fork, place in a jelly bag with 20 glass marbles for weight, tie closed, and put in primary. Meanwhile, put 1 quart water on to boil, remove from heat, and thoroughly dissolve sugar, acid, tannin, and yeast nutrient in the water. Pour over rosemary, add water to make 1 gallon, drip drain bag several times to allow the flavor of leaves to steep into water. Taste. If the flavor is not strong enough, dunk bag several more times or as long as necessary until satisfied with flavor—do not overflavor the water. Remove the bag and discard leaves, cover primary, and let cool to room temperature. Stir in pectic enzyme, re-cover primary and set aside 12 hours.

Add yeast: To 1 cup warm water (not to exceed 102 degrees F.), add a pinch of yeast nutrient, 1 teaspoon of sugar, and stir to dissolve. Add yeast to water, stir, and cover mixture for 30 minutes. Add mixture to primary, stir, and cover primary.

Fermentation: Stir twice daily until SG reads 1.020, or lower if the fermentation is still vigorous. Transfer to secondary, add 0.2 g potassium metabisulfite, stir well, fit airlock, and set aside in dark place for 30 days.

Post-Fermentation: Rack, top-up, and return to dark for 60 days. Rack, top-up, and affix airlock. Return to dark another 60 days and repeat racking. Return to dark a final 60 days, add 0.2 g potassium metabisulfite, ½ teaspoon dissolved potassium sorbate, stir well, and affix airlock. Sweeten to taste or to balance. If sweetened, wait 30 days to ensure no renewed fermentation and carefully rack into bottles. Allow to age six months. It will continue to improve for about two years.

Options: To add body, add one or two very ripe bananas, cut crosswise into ½-inch slices, before pitching yeast. For ease of removal, place it in a separate straining bag.

When sweetening at the end, try using premium honey instead of sugar. At the end of the final 30-day wait period (after stabilization), carefully check to see if pollen has precipitated out of the honey. Do not disturb any fine lees when bottling. If in doubt, rack again, wait three days and then bottle.

Rosemary blends well with ginger wine, but care must be taken not to allow the blended wine to become too prominent and diminish the flavor of the rosemary. The idea is to have just enough rosemary to add a suggestion of it being there. Taste trials are essential to getting this right.

As with all herbal and spice wines, because tasting can consume all of your wine, it is wise to bottle four 187-mL splits to use for that purpose.

Similar fruit: None.

11

CHAPTER ELEVEN
NOVELTY WINES

❖

Novelty wines are those that, for one reason or another, just don't fit in with a previous chapter. Some, like jalapeño, pawpaw, pumpkin, tomato, watermelon, and zucchini, are technically berries, but didn't seem to belong in the berries chapter, for obvious reasons. The other bases we'll cover here are quite novel in that they are not usually thought of in the context of wine, although rhubarb is borderline in that regard.

The truth is that we're leaving out a huge number of really novel wines because their distribution within the United States and Canada is too restricted or because the winemaking techniques required to make them are just a bit more advanced than this book permits.

Only one of the novel bases we'll explore in this chapter has a limited distribution, but even that is rather wide—the pawpaw, which is native to the Eastern United States and Canada.

When a recipe calls for 100% grape juice frozen concentrate, it is strongly advised that you add this ingredient. All other additives are based on its inclusion. You can use unfrozen concentrate obtained from a home brew shop, as these are formulated and pasteurized specifically for winemaking, but there is no assurance the additives called for here will be needed in the same measures as stated.

Jalapeño Wine ❖

As a cooking wine, this is a versatile choice. It can be used to marinade meats, spice up barbecue sauces or glazes, or added directly to foods and sauces. It does something to spaghetti sauce that is beyond description.

And as a sipping wine on a cold night, this is a superb choice. It will warm you like no other and even goes well when mixed with V8 juice, producing a Bloody Mary-like drink but with much less alcohol than vodka.

I made my first batch of jalapeño wine for cooking purposes, but when my wife and I tasted it during bottling, she said, "To heck with that. Let's drink it!" I enthusiastically agreed but set a bottle aside to enter in the next competition.

When I entered it in competition, my wife and I watched the judges judge all of the wines, saving mine until last. It was the first time they had encountered the wine and didn't know what to expect, so they were hesitant to taste it. They judged it and then turned in their judging sheets to be tallied. When all awards for categories had been presented, with jalapeño winning the novelty category, they made the Best of Show announcement.

The head judge mentioned each wine considered and came to the jalapeño. He spoke on and on about its quality, balance, flavor, and uniqueness, but finally ended by saying the judges thought the Best of Show wine ought to be a drinking wine and the jalapeño, at best, was a sipping wine. They awarded the Best of Show to another wine.

Such outcomes are to be expected, but my wife noted that they spent far more time talking about my wine than any other, including the wine that won Best of Show. A year later, at the same competition, there were five jalapeño wines entered. In hindsight, my wine had actually won.

Jalapeño wine has heat, to be sure. Back then, all jalapeños were hot. It was several years later that Texas A&M released its mild cultivar, which they had developed under a contract from the Pace Picante company. Today, most fresh jalapeños are TAM jalapeños—the mild variety. In fact, before buying jalapeños I always eat one just to find out if it is mild or hot. I prefer the hot ones in all my culinary and wine-making pursuits.

Jalapeños have a wonderful flavor, especially when baked as an ingredient of a casserole or other main dish or entrée— wonderful flavor, but you have to pay for it. In terms of relative heat compared to other hot chilies, it really isn't all that hot, but for those not raised on hot spices, it is hot enough.

That's why people approach jalapeño wine with a certain trepidation. You can't taste it and then move on to a Cabernet or Chardonnay. Your taste buds simply won't recognize or appreciate any other flavor for a while.

It is uncertain when jalapeño wine was first made. I know I wasn't the first to make it. I was inspired to make it one day in the produce section when I gazed upon the bright, shiny jalapeños and thought, "Why not?"

JACK'S TIP

AS I SAID BEFORE, jalapeños have a wonderful flavor. You just have to pay for it in heat. With TAM jalapeños available in almost every big-box supermarket, you don't have to pay as dearly. If those are the only jalapeños you can find, go ahead and make the wine with them. But if you run across the real thing, by all means, use them instead.

It makes no difference whether the jalapeños are large or small, as long as they are ripe. The flesh should be firm, and they should be plump or at least heavy for their size. That means lots of tasty flesh, which is exactly what you want.

If they are plump and turning dark, so much the better. If they are just starting to turn red, they are at their prime and heading toward their past-ripe phase. If they are already red, they are past ripe but still delicious when baked—just not as fleshy. If they are just a deep dark green, firm, plump and somewhat heavy, grab 'em and make wine.

Because this is a cooking wine or sipping wine, you do not want to bottle it in regular wine bottles if you don't have to. Bottling it in 375 ml splits or smaller, preferably with screw-on caps, makes it much more convenient for cooking.

Jalapeño Wine Recipe

WINE IS READY IN: **9 months**

YOU'LL NEED: **16 large jalapeños per gallon of wine**

ADDITIONAL EQUIPMENT: **1 nylon straining bag**

MAKES: **1 gallon, but can be scaled up**

INGREDIENTS

16 large jalapeños (for less heat, use 8 jalapeños)

1 lb. golden raisins, chopped or minced

2 lb. finely granulated sugar

1½ tsp tartaric acid

½ tsp grape tannin powder

¾ tsp pectic enzyme

water to one gal.

potassium metabisulfite, as needed

½ tsp potassium sorbate

1 tsp (3 g) yeast nutrient

Lalvin EC-1118 yeast

DIRECTIONS

Prepare must: Wearing rubber gloves, wash, split jalapeños lengthwise, cut out and discard pithy divisions and all seeds, and coarsely chop. Put 1 quart of water on to boil. Meanwhile, chop or mince raisins. Put raisins and jalapeños in nylon straining bag, tie closed, and lay in a primary. Remove water from heat and thoroughly dissolve sugar and add tartaric acid in it. Pour sugar-water over jalapeños, stir, cover primary, and leave until lukewarm. Add water to make 1 gallon and stir in tannin and yeast nutrient. Add 0.2 g potassium metabisulfite, stir well, re-cover primary, and set aside 12 hours. Add pectic enzyme, stir well and re-cover the primary. Set aside another 12 hours.

Add yeast: To 1 cup warm water (not to exceed 102 degrees F.) add a pinch of yeast nutrient, 1 teaspoon of sugar, and stir to dissolve. Add yeast to water, stir, and cover mixture for 30 minutes. Add mixture to primary, stir, and cover primary.

Fermentation: Wearing rubber gloves, gently squeeze bag daily until SG drops to 1.020, or lower if the fermentation is still vigorous. Remove the bag, squeeze firmly to extract all juices possible, discard chilies and raisins, transfer juice to secondary, and affix airlock. Ferment to dryness (45–60 days) and stir in 0.2 g potassium metabisulfite.

Post-Fermentation: Move wine to a dark, cool place and allow to sit untouched for 30 days. Carefully rack and stir well. Return to dark for 30 days and check clarity. If nor clear, wait another 30 days. If still not clear, add a two-part fining agent and stir well. If fined, wait four days and rack. Add 0.2 g potassium metabisulfite and ½ teaspoon dissolved potassium sorbate, then stir well. Sweeten to taste or to balance. If sweetened, wait 30 days to ensure no renewed fermentation and carefully rack into bottles. It can be used in cooking immediately, but should age 4 months if for sipping.

Options: If sweetening, try using honey instead of sugar. At the end of the final 30-day wait period (after stabilization), carefully check to see if pollen has precipitated out of the honey. Do not disturb any fine lees when bottling. If in doubt, rack again, wait three days and then bottle.

As with all novelty wines, because tasting can consume all of your wine, it is wise to bottle four 187-mL splits to use for that purpose.

Similar fruit: Any other chili can be substituted for jalapeños in this recipe. Some are hotter than jalapeños and require fewer chilies in the recipe. Experiment to find the right mix.

Nettle Tips Wine ❖

The common stinging or burning nettle (*Urtica dioica*) has long been used for food, tea, beer, and wine. Fibers in the stems have been used for making clothing for at least 2,000 years. The leaves, stems, and roots have all been used for dying textiles.

The leaves have long been and continue to be a popular food source in Europe and Asia. The older leaves, with stinging hairs, are rendered safe to eat when steamed, boiled or cooked. Unlike Canadian Wood-nettles (*Laportea canadensis*), which taste very similar to spinach, stinging nettles have a slightly saline or fishy taste that some people find unpleasant on their own. This is probably why they are popular in soups and other prepared dishes.

The stem and mature, dark green leaves are covered with tiny hairs ripe with histamines and other irritating compounds, the source of the stinging inflicted by these plants. The small leaf buds and flowers that form near the top of the plant are the edible portions, too immature to be capable of inflicting pain yet. Nonetheless, one should wear a thick, long-sleeved shirt and gloves when collecting them, as most other portions of the plants from which the tender tops are collected can cause hours of pain, itching, and discomfort.

Another edible nettle found in moist woods and river bottomlands throughout the eastern and southern United States is the itch weed or Canadian Wood Nettle (*Laportea canadensis*). At the height of three feet, the wood nettle is smaller than the stinging nettle, and the leaves are lighter in color but exhibit every bit of the stinging properties as the stinging nettle.

When the plant was first used to make wine is unknown, but nettle beer has a rather long history in Europe.

JACK'S TIP

GATHER THE YOUNG, growing tops and wash and drain them as soon as possible. Measure them without packing. By itself, nettle wine is said to lack body and character and so here we will add both.

Nettle Tips
Wine Recipe

WINE IS READY IN: **drinkable in 2 months; best within 18 months**

YOU'LL NEED: **2 quarts nettle tips, 2 cans frozen 100 percent white grape juice concentrate per gallon of wine**

ADDITIONAL EQUIPMENT: **1 nylon straining bag**

MAKES: **1 gallon, but can be scaled up**

INGREDIENTS

2 qt. fresh nettle tips, loosely packed

2 cans 100 percent white grape juice frozen concentrate, thawed

1 lb., 2 oz. very fine granulated sugar

1 tsp tartaric acid

½ oz. ginger root, grated

⅛ tsp grape tannin powder

1 tsp pectic enzyme

water to one gal.

potassium metabisulfite, as needed

½ tsp potassium sorbate

1 tsp (3 g) yeast nutrient

Lalvin EC-1118 yeast

DIRECTIONS

Prepare must: Place 1 pint water on to boil. Meanwhile, wash nettle tips and grated ginger and place both in nylon straining bag, tie closed and place in your primary. Pour grape concentrate over nettles. When water boils, remove from heat and completely dissolve sugar and acid in it. Pour sugar-water over nettles and cover primary. Set aside until lukewarm. Add tannin, acid, and yeast nutrient to primary and stir. Add water to make 1 gallon total liquid. Add pectic enzyme, re-cover primary, and set aside 12 hours.

Add yeast: To 1 cup warm water (not to exceed 102 degrees F.) add a pinch of yeast nutrient, 1 teaspoon of sugar, and stir to dissolve. Add yeast to water, stir, and cover mixture for 30 minutes. Add mixture to primary, stir, and cover primary.

Fermentation: After five days of vigorous fermentation, remove the bag, squeeze firmly to extract juice, discard nettles, and re-cover primary. When the wine begins to clear, transfer to secondary, add 0.2 g potassium metabisulfite, stir well, and affix airlock.

Post-Fermentation: Set aside in a dark place for 60 days. Carefully rack and replace airlock. Return to dark another 30 days. Check clarity and add pectic enzyme if needed. If still not clear add a two-part fining agent and stir well. If fined, wait four days and rack. After 30 days, add 0.2 g potassium metabisulfite and ½ teaspoon dissolved potassium sorbate and stir well. Sweeten to taste or to balance. If sweetened, wait 30 days to ensure no renewed fermentation and carefully rack into bottles. May drink in 2 months; it's best to consume within 18 months.

Options: If sweetening, try using Muscovado sugar or dark brown sugar for added complexity. Do not use much, however.

As with all herbal and spice wines, because tasting can consume all of your wine, it is wise to bottle four 187-mL splits to use for that purpose.

Similar fruit: The following can be substituted for stinging nettles in this recipe: Canadian Wood Nettles.

Pawpaw Wine ❖

The pawpaw is a small tree growing in the eastern half of the United States north to Ontario, Canada; it's native to at least 30 states. Growing from 10 to 40 feet in height, it produces the largest edible, native, tree-born fruit in North America. The fruit, which are green to yellowish when mature, are cylindrical to kidney-shaped with two rows of about five large black seeds each in a pulp-like flesh that has the consistency more like a custard than anything else. Ripe fruit bruise easily once separated from their stem they last only a few days without refrigeration before spoiling.

The flesh, for lack of a better word, is typically eaten out of hand with a spoon.

Its flavor is unique and almost beyond description, combining the flavors most associated with mangoes, bananas, and pineapple. It is related to a number of tropical fruits, including the custard-apple, the sweetsop, and the Cananga (ylang-ylang) of Asia down to Australia. It's the only member of its genus that isn't tropical.

The flavor and consistency of the flesh lend it to being used in any recipe where banana can be used in (think breads, cakes, muffins, cookies, pies, parfaits, puddings, custards, ice cream, milkshakes, etc.). If you expand your horizons a bit, think beer, wine, and mead.

Pawpaws have been cultivated for centuries in the U.S., first by Native Americans, and later by colonists and settlers. It's not know when the first pawpaw wine was created, but there was a readily available fruit and I'm sure it didn't take long for wine to be made from it.

JACK'S TIP

AN ACQUAINTANCE introduced me to pawpaw wine. His was better than my first attempt. Because pawpaws don't grow in my area, I was limited to the fruit obtained on trips to Eastern Texas and Louisiana. I have only made two batches, and my second batch was far superior to my first (which really wasn't all that bad).

The recipe that follows is from my second batch. Just make sure the pawpaws are ripe.

Pawpaw Wine Recipe

WINE IS READY IN: **13 months**

YOU'LL NEED: **3 pounds pawpaws, 1 can frozen 100 percent white grape juice concentrate per gallon of wine**

ADDITIONAL EQUIPMENT: **1 nylon straining bag**

MAKES: **1 gallon, but can be scaled up**

INGREDIENTS

3 lb. ripe pawpaws

1 can 100 percent white grape juice frozen concentrate, thawed

1 lb., 8 oz. very fine granulated sugar

1 tsp tartaric acid

⅛ tsp grape tannin powder

1 tsp powdered pectic enzyme

water to one gal.

potassium metabisulfite, as needed

½ tsp potassium sorbate

1 tsp (3 g) yeast nutrient

Lalvin EC-1118 yeast

DIRECTIONS

Prepare must: Place 1 quart water on to boil. Meanwhile, peel the fruit and cut it into pieces. Put the fruit into a fine-meshed nylon straining bag, tie closed, and place in a primary. Mash the fruit. Pour grape concentrate over nylon bag. When water boils, remove from heat and completely dissolve sugar, acid, tannin, and yeast nutrient in it. Stir well to thoroughly dissolve solids. Pour sugar-water over fruit and cover primary. Wait 1 hour and add water to make 1 gallon. Add 0.2 g potassium metabisulfite, stir well, cover primary, and set aside for 12 hours. Add pectic enzyme, stir well, re-cover primary, and set aside 12 hours.

Add yeast: To 1 cup warm water (not to exceed 102 degrees F.) add a pinch of yeast nutrient, 1 teaspoon of sugar, and stir to dissolve. Add yeast to water, stir, and cover mixture for 30 minutes. Add mixture to primary, stir, and cover primary.

Fermentation: When the must is fermenting vigorously, stir twice daily (do not squeeze bag) for seven days, remove the bag and suspend over a large bowl to drip-drain, gently squeezing bag every 15 minutes for 1 hour and then discarding the fruit. Transfer all juice to secondary and affix airlock.

Post-Fermentation: Set aside in a dark place for 60 days. Carefully rack and affix airlock. Return to dark for three months. Check clarity and add pectic enzyme if needed. If still not clear add a two-part fining agent and stir well. If fined, wait four days and rack. After 30 days, add 0.2 g potassium metabisulfite, ½ teaspoon dissolved potassium sorbate, and stir well. Sweeten to taste or to balance. If sweetened, wait 30 days to ensure no renewed fermentation and carefully rack into bottles. You may taste after six months but it's better to wait one year.

Options: When sweetening this wine at the end, honey or raw sugar adds both sweetness and complexity. Honey adds a little length to the finish but may precipitate pollen and require an extra racking.

This wine will blend with any wine that blends well with mango, banana, or pineapple wines.

Similar fruit: The following can be substituted for pawpaws in this recipe: Custard-Apple, Cherimoya, sweetsop, soursop, Cananga (Ylang-ylang).

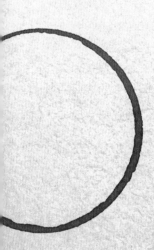

Pea Pod Wine ❖

Pea pod wine has been around a long time, most likely brought into existence from the desire not to waste anything from the garden. The earliest reference I could find is to "pods wine" in sixteenth-century England. But peas were cultivated in the Mediterranean Basin since at least 11,000 BC. That's a long time to have never made wine from a source available all that time.

Common garden pea pods and bean pods contain varying amounts of sugar and will support some fermentation. They do, of course, have to be supplemented with sugar to make what we call wine today.

It really does not matter whether the peas are snow peas, spring peas, sweet peas, black-eyed peas, crowder peas or whatever, or even if they are pods from beans (pinto beans, red beans, black beans, kidney beans, navy beans, white beans, broad beans, lima beans, etc.) rather than peas. Green pods make the best wine, but if the pods are just beginning to turn from green to yellow (on their way to brown) but have not yet dried out, they will work.

JACK'S TIP

HERE IS A BASIC "pea pod wine" recipe that will work for most pea or bean pods. Use fresh young pods as soon as possible after being picked and shelled. Freeze them if more than one shelling session is required to collect enough.

Pea Pod Wine Recipe

WINE IS READY IN: **10 months**

YOU'LL NEED: **4 pounds empty pea or bean pods, 2 oranges, 2 lemons per gallon of wine**

ADDITIONAL EQUIPMENT: **1 nylon straining bag**

MAKES: **1 gallon, but can be scaled up**

INGREDIENTS

4 lb. empty pea or bean pods

1 lb., 14 oz. very fine granulated sugar

2 oranges, zest, and juice

2 lemons, zest, and juice

1 tsp pectic enzyme

water to one gal.

potassium metabisulfite, as needed

½ tsp potassium sorbate

1 tsp (3 g) yeast nutrient

Lalvin EC-1118 yeast

DIRECTIONS

Prepare must: Place 2 quarts of water on to boil. Meanwhile, zest the citrus and put zest and pods in boiling water. Hold at a low boil for 30 minutes and remove from heat. Add sugar and yeast nutrient to water and stir until dissolved. Over primary, pour water through a nylon straining bag to collect pods and zest, which are then discarded. Add the juice of citrus to primary and water to make 1 gallon. Cover primary and set aside until lukewarm. Add pectic enzyme and stir. Cover the primary and set aside 12 hours.

Add yeast: To 1 cup warm water (not to exceed 102 degrees F.) add a pinch of yeast nutrient, 1 teaspoon of sugar, and stir to dissolve. Add yeast to water, stir, and cover mixture for 30 minutes. Add mixture to primary, stir, and cover primary.

Fermentation: When SG drops to 1.020, or lower if the fermentation is still vigorous, transfer to secondary, add 0.2 g potassium metabisulfite, affix airlock, and stir well.

Post-Fermentation: Set aside in a dark place for 30 days. Carefully rack and affix airlock. Return to dark another 30 days. Check clarity and add pectic enzyme if needed. Wait four hours. If still not clear, add a two-part fining agent and stir well. If fined, wait four days and rack. After 30 days, add 0.2 g potassium metabisulfite, ½ teaspoon dissolved potassium sorbate, and stir well. Wine should be bottled dry, but you can sweeten to taste or to balance. If sweetened, wait 30 days to ensure no renewed fermentation and carefully rack into bottles. Age six months before tasting. Drink within one year.

Options: Add ½ ounce thinly sliced ginger root and 20 green peppercorns to primary for spiciness.

If sweetening, try using raw sugar for complexity.

As with all herbal and spice wines, because tasting can consume all of your wine, it is wise to bottle four 187-mL splits to use for that purpose.

Similar fruit: The following can be substituted for pea or bean pods in this recipe: mesquite beans (green, unshelled, chopped to ½ inch pieces).

Pumpkin Wine ❖

This is a wonderful wine to serve any time in the autumn or winter, but especially at Thanksgiving or over the holidays. Since the pumpkin is native to the Americas, this wine wasn't made until settlers arrived, or traders returned to Europe with pumpkins in tow. Whenever it was, I'm sure the first winemaker who cut up the pumpkin was pleasantly surprised by the outcome.

JACK'S TIP

PUMPKIN makes a nice white wine, but it lacks body and character by itself. We will, therefore, add a little body with white grape juice concentrate and character with a few spices, making it a wine you will wish you had made more of. But first, a word about pumpkin.

Those medium and large pumpkins are fine for decorations and face carvings, but less so for cooking and baking, and certainly not for wine. The small sugar pie pumpkins are best for making wine. They come in various shapes and sizes, but I usually select the smaller ones, about 4 to 4½ pounds each, and I buy two. If they are smaller than that (3 to 3½ pounds) I buy three just in case I come up short and don't want to leave everything cluttering up the kitchen while I run to the store for another.

The pumpkins need to be ripe. The dark orange color is bred into the Sugar Pie Pumpkin, so look for that. To check for ripeness, give them a thump; that's an essential indicator of ripeness. They must have a hollow sound. The stem should be hard—whether green or dry, it must be hard.

Pumpkin Wine Recipe

WINE IS READY IN: **12 months**

YOU'LL NEED: **5–6 pounds pumpkin, spices, 1 can frozen
100 percent white grape juice concentrate per gallon of wine**

ADDITIONAL EQUIPMENT: **1 nylon straining bag**

MAKES: **1 gallon, but can be scaled up**

INGREDIENTS

5–6 lb. pumpkin flesh, shredded

1 can 100 percent white grape juice frozen
concentrate, thawed

1 lb., 10 oz. very fine granulated sugar

1 tsp tartaric acid

1 4-inch stick of cinnamon, broken and
crushed

1-inch ginger root, shredded

1 whole nutmeg

⅛ tsp grape tannin powder

1½ tsp pectic enzyme

water to one gal.

potassium metabisulfite, as needed

½ tsp potassium sorbate

1 tsp (3 g) yeast nutrient

Lalvin EC-1118 yeast

DIRECTIONS

Prepare must: Cut stem off the pumpkin, halve and clean out seeds, peel, and shred with
a food processor. Put in nylon straining bag and place in primary. Put 2 quarts of water
on to boil. Meanwhile, prepare spices, put in a jelly bag, tie closed, and put in primary.
When water boils, remove from heat and dissolve sugar and tannin, stirring well. Pour
grape concentrate over pumpkin and sugar-water over that. Add acid and yeast nutrient
and stir well. Add water to make 1 gallon. Cover primary and set aside until lukewarm.
Add 0.2 g potassium metabisulfite and stir well. Cover the primary and wait 12 hours.
Add pectic enzyme, stirring until completely dissolved. Set aside 12 hours.

Add yeast: To 1 cup warm water (not to exceed 102 degrees F.) add a pinch of yeast nutrient, 1 teaspoon of sugar, and stir to dissolve. Add yeast to water, stir, and cover mixture
for 30 minutes. Add mixture to primary, stir, and cover primary.

Fermentation: Stir primary twice daily and submerge nylon bag as necessary to keep pumpkin moist, for 3 days. Remove the jelly bag and discard spices. Remove nylon straining bag and suspend over a large bowl to drip-drain 30 minutes without squeezing. Discard pumpkin, transfer liquid to secondary, and affix an airlock. Rack after 2 weeks and affix airlock.

Post-Fermentation: Set aside in a dark place for 30 days. Carefully rack and reattach airlock. Return to dark another 30 days. Check clarity and add pectic enzyme if needed. If still not clear add a two-part fining agent and stir well. If fined, wait four days and rack. Return to dark for three months, add 0.2 g potassium metabisulfite, ½ teaspoon dissolved potassium sorbate, and stir well. Sweeten to taste or to balance, wait 30 days to ensure no renewed fermentation and carefully rack into bottles. Age 1 year before tasting.

Options: This wine can be sweetened with honey for greater complexity. Most honey contains pollen, so check the bottom of secondary after 30 days for signs of a very light dusting of pollen. If present, very carefully rack, add ⅛ teaspoon potassium metabisulfite, stir well, and immediately rack again into bottles.

As with all herbal and spice wines, because tasting can consume all of your wine, it is wise to bottle four 187-mL splits to use for that purpose.

Similar fruit: The following can be substituted for Sugar Pie Pumpkin in this recipe: Hubbard squash and blue Sweet Meat squash.

Rhubarb Wine ❖

Rhubarb wine has long been a winemaker's friend due to its ability to take on the flavor of just about anything with which it is blended. It not only stretches out a batch when there is not quite enough fruit to fill it but also adds a bit of body in the process. It also helps merge two or more flavors, such as Strawberry-Banana-Kiwi-Rhubarb.

Rhubarb can be frozen for later use if you don't have enough when first harvested, but one can save freezer space by pressing the stalks and freezing the juice in freezer-grade Ziploc bags. It is helpful to label the bags according to the date pressed and the amount of rhubarb used to yield the juice (*e.g.*, 4 lb. rhubarb, 6/25/2020).

JACK'S TIP

RHUBARB has a flavor you either love or hate. That distinctive taste is caused by oxalic acid. Oxalic acid is found in the leaves and is not supposed to reach down into the stalks, but a little sometimes will. The recipe that follows uses white grape juice concentrate to round out the flavor and make it more agreeable.

It is also worth noting that when blending this wine with another, much of whatever unpleasant taste remains (if any) will disappear.

Rhubarb Wine Recipe

WINE IS READY IN: **8 months**

YOU'LL NEED: **3½ pounds rhubarb, 1 can frozen 100 percent white grape juice concentrate**

ADDITIONAL EQUIPMENT: **1 nylon straining bag**

MAKES: **1 gallon, but can be scaled up**

INGREDIENTS

3½ lb. red rhubarb stalks

1 can 100 percent white grape juice frozen concentrate, thawed

1 lb., 12 oz. very fine granulated sugar

¼ tsp grape tannin powder

1 tsp powdered pectic enzyme

water to one gal.

potassium metabisulfite, as needed

½ tsp potassium sorbate

1½ tsp (5 g) yeast nutrient

Lalvin EC-1118 yeast

DIRECTIONS

Prepare must: Put 2 quarts of water on to boil. Meanwhile, wash rhubarb and cut into ½-inch lengths. Put into a nylon straining bag, put in primary, and crush. Remove water from heat, add sugar, and stir well to dissolve thoroughly. Pour over rhubarb, cover primary, and stir twice daily for three days. Remove the bag and squeeze firmly to extract all juice possible. Add tannin, yeast nutrient, grape juice concentrate, and water to make 1 gallon. Stir well, cover, and set aside 4 hours. Add 0.2 g potassium metabisulfite and stir well. Cover the primary and wait 12 hours. Add pectic enzyme, stirring until completely dissolved. Set aside 12 hours.

Add yeast: To 1 cup warm water (not to exceed 102 degrees F.) add a pinch of yeast nutrient, 1 teaspoon of sugar, and stir to dissolve. Add yeast to water, stir, and cover mixture for 30 minutes. Add mixture to primary, stir, and cover primary.

Fermentation: Stir primary twice daily until SG drops to 1.020, or lower if the fermentation is still vigorous. Transfer to secondary and affix airlock.

Post-Fermentation: Set aside in a dark place for 30 days. Carefully rack and affix airlock. Return to dark, and repeat every 30 days until wine clears. Carefully rack, affix airlock, and return to dark for 60 days. Carefully rack again, add 0.2 g potassium metabisulfite, ½ teaspoon dissolved potassium sorbate, and stir well. Sweeten to taste or to balance, wait 30 days to ensure no renewed fermentation and carefully rack into bottles. While wine is drinkable right away, it improves with age.

Options: This wine can be blended right away with other wines. If blended, age according to aging requirements of the blended wine.

As with all novelty wines, because tasting can consume all of your wine, it is wise to bottle four 187-mL splits to use for that purpose.

Similar fruit: None.

Tomato Wine ❖

Tomatoes were domesticated by the Aztec and Inca civilizations, and imported to Europe, where they were used in cooking long before they were used in the thirteen colonies. In the colonies, they were introduced via the Spanish colony of Florida into Georgia and then South Carolina, where it was especially appreciated. It is believed that tomato wine followed that same route. In the other colonies, however, there was a strong initial aversion to eating tomatoes thanks to the spread of many misconceptions about the plant.

When the idea of tomato wine is first expressed to a group, the reaction is always very mixed. For some, the initial reaction is "Yuck!", but the usual reaction is surprise, as in "Who'd have thunk it?!" There is also a lingering curiosity as to its taste. Let me assure you, it is nothing like you might expect.

When entered in competitions, well-made tomato wines tend to do fairly well. Having judged many of these wines, I have never hesitated to revel in the skill with which they are made. I have talked to many of these winemakers and have concluded that no one variety of tomato is favored, but rather the best wines tend to have 2–3 varieties in their pedigree, including cherry and heirloom.

JACK'S TIP

ON ITS OWN, tomato wine is thin and has little to recommend it other than its unique taste. Grape juice concentrate helps the wine tremendously with body and tends to normalize its taste.

Tomato Wine Recipe

WINE IS READY IN: **1 year**

YOU'LL NEED: **4 pounds tomatoes, 1 can frozen 100 percent white grape juice concentrate**

ADDITIONAL EQUIPMENT: **1 nylon straining bag**

MAKES: **1 gallon, but can be scaled up**

INGREDIENTS

4 lb. ripe tomatoes, mixed varieties favored

1 can 100 percent white grape juice frozen concentrate, thawed

1 lb., 10 oz. Demerara sugar or sugar-in-the-raw

¼ tsp grape tannin powder

1 tsp powdered pectic enzyme

water to one gal.

potassium metabisulfite, as needed

½ tsp potassium sorbate

1½ tsp (5 g) yeast nutrient

Red Star Côte des Blancs yeast

DIRECTIONS

Prepare must: Put 2 quarts of water on to boil. When boiling, remove from heat and dissolve sugar thoroughly. Meanwhile, wash tomatoes and cut into chunks, discarding any bruised or insect-scarred parts. Put tomatoes and any juice from cutting into a nylon straining bag in the primary. Tie closed and mash the tomatoes. Pour grape concentrate over tomatoes and hot sugar-water over that. Add water to make 1 gallon total, add tannin and yeast nutrient. Add 0.2 g potassium metabisulfite and stir well. Cover the primary and wait 12 hours. Add pectic enzyme, stirring until completely dissolved. Cover primary and set aside 12 hours.

Add yeast: To 1 cup warm water (not to exceed 102 degrees F.) add a pinch of yeast nutrient, 1 teaspoon of sugar, and stir to dissolve. Add yeast to water, stir, and cover mixture for 30 minutes. Add mixture to primary, stir, and cover primary.

Fermentation: Submerge bag several times a day (do not squeeze) for 7 days. Remove the bag and suspend over the primary 1 hour (do not squeeze). Discard tomatoes and transfer liquid to secondary, leaving sediments behind. Do not top-up but affix airlock.

Post-Fermentation: Set aside in a dark place for 60 days. Carefully rack and affix airlock. Return to dark, and repeat every 60 days until wine clears. Carefully rack, add an additional ½ teaspoon pectic enzyme, stir well, top-up, affix airlock, and return to dark for 60 days. Add 0.2 g potassium metabisulfite, ½ teaspoon dissolved potassium sorbate, and stir well. Check pH and correct it if necessary. Sweeten to taste or to balance, wait 30 days to ensure no renewed fermentation and carefully rack into bottles. Do not consume for a year. Serve chilled.

Options: Add 1 jalapeño, halved lengthwise and de-seeded, then cut into thin strips, to nylon straining bag.

Tomato wine blends well with a spice or herbal wine, such as rosemary, tarragon, ginger, or a chili wine such as jalapeño.

Serve with a dash or two of hot sauce, stirred.

As with all novelty wines, because tasting can consume all of your wine, it is wise to bottle four 187-mL splits to use for that purpose.

Similar fruit: None.

Walnut Leaf Wine ❖

Based on what I've read, it appears people were making wine with leaves from the English Walnut (actually, the Persian Walnut that was imported to England, likely by the Romans, and became naturalized centuries ago) for hundreds of years. A related species, the Black Walnut is native to the U.S. When European settlers made wine with the leaves of the Black Walnut, they found it superior to the leaves of the English Walnut, and Black Walnut then became the material of choice for making this wine.

Despite its pedestrian base, Walnut Leaf wine is a premium wine and it demands your respect when making it. If you don't give it that, you're wasting your time. It is also demanding to make, so read the recipe over and do not even think about making it if you cannot meet its demands. If you know where you can obtain the leaves, gather the other ingredients and specialized equipment (a mincer or good chopping block and arm) first—the Demerara sugar may be the biggest challenge. Premium honey should be located so you can pick it up just before harvesting the leaves.

JACK'S TIP

YOU WILL NEED a pint (packed down) of young Black Walnut leaves. Be responsible. Do not strip the leaves off of any branch. Instead, cut the growing end off with the five newest leaves on it so the tree will be able to recover by growing a new tip from the most forward leaf junction. Do this to 8 branches to collect 40 leaves suitable for this recipe—do not harvest tips that have immature walnuts on them.

The recipe says to macerate the leaves in the water for 24 hours. This is critically important. Do not try to outguess the recipe by thinking longer is better. It isn't. A longer immersion period will extract too much leaf tannin and cause the wine to take longer to become ready for bottling.

Also, the recipe calls for Demerara sugar and honey. Do not substitute brown sugar for Demerara. If you absolutely cannot find a source for Demerara sugar, use Turbinado sugar or Sugar-in-the-Raw (in that order of preference). Neither is a real substitute for Demerara's flavor, but either is better than white sugar and molasses.

Finally, a word about honey. The recipe calls for premium honey because it will have been processed by the beekeeper to remove pollen and other impurities that would slow down the maturation process and result in perhaps two or more additional months before the wine can be bottled. Don't skimp on these things. This wine will occupy two years of your time and cellar space before it can be consumed, and after such a long wait it would be a shame to end up with an inferior wine.

White raisins and golden raisins are the same. Sultanas will also work just fine. Raisins are a hassle to chop, but if you do not own a hand-cranked or electric mincer then you'll need to chop them. A meat grinder with a mincing face will work. It may be a chore to clean after the mincing, but it will do a better job than will chopping, and the wine will thank you for your trouble.

Walnut Leaf Wine Recipe

WINE IS READY IN: **26 months**

YOU'LL NEED: **1 pint Black Walnut leaves, 2 oranges, 1 pound premium honey per gallon of wine**

ADDITIONAL EQUIPMENT: **1 nylon straining bag**

MAKES: **1 gallon, but can be scaled up**

INGREDIENTS

1 pt. (packed) American black walnut leaves (about 40)

1 lb. white raisins or sultanas (chopped or minced)

1 lb. Demerara sugar

1 lb. premium honey

2 oranges (juice and zest)

¾ tsp powdered pectic enzyme

water to one gal.

potassium metabisulfite, as needed

½ tsp potassium sorbate

1¼ tsp (4 g) yeast nutrient

Lalvin EC1118 yeast

DIRECTIONS

Prepare must: Put 3 quarts of water on to boil, stirring in sugar and honey until completely dissolved. Meanwhile, wash the leaves and set them on the bottom of your primary. When water boils, remove from heat and skim any scum off the surface. Pour water over the leaves, cover primary, and set aside exactly 24 hours. Meanwhile, chop or mince the raisins and place in fine-meshed nylon straining bag. Zest the oranges and add zest to raisins. Tie bag closed and set aside in a sanitized bowl until needed. At 24 hours, remove the leaves from primary and discard. To primary, add yeast nutrient, and juice of both oranges. Add water to make 1 gallon. Immerse raisins and zest in primary, cover primary and set aside 12 hours. Add 0.2 g potassium metabisulfite and stir well. Cover the primary and wait 12 hours. Add pectic enzyme, stirring until completely dissolved. Cover primary and set aside 12 hours.

Add yeast: To 1 cup warm water (not to exceed 102 degrees F.) add a pinch of yeast nutrient, 1 teaspoon of sugar, and stir to dissolve. Add yeast to water, stir, and cover mixture for 30 minutes. Add mixture to primary, stir, and cover primary.

Fermentation: Submerge nylon straining bag several times a day (squeeze gently) for 7 days. Remove the bag, suspend over primary, and gently squeeze every 15 minutes for 1 hour. Discard pulp and transfer liquid to secondary, leaving sediments behind. Affix an airlock.

Post-Fermentation: Set aside in a dark place until fermentation completely stops and SG reading is below 1.000. Carefully rack and affix airlock. Return to dark for six months, checking the fluid in airlock occasionally. Carefully rack, add 0.2 g potassium metabisulfite, ½ teaspoon dissolved potassium sorbate, and stir well. Check clarity after 48 hours. Add an additional ½ teaspoon pectic enzyme if needed. Do not sweeten unless required for balance. If sweetened, set aside 30 days to ensure re-fermentation does not begin, Carefully rack into bottles. Do not taste for 18 months.

Options: Serve chilled with thin apple slices and your favorite cheese.

As with all novelty wines, because tasting can consume all of your wine, it is wise to bottle four 187-mL splits to use for that purpose.

Similar leaves: The following leaves can be substituted for American Black Walnut in this recipe: Arizona Walnut, California (Northern) Black Walnut, English (Persian) Walnut, Japanese Walnut, and Texas Black Walnut.

Watermelon Wine ❖

Long heralded as a delicate wine, watermelon wine is perhaps one of the most difficult wines to make. One can only wonder how they made it before refrigeration, as cold temperatures are required to prevent the juice from spoiling before the yeast can convert it to 12% alcohol by volume.

The most popular watermelon wine recipes, when they work, make a thin, somewhat lifeless wine. My early attempts to increase the juice ever closer to 100% all ended with spoiled must. When I was finally steered to a proven recipe, I saw in it an improved method, but also one that could be improved upon and I set out to do just that.

Warning: Malic acid is the major acid in watermelon, but it also contains a small amount of uric acid, so you should not consume it if you have gout (or serve it to someone who does). Wine should not inflict pain.

JACK'S TIP

A FEW THINGS must be said about the recipe that follows. It depends upon two essentials that cannot be stressed enough. The first is the watermelon. The second is the yeast. Elementary stuff? Yes, but more so than one thinks. The watermelon must not just be good, it must be excellent in flavor and sweetness.

And it must be large enough to yield a little more than a gallon in pure juice. A gallon of water weighs roughly 8.34 pounds. A gallon of watermelon juice, containing as it does a certain amount of sugar, organic acids, pectin, and trace vitamins and minerals weighs a bit more.

We're not interested in the rind or the flesh within a half-inch of the rind, so at the very least, we're talking about a medium-size melon. Look at the melon and try to imagine a gallon jug inside it. I ate three medium-size melons over two weeks that did not contain the flavor I wanted for wine before I finally sliced open a fourth one that I knew, by scent alone, was what I was looking for. When you find it, you must wrap the flesh in cellophane and refrigerate it at once before turning your attention to the yeast.

You want a very fast yeast without too many demanding requirements. You need to have 2–3 packets of it on hand in case you open one only to discover its percentage of viable cells is rather low. The only way to know this is to immediately begin a yeast starter solution. Start with lukewarm water, sugar, yeast nutrient, and a small pinch of malic acid (or a half-teaspoon of apple juice). Once it proves itself viable, increase its volume, sugar, and nutrients after 2 hours. When it has increased four-fold (eight hours), wait an hour and set it in the refrigerator for 10 minutes, then remove it. Do this three times and prepare for it some watermelon juice (which will be cold). Leave it out and when it is time to feed the starter again add watermelon juice so the yeast knows what it will be consuming.

Now it is time to prepare the juice and make the wine. Make sure you have Demerara sugar on hand (turbinado is a poor—but the best—substitute). Also, be cognizant that we are dealing with a malic must (we shall try to make it tartaric), so we do not want to allow MLF to occur. Sulfite additions will be appropriate to prevent that from happening. We will need to measure the pH to get it within the safe zone for wine. Watermelon is typically in the 5.10 to 5.60 pH range.

Watermelon Wine Recipe

WINE IS READY IN: **11 months**

YOU'LL NEED: **1 medium-to-large watermelon per gallon of wine**

ADDITIONAL EQUIPMENT: **1 fine-mesh nylon straining bag**

MAKES: **1 gallon, but can be scaled up**

INGREDIENTS

1 medium-to-large watermelon

2 lb. Demerara sugar

tartaric acid, as needed

½ tsp powdered pectic enzyme

⅛ tsp grape tannin powder

potassium metabisulfite, as needed

½ tsp potassium sorbate

1 tsp (3 g) yeast nutrient

1 g Fermaid-K

Lalvin EC1118 yeast (5 g)

DIRECTIONS

Prepare must: Cut the best flesh from watermelon into 1-inch cubes, place inside a fine-mesh nylon straining bag a portion at a time, and crush over a large bowl, squeezing to extract the most juice (discarding squeezed pulp each time), until you have collected a gallon of pure juice. Measure and record pH. Pour into your primary and stir in sugar until completely dissolved. Add tartaric acid to get pH down to 3.50 (3.4 is better), stirring as you add. Add tannin and yeast nutrient, stirring well to dissolve completely. Stir in 0.2 g potassium metabisulfite until completely dissolved. Cover primary and set aside 12 hours. Add pectic enzyme, stir well, and set aside another 12 hours.

Add yeast: Add prepared yeast starter solution (see above instructions) to primary, stir, and cover primary.

Fermentation: Stir juice daily. When SG drops to 1.020, or lower if the fermentation is still vigorous, carefully transfer to secondary, leaving three inches of ullage. Pour excess juice into an appropriately-sized container, screw the cap on tight enough to protect the juice but loose enough to allow any CO_2 to escape, and store in your refrigerator. Wait ten days, top up with reserved juice in the refrigerator, and affix airlock.

Post-Fermentation: Move wine to a dark, cool place for three months. Carefully rack and attach airlock. Check clarity in 24 hours. Return to dark additional 30 days until wine is crystal clear. Taste wine. Adjust acid higher if needed, add another ⅛ teaspoon tannin if needed, and sweeten to taste or to balance. Add 0.2 g potassium metabisulfite ½ teaspoon dissolved potassium sorbate. Stir well. Wait 30 days to ensure no renewed fermentation and carefully rack into bottles. Age 1 year in bottles before tasting.

Options: To add body, blend minimally with rhubarb (best choice) or banana wine (no more than 1 cup blending wine to a gallon of watermelon wine).

This wine blends well with other melon wines, such as canary melon, Crenshaw Melon, and sprite melon wine. Experiment.

Similar melon: Nothing can top watermelon, but the following melons can be substituted for watermelon: Muskmelon, Cantaloupe, Charentais melon, Honeydew melon, Galia melon, Crenshaw melon, Hami (Snow) melon, Canary melon, Sprite melon, Autumn Sweet melon, Korean melon, Bailan melon, and Sugar melon.

Zucchini Wine ❖

Zucchini, also known as marrow or a courgette, is a summer squash and a member of the gourd family (*Cucurbitaceae*). This family consists of about 965 species in approximately 95 genera (the botanical jury is still out on the exact numbers) and collectively represent one of the earliest and most important domesticated food sources in the world. Like all squash, *Cucurbita pepo* originated in Mesoamerica and was introduced to the Old World in the early sixteenth century. The variety we recognize as zucchini were developed in the early part of the nineteenth century.

Zucchini is the young, immature squash. When mature and reaching lengths of up to a meter, it is essentially treated as a different vegetable, known as marrow. Marrow lacks the fresh flavor and more yielding flesh of the zucchini.

The history of zucchini wine is murky. All we know at this point is that it was recorded in the latter half of the nineteenth century as marrow wine. It was not well thought of, being thin and without distinguishing flavor, and was considered a desperation wine that was made by those who had nothing else worth fermenting. This has changed as winemaking techniques evolved and improved all wines.

In the latter half of the twentieth century, zucchini wine began to gain a little more respectability, but old biases remained in many circles. Today, there is no reason to make a bad zucchini wine.

JACK'S TIP

ZUCCHINI WINE was much helped by co-fermenting it with raisins, and later with white grape juice concentrate. The addition of ginger also complements the zucchini flavor and gives it a spicy character. It simply is not the same wine of 60–70 years ago.

Malic acid is the predominant organic acid in zucchini with a pH ranging from 5.65 to 6.10. The pH must be reduced to at least 3.50 (3.40 is better), and the wine must not be allowed to undergo MLF (see page 58). The acidification is accomplished by adding tartaric acid, but if the taste gets too strong we can switch over to citric acid. It will simply take more citric than tartaric acid. We'll prevent MLF by maintaining an SO_2 level high enough to discourage it.

You'll be surprised how good this wine is.

Zucchini Wine Recipe

WINE IS READY IN: **7 months**

YOU'LL NEED: **5–6 pounds zucchini, ginger, 1 can frozen 100 percent white grape juice concentrate**

ADDITIONAL EQUIPMENT: **1 nylon straining bag**

MAKES: **1 gallon, but can be scaled up**

INGREDIENTS

5–6 lb. fresh zucchini, shredded

1 can 100 percent white grape juice frozen concentrate, thawed

1 lb., 10 oz. Demerara sugar

tartaric acid, as needed

1-inch ginger root, shredded

⅛ tsp grape tannin powder

1 tsp pectic enzyme

water to one gal.

potassium metabisulfite, as needed

½ tsp potassium sorbate

1 tsp (3 g) yeast nutrient

Lalvin EC-1118 yeast

DIRECTIONS

Prepare must: Put 2 quarts of water on to boil, add sugar and dissolve completely, and remove from heat. Meanwhile, wash and shred the unpeeled zucchini in a food processor. Shred the ginger and combine it with zucchini in a nylon straining bag. Tie closed and put in primary. Pour grape concentrate over the zucchini bag. Pour sugar-water over grape concentrate and stir in tannin and yeast nutrients. Add water to make 1 gallon. Cover primary and set aside until lukewarm. Add tartaric acid as needed to bring acidity to a pH of 3.5 or lower. Add 0.2 g potassium metabisulfite until completely dissolved. Cover primary and set aside 12 hours. Add pectic enzyme, stir well, and set aside another 12 hours.

Add yeast: To 1 cup warm water (not to exceed 102 degrees F.) add a pinch of yeast nutrient, 1 teaspoon of sugar, and stir to dissolve. Add yeast to water, stir, and cover mixture for 30 minutes. Add mixture to primary, stir, and cover primary.

Fermentation: Stir primary twice daily and submerge nylon bag as necessary to keep zucchini moist, for three days. Remove the nylon straining bag, suspend the bag over a large bowl to drip-drain, squeeze gently every 15 minutes for 1 hour, and discard pulp. Transfer liquid to secondary and affix an airlock. Rack after four weeks and affix airlock.

Post-Fermentation: Set aside in a dark place for 30 days. Carefully rack, top up, and affix airlock. Return to dark another 30 days. If the wine has not cleared, add amylase according to the manufacturer's instructions and stir well. Reattach airlock and return to dark for 30 days. Add 0.2 g potassium metabisulfite, add ½ teaspoon dissolved potassium sorbate, and stir well. Sweeten to taste or to balance, wait 30 days to ensure no renewed fermentation and carefully rack into bottles. Age 3 months before tasting.

Options: This wine can be sweetened with premium honey for greater complexity. Most honey contains pollen, so check the bottom of secondary after 30 days for signs of a very light dusting of pollen. If present, very carefully rack, add ⅛ teaspoon potassium metabisulfite, stir well, and immediately rack again into bottles.

Add 20 peppercorns to the primary for a bit more spiciness.

Add the juice only (no pulp) of 1 large or 2 average cloves of garlic to primary, but ferment in a well-ventilated place as the garlic smell will be pungent.

As with all novelty wines, because tasting can consume all of your wine, it is wise to bottle four 187-mL splits to use for that purpose.

Similar fruit: The following can be substituted for green zucchini squash in this recipe: yellow squash, Crookneck squash, Yellow (Golden) zucchini, Cousa squash, Costata Romanesco zucchini, Tatuna (Calabacita) squash, delicata squash, and Tinda squash.

CHAPTER TWELVE
WINEMAKING PROBLEMS

While all the recipes in this have been tested and fermented to dryness without incident, it sometimes happens that we have fermentation or post-fermentation problems. It happens to all of us, hopefully rarely. It's nice to know what to do next when a problem arises. That is the purpose of this final chapter—to identify, cope with, and resolve problems.

Stuck Fermentation

The fermentation either never starts or does but then grows progressively more sluggish, stopping altogether. There are a number of reasons this may occur.

- Lack of oxygen causes the culture to "wither on the vine" and grow inactive. If you added a dense culture in the form of a starter solution, the yeast will be oxygen-starved. They will need a well-aerated must to call home and resume propagation. Stir the must vigorously for several minutes. I stir my must in these critical times like I mix a cake dough—insert a sanitized wooden spoon deep at 3 o'clock and raise it while rotating around to 7 or 8 o'clock. Repeat many times. This brings oxygen-depleted must up to the surface where it picks up oxygen. If the yeast does not respond to this treatment, rack the wine into a new primary, allowing the juice to fall several inches into the new primary and cause surface splashing.
- Free SO_2 content is too high for the yeast strain selected. The solution is two-fold. First, stir the must exactly as you did above, only stir it longer. If you choose to rack, rack at least twice. Second, you can begin a new yeast starter using a more SO_2-tolerant strain such as Lalvin DV10.
- Specific gravity is too high—too much sugar. There is a temptation to kick the sugar content up a notch or two

and make a "killer alcohol" wine. This can be too much for the yeast. Yeast take in juice and nutrients through their cell walls and expel waste products—primarily CO_2 and alcohol—the same way. If the density of the juice is too high because of excessive sugar, this osmosis will not occur as the density outside is too high for the expulsion of the waste. The simplest way to correct this is to dilute the must with water until the SG is where it should have been. You will end up with a thinner, less flavorful wine. An alternative is to begin a new starter with Lalvin EC1118. If successful, you probably will end up with a sweet, high-alcohol wine.
- Fermentation temperature is too high or low for the yeast strain selected. You can cool the must or heat it by moving it to a cooler or warmer location, or you can switch to a yeast strain that tolerates the temperatures like you are experiencing. A combination of the two is usually a better solution.
- Alcohol by volume is too high for the yeast strain selected. Given the opportunity, all yeast strains used in winemaking will keep pumping out CO_2 until they reach their lethal toxicity level and the alcohol kills them. If the ABV level is not too high, you can switch to a yeast strain with better (higher) alcohol tolerance such as Lalvin EC1118, Lavin K1-V1116, or Lalvin DV10.

Very Hazy or Cloudy Wine

The initial addition of pectic enzyme is usually sufficient to prevent a lingering pectin haze, but the amount of pectin in a fruit or vegetable is an unknown variable. If the base is starchy, the haze could be either pectin or a starch. To test the haze for residual pectin, add 50 mL of wine to 200 mL of methylated spirit (methanol or denatured alcohol). The formation of a white, powdery substance indicates excessive pectin. Treat with additional pectic enzyme, a little at a time.

The absence of pectin indicates it may be excessive starch. Treat with small additions of amylase, always stirring and letting the wine rest for 45–60 minutes between additions. If the wine does not improve after three additions, it may be another problem.

If cloudiness occurs after racking, the very fine yeast lees may have been picked up during racking and distributed throughout the new secondary, and for several days the wine appears cloudy.

If the wine does not settle clear on its own within two weeks after racking, the problem may be heat instability of proteins. Treat the wine with bentonite or a two-part fining regimen, wait at least four days (a little longer after bentonite fining), and carefully rack.

If cloudiness persists, refer to your last potassium metabisulfite addition and add half that amount to your wine. If cloudiness persists after 24 hours, the problem is probably biological contamination, which means your wine might be spoiled. It's beyond the scope of this book to resolve such problems.

Sulfur Smell to a Rotten-egg Smell

There are two potential problems that can arise relating to sulfur. The first is the smell of sulfur dioxide (SO_2). The second is the smell of hydrogen sulfide (H_2S), a sulfur-based compound that will, if unchecked, evolved into a mercaptan, a serious but resolvable problem.

Sulfur smell usually arises from the addition of potassium metabisulfite far greater than the amount needed to produce the required molecular SO_2 for the pH of the must or juice. The excess molecular SO_2 is detected as a "burnt match" odor. If the excess arises in the secondary, the smell is detected at the airlock.

The solution is to rack the wine immediately, not once but twice, allowing it to splash as you siphon it to drive out as much of the excess molecular SO_2 as is sensible. If two hours later the smell is still detected, the wine should be racked again in the same manner.

A rotten-egg smell advertises the presence of hydrogen sulfide (H_2S), a volatile sulfur compound that can be further converted into a mercaptan (much worse than H_2S), or a disulfide.

If detected at the beginning of fermentation, the cause is probably the reduction of elemental sulfur from fungicidal sprays that came in on the fruit. The must should immediately be cold-settled—not easy to pull off in the average home or apartment. The must is then racked off the sulfur-containing sediment.

When yeasts are stressed for nitrogen, usually near the end of fermentation, they can expel sulfur taken in and metabolized into H_2S. Normally, if sufficient nitrogen were available, they would convert the H_2S into two amino acids.

If H_2S is noticed when the rotten egg smell is just detectable, the wine can be lightly aerated by removing some and pouring it back into the bulk, with terminal splashing. If the H_2S is not caught early and the rotten egg smell is strong, rack the wine (with a less vigorous racking than for the sulfur smell) off its gross lees. If fermentation is continuing, add ½ teaspoon of DAP with vitamins.

If, at any time before racking, the smell of garlic, cooked cabbage, or burnt rubber is detected, do not rack or otherwise aerate the wine. The problem is now mercaptans, and the wine is likely ruined.

A Vinegar Smell, Fingernail Polish Remover Smell, or a Bruised-Apple Smell

The following conditions are consequences of prolonged exposure to oxygen. This rarely is attributable to the time in the open primary at the beginning of our fermentation (unless extended far beyond the directions in this book) but is most likely an improperly sealed secondary—airlock short of sealing liquid or the bung not properly seated.

Every wine contains a little acetic acid, a by-product of fermentation, and since it adds to the wine's complexity, it is a good thing. However, when it can be smelled or tasted outright, the unmistakable signature of vinegar, it has gone above and beyond what is acceptable. The culprit is the bacteria *Acetobacter*, and if not checked

it will convert all of the ethanol in the wine into acetic acid. Note, I did not necessarily mean "if not reversed." Only very minor infections can be cured.

In very advanced cases of oxidation, acetic acid becomes esterified into ethyl acetate, which smells like a solvent, glue, or fingernail polish remover. There is no cure for a wine exhibiting ethyl acetate contamination. All one can do is prevent it through good winemaking practices.

Oxidation can also happen chemically, i.e. without the *Acetobacter* bacterium. Here, ethanol is oxidized into acetaldehyde, which imparts a bruised-apple smell and which reminds of sherry wine in advanced cases of such oxidation. Acetaldehyde is present in all wines and is welcome as it is produced in small amounts by yeast during fermentation, but in greater amounts it becomes problematic.

Another possibility is a too-high a pH wine fermented at too warm a temperature. Another cause is the presence of some rotten fruit in the must—it need only have been a brown bruise spot not excised. This is why it's really important to inspect damaged fruit before it leads to a problem.

For minor infections, inspect the wine for small floating white flakes. If present, or if the wine is still on its gross lees, rack the wine through very closed-weaved linen (200-count or higher), sulfite with 100 mg/L, and bottle the wine as soon as you can. This wine probably will not live long, so drink it promptly.

For heavy infections, all you can do is halt the process until you can dispose of the wine or make a batch of vinegar.

Neither should be carried out in the winemaking area, as *Acetobacter* is both an airborne and contact culprit and further residence in the winemaking area will only increase the likelihood of future infections.

After the wine is removed, the winemaking area and all equipment should be thoroughly cleaned with a sanitizer such as Bio-San, Bio-Clean, or sodium percarbonate.

Cleaning Up After a Spoiled Batch

If you need to clean up a large or confined space or equipment after *Acetobacter* contamination, thoroughly wipe clean with a good cleaning agent, such as sodium percarbonate, followed by a sulfite solution to sanitize surfaces. Do not neglect to clean the ceiling. If you must enlist aid to do this, do it.

Ethyl Acetate Formation

There is a logical chemical progression from wine to ethyl acetate, which smells like a solvent, glue, or fingernail polish remover. The progression is beyond the scope of this book, but it begins with the oxidation of ethanol into acetaldehyde. In trace amounts, this culprit is present in all wines and is welcome, but above trace amounts it becomes problematic.

There is no cure for a wine exhibiting ethyl acetate contamination. All one can do is prevent it through ***good winemaking practices***.

Good Winemaking Practices

- Only specific wines should be fermented and bottled with a TA below 6 g/L (see Chapter 1, ***Acidity***).

- Strenuously adhere to timely sulfite additions—be sure to measure sulfites, do not guesstimate.

- Keep pH between 3.1 and 3.55. Consider pH 3.25–3.55 a buffer zone, not to be crossed.

- Keep oxygen exposure to a minimum. There is no reason whatsoever to taste a wine daily during maturation.

Excess Astringency

Some astringency is welcome in all wine. Like acidity, it announces that this is wine, not Kool-Aid or fruit juice cocktail. Astringency is caused by specific tannins. There is currently no specific fining agent that will target these tannins alone, and removing all could adversely affect the quality and longevity of the wine, so it is best to run a bench trial to determine the correct dosage of the fining agent to use.

Among the fining agents suggested in Chapter 2 (**Fining agents**), gelatin and two-part fining agent are our choices for removing astringency. Gelatin is not recommended because the dosage would have to be very precise to be effective without causing other, potentially serious, problems with the wine. Getting gelatin to work is very difficult to achieve in a 1- to 3-gallon batch.

By default, that leaves the two-part fining combo. It is difficult to run a bench trial with this product because there is a required waiting period between adding the Kieselsol and adding the Chitosan— even using the manufacturer's minimum waiting period, which is 12 hours. This makes the bench trial impractical.

A recommended alternative is to use a reduced, measured dose on the wine. It is basically a 10% dose of each agent. First, dissolve the Kieselsol in 250 mL of warm water. When thoroughly dissolved, use a syringe to add 25 mL to the wine and stir well (use whatever syringe you have available—very inexpensive plastic syringes are readily available on Amazon and eBay in the 4-pack for $7-$9 range (a 30-mL size is very handy).

Wait at least 24 hours to add the Chitosan. Dissolve the powder in 250 mL of warm water. Make sure it is thoroughly dissolved. Draw off 25 mL in a syringe and add to the wine, stirring well.

This dosage is for a 1-gallon batch and seems to work well for astringency without stripping the wine of all its tannin, and it is easily scalable. Should the dose be too high and reduce overall tannins too much, one can add powdered grape tannin at the suggested rate of ¼ teaspoon increments for red wine, ⅛ teaspoon for whites.

Premature Browning

Some musts, particularly for white wines, experience browning almost as soon as they are constituted. To a degree, this is normal. In excess, it is not.

Many fruits are susceptible to browning when crushed to allow fermentation and pressing. Examples are pear, white grape, medlar, peach, apricot, apple, kiwi, muscatel grape, labrusca (native) grape, and its hybrids (Niagara, Cayuga, diamond), and raspberry.

Fruit juice is exposed to the surrounding air during crush operations, reacts with oxygen, and becomes oxidized. Oxidation causes browning, which is greatly accelerated by the presence of a naturally occurring enzyme in many fruit. The enzyme is polyphenol oxidase (PPO), the same enzyme that causes freshly cut apples and pears to turn brown.

Potassium metabisulfite is therefore needed at crush to deactivate PPO enzymes and block their browning effect. Ensuring an adequate supply of sulfite in wine throughout its journey from fermentation to bottling also avoids premature chemical oxidation (not related to PPO enzymes) and the wine turning brown.

Hot, Burning Wine

Wines containing more than 13.5% ABV are more difficult to balance than wines 12 to 13.5 percent ABV. The higher the alcohol, the more difficult the balance is to achieve. That being said, it should come as no surprise if those higher alcohol wines are difficult to balance, being either too sweet or too hot.

The way to prevent these problems is to avoid adding too much sugar in the beginning and instead creating a PA around 12.5% ABV, which is much easier to balance.

The solution for the current wine is to blend it with a low-alcohol wine. Alternatively, dilute the wine with water until the burning symptom disappears and then balance that.

Massive Volume of Gross Lees

An occasional wine will produce a massive amount of gross lees. Aggregate berries (raspberries, mulberries, blackberries, etc.) and strawberries are usual offenders, but soft-flesh pears and stone fruits (peaches, apricots, etc.), pawpaws, and any pulp prepared with a food processor are also frequent culprits. Any fruit that is overprocessed can also exhibit this condition.

The sheer amount of gross lees can be reduced by containing the fruit in a very fine-meshed nylon straining bag, which will allow the removal of the larger particles. Finer particles can be reduced in volume by passing the wine through a piece of very high-count (e.g., 500-count) sanitized linen. What remains can later be clarified using a 2-part fining regimen.

Autolysis

As dead yeast decomposes, it can impart an unpleasant yeasty smell and taste if allowed to remain in the wine for an extended time. The result is an unpleasant yeasty smell and taste. Since the period of co-existence is rather long (12–18 months), the development of the condition is through neglect.

There is no known cure for autolysis other than prevention. Obviously, racking is the most obvious prevention. An alternative is the periodic stirring of the lees—every 4–5 weeks is a reasonable periodicity—and racking after 18 months at the outside.

Gaseous or Fizzy Wine

We must draw a distinction between a gaseous and a fizzy wine.

All alcoholic (and malolactic) fermentations produce a great deal of carbon dioxide (CO_2) which bubbles up through the wine before exiting at the surface. The wine retains some of this gas until saturation is reached. Post-fermentation, the wine slowly gives up the CO_2 during agitations such as racking and stirring and over time. Atmospheric pressure also plays a part.

If a saturated wine is left under airlock for an extended period without agitation, it may have trouble ridding itself of the gas. A wine bottled in this condition is automatically faulted.

Agitate the wine in some way. Racking would probably be a good idea. If racking is not desired, the wine should be stirred vigorously several times a day for several days. Keep in mind that stirring like this, with the airlock removed, allows the wine to exchange, to a certain degree, O_2 for CO_2. In other words, the wine will oxidize sooner than it otherwise would have. After degassing, the wine should be stabilized and bottled as soon as possible and consumed early.

Fizzy Wine Due to Incomplete or Renewed Fermentation

A fizzy wine is another animal. Think of bubbles in Champagne or, to a lesser extent, a carbonated drink. This condition is caused by a fermentation that is not quite finished. It could be a primary (initial alcohol) fermentation or malolactic fermentation (MLF).

Wines made according to the recipes in this book are not supposed to be allowed to undergo MLF, so we need to check whether this might be the case. The first step is using the hydrometer to see if the wine is dry. If it is, examine the bubbles from outside the secondary. If they are small and look sort of silverish, MLF has commenced.

There are a couple of "ifs" we need to get past.

If an unwanted MLF is detected, the choice of allowing it to continue or terminating it needs to be made.

If the wine has already been stabilized, we need to stop the MLF immediately lest the wine develops a geranium smell. To stop the MLF, immediately add a dose of potassium metabisulfite sufficient to add 100 mg/L of free SO_2.

If the base is malic, as is the case for blackberry, apple, peach, plum, etc., we should stop the MLF lest the MLF strip the wine of its acidic backbone. However, since MLF will typically be 2–4 g/L lower in TA and 0.2–0.3 higher in pH, damage to the acidic backbone of the wine may not be so severe and indeed may be offset by an overall softer character and greater complexity. The overall fruitiness of the wine will be lessened.

Some berries, such as elderberry, gooseberry, and mulberry, are citric-malic, meaning the two acids are both prominent in nearly equal proportions, but citric is predominant. In these cases, MLF would strip the wine of a healthy portion of its acidity.

If the MLF is stopped using a free SO_2 addition, you are forewarned that this is just a temporary measure. A large application of free SO_2 will arrest the MLF, but only until the SO_2 subsides to a level the malolactic bacteria (MLB) can tolerate, at which point it will restart. Other measures can be taken.

The enzyme **Lysozyme** can be added at the dose of 300–500 ppm (1.14–1.90 g/gal.) to block MLB.

By measuring the loss of malic acid to MLF, either through pH or TA analysis, the reduction in acidity, if corrected, should be raised using another acid such as tartaric or citric.

An accidental, spontaneous MLF can be a good or a bad thing. However, a wide consensus among vintners is that a spontaneous MLF is not desired. Since no proven culture of MLB was added, the spontaneous MLF would be caused by wild MLB, and the chances are great that undesirable strains would be cultured.

Wines with an Off-color

Initial color in white wines is often brown, either slightly or deeply. See *Premature Browning* in this chapter. Red wines often are too light or too dark. The red wine color is dictated by the specific anthocyanins in the skin, pulp, and seeds. The stems may or may not contribute to color depending on the fruit. In some fruit, natural enzymes play a role in extracting and setting the color while in other fruit such enzymes are absent.

In red wines, particularly, there are color biases in the grape wine world. The bias is that specific grape wines need to be specific colors and that is that. Breaking out of this paradigm is often difficult. Take the example of White Zinfandel.

Bob Trinchero (Sutter Home Winery) had made a dry white Zinfandel (it was actually white) in 1972 and 1974 from first-run juice of the very dark Zinfandel grapes. When he attempted to make it again in 1975, the fermentation stuck with 2% residual sugar and a blush color also resulted. It tasted pretty good, so he stabilized and bottled it and the rest is history.

There is a side note to the story. Bob entered it in a number of wine competitions and the wine was always faulted on color. The judges knew what Zinfandel was supposed to look like and this wasn't it. At the California State Fair Commercial Wine Competition, the head judge, who had been following the wine's progress in both sales and in competitions, instructed his judges to leave their prejudices behind and judge the wine as it is entered—in other words, accept the category as correct and judge the wine against that category. Sutter Home Winery White Zinfandel won the highest award and broke out of Zinfandel's deep red paradigm.

But not all wrong colors are right. Blackberry, Blackcurrant, and Elderberry need to be dark. Blueberry never is dark unless blended with a darker berry, which is why blackberry-blueberry blends are so popular. Strawberry can be any color of red except blush—definitely not orange. But a really flavorful strawberry blush can overcome the color bias on the strength of its fruitiness and overall balance.

Blending too-deep a color with too-light a color of the same wine, all other character traits being approximate, can rescue both wines.

There is an old trick that can improve the depth of redness, but it can only work if used minimally, and that is to drop a couple of dried elderberries in the maturating wine. The color must be checked at least weekly, and the berries removed as soon as an appropriate color appears. Too deep a red will raise eyebrows, especially if the wine does not offer a flavor commensurate with the color.

Never, ever, use food colorings. Every one of them is wrong for wine and will be spotted immediately.

Color tends to bleach when sulfite additions are made, especially in the immediate area where added. Stir the wine very well to integrate the addition and the color will return in a day or two—sometimes within hours.

All colors tend to lighten as wine ages. Accept it and plan for it. You will have to make a few batches to judge how much a particular wine lightens. It won't be much, but it will be noticeable.

CHAPTER THIRTEEN
HELPFUL RESOURCES

Appendix A.
Abbreviations and Equivalent Measures

Abbreviations used in this book

Cup = c
degrees Celsius = degrees C
degrees Fahrenheit = degrees F
fluid ounce = fl. oz.
Gallon = gal.
Gram = G
Liter = L
Milligram = mg
Milliliter = mL
Ounce = oz.
parts per million = ppm
Pound = lb. (plural lb.)
specific gravity = SG
tablespoon = tbsp
teaspoon = tsp
trademark = ™

U.S. Equivalents (Rounded)

1 oz. = 28.35 g
1 g = 0.035 oz.
1 lb. = 16 oz. = 454 g
1 L = 0.26 gal.
1 fl. oz. = 29.57 mL
1 gal. = 128 fl. oz. = 3.785 L
1 qt. = 32 fl. oz. = 946.24 mL
1 mL = 0.034 fl. oz.
1 tsp = 5 mL
1 tbsp = 15 mL
1 cup = 8 fl. oz. = 237 mL

Raise TA

Tartaric acid
raise TA by 0.1%
1 g/L
3.785 g/gal.
Malic acid

raise TA by 0.1%
0.9 g/L
3.407 g/gal.

Lower TA

Calcium carbonate
lower TA by 0.1%
0.67 g/L
2.536 g/gal.

Appendix B.
231 Edible Flowers Suitable for Making Wine

Many years ago I began compiling a list of edible flowers. Because they are edible, I reasoned, they should be suitable for making wine. After several years of adding occasional flowers to that list, which was a prolonged, piecemeal effort, I published it on my website. It is not the exact list as in the table below, but it is almost the same.

There are three comments I'd like to say about the list at right. First, all the flowers listed have been validated as both edible and non-toxic to humans, although they may be toxic to certain domesticated animals.

Second, the word "suitable" may be theoretical in certain cases, as some flowers are very small, and it would take a long while to collect enough to make wine. Yet, I have done so with the small flowers of the Kudzu vine. It took more than a couple of hours to collect enough flowers to attempt a batch, which was delicate and could have used a couple hundred more flowers.

Finally, I completed this list after reviewing the literature over years, and I haven't made wine out of everything on this list. The list is a sample of what is probable, but be sure to confirm edibility yourself first.

231 Edible Flowers Suitable for Making Wine

Allegheny barberries
Alliums
Angelica flowers
Anise hyssop flowers
Apple blossoms
Apricot petals
Arugula flowers
Bachelor's button petals
Banana blossoms
Basil flowers
Bean blossoms
Bee balm petals
Begonias
Bellflowers
Bergamots
Bermuda buttercups
Birch flowers
Bird cherry flowers
Black locust blossoms
Borage blossoms
Broccoli flowers
Buffalo gourd blossoms
Burnet flowers
Butterfly ginger flowers
Cactus blossoms
Calendula petals
Camellias
Carnations
Chamomile flowers
Charlocks
Cherry blossoms
Chervil flowers
Chicory petals
China rose petals
Chinese catalpas
Chinese chives
Chinese hibiscus
Chinese lanterns
Chive blossoms
Chocolate lilies
Chrysanthemums
Cinnamon rose petals
Clary flowers
Clovers
Cloudberry petals
Coltsfoots
Columbines
Common milkweed
Common thistles
Coreopsis
Coriander flowers
Cornflower petals
Corn poppies
Cowslips
Crab apple blossoms
Currant flowers
Dahlias
Daisies
Dandelion petals
Day flowers
Daylilies
Dianthus
Dill flowers

Dog violets
Elderberry flowers
English daisy petals
English primroses
Evening primroses
Feijoa flowers
Fennel flowers
Field garlic flowers
Gardenia blossoms
Garden sorrel flowers
Garlic flowers
Geraniums
Ginger petals
Gladiolus flowers
Golden wattles
Good King Henries
Gorse flowers
Grapefruit blossoms
Grape hyacinths
Green wattles
Hawthorn flowers
Hibiscus flowers
Hog plum flowers
Hollyhocks
Honeysuckle flowers
Huisache
Hyacinth bean flowers
Hyssops
Impatiens
Indian cress flowers
Indigo bush flowers
Iron cross plant flowers
Jamaica sorrels
Japanese apricot blossoms
Japanese honeysuckle flowers
Japanese plum blossoms
Jasmine flowers
Johnny jump-ups
Joshua tree blossoms
Judas tree flowers
Kenaf flowers
Kudzu flowers
Kumquat blossoms
Lavateras
Lavender flowers
Leek flowers
Lemon blossoms
Lemon verbenas
Lespedezas
Lilacs
Lilac oxalis
Lily buds
Lime blossoms
Linden flowers
Locust blossoms
Lovage flowers
Magnolia petals
Mallow blossoms
Marigolds
Mariposa lilies
Marjoram flowers
Marsh marigolds
Marsh violets

Maypops
Meadowsweets
Melilots
Mimosa flowers
Mint flowers
Monardas
Morning star lilies
Mountain bells
Mush mallows
Mustard flowers
Nasturtiums
Nectarine blossoms
Okra blossoms
Onion flowers
Orange blossoms
Oxeye daisies
Oyster plant flowers
Pansies
Passion flowers
Pea blossoms
Peach blossoms
Pear blossoms
Peonies
Pineapple guava flowers
Pineapple sage flowers
Pink sorrels
Plum blossoms
Prairie onion flowers
Prickly pear blossoms
Primroses
Pumpkin blossoms
Purple milkweed flowers
Purple sage blossoms
Queen Anne's lace
Quince blossoms
Radish flowers
Red alders
Redbuds
Red clover
Rhubarb flowers
Rose petals
Roselle flowers
Rosemary flowers
Rose of Sharon petals
Russian sage flowers
Safflowers
Sage blossoms
Salmonberry petals
Salsify flowers
Savory flowers
Scarlet runner bean blossoms
Scotch brooms
Scotch thistles
Shallot flowers
Sloe blossoms
Snapdragons
Sorrels
Southern magnolia petals
Spiderwort petals
Spring beauty flowers
Squash blossoms
Strawberry flowers
Sunflower buds

Sunflower petals
Sweet briars
Sweet coltsfoots
Sweet pepper flowers
Sweet violets
Sweet Williams
Sweet woodruff flowers
Tangerine blossoms
Tansies
Thimbleberry petals
Thyme flowers
Tiger lily buds
Tree peonies
Trout lilies
Tulip petals
Verbenas
Violas
Violets
Water hyacinths
Water lily petals
Water lotus petals
Wax gourd blossoms
Western columbine
Western redbuds
White alders
White clovers
White trumpet lilies
Wild columbines
Wild onion flowers
Wild plum blossoms
Wild raspberry petals
Wild rose petals
Winter sweets
Wood rose petals
Wood sorrels
Woody thistles
Yarrow flowers
Yellow bells
Yellow butterfly bush flowers
Yellow rockets
Yellow sorrels
Yucca blossoms

Use the list as you will. There are many flowers on it that have long been made into wine. Finding the recipes grows more difficult with time, as the major search engine most of us use (Google) is increasingly more commercial—search the name of a flower, and you're very likely to get pages of products with the flower in their names.

Note: When foraging for flowers or any other materials for making wine, always confirm your identification and rule out toxic look-alikes.

Appendix C.
Selected References

The following print editions were consulted in some manner while writing this book.

Acton, Brian. *Recipes for Prizewinning Wines*. Andover: The Amateur Winemaker, 1971.

Acton, Brian, and Peter Duncan. *Making Wines Like Those You Buy*. Ann Arbor: G.W. Kent, 1985.

American Wine Society. *The Complete Handbook of Winemaking*. Ann Arbor: G.W. Kent, 1993.

Amerine, M.A., and E.B. Roessler. *WINES Their Sensory Evaluation*. San Francisco: W.H. Freeman & Co, 1976.

Anderson, Stanley F., and Raymond Hull. *The Art of Making Wine*. New York: Plume Books, 1991.

Belt, Thomas Edwin. *Vegetable, Herb & Cereal Wines*. London: Mills & Boon, Ltd, 1971.

Belt, Thomas Edwin. *Plants Unsafe for Winemaking*. Andover: The Amateur Winemaker, 1972.

Bender, Richard W. *Wild Winemaking*. North Adams: Storey Publishing, LLC., 2018.

Berry, C.J.J. *130 New Winemaking Recipes*. Ann Arbor: C. W. Kent, 1993.

Berry, C.J.J. *First Steps in Winemaking*. Andover: The Amateur Winemaker, n.d.

Berry, C.J.J. *Winemaking with Canned & Dried Fruit*. Andover: The Amateur Winemaker, 1971.

Boulton, Roger B., Vernon I. Singleton, Linda F. Bisson, and Ralph E. Kunkee. *Principles and Practices of Winemaking*. New York: Chapman & Hall, 1996.

Carey, Mary. *Step by Step Winemaking*. New York: Golden Press, 1973.

English, Sarah J. *The Wines of Texas*. Austin: Eakin Press, 1995.

Garey, Terry A. *The Joy of Home Winemaking*. New York: Avon Books, 1996.

Goode, Jamie. *The Science of Wine*. Berkeley: University of California Press, 2005.

Herter, George Leonard. *How to Make the Finest Wines at Home*. Waseca: Herter's, Inc, 1969.

Hornsey, Ian S. *The Chemistry and Biology of Winemaking*. Cambridge: The Royal Society of Chemistry, 2007.

Hudelson, John. *Wine Faults Causes, Effects, Cures*. San Francisco: The Wine Appreciation Guild, 2011.

Irion, Curtis W. *Home Winemaking Chem 101*. Self-published, 2000.

Irwin, Judith. *Home Made Wine*. Stamford: Longmeadow Press, 1991.

Iverson, Jon. *Home Winemaking Step by Step*. Medford: Stonemark Publishing Co., 2009.

Jackisch, Philip. *Modern Winemaking*. Ithaca: Cornell University Press, 1985.

Kallas, John. *Edible Wild Plants*. Kaysville: Gibbs Smith, 2010.

Kania, Leon W. *The Alaskan Bootlegger's Bible*. Wasilla: Happy Mountain Publications, 2000.

Katz, Sandor Ellix, and Michael Pollan. *The Art of Fermentation*. White River Junction: Chelsea Green Publishing, 2012.

Kraus, Steven A. *Wines from the Wilds*. Mechanicsburg: Stackpole Books, 1996.

Marie, Dawn. *Wild Wines*. Garden City Park: Square One Publishers, 2008.

McIlnay, Annabelle. *Making Wine at Home*. Secaucus: Citadel Press, 1974.

Mitchell, John Richard. *Scientific Winemaking Made Easy*. Andover: The Amateur Winemaking, 1972.

Ough, C.S. *Winemaking Basics*. New York: Food Products Press [an imprint of The Haworth Press, Inc.], 1992.

Pambianchi, Daniel. *Techniques in Home Winemaking*. Montreal: Véhicule Press, 1999.

Peragine, John N. *The Complete Guide to Making Your Own Wine at Home*. Camden: Atlantic Publishing, Inc, 2015.

Peynaud, Emile. [translated from French by A. Spencer]. *Knowing and Making Wine*. New York: John Wiley & Sons, Inc, 1984.

Rivard, Dominic. *The Ultimate Fruit Winemaker's Guide*. No location, Bacchus Enterprises Winemaker Series, 2009.

Vargas, Pattie, and Richard Gulling. *Making Wild Wines & Meads*. North Adams: Storey Books, 1999.

Ward, Philip. *The Home Winemaker's Handbook*. New York: Lyons & Burford, Publishers, 1994.

Warrick, Sheridan. *The Way to Make Wine*. Berkeley: University of California Press, 2006.

Zanelli, Leo. *Home Winemaking from A to Z*. New York: A.S. Barnes & Co., 1972.

The following websites were consulted in some manner while writing this book.

"Aging Wine," in *MoreWinemaking*, https://morewinemaking.com/articles/Aging_red_wine.

"Ameliorating Wine," in *Presque Isle Wine Cellars*, www.piwine.com/ameliorating-wine.html.

Comfort, Shea. "About Acidity and Adding Acid to Must/Wine." In *MoreWine*, https://morewinemaking.com/articles/Acidifying_must.

Dharmadhikari, Murli. "Wine Aging," in *Iowa State University, Midwest Grape and Wine Industry*, www.extension.iastate.edu/wine/wine-aging.

Eisenman, Lum. "The Home Winemaking Manual," in *Erowid*, www.erowid.org/chemicals/alcohol/alcohol_article2_winemakers_manual.

Eisenman, Lum. "Sulfur Dioxide in Wine," in *Garage Enologists of North County (Sonoma County, CA)*, www.gencowinemakers.com/docs/Sulfur%20Dioxide.pdf.

Gardner, Denise. Sulfur-Based Off Flavors in Wine," in *Penn State Extension*, https://extension.psu.edu/sulfur-based-off-flavors-in-wine.

Giglio, Lise. "pH Levels of Fruit," in *Hunker*, www.hunker.com/13427831/ph-levels-of-fruit.

Hartung, Alexis. "Country Wine: Non-Grape Winemaking," in *WineMaker Magazine*, https://winemakermag.com/article/country-wine-country-wine.

"Instabilities, Hazes and Deposits," in *Australian Wine Research Institute*, www.awri.com.au/industry_support/winemaking_resources/fining-stabilities/.

Keller, Jack. "Aging Country Fruit Wines," in *WineMaker Magazine*, https://winemakermag.com/technique/aging-country-fruit-wines.

Keller, Jack. "A Taste of the Tropics," in *Wine-Maker Magazine*, https://winemakermag.com/article/1422-a-taste-of-the-tropics.

Keller, Jack. "Taming the Wild Elderberry," in *WineMaker Magazine*, https://winemakermag.com/article/841-elderberry-wine.

Keller, Jack. *The Winemaking Home Page*, https://winemaking.jackkeller.net/index.asp.

Krebiehl, Anne. "What Really Happens as Wine Ages?" in *Wine Enthusiast*, www.winemag.com/2018/10/09/what-happens-wine-ages/.

"Master List of Typical pH and Acid Content of Fruits and Vegetables for Home Canning and Preserving," in *PickYourOwn*, www.pickyourown.org/ph_of_fruits_and_vegetables_list.htm.

Matthews, Erik. "Aging Gracefully," in *Wine-Maker Magazine*, https://winemakermag.com/article/55-aging-gracefully.

Pambianchi, Daniel. "Make Wines to Age," in *WineMaker Magazine*, https://winemakermag.com/technique/1498-wines-to-age-advanced-winemaking.

Pambianchi, Daniel. "pHiguring out pH," in *WineMaker Magazine*, https://winemakermag.com/article/547-phiguring-out-ph.

Pambianchi, Daniel. "Solving the Sulfite Puzzle," in *WineMaker Magazine*, https://winemakermag.com/article/634-solving-the-sulfite-puzzle.

Pambianchi, Daniel. "The Strain Game," in *WineMaker Magazine*, https://winemakermag.com/article/681-the-strain-game.

Pambianchi, Daniel. "Sulfite Calculator," in *WineMaker Magazine*, https://winemakermag.com/resource/1301-sulfite-calculator.

Patterson, Tim. "Aim for Age," in *WineMaker Magazine*, https://winemakermag.com/article/828-aim-for-age.

Peak, Bob. "Bulk Wine Aging," in *WineMaker Magazine*, https://winemakermag.com/technique/1472-bulk-wine-aging.

"pH Values of Common Foods and Ingredients," in *Clemson University Extension*, www.clemson.edu/extension/food/food2market/documents/ph_of_common_foods.pdf.

Rotter, Ben. "Deacidification Techniques," in *Improved Winemaking*, www.brsquared.org/wine/Articles/deacid.htm.

Rotter, Ben. "Fruit Maturity Assessment," in *Improved Winemaking*, www.brsquared.org/wine/Articles/fruitmat/fruitmat.htm.

Rotter, Ben. "The Influence of pH," in *Improved Winemaking*, www.brsquared.org/wine.

Rotter, Ben. "Sulfur Dioxide," in *Improved Winemaking*, www.brsquared.org/wine/Articles/deacid.htm.

"Use and Measurement of Sulfur Dioxide in Wine," in *Presque Isle Wine Cellars*, www.piwine.com/use-and-measurement-of-sulfur-dioxide-in-wine.html.

"Using a pH Meter in Titration to Measure TA," in *The Valley Vintner*, http://valleyvintner.com/Merchant2/DataSheets/LabKit.pdf.

"Wine Fermentation," in *Australian Wine Research Institute*, www.awri.com.au/industry_support/winemaking_resources/wine_fermentation/.

"Wine Yeast Selection Chart," in *Presque Isle Wine Cellars*, www.piwine.com/media/pdf/yeast-selection-chart.pdf.

INDEX

Photo credits

About the Author

Jack Keller lived in Pleasanton, Texas a half-hour south of San Antonio. Winemaking was his passion and for decades he made wine from just about anything both fermentable and nontoxic. Jack developed scores of recipes and tended to gravitate to the exotic or unusual, having once won first place with jalapeño wine, second place with sandbur wine, and third with Bermuda grass clippings wine.

Jack was six times elected President of the San Antonio Regional Wine Guild, was a certified home wine judge, periodic contributor to *WineMaker Magazine*, and creator and author of *The Winemaking Home Page*, which was the largest home winemaking website in the world and the first winemaking blog on the internet.

Jack grew a few grapes and was married to his high school sweetheart Donna (née: Bennett). He was a mentor to thousands of amateur winemakers and communicated through his Facebook page, Jack Keller Winemaking (https://www.facebook.com/JackKellerWinemaking/). He passed away in 2020.

About the Technical Editor

Daniel Pambianchi is a well-known winemaking author, lecturer and consultant, and seasoned winemaker both as an amateur and professional having owned and operated a small commercial winery in Niagara Wine Country in Ontario, Canada. His bestselling book *Techniques in Home Winemaking* has become the go-to reference textbook by advanced amateurs and small-winery operators alike. His area of expertise is wine chemistry in which he performs extensive studies in his wine analysis lab. He is a member of the American Society for Enology and Viticulture, the Australian Society of Viticulture and Oenology, and the American Wine Society. Daniel lives in Montreal, Quebec (Canada).